The Rise of Transnational Corporations from Emerging Markets

STUDIES IN INTERNATIONAL INVESTMENT

Series Editor: Karl P. Sauvant, *Executive Director, Columbia Program on International Investment (a joint undertaking of Columbia Law School and the Earth Institute at Columbia University), Columbia University, USA*

Columbia Law School
Columbia Law School, founded in 1858, stands at the forefront of legal education and of the law in a global society. Columbia Law School graduates have provided leadership worldwide in a remarkably broad range of fields: government, diplomacy, the judiciary, business, nonprofit, advocacy, entertainment, academia, science and the arts. Led by Dean David M. Schizer, Columbia Law School joins its traditional strengths in international and comparative law, constitutional law, administrative law and human rights law with pioneering work in intellectual property, digital technology, sexuality and gender, and criminal law. For further information, visit http://www.law.columbia.edu.

The Earth Institute at Columbia University
The Earth Institute at Columbia University is the world's leading academic center for the integrated study of Earth, its environment and society. Led by Professor Jeffrey D. Sachs, The Earth Institute builds upon excellence in the core disciplines – earth sciences, biological sciences, engineering sciences, social sciences, and health sciences – and stresses cross-disciplinary approaches to complex problems. Through research, training and global partnerships, it mobilizes science and technology to advance sustainable development, while placing special emphasis on the needs of the world's poor. For more information, visit: http://www.earth.columbia.edu.

The Columbia Program on International Investment
The Columbia Program on International Investment (CPII), launched in January 2006, seeks to be a leader on issues related to foreign direct investment (FDI) in the global economy. Led by Dr. Karl P. Sauvant, its objectives are to analyze important topical policy-oriented issues related to FDI, develop and disseminate practical approaches and solutions, and provide students with a challenging learning environment. CPII is a joint program of Columbia Law School and the Earth Institute at Columbia University. For more information, visit: http://www.cpii.columbia.edu.

The Rise of Transnational Corporations from Emerging Markets

Threat or Opportunity?

Edited by

Karl P. Sauvant

Executive Director, Columbia Program on International Investment, Columbia University, USA

With

Kristin Mendoza and Irmak Ince

STUDIES IN INTERNATIONAL INVESTMENT

Edward Elgar

Cheltenham, UK • Northampton, MA, USA

Published by
Edward Elgar Publishing Limited
Glensanda House
Montpellier Parade
Cheltenham
Glos GL50 1UA
UK

Edward Elgar Publishing, Inc.
William Pratt House
9 Dewey Court
Northampton
Massachusetts 01060
USA

A catalogue record for this book
is available from the British Library

ISBN 978 1 84720 766 1 (cased)

Printed and bound in Great Britain by MPG Books Ltd, Bodmin, Cornwall

Contents

PART III   WHAT'S IN IT FOR HOST COUNTRIES?

PART IV   WHAT'S IN IT FOR HOME COUNTRIES AND
THE INTERNATIONAL COMMUNITY?

PART V   CONCLUSION

Contributors

Helena Barnard completed her PhD at Rutgers University, US, in October 2006 on developing country firms' use of outward investment in the developed world as a mechanism for economic upgrading. In January 2007, she became a Senior Lecturer at the Gordon Institute of Business Science, University of Pretoria, South Africa. Her overarching research interest is the upgrading strategies of developing country firms. She has published in the *Journal of Management and Governance, International Journal of Technology Management* and *Advances in Qualitative Organizational Research*. (Email: barnardh@gibs.co.za)

Peter J. Buckley is Professor of International Business, Director of the Centre for International Business (CIBUL) and Director of the Institute for Research on Contemporary China at the University of Leeds, UK. He is also Visiting Professor in the Department of Economics, University of Reading, UK, and Honorary Professor at the University of International Business and Economics (UIBE), Beijing, China. Buckley was President of the Academy of International Business (2002–4). He is editor of the Edward Elgar book series *New Horizons in International Business*, Associate Editor of *International Business Review*, Consulting Editor of the *Journal of International Business Studies* and on the editorial board of the *International Journal of the Economics of Business*, *Asia Pacific Business Review* and the *Journal of Chinese Economic and Business Studies*. Buckley has consulted for governments, UNCTAD's Division on Investment, UNIDO and leading companies. In 2007, he was awarded the Viipuri Prize in Strategic Management and Business Economics. (Email: pjb@lubs.leeds.ac.uk)

John Cantwell has been Professor of International Business at Rutgers University, US, since 2002. He has also been Visiting Professor at the University of Rome 'La Sapienza', Italy, the University of the Social Sciences, Toulouse, France, and the University of Economics and Business Administration, Vienna, Austria. He is a pioneer in the field of research on transnational corporations and technology creation, beyond merely international technology transfer. He has published 11 books, over 50 articles in refereed academic journals and over 60 chapters in edited collections. He served as President of the European International Business Academy

(EIBA) in 1992, and in 2001 was elected one of four EIBA Founding Fellows. In 2005 he was elected a Fellow of the Academy of International Business (AIB), and its Vice President in 2006. (Email: cantwell@rbsmail.rutgers.edu)

Jeremy L. Clegg is Jean Monnet Professor of European Integration and International Business Management in the Centre for International Business, Faculty of Business, University of Leeds, UK. His Chair is supported by the European Commission. His research interests include the determinants of foreign direct investment by and into developed and developing countries, and the impact of European and foreign-owned firms on the productivity and performance of Chinese firms. He is currently working on a research project on the determinants of productivity and international productivity differences in the retailing (particularly food retailing) industry. Previously he held appointments at the universities of Bath, Reading, Swansea and Exeter, in the United Kingdom. He served as Chair of the Academy of International Business, United Kingdom and Ireland Chapter, from 2001 to 2007. (Email: L.J.Clegg@lubs.leeds.ac.uk)

Adam R. Cross is a Senior Lecturer in International Business at the Centre for International Business (CIBUL), Leeds University Business School, and Director of the Centre for Chinese Business and Development, University of Leeds, UK. With degrees in geology and management science, he worked in the Manchester School of Management and Manchester Metropolitan University in several research and teaching positions before joining CIBUL in 1996. His research on cross-border licensing, intellectual property as a business asset and outward foreign direct investment from emerging markets has been published in a number of articles and edited books. He teaches international business and intellectual capital management on a number of undergraduate and MBA programmes, both in the United Kingdom and overseas. (Email: arc@lubs.leeds.ac.uk)

Alvaro Bruno Cyrino is Professor of International Business and Researcher at Fundação Dom Cabral, Brazil. He is also Associate Professor at the Pontifical Catholic University of the State of Minas Gerais. He has a B Sc in business and public administration from the Federal University of the State of Paraná; a Diplôme d'Etudes Approfondies (M Sc equivalent), from the Université de Technologie de Compiègne, France; and a PhD in Business Administration from the École des Hautes Études Commerciales (HEC), France, with a major in strategy. He has served in executive positions in universities, the public sector and private companies, including international assignments. He has also worked as a strategic management consultant for major Brazilian companies. His current research interests include the field of strategy, with an emphasis on the resource-based view, and the field of international business, where he has concentrated on the internationalization process of companies from emerging markets. (Email: alvarobc@fdc.org.br)

Emerson de Almeida has been the Dean of Fundação Dom Cabral (FDC), Brazil, since its creation in 1976. He has a Bachelor's degree in economics from the College of Economic Sciences, Universidade Federal de Minas Gerais, and a Maitrise from the University of Paris, Institut Français de Presse (1972). De Almeida guided the negotiations to implement alliances between FDC and INSEAD (France), Kellogg (US) and UBC (Canada). He directed the implementation of the FDC partnership projects with companies. He is a member of the international INSEAD Council and a permanent member of the Plenary Assembly of *Gazeta Mercantil*'s Entrepreneurial Leaders Forum. He is the author of *Fundamentos da Empresa Relevante: Meu aprendizado na FDC* (Elsevier, 2006) and numerous articles. (Email: ealmeida@fdc.org.br)

John H. Dunning has been researching the economics of FDI and transnational corporations since the 1950s. He has authored, co-authored, or edited 43 books on this subject and on industrial and regional economics. Dunning is Emeritus Professor of International Business at the University of Reading, UK, and State of New Jersey Professor of International Business at Rutgers University, US. In addition, he has been Visiting Professor at several universities in North America, Europe and Asia. He has honorary doctorates from five leading European and Asian universities and is an honorary Professor of International Business at the University of International Business and Economics at Beijing, China. In 2002, he received the Distinguished Scholar in International Management award at the Academy of Management. In 2004, he was honored with a lifetime award for his contribution to international business studies from the European Academy of International Business. (Email: jill.mturner@virgin.net)

Lorraine Eden is Professor of Management at Texas A&M University, US. She focuses her research on the political economy of transnational corporations, specializing in transfer pricing, international taxation and regional integration. She has more than 100 publications in several journals. Her best-known book is *Taxing Multinationals* (University of Toronto Press, 1988). Her current research focuses on TNC strategies in corrupt economies and tax havens, responses to liability of foreignness and regional integration, and estimates of transfer price manipulation. Eden is Editor in Chief Elect of the *Journal of International Business Studies*. She has been a Fulbright Scholar, a Pew Fellow and a recipient of multiple teaching and research awards, including election as a Fellow of the Academy of International Business. (Email: leden@tamu.edu)

Rainer Geiger is the Deputy Director for Financial and Enterprise Affairs and Head of the Middle East and North Africa Programme at the Organisation for Economic Co-operation and Development (OECD) in Paris. He is a graduate of the University of Heidelberg in Germany and Columbia Law School in New York, with a PhD and an advanced law degree. He has been a Counselor in the Ministries of Economics and Economic Cooperation in Germany and Secretary of the Finance Commission of the Conference on International Economic Co-operation in Paris. Geiger is Co-Chair of the Investment Compact Stability Pact for South East Europe. He is an Associate Professor of International Economic Law at the University of Paris I (Panthéon-Sorbonne), and he has published numerous articles on international economic law issues. He is a member of the German American Lawyers Association and the French Society of International Law. (Email: rainer.geiger@oecd.org)

Steven Globerman is the Kaiser Professor of International Business and Director of the Center for International Business at Western Washington University, US. His research on topics in international business and public policy has been published in a wide range of professional journals and edited books. Globerman has served as a consultant to governments and international organizations, including the Government of Canada, the World Bank and the OECD. He is listed in *Who's Who Among Economists* and *Who's Who in International Business*. (Email: steven.globerman@wwu.edu)

Andrea Goldstein is a Senior Economist at the OECD Development Centre, working on private development and foreign direct investment in sub-Saharan Africa and other regions. In 2004, he worked at the World Bank Group as Senior Investment Policy Officer at the Foreign Investment Advisory Service, where he task-managed projects in Burkina Faso and the Democratic Republic of Congo. He was previously in the OECD Economics Department and Consob, the Italian Securities and Exchange Commission, and has consulted for the Inter-American Development Bank and the United Kingdom Department for International Development. He received a Laurea in Economia Politica from Bocconi University in Milan, Italy, and a Masters in International Affairs from Columbia University in New York. (Email: Andrea.goldstein@oecd.org)

Edward M. Graham was Senior Fellow at the Peterson Institute for International Economics in Washington, DC and was also an Adjunct

Professor at Columbia University's School of International and Public Affairs, US. He wrote extensively on foreign direct investment and was author, co-author, editor, or co-editor of nine books, including *Does Foreign Direct Investment Promote Development* and *US National Security and Foreign Direct Investment* (Institute for International Economics, 2005 and 2006). Graham also published more than 50 articles in the academic press and contributed articles to the financial press. He held a BA from Massachusetts Institute of Technology and a Master's degree and PhD from Harvard University, US. (Graham passed away on 12 September 2007, and this volume is dedicated to him.)

Carrie Hall is a Communications and Public Affairs Officer at the United Nations Global Compact, the world's largest voluntary corporate citizenship initiative. She joined the Compact in 2004 and has served as Editor of the *Compact Quarterly* since its launch in January 2005. Previously, Hall was a Vice President at Hill and Knowlton, an international public relations agency, where she specialized in crisis communications. She holds a Masters in Public Administration from Columbia University's School of International and Public Affairs, US. (Email: hallc@un.org)

Zenaida Hernández is an Investment Policy Officer at the Foreign Investment Advisory Service (FIAS), a multidonor service of the Financial and Private Sector Development Vice Presidency of the World Bank Group. She has worked in advisory projects to help improve the business environment in Latin America and the Caribbean as well as Africa. Previously, she was part of the team that produced the *World Development Report 2005: A Better Investment Climate for Everyone* (World Bank, 2004). Prior to joining the World Bank, Zenaida worked in international business consulting and international trade promotion. She holds an economics degree from the University of Zaragoza (Spain) and a Masters of Science in Foreign Service from Georgetown University, US. (Email: zhernandez@ifc.org)

Irmak Ince was recently awarded a JD at Columbia University, School of Law (2007). Previously, she received a BA in political science at the University of California, Los Angeles, US, Magna Cum Laude and Phi Beta Kappa (2004). During her time at Columbia, she was Managing Editor of the *Journal of European Law* and Co-Chair of Qanun, the Middle Eastern and North African Law Students Association. As part of the Human Rights Internship Program, she spent a summer working for the Chambers at the International Criminal Tribunal for Rwanda. She also interned with the District Attorney and the US Attorney's Offices while attending law school. Starting in Fall 2007, she will begin serving as an associate at the law firm of Latham and Watkins LLP in New York City. (Email: ii2111@columbia.edu)

Ravi Kant is Managing Director, Tata Motors Ltd. He has extensive experience in consumer durables and the automobile industry. Prior to joining Tata Motors Ltd, in 1999, Kant was Director, Phillips India Limited. He contributed significantly to turning around an ailing scooter manufacturer and to the launch of Titan, now India's leading watch brand. He is the Chairperson of Tata Daewoo Commercial Vehicles, Republic of Korea, Hispano-Carrocera, Spain, and Tata Motors Thailand Ltd, Bangkok. He is also the Chairperson of Tata Cummins Limited, a joint venture with Cummins, US, Tata Marcopolo Motors Ltd, H.V. Transmissions Ltd and TAL Manufacturing Solutions Ltd. He graduated from Mayo College, Ajmer, the Indian Institute of Technology, Kharagpur (both in India) and Aston University, Birmingham, United Kingdom, where he received a Masters in management in industry. (Email: ravikant@tatamotors.com)

Changsu Kim is a Professor in the College of Business Administration, Ewha Womans University, Republic of Korea. He was formerly an Assistant Professor of International Business at Nanyang Technological University, Singapore. His research areas include cross-border research and development alliances, technology learning and innovation, and FDI from emerging markets. (Email: cskim@ewha.ac.kr)

Kristin Mendoza is a JD/LL M candidate at Columbia University School of Law, US, and the University of London School of Oriental and African Studies (2008). She graduated with a BA in history, with distinction, from Yale College, US (2001). She also received an AM in Middle Eastern Studies from Harvard University (2004). Ms Mendoza is currently working with the International Senior Lawyers Project on various rule of law and economic development issues, and worked as a summer associate at Clifford Chance US LLP. Prior to law school, she was an intern to the President of the American University in Cairo, a teaching fellow at Harvard College and project coordinator for the Afghan Legal History Project. (Email: kristin.mendoza@aya.yale.edu)

Theodore H. Moran is the Marcus Wallenberg Professor, International Business and Finance, Georgetown University, US, and the founding Director of the Landegger Program, where he teaches and conducts research at the intersection of international economics, business, foreign affairs and public policy. Moran received his PhD in government from

Harvard University, US, and is widely known for his work on international economics and national security, political risk analysis, corporate strategy and transnational corporations, including nine books and some 60 scholarly articles. He is a consultant to the World Bank Group, the United Nations, various governments in Asia and Latin America, and the international business and financial communities. (Email: morant@georgetown.edu)

Donghyun Park has been Associate Professor, Nanyang Technological University, Republic of Singapore, since June 1995. He has a PhD in economics from the University of California Los Angeles, US. His research interests include international economics, development economics, political economy, applied microeconomics and East Asian economies, focusing on empirical testing of purchasing power parity, the impact of exchange rates on foreign direct investment, and economic geography in the presence of regional trade agreements. Park has published in numerous refereed international journals and has taught a number of courses at both the graduate and undergraduate levels. (Email: adpark@ntu.edu.sg)

Paulo T.V. Resende is Associate Dean for Research and Development and a Professor in Logistics, Transportation Planning and Supply Chain Management at Fundação Dom Cabral in Brazil; he is also a researcher and the coordinator of its Center for Logistics and Supply Chain Studies. He is the coordinator of the Masters Degree Program of Fundação Dom Cabral and the Catholic University of Minas Gerais, Brazil. Resende is author and co-author of several publications in Latin America, including *Mejores Practicas en Latinoamerica* (Thompson, 2004). He is a consultant in logistics and supply chain for several Latin American TNCs. (Email: pauloresende@fdc.org.br)

Mark Rhodes is a Lecturer in Economics and Programme Leader of the Masters in Finance programmes at the University of Wales. He received his doctorate from the University of Manchester Institute of Science and Technology (UMIST) in 1995. His research areas are financial and industrial economics, and applied econometrics. He has had previous appointments with the University of Warwick and the Financial Services Authority, UK. (Email: mkr@aber.ac.uk)

Alan Rugman holds the L. Leslie Waters Chair of International Business at the Kelley School of Business, Indiana University, US, where he is Professor of International Business and Professor of Business Economics and Public Policy. Rugman has published over 200 articles, appearing in leading journals that deal with economic, managerial and strategic aspects of TNCs and with trade and investment policy. His over 40 books include: *Inside the Multinationals*; *The Theory of Multinational Enterprises* (Columbia University Press, 1981 and Palgrave, 2006); *Multinational Enterprises and Trade Policy* (Elgar, 1996); and *The Regional Multinationals* (Cambridge University Press, 2005). He has just completed his term as President of the Academy of International Business, 2004–2006. (Email: rugman@indiana.edu)

Jeffrey D. Sachs is the Director of The Earth Institute, Quetelet Professor of Sustainable Development, and Professor of Health Policy and Management at Columbia University, US. He is also Special Advisor to United Nations Secretary-General Ban Ki-moon. From 2002 to 2006, he was Director of the UN Millennium Project and Special Advisor to United Nations Secretary-General Kofi Annan on the Millennium Development Goals, the internationally agreed goals to reduce extreme poverty, disease and hunger by the year 2015. Sachs is also President and Co-Founder of Millennium Promise Alliance, a nonprofit organization aimed at ending extreme global poverty. He is widely considered to be the leading international economic advisor of his generation. He is author of hundreds of scholarly articles and many books, including New York Times bestseller *The End of Poverty* (Penguin, 2005). He has won many awards and received many honorary degrees around the world. A native of Detroit, Michigan, Sachs received his BA, MA and PhD degrees at Harvard University, US. (Email: sachs@columbia.edu)

Karl P. Sauvant is the founding Executive Director of the Columbia Program on International Investment, Research Scholar and Lecturer in Law at Columbia Law School, Co-Director of the Millennium Cities Initiative, Columbia Program on International Investment, US, and Guest Professor at Nankai University, China. Before that, he was Director of UNCTAD's Investment Division. He is the author of, or responsible for, a substantial number of publications. In 2006, he was elected an Honorary Fellow of the European International Business Academy. (Email: karl.sauvant@law.columbia.edu)

David M. Schizer is the Dean of Columbia Law School, US, and the Lucy G. Moses Professor of Law. He graduated from Yale College and Yale Law School and clerked for Judge Alex Kozinski, US Court of Appeals for the Ninth Circuit, and for Justice Ruth Bader Ginsburg, Supreme Court of the United States. He then practiced law in the tax department of Davis Polk and Wardwell LLP. Schizer joined the Columbia faculty in 1998 and currently teaches federal income taxation, the taxation of financial instruments, corporate tax, professional responsibility and deals. (Email: dschiz@law. columbia.edu)

Daniel M. Shapiro is Dennis Culver EMBA Alumni Professor in the Faculty of Business Administration, Simon Fraser University, and Director of the CIBC Centre for Corporate Governance and Risk Management, Canada. He has published five books and monographs and over 50 scholarly articles on corporate performance and strategy, corporate ownership and governance, foreign investment and TNCs, industrial structure and various aspects of public policy. His current research is in the areas of corporate governance and the determinants of foreign direct investment. In 1995, and again in 2002, he was awarded the TD Canada Trust Teaching Award. He has been visiting professor at McGill University, Hong Kong Baptist University, Rotterdam School of Management (Erasmus University, the Netherlands), Monash University, Australia, and CEIBS (China). (Email: dshapiro@sfu.ca)

Joseph E. Stiglitz is University Professor at Columbia University, US, Chair of Columbia University's Committee on Global Thought, and Co-founder and President of the Initiative for Policy Dialogue. A winner of the Nobel Prize in Economics in 2001 for his analyses of markets with asymmetric information, he was chairperson of President Clinton's Council of Economic Advisers from 1995–97 and a member of his cabinet. From 1997 to 2000 he was Senior Vice President and Chief Economist of the World Bank. His book, *Globalization and Its Discontents* (W.W. Norton, 2003), was translated into 35 languages and has sold more than one million copies worldwide. His most recent book, *Making Globalization Work*, was published by W.W. Norton in September 2006. (Email: jes 322@columbia.edu)

Hinrich Voss is currently Post-Doctoral Fellow at the White Rose East Asia Centre, University of Leeds, UK. He received his doctorate from the University of Leeds in 2007, where he studied at the Centre for International Business (CIBUL). His research, which has been funded by scholarships from the Economic and Social Research Council and Leeds University Business School, concerns the international investment strategies and behavior of Chinese transnational corporations and the institutional environment in which they operate. Voss has presented his research at doctoral colloquia of the Academy of International Business Conferences in Beijing, China, Bath and Manchester, UK, and the European International Business Academy in Oslo, Norway. (Email: bushv@leeds.ac.uk)

Ping Zheng studied in China, where she received both a Bachelor's and Master's degree in economics. She received a doctorate in economics from the University of Abertay Dundee (UAD), United Kingdom. Zheng was a Teaching Fellow in 1988 at Dongbei University of Finance and Economics (DUFE), China. From 1991 to 1998, she was a lecturer at DUFE, and went on to become a part time Lecturer at UAD. Since 2004, Zheng has been a Research Fellow at Leeds University Business School. Her research interests include foreign direct investment, business, management and comparative development of India and China, Chinese economic development and competitiveness, and international economics. (Email: pz@lubs.leeds.ac.uk)

Yiping Zhou is Director of the Special Unit for South–South Cooperation (SU/SSC) at the United Nations Development Programme, which has the mandate from the General Assembly to promote and coordinate South–South and triangular cooperation on a global South and United Nations system-wide basis. He is also Editor-in-Chief of the development journal, *Cooperation South*. He served in the SU/SSC from 1997 to 2004, and was previously in the Regional Bureau for Asia and in the Office for Project Services. Before joining the UN, Zhou worked as Policy Officer in the Department of International Relations, Ministry of Foreign Economic Relations and Trade, Government of the People's Republic of China. He also served as a diplomat in the Permanent Mission of China to the UN from 1984 to 1985. (Email: yiping.zhou@undp.org)

Foreword

Supachai Panitchpakdi*

The world economy is undergoing a profound transformation, driven by globalization, the spread of the market economy to virtually all countries and the liberalization of international economic transactions. Part of this transformation involves the rise of emerging markets, led by developing Asia. The growth of exports from that region, its attractiveness to foreign direct investment (FDI) and its economic growth in general have drawn the attention of analysts and policy makers worldwide, as prime indicators of this transformation.

In the shadow of these developments, another change is taking place: emerging markets increasingly not only attract FDI, but are also becoming the source of such investment. Largely unnoticed, the proportions of this investment have become quite significant: as UNCTAD's *World Investment Report 2006* documents, FDI outflows from emerging markets in 2005 were some $130 billion (almost three times *world* FDI flows some 25 years ago), and the stock of this investment had reached $1.4 trillion. This means that emerging market firms have not only become internationally competitive in terms of trade, but a good many of them now also have the tangible and intangible assets needed to be successful through FDI – and more firms will join the already established global or regional players in the future.

This is a good thing: outward FDI from emerging markets (as is shown in the contributions to this volume) strengthens the competitiveness of the firms involved; it helps the economic performance of their home countries; it opens new sources of long-term capital flows (and the benefits associated with them) for other countries; and, more broadly, it becomes another avenue for the integration of emerging markets into the globalizing world economy.

Despite the importance of this phenomenon, it has not received the analytical and policy attention it deserves. The policy challenges, in particular, stand out. Emerging markets themselves need to come to grips with their new role as home countries, including by balancing their interests as host and home countries. Host developed countries, for their part, must recognize that emerging market transnational corporations are here to stay and need to be accepted as increasingly important players in their markets. Furthermore, there is the challenge of integrating the new players smoothly into the international economic system within a framework of rules that gives due attention to the interests of all involved.

These are formidable challenges, especially since they need to be seen as part of a broader transformation of the world economy – what I would like to term the second generation of globalization. They call for more research and policy analysis, and this volume is an important step in that direction.

Geneva, August 2007

NOTE

*   Secretary-General of UNCTAD and former Director General of WTO.

Preface

Emerson de Almeida, David M. Schizer and Yiping Zhou

The First Columbia International Investment Conference, held at Columbia University, US, on 24–25 October 2006, focused on a topic that is receiving increasing attention in the media and academic circles, as well as from policy makers: *The Rise of Transnational Corporations from Emerging Markets: Threat or Opportunity?* Fittingly, it was organized by three institutions, each of which has a special interest in this new phenomenon and a core competency that bears on one of its vital aspects:

- The Columbia Program on International Investment, a joint undertaking of Columbia Law School and The Earth Institute at Columbia University. It follows closely the growth of transnational corporations (TNCs) from emerging markets and the foreign direct investment (FDI) they undertake, with a view to examining its policy, legal and economic development, and academic curriculum implications. This is part of the mission of the Columbia Law School and The Earth Institute: to address, through intellectual discourse, cutting-edge global developments.
- Fundação Dom Cabral, a leading business school in Brazil, one of the BRIC countries (Brazil, Russia, India, China), which are the ones that attract most attention when it comes to outward FDI from emerging markets. It develops corporate executives to face the challenges of today's world. Increasingly, this entails preparing these executives for venturing out of their home country not only through trade but also through FDI, and for managing integrated international production networks on a regional or global basis.
- The Special Unit for South–South Cooperation, United Nations Development Programme (UNDP), the focal point for cooperation among developing countries in the United Nations system. It has a special interest in exploring the implications of the growth of emerging-market TNCs for developing countries in general and their beneficial integration into the globalizing world economy.

An increased understanding of this phenomenon is all the more important, as a good part of FDI by emerging-market TNCs is directed toward other emerging markets.

Combining these interests and core competencies, these three institutions brought together the leading scholars in the field to examine what may well be the beginning of an accelerating process that contributes to the transformation of the world economy and the policy and legal systems governing it. We hope that this volume, which contains the Conference papers as finalized in the light of the discussions, helps to bring about a better understanding of the range of issues related to the rise of transnational corporations from emerging markets.

New York and Belo Horizonte, August 2007

Acknowledgements

Karl P. Sauvant, Kristin Mendoza and Irmak Ince

This book consists of the finalized papers prepared for the First Columbia International Investment Conference entitled *The Rise of Transnational Corporations from Emerging Markets: Threat or Opportunity?* held in October 2006 at Columbia University, US.[1] The event was organized by the Columbia Program on International Investment (a joint undertaking of Columbia Law School and The Earth Institute at Columbia University), Fundação Dom Cabral, Brazil, and the Special Unit for South–South Cooperation, United Nations Development Programme. We want to thank, first of all, the institutions that co-sponsored the Conference: without their financial and overall support, and that of Mark and Gail Appel, the event itself and this volume would not have been possible.

The intellectual burden of this volume and its strength rest, of course, on its individual contributors and their contributions. Each of them helps to advance the international debate on the subject of this Conference. They, in turn, benefited from presentations by James P. Shaughnessy, Alessandro Giuseppe Carlucci and Friedrich von Kirchbach; comments from the participants in the Conference; and especially, the discussants, namely, Eddie Chen, Jorge H. Forteza, Todd Malan, Manfred Schekulin and James Zhan. The rich discussions were led by Richard N. Gardner, Lisa Anderson, John C. Mutter and José Alvarez.

The Conference itself was organized expertly by Matthew Quint, working with Luiz Carvalho, Tracy Zhou and André Almeida. They were supported by Todd Arena, Jenny Chao, Victor Chan, Ludmilla Maria Coccia, Maria Esstenssoro, Lisa Sachs, Timothy Sparkman and Jyotsna Vasisht – almost all of them participants in Columbia's *Foreign Direct Investment and Public Policy* seminar. Their efforts ensured the smooth proceeding of the Conference, and, in the case of Matthew Quint, also the preparation of this volume.

Thank you very much to all of them!

New York, August 2007

NOTE

1. Throughout the book, the use of names of countries and territories follows official UN usage. Please also note that figures in tables do not always add up to 100 due to rounding.

This volume is dedicated to the memory of Edward M. Graham

PART I

Overview

1. The rise of TNCs from emerging markets: the issues

Karl P. Sauvant

INTRODUCTION

The subject of this volume – the rise of transnational corporations (TNCs) from emerging markets: threat or opportunity? – is topical and important, and it poses a number of challenges that will require considerable policy attention in the future.

1.1 TOPICALITY

The topicality of the subject is exemplified by a spate of recent high-profile takeovers by emerging-market TNCs of firms in developed and developing countries. Examples are:

- Lenovo's (China) acquisition of the personal computers division of IBM (United States). When the deal was completed in 2005, Lenovo paid $1.25 billion with a total cost of $1.75 billion, including assumed debt.
- CVRD's (Brazil) takeover of INCO (Canada) in 2007, for $16.7 billion.
- Tata's (India) successful bid (against the competition of Companhia Siderúrgica Nacional of Brazil) for Corus (United Kingdom/ Netherlands). The deal was reached in 2007, for a total price of $13.5 billion.
- Hindalco (India) bought Novelis (US) in 2007 for $6 billion.
- Dubai Ports World's acquisition of P & O Steam Navigation Company (United Kingdom), an event that led to an excited policy debate in the US as Dubai Ports World would then have controlled a number of ports in that country (Dubai Ports World eventually had to divest itself of its US assets). The sale for $6.8 billion dollars was approved in 2006.

- Cemex (Mexico) bought Rinker (Australia) for $15.5 billion in 2007, the largest takeover in Australia's history.
- Lukoil Overseas Holding Ltd (Russia) purchased Nelson Resources Ltd (United Kingdom) in 2005 for $2 billion.
- Oger Telecom (Saudi Arabia) purchased Turk Telekomunikasyon AS (Turkey) for $6.55 billion in 2005.
- America Movil SA de CV (Mexico) acquired Telecom Americas Ltd (Brazil) for $2.27 billion in 2002.

These are just a few examples of how a new breed of firms from emerging markets, the new kids on the block, are becoming important players in the world foreign direct investment (FDI) market. Fittingly, an editorial in the *Financial Times* – enigmatically entitled 'Empire strikes back as Tata bids for Corus' – concluded as follows:

> The new trend for foreign purchases [by TNCs from emerging markets] has only just begun: the Tata-Corus deal is a dramatic demonstration of the new, self-confident mood of Indian business. Over the next 30 years, China and India will grow to dominate the world economy. They will give birth to great industrial companies that own plants all around the world. National pride may suffer a little but economic nationalism and imperialism have had their day and that can only be a good thing.[1]

This quote captures the underlying dynamic that is driving the rise of emerging-market TNCs, namely the re-emergence of China and India as important players in the world economy. As Jeffrey D. Sachs reminds us (in Chapter 2), the Asian economy accounted for some 60 per cent of world GDP at the beginning of the 19th century, and the region is in the process of regaining this share. (China alone accounted for over 30 per cent of world GDP (at purchasing power parity) at the beginning of the 19th century, a share that declined to about 5 per cent in the 1950s and recovered to 15 per cent in 2006.) But as we can observe, this process is broader (reflected, for instance, in the growing share of emerging markets in world exports), and encompasses a growing number of developing countries and economies in transition. It is therefore not surprising that this underlying structural shift finds its expression also in the rise of TNCs from emerging markets and hence outward foreign direct investment (OFDI) from them. The subject of this volume is therefore not only topical, but it is also important, and it will remain with us for the foreseeable future.

1.2 IMPORTANCE

OFDI from emerging markets is not a new phenomenon: firms based in these countries have invested abroad for decades; this is reflected in their almost 13 per cent share in the world FDI stock in 1980 (Table 1.1).[2] What is new is the absolute magnitude that this phenomenon has achieved, growing rapidly, but largely unobserved, over the past 20 years or so in the shadow of the global expansion of FDI in general, driven primarily by TNCs from developed countries. More specifically, world FDI flows were about $50 billion during the early 1980s, of which flows originating in

Table 1.1   Distribution of OFDI by region and selected countries, 1980–2005 (%)

Region	Stock			
	1980	*1990*	*2000*	*2005*
Developed economies	87.3	91.7	86.2	86.9
European Union	37.2	45.2	47.1	51.3
Japan	3.4	11.2	4.3	3.6
United States	37.7	24.0	20.3	19.2
Emerging markets	12.7	8.3	13.5	11.9
Africa	1.3	1.1	0.7	0.5
Latin America and the Caribbean	8.5	3.4	3.3	3.2
Asia and Oceania	2.9	3.8	9.5	8.2
Southeast Europe and CIS	..	0.01	0.3	1.2
World	100.0	100.0	100.0	100.0

Region	Flow			
	1978–1980	*1988–1990*	*1998–2000*	*2003–2005*
Developed economies	97.0	93.1	90.4	85.8
European Union	44.8	50.6	64.4	54.6
Japan	4.9	19.7	2.6	4.9
United States	39.7	13.6	15.9	15.7
Emerging markets	3.0	6.9	9.4	12.3
Africa	1.0	0.4	0.2	0.2
Latin America and the Caribbean	1.1	1.0	4.1	3.5
Asia and Oceania	0.9	5.6	5.1	8.6
Southeast Europe and CIS	..	0.01	0.2	1.8
World	100.0	100.0	100.0	100.0

Source: UNCTAD 2006.

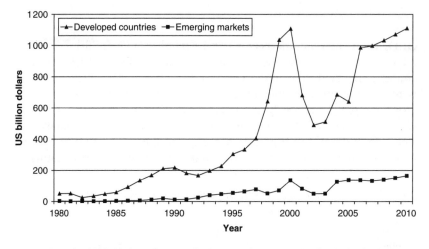

Note: Data for 2006–2010 are forecasts for 82 countries responsible for the bulk of all OFDI flows from both developed and emerging markets; Data for 2006–2010, Kekic and Sauvant (2006).

Source: Data for 1980–2005, UNCTAD 2006.

Figure 1.1   OFDI flows from developed countries and emerging markets, 1980–2010

emerging markets were negligible. By 2005, world OFDI flows had risen to $779 billion, of which $133 billion originated in emerging markets – almost three times world FDI flows two decades earlier.[3] Estimates are that the level of OFDI from emerging markets will remain at this level at least until 2010, although they may well be higher (Figure 1.1).[4] These flows had accumulated to a stock of $1.4 trillion by the end of 2005. Overall, emerging markets now account for roughly 15 per cent world's FDI flows, FDI stock, cross-border mergers and acquisitions and greenfield investments.

The regional distribution of OFDI from emerging markets has undergone a dramatic change over the past 25 years (Table 1.1). In particular, the role of Latin America and the Caribbean versus that of Asia as dominant home region has been reversed: the former accounted for two-thirds of OFDI stock of emerging markets in 1980, a share that declined to one quarter in 2005; over the same period, the share of Asia rose from nearly one quarter in 1980 to almost two-thirds in 2005. Moreover, a good part of this investment is in other emerging markets. In developing Asia, for example, perhaps some 40 per cent of FDI originates in other emerging markets.[5] More broadly, emerging market TNCs have become important investors in many of the poorest countries in Africa and Asia. This reflects the tendency of TNCs, including emerging-market TNCs, to invest typically in their own region, as Alan Rugman examines below (Chapter 6), and explores in particular for Chinese TNCs. Part of the reason for this pattern is that firms typically have better regional than global knowledge; however, it also shows how difficult it is to become a truly global player. Firms headquartered in China are also the subject of discussions by Peter J. Buckley *et al.*, who investigate factors explaining China's OFDI (Chapter 7).

Moreover, while a fairly limited number of economies accounts for the bulk of this OFDI,[6] with firms from Brazil, Russia, India and China (the BRIC countries)[7] being particularly visible, over 90 emerging markets reported at least some OFDI flows in 2005. In fact, the number of emerging markets with an OFDI stock of over $5 billion has risen from 6 in 1990 to 24 in 2005 (Table 1.2). This reflects the fact that there are at least 20 000 emerging-market TNCs (defined as firms controlling assets abroad). Most of this OFDI is in services, including trade-supporting services.

It is not surprising that there is such a high number of emerging-market TNCs: like their competitors from developed countries, they too face the same opportunities and pressures of the globalizing world economy. More specifically (and apart from the structural changes mentioned earlier), the strategies of firms, whether large or small, from developed countries or emerging markets, are increasingly driven by a combination of three factors:

- the worldwide liberalization of FDI regimes, which opens new opportunities for firms to expand;
- advances in transport, communication and information technologies, which create opportunities to manage integrated international production networks consisting of parent firms and their foreign affiliates located in various countries; and
- competition among firms, which drives firms to take advantage of these new opportunities and possibilities.

These factors were also present 30 years ago or so, when the transnationalization process of firms from developed countries gathered speed. But the economic globalization process (itself partly driven by the growth of FDI), as John H. Dunning, Changsu Kim and Donghyun Park explore below (Chapter 8), created a new environment within which emerging-market firms (as well as those from developed countries) are under greater pressure than ever before to transnationalize. Increasingly a portfolio of locational assets in the form of a regional or global network of foreign affiliates becomes one source of the international competitiveness of firms. No wonder, then, that firms from emerging markets are increasingly investing abroad.

Table 1.2   *Emerging markets with an OFDI stock of $5 billion or more,*
1990, 2005 (US$m)

Economy	1990	Economy	2005
Brazil	41 044	Hong Kong (China)	470 458
Taiwan Province of China	30 356	British Virgin Islands	123 167
South Africa	15 004	Russian Federation	120 417
Hong Kong (China)	11 920	Singapore	110 932
Singapore	7 808	Taiwan Province of China	97 293
Argentina	6 057	Brazil	71 556
		China	46 311
		Malaysia	44 480
		South Africa	38 503
		Korea, Republic of	36 478
		Cayman Islands	33 747
		Mexico	28 040
		Argentina	22 633
		Chile	21 286
		Indonesia	13 735
		Panama	12 891
		Venezuela	10 665
		UAE	10 087
		India	9 569
		Colombia	8 876
		Bermuda	5 982
		Kuwait	5 403
		Bahrain	5 058
		Nigeria	5 026

Note: As already noted earlier, data on OFDI from emerging markets need to be interpreted with caution. The phenomenon of trans-shipment FDI has already been noted; it is reflected in the stock data as well. Another difficulty is that flow data (although recent) do not accumulate, even closely, to stock data; that appears to be the case for Russia. As for the 1980 data, Brazil accounted for nearly half of the stock reported here; it is quite possible that most of it was in tax havens.

Source: UNCTAD 2006.

1.3   CHALLENGES

But the growth of this investment poses a number of challenges. There is, first of all, the challenge for the firms themselves. To be competitive in the international FDI market, firms need ownership-specific advantages. When combined with the locational advantages of host countries and those of internalizing transactions within their own corporate networks (as opposed to, say, servicing a foreign market through exports), ownership-specific advantages allow firms not only to survive in foreign markets, but also to prosper in competition with domestic rivals.[8] The bottleneck in this respect is often not so much finance or even technology, but human resources with the experience of managing regional or global production networks and the various challenges and risks associated with that; this experience becomes all the more important if international expansion takes place through mergers and acquisitions (M&As) as these typically pose the additional challenge of integrating already-established operations, often with their own distinct corporate culture, into a new corporate environment. And success as regards M&As is, as John Cantwell and Helena Barnard discuss (Chapter 5), one indicator of the competitiveness of emerging market TNCs. This volume does not explore these issues, although Ravi Kant's account (Chapter 3) of the experience of Tata touches upon some of these matters in the broader context of the transnationalization of that firm, and Paulo Resende and Alvaro Cyrino's discussion (Chapter 4) of the internationalization of the supply chain provides a taste of one of the specific managerial tasks involved.

Host countries too, face challenges of a mixed nature. For one, emerging markets have now become an important source of FDI that can be tapped. To do that, host countries must get away from a mindset that FDI flows originate only in developed countries, and from, as a result, gearing their efforts to attract such investment only (or overwhelmingly) from those countries. This is already beginning to take place. Thus for example, a number of countries have established branches of their investment promotion agencies (IPAs) in China, precisely to tap into that country's reservoir of FDI. Furthermore, IPAs in Africa expect that, in the future, a good part of their FDI will come from Asia, and presumably, will direct their promotional efforts more toward that region (UNCTAD 2006, p. 220).

While the impact of emerging-market TNCs on host countries may not be systematically and substantially different from that of their developed-country competitors, it may well be that especially smaller firms among them may at times be less sensitive to some host country concerns, or engage in practices that may compare unfavorably with those of other foreign firms. At the same time, as Carrie Hall documents (Chapter 11), it may be that such negative aspects are, at least for some larger emerging-market TNCs, counterbalanced by more sharply developed corporate social responsibility practices, as firms from emerging markets are presumably more attuned to the conditions of poverty characterizing most of their home economies.

But there is also a broader and in some ways more difficult challenge, particularly for host countries in the developed world: they need to see the rise of TNCs from emerging markets not as a threat but as an opportunity, as an additional avenue to integrate emerging markets fully into the world economy. In other words, they need to accept that emerging-market TNCs are here to stay.[9] In fact, they will become more important and need to be integrated as smoothly as possible into the world FDI market dominated so far by developed-country TNCs. It is not easy to integrate rising powers (as we know from other contexts), especially if they challenge established players across a growing range of industries. The defensive reactions to some of the takeovers mentioned earlier in this chapter – or attempts thereof, such as CNOOC's (China) bid to acquire UNOCAL (US), or the possibility of Haier (China) taking over Maytag (US) – bear this out, and are examined by Andrea Goldstein (Chapter 9). They are particularly acute if market entry takes place through cross-border M&As as, by definition, these do not lead to the immediate creation of new production capacity but rather represent only a change in ownership, from domestic to foreign hands. Moreover, M&As are often accompanied by restructuring, which can involve the closing down of business activities and lay-offs of personnel (even though such actions may be needed to ensure the survival of the entity involved). M&As can acquire an additional edge and become especially controversial when the acquiring firms are state-owned enterprises and acquisition targets are in sectors considered sensitive by host countries, be it for security or economic development reasons, or because they are national champions. Related issues concern the internal governance of emerging-market TNCs in the light of the perception that these firms may have limited experience in managing international production networks and may sometimes not be as well governed as would be desirable; the latter issue is examined by Rainer Geiger (Chapter 10).

All this means that there is a growing tension, especially in host countries in the developed world, between their desire to attract FDI and their uneasiness with respect to the 'new kids on the block' that disturb the established order.[10]

Tensions – although not yet visible – are also likely to emerge in the home countries of emerging-market TNCs. The basic reason is that the overwhelming number of emerging markets, be they developing countries or economies in transition, are capital-importing countries, that is, economies that need capital to advance their development. Allowing OFDI, let alone encouraging it, is counterintuitive and therefore not an obvious policy choice for home country governments, even if they understand that their firms, to remain internationally competitive, require a portfolio of locational assets. So far, this tension has not surfaced, as it is partially obscured by national pride in the success of one's own firms in acquiring major assets in developed countries. But it may only be a question of time until pride is

replaced by concern, in particular, about productive capacity and jobs being created abroad and not at home, and about 'hollowing out'.

What this calls for is a policy debate in emerging markets that are home countries, involving all stakeholders – business, unions, non-governmental organizations, the government. Such a dialogue requires of course an understanding of the impact of OFDI on the international competitiveness of domestic firms and the economic performance of home countries. Reference has already been made to the analysis by John Cantwell and Helena Barnard (Chapter 5), dealing with the former issue. Steven Globerman and Daniel M. Shapiro examine (Chapter 12) the latter issue. Theodore H. Moran (Chapter 13) takes this analysis a step further by dis- cussing policy implications. As Moran points out, these analyses partly build on work that was done some 30 years ago for developed countries, when OFDI from them became a hotly debated issue. Work at that time showed that, on balance, such investment is beneficial for home countries, with the benefits accruing through a number of channels. Little work on that subject has been done since then, and virtually no work in the context of emerging markets. The chapters in this volume are, therefore, pioneer- ing. They can serve as building blocks for a more comprehensive under- standing of this subject and the policy options that emerge from it.

For governments of developed countries, these policy options all pointed in one direction: to liberalize OFDI flows (and, by now, they have almost all completely done so) and to develop a set of instruments designed to protect and encourage such flows. At the national level, these instruments include the provision of information on investment opportunities, insur- ance against certain risks offered to firms investing abroad, and the provi- sion of certain types of finance for overseas projects.

At the international level, developed countries pioneered bilateral investment treaties (BITs), with the first one concluded between Germany and Pakistan in 1959, to promote and protect FDI.[11] Originally concluded virtually entirely between developed and developing countries, the number of BITs between emerging markets accounted for 26 per cent of the total number of BITs at the end of June 2006, and 30 per cent of the BITs con- cluded between 1 January 2005 and 30 June 2006 (UNCTAD 2007a). This is, in and by itself, a sign that governments of emerging markets see the need to protect and promote the outward investment of their firms in a bilateral context; in fact, a number of them have also done so in a regional context, for example, in NAFTA, MERCOSUR and ASEAN.

But emerging markets, and particularly developing countries as a group, have resisted efforts led by developed countries to do the same at the mul- tilateral level of the World Trade Organization (WTO).[12] It remains to be seen whether this attitude will change in the light of developing countries

themselves becoming important outward investors (including those that were among the leaders of an investment agreement in the WTO, India and Malaysia). Edward M. Graham (Chapter 14) is skeptical in this respect, while Joseph E. Stiglitz (Chapter 15) points in particular to the importance of such an agreement taking into account the needs of developing countries. While the question of a multilateral framework on investment is currently not on the agenda of the world community, it may well be that the rise of TNCs from emerging markets changes the underlying interest situation of key emerging markets in such a manner that they too seek a multilateral framework for this international economic activity, complementing the institutional arrangements that already exist for international trade and finance. Other emerging markets, for their part, may find it in their interest, and to their benefit, to deal with investment matters in a multilateral rather than a bilateral (or regional) context, as the former typically is more favorable for smaller countries. The explosion of international investment disputes in recent years and the discussions of a review mechanism this has triggered[13] may well give additional impetus to a multilateral approach.

CONCLUSION

The rise of TNCs from emerging markets poses threats and offers opportunities. The threats consist mostly of challenges to integrate the newcomers smoothly into the international FDI market and the world economy, at levels eventually on par with the best-managed TNCs. The opportunities consist mostly of the potential for OFDI from emerging markets to strengthen the economic performance of their home countries, and the fact that emerging-market TNCs represent a new source of capital, technology, skills and access to markets for host countries to advance their own development.

The contributions in this volume – all of which are mentioned in the course of this chapter – examine a number of issues related to the rise of emerging-market TNCs. They were discussed during the International Conference on *The Rise of Transnational Corporations from Emerging Markets: Threat or Opportunity?* held at Columbia University on 24–25 October 2006, and subsequently finalized in the light of these discussions; the event was organized by the Columbia Program on International Investment, Fundação Dom Cabral (Brazil) and the South–South Unit in the United Nations Development Programme (UNDP). The essence of these discussions is captured by Lorraine Eden (Chapter 16). As the subject of this Conference and this volume is complex and has not yet received the attention it deserves, this book can only be a step in the direction of

fostering a much better understanding of, and developing appropriate policy options for the rise of TNCs from emerging markets.

ACKNOWLEDGEMENTS

This chapter was finalized while the author was Visiting Professor at Nankai University, Tianjin, China. I acknowledge with thanks the helpful comments provided by John H. Dunning, Andrea Goldstein, Laza Kekic and Masataka Fujita and the assistance provided by Matthew Quint.

NOTES

1. 'Empire strikes back as Tata bids for Corus', *Financial Times*, 21 October 2006.
2. There was a burst of literature in the 1980s drawing attention to FDI by firms from developing countries. See Kumar and McLeod (1981); Lall (1983); Lecraw (1981); Oman (1986); Wells (1983). An example of later writing is Dunning, Van Hoesel and Narula (1998).
3. For extensive recent discussions of OFDI from emerging markets, see UNCTAD (2006) and Goldstein (2007); some of the chapters below also document various aspects of this development. Unless otherwise noted, the data below are from the *World Investment Report* and especially UNCTAD (2007). It should be noted that some 10 per cent of OFDI flows from emerging markets originate in offshore financial centers, often consisting of trans-shipment FDI from other emerging markets and from developed countries.
4. In the case of Brazil, for example, outflows of FDI in 2006 actually surpassed FDI inflows, and the same is predicted for India in 2007. See ECLAC (2007, p. 68) and Bhutani (2007). The same situation is more difficult to imagine for China, given its high levels of FDI inflows. However, it is conceivable that as inflows stabilize while outflows soar, driven not only by the government's 'Go Global' policy, but also by China's State investment company, to be established in the course of 2007 to invest part of China's official reserves more profitably abroad. Even before that company was formally established, it acquired in May 2007 non-voting shares worth $3 billion (9.9 per cent) of The Blackstone Group (the second largest US private equity firm), in this manner not triggering an examination by the Committee on Foreign Investment in the United States (*China Daily*, 22 May 2007).
5. Some of this FDI, though, is indirect FDI, the ultimate parent firms of which may be headquartered in a developed country. A good part of OFDI from Hong Kong (China) and Singapore, for example, is from foreign affiliates located there. (Reference has already been made (note 3) to trans-shipment FDI in offshore financial centers.)
6. In 2005, the five most important emerging-market home economies accounted for about two-thirds of the OFDI stock of all emerging markets, and the top ten for 83 per cent.
7. See Sauvant (2006).
8. For an explanation of what drives FDI, see Dunning and Lundan (forthcoming).
9. In 2005 there were 47 firms from emerging markets listed in *Fortune*'s Global 500, as compared to 19 in 1990 (UNCTAD 2006, p. 122).
10. This uneasiness can fuel a broader backlash against FDI, see Sauvant (2006).
11. Double taxation treaties are also important; they are meant to avoid, as their name suggests, the imposition of double taxation on the profits of TNCs. By the end of June 2006, 2799 such treaties existed; see UNCTAD (2007a).

12. Beyond the General Agreement on Trade in Services (which covers FDI in services) and the Agreement on Trade-related Investment Measures (which covers certain performance requirements).
13. See Sauvant with Chiswick-Patterson (forthcoming).

REFERENCES

Bhutani, Jyoti (2007). *ASSOCHAM Eco Pulse Analysis: FDI Outflow of USD 15 Billion Seen in 2007; Manufacturing to Lead the Drive* (New Delhi: ASSOCHAM), mimeo.

Dunning, John H. and Sarianna M. Lundan (forthcoming). *Multinational Enterprises and the Global Economy* (Cheltenham, UK: Edward Elgar) 2nd edition.

Dunning, John H., R. Van Hoesel and R. Narula (1998). 'Third world multinationals revisited: new developments and theoretical implications', in John H. Dunning, ed., *Globalization, Trade and Foreign Direct Investment* (London: Pergamon).

ECLAC (Economic Commission for Latin America and the Caribbean) (2007). *Foreign Investment in Latin America and the Caribbean, 2006* (Santiago, Chile: United Nations).

Goldstein, Andrea (2007). *Multinational Companies from Emerging Economies: Composition, Conceptualization and Direction in the Global Economy* (Basingstoke, UK and New York: Palgrave Macmillan).

Kekic, Laza and Karl P. Sauvant, eds (2006). *World Investment Prospects to 2010: Boom or Backlash?* (London, UK: The Economist Intelligence Unit Ltd).

Kumar, Krishna and M.G. McLeod, eds (1981). *Multinationals from Developing Countries* (Lexington, MA: Lexington Books).

Lall, Sanjaya (1983). *The New Multinationals: The Spread of Third World Enterprises* (Chichester: Wiley).

Lecraw, Donald J. (1981). 'Internationalisation of firms from LDCs: evidence from the ASEAN region', in K. Kumar and M.G. McLeod, eds, *Multinationals from Developing Countries* (Lexington, MA: Lexington Books), pp. 37–51.

Oman, Charles, ed. (1986). *New Forms of Overseas Investment by Developing Countries: The Case of India, Korea and Brazil* (Paris: OECD Development Centre).

Sauvant, Karl P. (2006). 'A backlash against foreign direct investment?' in Laza Kekic and Karl P. Sauvant, eds, *World Investment Prospects to 2010: Boom or Backlash?* (London, UK: The Economist Intelligence Unit Ltd), pp. 71–77, available at www.cpii.columbia.edu/pubs/documents/WIP_to_2010_SPECIAL_EDITION.pdf, last visited 24 October 2007.

Sauvant, Karl P. with Michael Chiswick-Patterson, eds (forthcoming). *Coherence and Consistency in International Investment Law* (Oxford: Oxford University Press).

UNCTAD (2006). *World Investment Report 2006: FDI from Developing and Transition Economies: Implications for Development* (Geneva: UNCTAD).

UNCTAD (2007). *The Emerging Landscape of Foreign Direct Investment: Some Salient Issues: Note Prepared by the UNCTAD Secretariat*, TD/B/COM.2/77 (1 February 2007), mimeo.

UNCTAD (2007a). *International Investment Rule-Setting: Trends, Emerging Issues and Implications*, TD/B/COM.2/73 (5 January 2007), mimeo.

Wells, Louis T. Jr (1983). *Third World Multinationals: The Rise of Foreign Direct Investment from Developing Countries* (Cambridge, MA: MIT Press).

2. The rise of TNCs from emerging markets: the global context

Jeffrey D. Sachs

I would like to frame a few of the broader global conditions in which this topic will proceed in substance for some time to come. I want to give a kind of macroeconomic overview, and a very brief one indeed, rather than a microeconomic assessment of the particular issues of outward foreign direct investment (FDI) from emerging markets.

There is little doubt that, barring a catastrophe, we are living in an age that will be marked by the biggest economic change in the history of recent centuries. It will have, in its geopolitical impact, a role comparable to that of the Industrial Revolution, which is one of the great ruptures of history. We are now living in the age of convergence of economic performance, after several centuries of divergence. Since around 1500, the North Atlantic economies – for a lot of very complicated economic, political and military reasons – rose in dominance over the course of 450 years, so that, by the middle of the twentieth century, the shared dominance of the United States and Europe completely defined the global economic reality. Of course, the Cold War was the dominant survival issue for the world, but the dominant economic issue was the unprecedented concentration of economic power in the North Atlantic economies, and all that it meant for society, technology, culture and so on.

The rise of the North Atlantic countries was a long process. It was most fundamentally made powerful by the discovery of trade routes to the Americas and, even more importantly, it was accelerated dramatically after 1800 by the Industrial Revolution in the nineteenth century. It was an age of profound divergence. Starting from rough equality of economic activity around the world as late as 1800, one small part of the world, the North Atlantic, surged in economic weight: according to estimates by Angus Maddison, the Asian economy went from about 60 per cent of world GDP in 1820 to about 23 per cent by 1970 (Maddison 2001).

That was extraordinary, and rather unusual in economic terms, because generally, there are powerful reasons to believe that divergence should not be a hundred-year process, but rather, that it should be a process that is overtaken by powerful forces of convergence. That did not happen for a long time. The unprecedented thrust of science-based, technological advance that took place in Western Europe, and the ensuing military advantage, gave divergence 150 years or so of life. That is unusual in any grand sense and almost impossible in any economic model. The world is not supposed to be like that. In one of the most important passages of modern social thinking, Adam Smith ([1776] 1904) wrote about the discovery of the trade routes to the Americas and to Asia from Europe as being the two most significant events in the history of the world. He wrote that these two events should have strengthened all of the world, but by an accident of history, they occurred at a time when the military advantage of Europe was so large that it ended up wrecking the native economies and societies of the East and West Indies. Smith also wrote that we have to look forward to the day when this accident will be righted, and when there will be a balance of fear sufficient to provide mutual benefit that should come from globalization. And Smith went on to say, in this unbelievable paragraph of wisdom, that it is trade itself, and the flow of ideas, that will be the re-balancer in the world eventually, so that there will be a return to convergence, and it will be mutual fear that will eventually lead to the mutual respect and the mutual benefit that can come from the globalization process.

My essential point is that the 'tricks of the trade' of technology-based, market-led development are now known everywhere, and they are basically being implemented everywhere. The very specific historical period in which the West, meaning the North Atlantic, was dominant, is over, because what fueled that process is now being overtaken by extremely powerful forces of convergence. The main forces of convergence are technology, which is available everywhere in the world, and the essential instruments of economic development, which are now shared by most of the world, and certainly by the largest nations, China and India. We are on a path that is different from the path of the past 450 years, which ended roughly around 1950. For China, the real convergence only started after 1978. One could say that in India, it had a long, very slow start until 1991. But convergence is now a very deep process.

Economics, or the kind of economics that I was raised in and that I practice in my general thinking, takes convergence as a much more natural phenomenon than divergence. Divergence depends on two things. It depends first on only one part of the world having the magic elixir of science-based innovation and, second, on political dominance. Those are both ending. Political dominance really has been unraveling. There is no longer such a thing as a successful occupying army anywhere in the world. At the same time, the economic organization required for innovative growth is also broadly shared. According to my estimates, China's share, or Asia's share, of world GNP will rise to more than 50 per cent of world GNP by 2050, up from 23 per cent in 1970, and roughly 38 per cent in 2000.[1] The reason that more than half of the world GNP will be in Asia is that more than half of the world's people live in Asia. So the real question is why not? What would stop that kind of convergence from happening? Asia is where the people are, and the people now are empowered with tools, competent universities, research labs, research and development (R&D), and all sorts of modern tools, especially cell phones, computer terminals and the internet.

Thus, my starting point for our topic is that there really is fundamental change. The idea of FDI coming from emerging markets is going to be the norm. Again, why not? Of course we are going to have major firms head-quartered in emerging markets – it is just unusual for us to think in those terms. Since social attitudes lag reality by 15 years, the public ethos will lag behind for a while. Trends that seem surprising now will not be quite so surprising over time.

The second important, basic macroeconomic fact is that China and India are moving beyond the Asian model of catching up. That model is essentially a workshop model, which involves bringing in capital and technology, assembling it and then re-exporting it. From 1960 to 1985, the workshop model fueled Asia's rapid catching up. It was a good model that made sense with skilled, numerate, literate, low-wage labor. There is still is a lot of that kind of growth left. But there is no doubt in my mind that we are already well past the threshold at which Asia has entered the era of endogenous growth, fueled by its own innovation and heavy investments in R&D. Much more of that is going to happen.

Of course, Japan has demonstrated this for three-quarters of a century or more, and it was Japan's knowledge base that fueled a part of Asian industrialization in the flying geese model.[2] But it is already evident that there is a great deal of innovation in China and India (not to mention in the Republic of Korea, Singapore, Taiwan Province of China and so on), as well as substantial R&D investment, in the context of movements for integration of the Asian economy. As a result, the idea that these economies will merely continue to serve the US market or the European market is going to be passé in a relatively short time. We are seeing the development of an independent, major growth pole of the world economy. It will probably become the biggest growth pole by the mid-century, a knowledge- and R&D-led development process in the framework of a substantially integrated Asian economy. In fact, there is also the inevitable increase in importance of South–South trade and investment. There is, for example, an increasing presence of China in Africa. As someone interested in African development, I think this is good. The South–South dimension is real, and it is part of the shift to knowledge-based growth in the emerging economies.

My third point is that we do not have dual economies, but triple economies, in China and India. They are quite complicated and we do not have good models for them. First, we have a very high-tech, world-class R&D end, which will grow. Second, we have the workshop of the world, standardized mass production of a lot of manufacturing. Third, we have hundreds of millions of poor people in the countryside. That is the triple economy. We need to recognize how rich the economic structures of Asian economies are. As a result, we need something more than Lewis's two-sector model (Lewis 1954): we need at least a three-sector model to even understand these economies. In reading the chapters of this book, I think a lot of the mixed signals that are coming through in some of them are because many different effects are coming through in the data. Outward investment is not only coming from plain vanilla manufacturing, low-cost investors; it is also coming from high-tech firms. In fact, since a part of these economies is already at the high-end, R&D, knowledge-based stage, one would expect outward investment for all the reasons that the knowledge-based industries of the developed countries have invested abroad. That Infosys (India), for example, is investing in the United States is therefore not surprising. It is happening for the same reason that knowledge-based industries in the US have long been expanding abroad. Overall, convergence is so powerful that convergence in FDI behavior will be evident as well.

My final point is that everything is based on the idea that things will go forward without major upheavals. In other words, if things remain peaceful enough and open enough and there is no major rupture, the forces of convergence will be the dominant forces of the era.

There are many things that could go seriously wrong. For example, making the war on terror the centerpiece of our thinking shows a profound misunderstanding of the fundamental forces that shape the world. A more traditional problem is that the world economy had difficulties in the twentieth century absorbing the rising powers. There were two World Wars that were related – in some way, though not in a mechanistic or deterministic way – to the challenge of rising powers. The First World War was clearly related to the competition between Germany and England, and the inability to harness that competition in a way that created a large enough comfort zone to avoid war. And I think there is little doubt that the competition with Japan was the underpinning of the war of the Pacific in the Second World War.

These are sobering facts, because we are facing a major rebalancing of global power, and it is very difficult for that process to happen smoothly.

Things are prickly even in matters concerning emerging-market transnational corporations (TNCs). Very specific, small transactions in a very large economy can already generate high levels of anxiety. There is almost an inability to think from the other person's perspective, which is the real danger when trying to understand your competition or to avoid war.

Another huge risk for the planet is environmental, namely the threat of a cascading effect producing profound environmental crises. Already in 2006 – this is just a minor blip – we saw droughts all over the world. In the main wheat-producing regions we saw wheat prices soar in October 2006 (for example, half the Australian crop was lost); there were major droughts throughout Asia; and there were major water stresses in the United States – probably all related to climate change. There is more of that to come. So far we have done a miserable job of handling the energy transition, the water transition, climate change and so on. These are of first-order geopolitical significance. While it seems strange that they could really derail global growth or global convergence, it is possible that they will – not because the practical solutions do not exist, but because we might not take them.

We need to think about the dangers. But we also need to realize that, if we are successful in what we want to achieve in global development, we are talking about the biggest change of global society and reorientation of power in economics in at least 250 years. Today, we are talking about one of the very important transmission belts of that change. From that perspective, I think this is an extraordinarily important book.

NOTES

1. Author's calculations based on Maddison (2001) and United Nations (2005).
2. As developing countries benefit economically from FDI, they in turn engage in outward FDI with less-developed countries.

REFERENCES

Lewis, Arthur (1954). 'Economic Development with Unlimited Supplies of Labour', *The Manchester School*, 22, pp. 139–191.
Maddison, Angus (2001). *The World Economy: A Millennial Perspective* (Paris: OECD).
Smith, Adam ([1776] 1904). *The Wealth of Nations*, edited by Edwin Cannan (London: Methuen and Co. Ltd.).
United Nations (2005). *World Population Prospects: The 2004 Revision* (New York: United Nations).

PART II

Exploring the growth and pattern of outward
FDI from developing countries

3. The rise of TNCs from emerging markets: challenges faced by firms from India

Ravi Kant

INTRODUCTION

In the past 50 years, Indian industry has transformed itself from a government-led, license-based and public sector unit-dominated entity into an open, vibrant and globally competitive industry. During these 50 years, Indian companies have overcome many challenges by acquiring unique capabilities. When Indian industry was hit by an economic downturn between 1998 and 2002, with the simultaneous entry of many competitors from abroad and increased customer expectations of quality products and services, many Indian companies enhanced their capabilities to surge above the odds, not only for their own survival but with specific strategies for sustained growth. Indian companies today are becoming very competitive entities. For example, they are currently the lowest cost telephone and internet service providers in the world, and Indian banks have the lowest cost of technology per transaction, which is nearly one-tenth of their Western counterparts.

3.1 INDIAN TNCs MOVE BEYOND SHORES

Indian companies are increasingly competing with major global firms for businesses and customers. Outbound investment by Indian companies increased continuously between 2003 and 2006 (Figure 3.1). After tripling to $4.5 billion in one year in 2005, it grew by 60 per cent in the first nine months of the next fiscal year. The average deal size in the 2006 fiscal year also tripled over that of the previous year. Indian companies invested over $10 billion overseas in 2006, which is a substantial amount in view of the total capital expenditure of $24 billion in 2005 by nearly 1400 Indian companies.

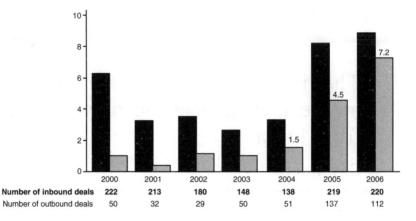

	2000	2001	2002	2003	2004	2005	2006
Number of inbound deals	**222**	**213**	**180**	**148**	**138**	**219**	**220**
Number of outbound deals	50	32	29	50	51	137	112

Notes:
1. Inbound deals are in black and outbound deals in grey.
2. 2006 Figures are for 9 months only.

Source: New Economist (2006).

Figure 3.1   India's inbound and outbound deals, 2000–2006: announced deal value (US\$ b)

The increase in outbound investment by Indian companies raises a pertinent question: why are Indian companies increasingly moving out to foreign markets? Four main reasons explain this outward movement:

1. **Gaining access to newer markets**. This provides Indian companies with an opportunity to grow revenues and capture a larger part of the global market share for their products and services. Indian companies are emerging as important competitors to the world's largest companies in global markets. Tata Tea, with sales of approximately \$300 million, spent nearly \$1.4 billion for its three major acquisitions in packaged tea, coffee and flavored water to gain access to developed countries.
2. **Overcoming constraints of the domestic market**. The Indian economy witnessed robust growth for the third consecutive year in 2005–06, in a stable macroeconomic and financial environment, even as international crude oil prices scaled new peaks. Real GDP growth averaged over 8 per cent in 2004–6 and over 7 per cent in 2003–6.

    Indian companies have been supported by the large and fast-growing Indian market. Almost all Indian companies that are aspiring to a higher global market share have a dominant position in the domestic market. But this is becoming a constraint to further growth. Financial markets and investors' aspirations are expecting companies to grow at

10–15 per cent every year, necessitating Indian companies to expand their business from one economy to many by developing a presence in the international arena.

The cyclicality of recent growth after an economic slump affects some industries considerably. In particular, the commercial vehicle industry is cyclical in nature, and India is no exception. A few years back, TATA Motors was hit badly by the down cycle, which coincided with its investments in its new passenger car business. The company reported a loss (of over $0.1 billion) for the first time since its inception in 1945. It crafted a recovery strategy with international business growth as a key thrust area. The execution of this strategy has helped the company establish its presence in many markets across the globe. As the cyclicality of these markets is not expected to coincide with that of the Indian market, the risk of the downturn of the domestic market is minimized. Thus, the business model is being put on a safer footing.

3. **Gaining new products, processes and technology**. Indian companies are gaining access to new products, processes and technology through acquisitions and joint ventures. India's largest forging company has successfully used the acquisition route to gain new products and businesses and has become a key forging supplier to many automobile majors in Europe. TATA Motors, through its acquisition of Daewoo Commercial Vehicle Ltd, Republic of Korea, in 2004, gained access to technology and complementary products to increase its strength. As a result of the synergy between the two, a range of heavy commercial vehicles has been introduced in the Indian market, and a range of medium-size commercial vehicles has been introduced in the Korean market; both have been well-received. Another example is the 2006 acquisition by TATA Motors of INCAT (UK), a global provider of product life cycle management and engineering and design services primarily to manufacturers and suppliers in the international automotive, aerospace and engineering markets.

4. **Securing access to raw materials**. A few Indian companies, mostly in the energy and basic materials domain, are expanding overseas not to increase their revenue but to gain access to raw materials for their operations. For example, the $13.8 billion Oil and Natural Gas Company (ONGC), India, which has 131 well platforms, 28 process platforms and 75 drilling rigs, and operates more than 11 000 kilometers of pipelines, has expanded into foreign markets to gain access to foreign oil with investments of $4.3 billion in overseas exploration projects.

The movement of Indian companies beyond shores is also supported by the following factors:

1. **The presence of congruent customer segments across geographies**.
    An internal research project, conducted by TATA Motors with
    Krishna Palepu of Harvard Business School, showed that customers
    in various markets around the world could be classified into a few clus-
    ters according to their needs and purchase motivators, and that the
    size of these clusters was different for different geographies. The
    company has been exploiting this opportunity by taking its home
    products, customized to meet the local needs of similar segments, to
    these geographies.
2. **India's low cost advantage**. The core advantage that Indian companies
    have is their access to low cost resources which could help them to gain
    and maintain a competitive advantage in the global market place. The
    cost advantage primarily is in labor, property, equipment, and raw
    materials. These resources are:

    a. *Low cost labor*. Labor costs in India are significantly lower than in
        developed markets. For example, full employment costs for manu-
        facturing workers in India are between $1 and $6 per hour, a frac-
        tion of the $20 to $40 per hour in most developed countries,
        including North America, Western Europe and Japan. This cost
        differential is also similar for the labor costs in service industries.
    b. *Low cost of design and development*. The abundant availability of
        educated and talented manpower in India is a major competitive
        strength that is well-leveraged by information technology and soft-
        ware industries that see this as the foundation of their success. This
        environment could naturally be leveraged for product design and
        development, which is increasingly dependent on computer-aided
        and virtual environments, thus reducing the cost of development.
    c. *Low cost property and equipment*. The total cost of establishing a
        green field manufacturing facility in India is 60 per cent to 80 per
        cent lower than setting up a similar facility in a developed country.
        The easy and abundant availability of labor at lower cost also gives
        companies the flexibility to reduce capital investments for complex
        and automated machinery.
    d. *Low cost raw materials*. India is rich in minerals like iron ore and
        bauxite, which are key to the competitiveness of the country's steel
        and aluminum companies.

3. **The availability of a highly educated, English speaking talent pool**. India
    produces over 3 million graduates and over 700 000 postgraduates
    every year. According to the Institute of Management Development,
    India ranks among the top three among 30 nations in terms of the

availability of a skilled workforce (Mahapatra and Padmanabhan 2005). Another edge is the vast use of English as *lingua franca* among Indians. India's technical talent pool also offers immense opportunities for Indian companies. The information technology industry recruits thousands of engineers not only from metropolitan areas but also from smaller towns.

Managerial talent of Indian origin is emerging as among the best in the world within as well as outside India. Indian managers have successfully demonstrated their capability of operating in a multi-lingual, multi-cultural and multi-religious environment which is full of uncertainty due to infrastructure bottlenecks. These challenges have shaped their ability to see the immediate issue as well as the broad picture. The diversity of the Indian context has also enabled Indian managers to deal with ambiguity. As a result, they have been able to steer successfully their Indian companies against competition in the domestic market; this has proved to be an asset for companies moving to foreign markets.

4. **India's influence for 'soft power'.** The term 'soft power' was used by Harvard academic Joseph Nye to describe the international influence that a country acquires when others are drawn to its culture and ideas. When David Beckham had his wife's name tattooed in Hindi on his forearm six years ago, it gave a small boost of encouragement to India's cultural commissars. India is making concerted efforts to realize its ambition of becoming a 'soft power'. India's 'soft power' is growing more rapidly than that of its communist neighbor since India has a democratic constitution and a well-established political structure. Since the liberalization of the Indian economy in 1991, people across the world are increasingly showing interest in understanding what makes this multi-lingual, multi-cultural and multi-religious democracy tick. Bollywood movies, Bhangra pop hits, Indian cuisine, yoga, and Indian art are gaining acceptability and are increasingly making inroads in Western countries.

3.2 CHALLENGES FACED BY INDIAN COMPANIES

As Indian companies continue their efforts to increase their global footprint, they have to overcome the following challenges to be successful:

1. **Developing products and services with a worldwide appeal.** Indian companies have long been operating in a protected environment. Their products and services, which are acceptable in the home country, might

not be an attractive proposition to customers abroad. Therefore, it is imperative for Indian companies to offer innovative products and services with global appeal and to improve the quality of their existing products and services to the next level to meet global expectations. This would require increased basic research and development and the encouragement of innovation. Simultaneously, it is also imperative that Indian companies establish appropriate systems for protecting intellectual property rights.

Another challenge that Indian companies face is attracting non-Indian customers with products or services having the 'best of both worlds', or having a 'European or Japanese quality at Chinese prices'. Indian companies have to modify or realign their entire value chains to meet this objective. The ones which accomplish this feat could lead world markets.

2. **Overcoming regulatory issues**. A few regulatory bottlenecks listed below are constraining the ambitions of Indian companies and require urgent attention:

    a. Developed countries' regulations for higher levels of product compliance with respect to emissions, safety and performance demand significant investments and efforts by Indian companies to upgrade existing products and to develop new ones.
    b. According to Reserve Bank of India regulations, companies cannot bid for an overseas acquisition under the automatic route if the total funds required for an acquisition exceed 200 per cent of the Indian company's net worth. According to the Indian Companies Act, if the acquisition value exceeds 60 per cent of an Indian company's net worth or 100 per cent of its free reserves, then the company is required to obtain prior approval from its shareholders for making an investment in a target company. This means disclosing vital details about the target company to shareholders, including the price offered, and results in disclosing certain critical, sensitive and confidential information.
    c. Stringent inward investment norms in certain countries like China, where, for example, foreign companies need to invest in excess of $200 million and also need to relinquish at least a 50 per cent stake to an identified Chinese partner, according to China's automotive policy.

3. **Cultural issues**. Many Indian companies have faced cultural issues during the course of acquisitions or joint ventures with foreign partners. An Indian company is seen in a slightly different manner from a

European or a US company by many stakeholders. The experiences TATA Motors had during its first acquisition (Daewoo, Republic of Korea) have helped company leaders appreciate the need and importance of influencing the mindset of all stakeholders involved in an acquisition, as the purchase was not of an asset but of a functioning company. This included communicating information about the country, business group, company and culture not only to the employees of the target company but also to its suppliers, government officials and other business partners. This was achieved through a mix of formal and informal initiatives such as presentations, documents, movies, food, and film festivals. The philosophy of TATA Motors is to be a Korean company in Korea, a South African company in South Africa and a Spanish company in Spain. The company seeks to give back gains to the society it operates in.

4. **Building brand 'India'**. The biggest challenge facing Indian companies is gaining a recognition share in the minds of foreign consumers. Today, in a consumer's mind, the brand 'Japan' is associated with electronics, high technology, efficiency, process orientation and so on. Similarly, the brand 'Germany' is associated with technology, automobiles, engineering precision, robust design and so on. This association is a result of these countries' companies offering a consistent experience to consumers over a long period. Indian companies that have started arriving on the global scene have to undertake massive efforts to offer the global consumers a consistently superior product or service experience to build the brand 'India'.

3.3 CHALLENGES FOR TATA MOTORS

TATA Motors wants to increase its share of international business with a growing product portfolio. It plans to leverage its association with the TATA Group in select countries in which the TATA brand has a presence. The TATA Group had operations in more than 54 countries across six continents, and international sales of over $6.7 billion worth of products and services to over 120 countries during the fiscal year 2004–5; this was almost 30 per cent of the Group's revenue of $21.9 billion.

As mentioned earlier, TATA Motors has identified key customer segments in these markets and has initiated a product plan for developing automobiles to fulfill customer requirements in a competitive manner, complying with various emission, safety and regulatory norms. Therefore, the three biggest challenges that TATA Motors faces as an Indian company entering foreign markets are:

1. **Product: developing competitive products for international markets**.
    TATA Motors has carefully crafted a strategic plan to meet this chal-
    lenge. It has augmented its in-house product design and development
    capability through its acquisition of Daewoo Commercial Vehicle Ltd
    (Republic of Korea) for trucks, Hispano Carrocera (Spain) for buses
    and coaches and INCAT Technologies (UK) for automobile develop-
    ment, and the establishment of its European Technical Centre (UK)
    for product design. The company is widening the scope of its research
    and development activity from in-house product and technology devel-
    opment to managing the product development process across its
    affiliates, as well as various parts suppliers and outsourcing partners. It
    perceives this kind of distributed product development environment
    across the globe as aiding the development of contemporary products
    at competitive costs that would attract customers.
2. **People: supporting international expansion plans with managers having
    an international mindset**. To deal with the second challenge, the
    company is reformulating its human resource policy in line with its
    business requirement of having an international mindset for its work-
    force. Selected managers are exposed to higher and more complex chal-
    lenges, thereby gaining experience in dealing with foreign markets.
    Special emphasis is also put on developing 'soft skills' and handling
    cultural diversity. Concerted efforts are made to change the mindset of
    the blue collar workforce from manufacturing automobiles 'only for
    India' to producing for other parts of the world. The company is
    working toward creating a 'preferred employer' brand and is also
    realigning its policies to win the war of talent by attracting youth
    amidst a booming information technology industry.
3. **Process: introducing and implementing world-class processes**. To address
    the third challenge and to expose itself to the rigors of the international
    market, the company is taking various initiatives such as listing itself
    on the New York Stock Exchange (in 2004) and thus creating a greater
    discipline and rigor in its audit processes, reporting and corporate gov-
    ernance. The company is pursuing an e-sourcing initiative with ARIBA
    (previously Freemarkets) and has deployed a comprehensive Customer
    Relationship Management program with SIEBEL, enabling it to gain
    market insights by exploiting the huge online customer transaction
    database. In the enterprise resource planning area, SAP[1] was rolled out
    in 1999 across various functions and areas for enhancing transaction
    effectiveness.

    The company has adopted the Tata Business Excellence Model[2]
    process, which is based on the Malcolm Baldridge Quality Award for
    Business Excellence and the Balanced Score Card developed by Robert

Kaplan and David Norton for the deployment of strategic initiatives. The company participates in 'Triple Bottom Line Reporting', which is a measure of future sustainability with regard to environmental, social and economic accountability enunciated by the United Nations.

CONCLUSION

The newfound strength and resurgence of the Indian manufacturing sector necessitates Indian firms and the Government of India to develop a mission plan to support growth and become internationally competitive. In particular, while the Indian automotive industry is expected to continue to enjoy its eminent position of being the largest tractor and three-wheeler manufacturer and the second largest two-wheeler manufacturer in the world, it will also seek to attain a significant position in the car, bus and truck segments by the middle of the next decade. By 2016, when India's automotive industry's output is estimated to be $150 billion, the value of exports of automotives and components is estimated to be $40 billion.

This vision can only be achieved through a partnership approach between original equipment manufacturers, automotive component manufacturers (including SMEs) and the Government of India. To realize this vision, the Indian automotive industry must focus primarily on developing and manufacturing products that meet international standards, sustain cost competitiveness and showcase Indian products in potential global markets. The Government of India could play a key enabling role by facilitating infrastructure creation, promoting the country's capabilities, creating a favorable and predictable business environment, attracting investment and promoting research and development.

NOTES

1. SAP Germany is a globally renowned ERP solutions provider.
2. Tata Motors is one of the largest users of SAP systems in India.

REFERENCES

Mahapatra, Arun Das and Gauri Padmanabhan (2005). *India: Beyond Cost Arbitrage* (New Dehli: Heidrick and Struggles International, Inc.), mimeo.
New Economist (2006). 'Corporate India: going global', 4 October. Available at: http://neweconomist.blogs.com/new_economist/2006/10/corporate_india.html, last visited 24 October 2007.

4. The transnationalization of supply chain management: the experience of Brazilian industrial companies

Paulo T.V. Resende and Alvaro Bruno Cyrino

INTRODUCTION

Corporate decisions to push business deeper into foreign markets have important implications for the *modus operandi* and the performance of any company. Traditionally, the motivation to internationalize is largely based on economic reasons (for example, business growth, lower costs), with effects for other areas. The logic behind the ambition to become a global company, then, is to increase market share, while concurrently achieving cost reductions through scale economies. The expansion into uncharted territories involves a rethinking of most business functions, including activities related to supply chain management, such as purchasing, logistics, production, sales and distribution. But compared to the expansion in domestic markets, the risks and uncertainties of global markets are much higher, in spite of the potential growth of revenues and profit margins.

Given various risks and uncertainties, emerging transnational corporations (TNCs) from developing countries (companies expanding their international presence beyond exports) first seek possibilities for gaining market share in their domestic markets before tapping foreign ones. Yet since the 1990s, several Brazilian companies have searched for new opportunities in international markets through outward foreign direct investment (OFDI), facing in the process new challenges to avoid potential failures.

One of the most important issues in the context of reducing risks and uncertainties is supply chain management. First, because global markets are not homogenous, the product and business model needs adaptation to different conditions. Second, companies have to add capacity, often at breakneck speed and at a global level, which often results in higher costs. Christopher (2005) argued that the key success factors in supply chain management involve two contrasting demands simultaneously: (1) how to offer variety to local markets while maintaining the advantages of standardized global production; and (2) how to manage networks connecting suppliers and consumers. Consequently, in global operations, the trade-off between low-cost supply sources and a higher level of service to customers is a recurring issue for managerial decision making. That is why companies seeking to transnationalize through OFDI must take supply chain challenges seriously to assure that the results are revenues based on a higher level of service and margins that are not permanently eroded by high-cost logistics.

This chapter focuses on how Brazilian companies are dealing with the supply chain challenge in their transnationalization process. A series of analyses are conducted to explore different stages of transnationalization, using as examples some Brazilian companies, in association with investigations of their main shortcomings in achieving efficiency of supply chain management.

Accordingly, this chapter has the following objectives:

- to analyze the main strategies pursued by Brazilian companies in their transnationalization process;
- to investigate supply chain management configurations given those strategies;
- to examine what is missing in the area of supply chain management for this activity to become an ally in the search for efficiency, instead of a barrier to growth.

Before beginning the actual analysis of transnationalization strategies and supply chain management issues, it is important to introduce the concepts of 'supply chain' and 'integrated logistics'. Accordingly, the following section contains a short discussion of the basic definitions and the scope of supply chain management and how it fits into strategic movements toward transnationalization.

4.1 SUPPLY CHAIN MANAGEMENT: ON THE SCOPE OF TRANSNATIONALIZATION PROCESSES

The first concept discussed in this chapter is the connection between supply chain management and integrated logistics. Integrated logistics is essentially a plan to move products and services to where the equilibrium between inventory levels and transportation costs is best achieved, given an expected level of information and risk. Hence, supply chain management is built upon logistics, but it is expanded to involve linkages and coordination with other entities of the productive chain, such as those with suppliers and customers. This chapter uses the same definition of supply chain management as Christopher (2005, p. 5):

> The management of upstream and downstream relationships with suppliers and customers to deliver superior value and less total cost ownership to the supply chain as a whole.

Based on this definition, supply chain management is a concept broader in scope when compared to integrated logistics, and it must precede transportation and inventory plans. This is because the number and location of all inventory sites, mainly in consideration of global operations, are not fixed until all sourcing and outsourcing decisions have been made. Moreover, worldwide aggressive competition is an unrelenting threat to business. This implies that winning supply chains need to move faster from product development to product delivery. To achieve a full understanding of supply chain management, Figure 4.1 shows the main activities incorporated in it. These interrelated activities constitute the ground upon which the flow of information and products should be built when it comes to operating in international markets.

Once an optimal framework for supply chain management has been defined, taking into consideration the integration of all of these activities, a logistics plan can be developed. This plan is characterized by clear definitions of short- and long-term metrics, information system requirements, inventory levels, transportation structures and all logistics parameters to assure customer response associated with cost-saving strategies.

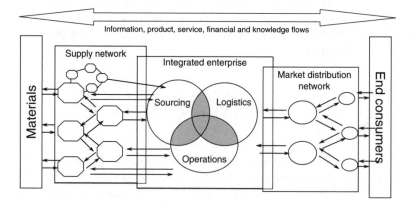

Source: Resende (2003), adapted from Bowersox (1996).

Figure 4.1   The scope of supply chain management

The most important characteristic of the framework contained in Figure 4.1 is the network feature of supply chain management. The complexity of each linkage is depicted as the number of linkages increases within each network. Moreover, the organization fields of operations, sourcing and logistics must not only be internally integrated, but must also be coordinated with the downstream and upstream groups of suppliers and end customers, respectively.

Once the scope of the supply chain is determined, as demonstrated in Figure 4.1, certain areas of the corporate arena arise as essential to the management of the supply chain, as shown in Figure 4.2.

The scope of supply chain management starts with relationships to suppliers and continues to where products are made available to consumer markets. A consideration of the six dimensions shown in Figure 4.2, demonstrates that strategic actions are required to achieve efficiency. This includes:

- the search for continuous collaboration with suppliers;
- highly efficient material handling and administration;
- effective strategies to accommodate the trade-off between level of service and cost arrangements related to inventories;
- distribution channels designed to provide efficiency in service levels and costs;

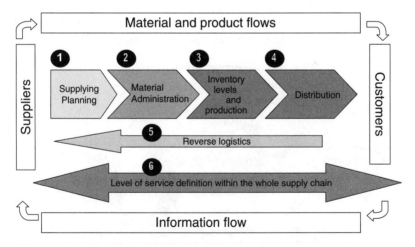

Note: The arrows show the dynamics of the supply chain, where communications should be built in a cycle that begins at the market, goes into the company, reaches the suppliers, and goes back to the market, in a closed cycle.

Source: Resende (2003), adapted from Bowersox (1996).

Figure 4.2 The scope of supply chain management

- reverse logistics that do not interfere with the cost structure of the entire system; and
- an information flow that provides data and support to decision making for supply chain management.

Understanding the scope of a supply chain provides a sense of the challenges that companies face when entering international markets. Accordingly, a myriad of issues need to be analyzed; but for the purposes of this chapter, just some of them are investigated. The main ones are:

- the challenges in integrated logistics within domestic markets, taking Brazil as an example;
- analysis of strategic decisions regarding integrated logistics and supply chain management in the transnationalization process;
- analysis of the stability of supply processes and demand uncertainties; and
- the effects of the decision-making process on push and pull systems through supply chains in foreign markets.

The next section contains a short discussion on integrated logistics within domestic markets. The main reason for beginning to analyze transnational supply by looking at domestic approaches is that the latter contain the core characteristics, the 'DNA', of a company's historical efficiency or inefficiency in its logistics operations (Figure 4.3).

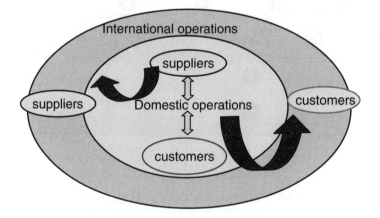

Source: Resende (2006).

Figure 4.3   The history of domestic operations influences newly designed transnational operations

4.2 CHALLENGES OF DOMESTIC LOGISTICS FOR TRANSNATIONALIZATION: THE BRAZILIAN CASE

The first supply chain challenge in the transnationalization process is related to domestic operations, with transportation as the main element. Especially in Brazil, transportation represents the most important bottleneck, in particular when a Brazilian company expands its operations to foreign markets. No matter what the magnitude of a company's overseas expansion, a part of the productive chain will be located in Brazil and depend upon the Brazilian transportation infrastructure. Hence, a short analysis of the status of the Brazilian transportation network follows.

The Brazilian transportation network is characterized by highly concentrated flows of products in its highway system, whereas the railroad and the inland waterway systems are of secondary importance. Notwithstanding the high usage within the past two decades (more than 65 per cent of the general freight is carried by heavy trucks), there have been few efforts toward continuous planning for the maintenance, operation and safety of the highway network. Other modes, such as railways, inland waterways and coastal navigation, have shown much lower productivity levels (see the comparative analysis between the percentage of total freight volumes for railroads and highways in Figure 4.4).

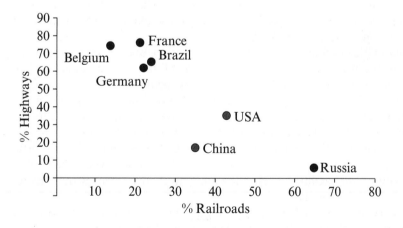

Source: Resende (2006).

Figure 4.4   The current transportation distribution in Brazil as compared to other countries (% of total freight)

Moreover, the inland waterways account for just 1 per cent of general freight, despite the fact that the country has approximately 20 000 miles of navigable rivers. The railroad system, once considered to have a dominant role in territorial integration, has experienced a significant deterioration in its equipment, personnel productivity and operational network. During the past eight years, hopes have been raised as a result of privatization, as private funds have been made available for reconstruction and rehabilitation of the physical network.

This short overview of the Brazilian transportation system shows that there is an urgent need for planning: there must be a detailed inventory of the critical links, bottlenecks and strategic inputs to help in decisions related to location and terms of corporate investments. If such a program becomes a reality, then the transportation field can be adjusted to enhance Brazil's competitiveness, both in internal and external markets. To achieve this purpose, it is important that the current short-term approach of Brazilian decision makers be changed to a more comprehensive view, so that investments are not made in inefficient transport segments.

With the dominant focus on highway development, Brazilian decision makers have ignored the most basic rules of planning, forgetting that any transportation system needs design, implementation, evaluation and, most of all, maintenance (and not just construction). As a result, the entire highway system has deteriorated since the 1980s, reaching levels of service much lower than minimum worldwide standards of operation. Today, this deteriorated highway network is responsible for tremendous economic losses and extremely high accident figures. It also has negative effects on the competitiveness of companies, including those planning to expand their operations to foreign markets.

Notwithstanding various historical disruptions and poorly planned decisions, the Brazilian transportation system still faces unquestionable challenges to overcome longstanding logistics inefficiencies. What has been observed in Brazil today is a dynamic process of infrastructure privatization that has already led to several planning programs involving intermodal systems, multimodal facilities, private participation in decision making and so on. These initiatives have tended to change the mentality of transportation planners toward a more comprehensive approach, where the level of service of the facilities dictates the amount of investment within macroregions of the country.

Based on this brief analysis of the Brazilian transportation system, a number of actions can be suggested to improve domestic logistics so that the competitiveness of companies involved in the transnationalization processes is not so negatively affected. Such actions include the expansion of intermodal systems with due consideration for the operational capacity of each mode; massive investments in the privatized railroad system, mainly in cargo transfer points, so that larger volumes can be transferred to the railway system; regulation of the 'multimodal operator's' role, which could facilitate the bureaucratic process of freight transport; higher participation of the railroad and inland waterway systems in the Brazilian transportation matrix; acceleration of the process of highway privatization to generate more investment in the system; and capacity expansion of some highway segments.

One other area worth analyzing is foreign direct investment (FDI) opportunities in the logistics field in Brazil. The country has enormous potential to accommodate FDI, mainly in transportation facilities (for example, highways, ports, railroads), resulting in attractive returns on investments to foreign companies. Once legislation is changed to provide regulatory guarantees for long-term investments, the Brazilian logistics network can and will be one of the most attractive regions for FDI. And these investments will surely contribute to improved logistics facilities, thereby leading to important reductions in the bottlenecks that companies face during transnationalization processes.

Once a country has achieved a certain level of efficiency in its domestic logistics, strategic decisions must be made regarding integrated logistics and supply chain management, considering the international environment. This is the subject of the next section, where examples of Brazilian companies will provide elements for a corporate analysis.

4.3 STRATEGIC DECISIONS ON INTEGRATED LOGISTICS AND SUPPLY CHAIN MANAGEMENT IN THE INTERNATIONAL ARENA

According to Bovet (2005, p. 5):

> no matter the risks, global supply chains grow longer and more complex as companies push deeper into uncharted territory in search of lower costs and higher level of service. Then questions such as adding tons of inventories, quietly ripening toward obsolescence, and retreating the cost-saving deals that are driving companies into far-flung lands become essential.

Transnationalization is the result of these considerations.

4.3.1 Integrated Logistics and Supply Chain Management: the Balance Between Risk and Return

Managing supply chains to achieve integrated logistics in global markets revolves around the need to operate a network of manufacturing and

Exploring the growth and pattern of outward FDI

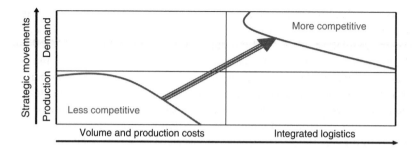

Source: Resende (2005).

Figure 4.5   Strategic and operational movements in the supply chain

inventory facilities spread over different locations, and separated from each other by thousands of miles. Since supply chain management involves procurement, sourcing, manufacture and the logistics of distribution, the number of external variables increases as operations reach different regions and increasingly heterogeneous markets. Accordingly, strategic moves historically based only on production efficiencies are forced to incorporate demand planning in their core. At the same time, operations based on volume and costs are required to move to integrated logistics, where volumes may be lower and costs may be higher (see Figure 4.5 for a graphic demonstration of these movements).

This figure shows that companies in the process of transnationalizing must consider the fact that, in order to be more competitive, they must move to a position in which demand planning dictates their strategic supply chain movements associated with the incorporation of integrated logistics throughout their global operations. Bovet (2005) maintained that demand management must aim at reducing the risk of being blindsided by demand shifts.

This is not the reality for most Brazilian companies involved in transnationalization processes. Most are not paying sufficient attention to the following aspects of strategic movements within the supply chain dimension:

- A supply chain in global markets is an inter-functional entity; the great majority of difficulties associated with supply chain management derive from uncoordinated and fragmented activities in functional areas.
- A supply chain is a strategic client of inventories and other productive resources; supply chain management can and should be used as a potential tool to balance demand and supply capacity throughout global operations.

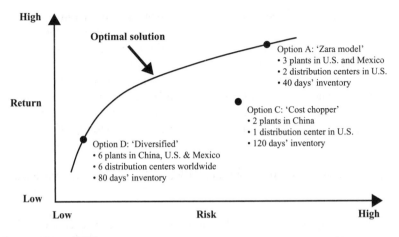

Source: Bovet (2005).

Figure 4.6   The efficient frontier of the supply chain in global markets

- A supply chain must function as a system to integrate and coordinate the activities of production and logistics; this coordination aims at efficiency in logistics costs, shorter lead times and higher customer service levels.

Considering the balance between return and risk, Bovet (2005, p. 4) presented the analysis shown in Figure 4.6 as an optimal solution for the efficient frontier of the supply chain in global markets: 'there are two ways to strategically address the burgeoning nature of risk in the supply chain of global markets: (1) shorten the supply chain in order to reduce cycle time and disruption risks, or (2) optimize the portfolio of supply chain sources and locations in order to gain flexibility through diversification'.

An analysis of Brazilian companies' moves toward transnationalization reveals that they have not taken advantage of the economic benefits of extending their supply chains globally. Taking Figure 4.6 as the basis, Brazilian companies have not diversified and created a global network capable of achieving higher performance on cycle time, reliability, flexibility, cost, capital deployed and other factors. In fact, Brazilian companies have internalized themselves through production line acquisition, rather than building supply chain networks.

If one considers these strategies and compares them to some international examples, the risks for Brazilian companies become clear. For example:

- Continental Teves, a major automotive supplier, has prepared contingency plans in the wake of 11 September 2001 to supplement US production facilities through air shipment of parts from Europe. If any other Brazilian company faces such an event, the Continental Teves strategy could not be used, since these companies have not built global supply networks but rather buy locally.

- Electronics companies have adopted dual sourcing policies. They either retain an existing supplier as a secondary source, or develop second sources in Asia or East Europe. Again, the strategy is not applied by any Brazilian company, exposing them to high risks of disruption in their productive chains.

4.3.2 Integrated Logistics and Supply Chain Management: the Push and Pull Factors

When the management of a supply chain achieves a certain level of coordination and integration, strategic decisions can be made to balance the level of service with costs. There are basically two extremes of strategic logistics: building inventories (make-for-stock), or waiting for orders to arrive and then produce (make-to-order). These two strategies lead to an environment that characterizes one of two systems: push (based on inventory building) or pull (based on demand response). Figure 4.7 adds an external variable (the number of products – in logistics known as stock-keeping units), and contains an analysis of trade-offs between the breadth of product lines and the push and pull factors in respect to global markets.

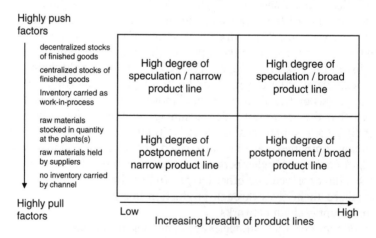

Source: Resende (2005), adapted from Lee and Billington (1992).

Figure 4.7　Strategies for push and pull factors and the breadth of product lines

With respect to the pull factors, a strategy of postponement consists of waiting for the final order before producing and delivering a certain product to a customer. This strategy complies with the notion that the longer the lead-time to production, the more reduced the risk of demand uncertainties. This strategy can apply to low- or high-breadth product lines, but each situation has its own set of uncertainties.

When a company decides to operate internationally under the pull strategy, the following challenges must be taken into account:

- The production lines have to be increasingly flexible as the breadth of products grows. There will be times for operating in full capacity and other times when operations are under capacity, resulting from low demand. Either way, the strategy calls for an efficient system to predict demand and to make decisions on production flexibility.
- The higher the breadth of products, the more complex is the production control and planning. When a company operates internationally, such complexity can serve as a barrier to flexibility and outsourcing.
- Logistics costs tend to be higher, mainly as a result of transportation, since reduced cycle times must be the top objective to guarantee high service levels.
- The sourcing issue must be to consider standardization of logistics and supply processes through the selection of global suppliers.

When a company operates under the push strategy, other challenges come into play, such as:

- A company works with high inventory levels, which also call for an increasing knowledge of demand patterns in each market where the company operates.
- The higher the breadth of products, the higher the risk of cost overruns due to obsolescence and demand variability over inventory levels.
- In this case, logistics costs rely on inventory capital and warehousing expenditures. If a company operates in developed markets, warehousing expenditures tend to be even higher.
- Global supply contracts should consider risk sharing, mostly with respect to inventories along the supply chain.

When looking at Brazilian companies in a comparative perspective, some imperfections appear in their transnationalization process, as shown in Table 4.1. In order to avoid naming the companies, activities which they undertake are indicated. However, it is important to emphasize that these

*Table 4.1   An analysis of pull and push factors for Brazilian industrial
companies involved in the transnationalization process*

Activity	Global operations	Supply chain analysis
Electrical motors, transformers and automation	Transnationalization through cross-border acquisitions or operations in Argentina, Mexico, Portugal, China.	• The acquisition of production lines points to a pull system. • North American and some European markets are still served by Brazilian exports. • Brazilian plants work under a push system, using some global facilities as inventory buffers to supply foreign markets.
Small compressors	Transnationalization through cross-border acquisitions in Italy, brownfield in Slovakia and joint ventures with the Government of China.	• Foreign production lines are designed for regional markets where they are located, therefore showing low levels of worldwide logistics and supply chain management. • North American and some European markets are still served by exports from Brazilian plants. • The choice to go international is more related to the saturation of the domestic market, with very weak supply chain coordination among the production plants.
Steel products	Subsidiaries through acquisitions in Argentina, Canada, Chile, Colombia, Peru, Spain, the United States, Uruguay.	• Part of the strategy is to access other sources of raw materials to be used on the closest plants. There is no strategy to create a global raw material network to guarantee global supply. • Since the production lines are capital intensive, inventory levels are low during high demand periods, but high during low demand periods, since the push strategy is strictly related to the characteristics of the production system.
Meat processor	Subsidiaries in Argentina, Chile, China, Germany, Japan, Panama, Russia, Turkey, United Arab Emirates, the United Kingdom, Uruguay.	• Local commercial affiliates are supplied from Brazil. The industry carries high raw material inventories that depend on high demand at all times. • This strategy is weak since there is no movement to develop local suppliers in foreign markets.

Source: Resende (2006).

activities are representative of one or more Brazilian companies that are currently involved in the process of transnationalization.

In the light of the experience of Brazilian companies and their transnationalization strategies, some issues emerge as regards supply chain management and integrated logistics:

- Production lines fed by distant sources must rely on a stable supply process, since they depend on short lead times to avoid high inventory levels.
- Companies driven by push strategies must have an efficient way to understand demand patterns and to avoid demand uncertainties in their decision-making processes.
- Finally, companies operating in international markets must combine strategies to stabilize supply processes and efficient demand planning.

Considering these issues, decisions to adopt pull or push strategies when it comes to the transnationalization of operations must rely on a combination of investigating the stability of the supply process and the uncertainties of demand (as shown in Figure 4.8).

According to this figure, a decision must be made to achieve the best supply chain strategy in terms of pull factors (in a make-to-order dimension) or to push factors (in a make-for-stock dimension). However, Brazilian companies represented by the activities listed and analyzed in

	Demand Uncertainty	
	Low (functional products)	High (innovative products)
Low (stable process) High economies of production	push to: minimize manufacturing and logistics costs with little risk of high speculation costs	find push/pull boundary to balance costs
High (unstable process) Low economies of production	find push/pull boundary to balance costs	minimize speculation costs with little loss in manufacturing and logistics efficiency

(Supply Uncertainty — left axis label)

Source: Resende (2005), adapted from Lee and Billington (1992).

Figure 4.8 Strategies for push and pull systems according to demand uncertainty and supply process stability

Table 4.1 have encountered several difficulties in making these decisions. The most important of these include:

- The domestic logistics system does not contribute to transport efficiency, which is essential to supply foreign plants working under pull systems.
- Brazilian companies do not have a history of long-term supplier contracts with specific clauses for just-in-time delivery, including keeping inventories near clients' production facilities.
- First tier and preferred vendors in domestic markets do not have the financial, technological and operating capabilities necessary to move closer to their clients' production plants in foreign markets.

Hence, decisions that are necessary to define push and pull boundaries in foreign markets that should follow the recommendations contained in Figure 4.9 below are affected by those difficulties listed when it comes to Brazilian companies. Brazilian companies cannot strictly consider these recommendations as to the boundaries of push and pull systems because:

- their transnationalization experience is not sufficient to guarantee full understanding of demand uncertainties for the entire global supply chain.
- domestic logistics and low volumes of raw materials due to low market shares negatively affect lead times.
- their domestic experience is highly dependent on cost reductions, rather than on service level tactics.
- resource allocation unbalances the boundaries of responsiveness.

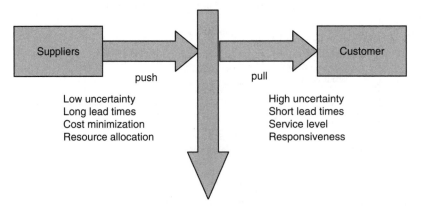

Source: Resende (2005), adapted from Lee and Billington (1992).

Figure 4.9   Push and pull boundaries

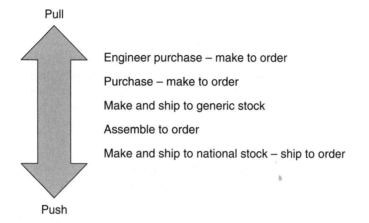

Pull

Engineer purchase – make to order

Purchase – make to order

Make and ship to generic stock

Assemble to order

Make and ship to national stock – ship to order

Push

Note: Engineer purchase orders are those that demand technical customization through special engineering projects.

Source: Resende (2005), adapted from Lee and Billington (1992).

Figure 4.10   Characteristics of the production lines along the push and pull axis

Considering the various characteristics of production lines (Figure 4.10), Brazilian companies in the process of transnationalization tend to adopt the following strategies:

● Domestic plants continue to push inventories to foreign plants, using those plants as buffers to supply global markets.
● Low market shares in foreign markets negatively affect logistics costs and supply chain integration.
● The international expansion of some Brazilian companies has meant that many of their suppliers follow clients' footprints in some activities (general warehousing, after-sale presence) and, in some cases, even in their production activities. However, these movements are very embryonic.

In sum, going back to the examples analyzed before, the pull effect is stronger in more concentrated and oligopolistic industries (for example, refrigerators). This happens because there are few buyers with high bargaining power – which is not the case for industries in the processed meat and electronic motors segments. Moreover, Brazilian industrial TNCs still largely rely on exports; home-base logistics infrastructure and bureaucratic barriers are the main constraints to using export know-how as a supply chain advantage.

In order to reach higher supply chain standards in international markets, Brazilian companies must overcome their shortages related to operating on a stand-alone basis, without integration or collaborative movements to becoming global suppliers. Therefore, global sourcing must be their most important objective through the process of understanding global supply chains and the development of integrated logistics networks. Hence, sourcing is essential to any Brazilian company in the transnationalization process. This is discussed in greater detail in the next section.

4.4   STRATEGIC SOURCING AND THE TRANSNATIONALIZATION PROCESS

When it comes to international markets, sourcing strategies should take into account long-term plans, core competencies, capabilities of alternative sources, total ownership costs and quality implications associated with domestic versus foreign sourcing. A balanced sourcing strategy employing an optimal mix of global and domestic sources should be based on total acquisition cost, a global business strategy and high-level sourcing policies.

It is important to consider collaborative initiatives to compress cycles through vendor management inventories and collaborative planning for forecast and replenishment. Additionally, it is essential to speed up information exchange, create chain visibility, evaluate potential role shifts and build unique competencies.

Brazilian companies undergoing transnationalization processes do not concern themselves with creating consolidated global supply networks. Once they move to foreign markets, the process works almost in complete isolation: a Brazilian company takes over a foreign company and starts operating, but without any contributions from a previously built global network of international suppliers.

The combination of different strategies involving strategic sourcing and procurement that are associated with internal supply chain management aim to reduce the number of suppliers while satisfying all the quality and cost objectives of sourcing policies. Therefore, some companies undergoing transnationalization are reducing the number of suppliers, while improving supply quality and minimizing the total cost of acquisitions. Raising quality standards means directly disqualifying many suppliers while trade volumes increase with a smaller supplier base. This should also yield unit purchase price reductions.

Long-term logistics initiatives aimed at enhancing customer service and reducing total logistics costs are much easier to achieve with a few, highly-integrated and highly-capable suppliers. And this happens easily when a company has a smaller supplier base. When it comes to companies going through transnationalization processes, supply base rationalization and consolidation should be an ongoing, cross-functional practice, supported by updated supplier performance metrics on the logistics information system of a company.

Specifically in the logistics field, it is important to consider some recommendations for companies that are facing the transnationalization of outsourcing. Important considerations include: searching for a proven third party logistics provider in the industry's segment; understanding economies of scope and scale for third party logistics; making sure that outsourcing is acceptable to the customer base; and defining the cultural match between the third party logistics and the company.

One of the best tools to rationalize and consolidate a company's supplier base is shown in Figures 4.11 and 4.12, where the complexity of a supply market and the impact on the business of what has been supplied are put together in the same matrix.

Considering the matrix exhibited in Figure 4.11, which is widely used throughout the world by consulting companies (for example, A.T. Kearney), sourcing and outsourcing for companies trying to improve their international supply chain management can be built based on the following strategies:

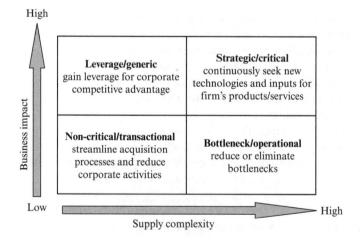

Source: Resende (2005), adapted from Slaight, Naramore and Bouchet (2004).

Figure 4.11   Supply market complexity and impacts on business-framework

High

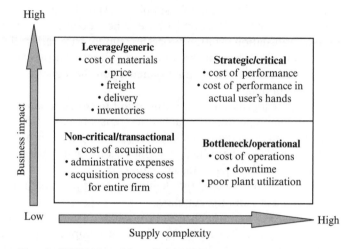

Business impact

Leverage/generic	Strategic/critical
• cost of materials • price • freight • delivery • inventories	• cost of performance • cost of performance in actual user's hands
Non-critical/transactional	Bottleneck/operational
• cost of acquisition • administrative expenses • acquisition process cost for entire firm	• cost of operations • downtime • poor plant utilization

Low 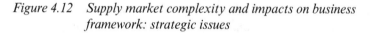 High

Supply complexity

Source:　Resende (2005), adapted from Slaight, Naramore and Bouchet (2004).

Figure 4.12　Supply market complexity and impacts on business framework: strategic issues

- Non-critical supplied items: supplier substitution is relatively easy, with low transaction costs and low impact on business. Companies should then work with local suppliers.
- Leverage items: supplier substitution is relatively easy, with low transaction costs but high impacts on business. Companies should develop collaborative strategies with local suppliers.
- Bottleneck items: they show high complexity within a supplier market, with high transaction costs but with low impact on business. Companies should search for a smaller supplier base together with higher economies of scale.
- Strategic items: they show high complexity within a supplier market, with high transaction costs and higher impacts on business. Companies should aim at developing global suppliers, with collaborative planning for forecasting and replenishment.

Taking into account these strategies, it is important to note Brazilian companies' main deficiencies concerning sourcing and outsourcing movements in global markets:

- Brazilian companies do not have the experience to integrate suppliers in their supply chain management.

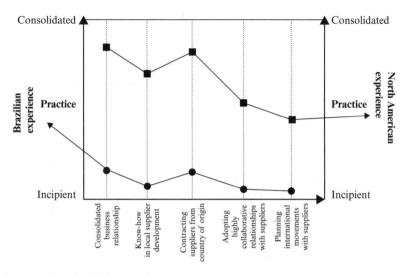

Source: Resende (2006).

Figure 4.13   Issues on global sourcing, North American and Brazilian companies

- Brazilian companies do not have the know-how on local supplier development in foreign markets.
- Brazilian companies lack long-term plans to keep consolidated relationships with suppliers.
- A long history of predatory supplier–client relationships has prevented Brazilian companies from adopting collaborative approaches to their supply chains.

A comparative analysis of the history of collaborative relationships with suppliers can provide a good perspective on the level of development of Brazilian and North American companies. Figure 4.13 contains a comparative analysis of North American and Brazilian companies with respect to five issues related to sourcing.

4.5   RECOMMENDATIONS TO BRAZILIAN COMPANIES INVOLVED IN TRANSNATIONALIZATION PROCESSES

The supply chain field is closely related to decision making in the logistics management area. Therefore, recommendations regarding the supply chain must consider the balance between global and local patterns – the so-called 'glocal logistics'. Accordingly, the framework within which strategies for integrated logistics and supply chain management work in global markets must take into account centralized and decentralized operations, as well as harmonizing management of the day-to-day exchange of goods, services and information.

Considering these issues, this chapter closes with a series of recommendations to Brazilian and other developing world companies that are involved in the transnationalization process. These recommendations are shown in Table 4.2 and are based on conceptual and practical analyses of Brazilian cases studied by internal and external researchers in the supply chain management field. The recommendations point to some strategies that companies can pursue to achieve efficiency in their global operations within foreign markets.

However, before dealing with specific recommendations, companies should realize that with the reduction of trade barriers and the development of global systems to operate worldwide logistics, fewer production lines can produce larger quantities to meet global, rather than local demand. On the other hand, sources of global competition have increased, thereby leading to increasing capacities in most industries and augmented competitive pressures. Increasingly, remaining competitive means that companies must lower costs and enhance services – two actions central to the field of supply chain management and integrated logistics.

Once most of these recommendations are followed, risks associated with achieving higher supply chain and integrated logistics performance are reduced. Naturally, each segment has its own business characteristics that will always call for accommodations regarding specific actions. In general, however, these recommendations can be followed to reach an efficient balance between costs and service levels.

Finally, four principles have emerged as companies have dealt with the challenges of operating in foreign markets. These are:

- Centralized control of logistics flows is gaining more and more attention because of elevated achievements in worldwide optimization costs.
- Service levels must be adapted and met according to the requirements of local markets to ensure competitive advantage.
- Increasing outsourcing necessarily leads to global coordination.
- In the words of Christopher (2005, p. 205), 'a global logistics information system is the prerequisite for enabling the achievement of local service needs whilst seeking global cost optimization'.

Table 4.2   Main recommendations to Brazilian and other companies to achieve supply chain excellence in global markets

Main issues	Product strategies	Customer strategies	Cost strategies
Goals of logistics systems	• Flexibility to volume shifts • Flexibility to product changes • Ability to handle small orders • Ability to handle erratic orders • Availability	• Rapid delivery • Consistent delivery • Flexibility to customer changes	• Minimum costs with acceptable level of service
Procurement	• Continuous and stable supply • Quality • Flexibility to deal with changes in specification	• Consistent delivery • Full-line delivery • Responsiveness • Integration and collaboration	• Maximum use of economies of scale • Centralized purchase organization • Low price strategy
Inventory policies	• Trade-off analysis between stocks kept locally to ensure availability and stocks kept at low levels to retain flexibility and guard against obsolescence and high inertial capital	• Local inventories to secure market presence for rapid and consistent delivery	• Investment in inventories at minimal levels to ensure acceptable service
Transport policies	• Premium on rapid service • Use of common carriers instead of investment in private fleet	• Emergency shipment network planned and available when needed	• Low-cost transport • High utilization of transport capacity • Volume discounts to encourage direct-from-the-plant shipments

Source: Resende (2006).

Companies will continue trying to become global players because this is a strategy that pays off if it is done with competence. At the same time, this strategy carries with it challenges that are at the core of international supply chains. Overcoming these challenges means that companies must confront the issue of how to structure their global logistics organization. Brazilian and other developing-world companies are no different and must face the same challenges. Therefore, being aware of them and planning to resolve their shortages and uncertainties is the first step in achieving sustainable competitiveness for the long run.

REFERENCES

Bovet, David (2005). 'Balancing global risk and return', *Harvard Business Review: Supply Chain Strategy*, 1(3), pp. 2–3.

Bowersox, Donald. J. and David J. Closs (1996). *Logistical Management: The Integrated Supply Chain Process* (New York: McGraw-Hill).

Christopher, M. (2005). *Logistics and Supply Chain Management: Creating Value-Adding Networks* (London: Financial Times Press).

Lee, H.L. and C. Billington (1992). 'Managing supply chain inventory: pitfalls and opportunities', *Sloan Management Review*, 33(3), pp. 65–73.

Resende, P.T.V. (2003, 2005 and 2006). *Results from Research Projects Conducted by the Author at The Center for Logistics and Supply Chain Studies* (Belo Horizonte: Fundação Dom Cabral), mimeo.

Slaight, Tom, Tom Naramore and Guy Bouchet (2004). 'China's role in a global supply strategy', in *Business Briefing: Global Purchasing and Supply Chain Strategies 2004*, Touch Briefings (International Federation of Purchasing and Materials Management).

5. Do firms from emerging markets have to invest abroad? Outward FDI and the competitiveness of firms

John Cantwell and Helena Barnard

INTRODUCTION

In the field of international business, a broad consensus has been reached that, although not every instance of inward foreign direct investment (IFDI) necessarily benefits developing countries, in most cases IFDI acts as a useful source of jobs, capital and especially new knowledge and technology. However, there is little academic work on the relationship between development and outward FDI (OFDI) from developing countries, especially when such FDI involves relocation to the developed world. Should it be seen as institutionalized capital flight, fundamentally an expression of negative sentiment, or is OFDI a potentially positive development that may serve to increase the competitiveness of the investing firm, and eventually its home country?

The emergence and now persistence of the phenomenon of developing-country firms investing abroad suggests that OFDI benefits at least the individual firm. If firms do not benefit from international expansion, they are unlikely to continue (not to mention extend) their efforts abroad. In most cases, OFDI confers net benefits to the investing enterprise in the form of improved access to markets, resources and knowledge. However, the benefits that firms derive from their FDI may not be immediately apparent, and may even sometimes seem counterintuitive in terms of the immediate net advantages. Thus, a firm from a less-developed country may engage in FDI in the developed world in order to build a reputation as a global player, perhaps even at the cost of shorter-term profitability. Over the longer term, the firm may upgrade its own capabilities in order to survive in the more competitive environment, and thus evolve into a successful global player.

But even in such cases, firms do not have an indefinite window for demonstrating the benefits of their international expansion, as developing-country firms are often from countries with balance-of-payment constraints. If the positive effects of OFDI remain negligible, adverse policy reactions are possible as governments intervene to limit the use of what may be regarded as a dubious purpose for scarce funds. This chapter considers how firms from developing countries use OFDI to reconcile their relatively more limited capability base with the increasing prerequisite of global economic integration and to enhance their corporate competitiveness.

In understanding the link between outward investment and the competitiveness of developing-country firms, it is necessary to consider both the ownership advantages that firms develop in their home country and the locational advantages that they derive from expansion to different types of host countries. Tolentino (2000) made a distinction between natural resource-rich and natural resource-poor, and also large and small countries, and documented that they follow different trajectories in terms of their economic development, the nature of their strongest transnational companies (TNCs) and their OFDI. The effects of the size of home countries and their natural resource base must therefore be kept in mind when considering the ownership advantages of developing-country firms.

In considering the destination of FDI, the main distinction to keep in mind is between developed and developing countries, although the early work of Tolentino (1993) suggested that the distinction between intra-regional and extra-regional OFDI from developing countries may also be relevant in certain cases. Whether OFDI is directed to a neighboring developing country, to a developing country in another region (South–South development) or to the developed world, the destination of FDI is likely to affect the types of challenges faced by firms, and therefore also the types of corporate learning that may affect their continuing competitiveness.

The chapter is organized as follows. In the first section, we review the prior literature and in section 5.2, we examine the extent of OFDI from developing countries. Then we consider the effects of differences in the originating location, that is, the home country, and following that, we look at the effects of differences in the location to which FDI is directed, that is, the host country. In the final section, we summarize our argument and present some conclusions.

5.1   PRIOR LITERATURE

Existing macro developmental models suggest that FDI by developing countries will tend to occur only relatively later in their development and also focus primarily on other developing countries. Dunning (1981, 1986) argued that the investment profile of a country is a dynamic reflection of the country's level of development. The Investment Development Path (IDP) model holds that, at the lowest levels of development, stages 1 and 2, IFDI tends to be directed at accessing natural resources or benefiting from low wages, and no OFDI takes place. As the country develops and its domestic industry strengthens so that it can be described as a middle-income developing country (stage 3), local firms increasingly develop the necessary capacity to allow them to invest abroad. By stage 4, the growing competitiveness of the country leads to OFDI exceeding IFDI, with a fluctuating equilibrium reached by stage 5.

A similar model to the Investment Development Path, but with a more explicit emphasis on developing countries, can be found in the flying geese model of Kojima-Ozawa (Kojima 2000; Ozawa 1992). The model was initially developed to explain the processes that were associated with the increasing complexity of Japan's manufacturing sector (Akamatsu 1962), but also found application in the sequential upgrading of Japan, South Korea and other South-East Asian countries like Malaysia and the Philippines in the post-war era. In each case, IFDI, prompted by the relocation of mature industrial activity to a country at an earlier stage of development, set in motion a process of economic development. IFDI over time led to increases not only in economic activity, but also in the general level of education and wages, transforming the character of the locational advantages that attract and then sustain IFDI. According to the flying geese model, the developing country itself will then engage in OFDI to other less developed and lower cost locations at the next rung down of the development ladder in order to remain competitive itself over time.

The two models are similar in a number of ways. Both see IFDI as an initial spur for development and both see OFDI as a response once countries have achieved a certain level of competitiveness. Subsequent research has confirmed the continued empirical relevance of both the flying geese model (Dowling and Cheang 2000; Ginzberg and Simonazzi 2005) and the Investment Development Path (Durán and Ubeda 2001, 2005; Liu, Buck and Shu 2005), even though changes in the economic environment have led to some changes in how the models function. So far as the flying geese model is concerned, the importance of FDI from outside the region needs also to be taken into account (Reynolds 2001). In addition, the development of export industries, such as in electronics, is not necessarily preceded by a process of 'import substitution'. Instead, firms may be focused on producing for global markets from the outset (Ginzberg and Simonazzi 2005). In the context of the Investment Development Path, the work of Tolentino (1993) and Narula (1996) both pointed to an increase in internationalization across countries in every category. Compared to earlier periods, FDI activity takes place at an increasingly lower level of development. In addition, there has been an increasing shift to a knowledge-based economy, which has reduced the importance of the natural resource base and even low-cost unskilled labor (in a suitably productive environment) as a source of comparative advantage. As indicated by Narula and Dunning, 'value-added activities have become increasingly knowledge- or information-intensive, not just in high research-intensive sectors, but also in those that were previously regarded as natural resource or labor-intensive' (2000, p. 142).

The recent revisions to these frameworks do not address the increased complexity in the motives for FDI. In the initial formulation of the Investment Development Path, there was a relatively clear association of motives for FDI with each stage of the IDP. Thus, the first stage is characterized by natural resource seeking, the second by increased market seeking and so on. The search for capabilities and competencies – 'created assets' in the formulation of Dunning (1998) – became important only in stages 4 and 5, in other words, only for developed countries. Similarly, according to the flying geese model, OFDI by developing countries is spurred by the search for lower costs in more mature types of activity, not by the search for created assets, and FDI takes place in even lesser-developed countries at the next rung down of the ladder. Although this broad progression of motives characterized the industrialization process of the current industrial leaders and the gradual transformation of their leading firms, in the recent era motives may increasingly co-exist, for example, in the simultaneous search for natural resources and created assets by Chinese firms. The increasingly complex relationship between developing-country firms' resource endowments and capabilities (established and sought after) and their FDI location must therefore be examined carefully.

Research looking at specific TNCs from developing countries, rather than at general country-wide trends, has long documented instances of those firms' search for created assets in the developed world. Tolentino (1993) demonstrated that 'Third World' TNCs follow a recognizable pattern in their OFDI. At first, they export only to a few neighboring and ethnically similar countries. They increasingly expand to more neighboring and ethnically similar countries, and also to non-ethnically related developing countries. In the third and final stage, they invest 'in countries further away from their home base and in those further away in terms of psychic distance, including developed countries' (Tolentino 1993, p. 364). Such investment could reflect either the search for markets or the search for new capabilities and competencies, for example, through the location of research facilities abroad.

In fact, already a decade earlier, in Lall's early work on Third World TNCs, evidence had been provided of OFDI with the aim of gaining access to the capabilities of more developed countries:

There is also a different kind of investment by Hong Kong enterprises emerging: joint ventures in established technology industries which are neither well-established at home nor important export products of the colony. These investments are mainly to find and transfer back manufacturing technologies. As such, they represent something of an exception to the normal pattern of international activity by both developed and developing country enterprises (Lall 1983, p. 256).

At the time, FDI motivated by the search for capabilities was indeed 'something of an exception' among firms from both developing and developed countries. In the more recent literature, numerous examples of created asset seeking – also termed home base augmenting (Kuemmerle 1999) or knowledge seeking (Chung and Alcacer 2002) – have been documented. Cantwell and Piscitello (2000) argued that changes in the business environment, coupled with a shift in the techno-socio-economic paradigm that governs the nature of innovation in production, are responsible for the change from an ad hoc to a more direct and positive linkage between internationalization and corporate technological diversification (the diversification of the competence base of the firm through increased subsidiary creativity in its international network) since the late 1980s.

Created asset seeking in the developed world has also been documented for firms from Hong Kong (China), Singapore, Taiwan Province of China, and especially South Korea – the Asian Tigers. A number of excellent case studies, for example, Kim and Nelson (2000) and Sachwald (2001), documented the important role of OFDI to the developed world. It was key to the success of Samsung's camera business (Lee 2001), and Hyundai's investments in the US and Japan have been seen as the final steps in a lengthy, ambitious catching-up process that relied on 'crisis construction' to force organizational learning (Kim 1998). However, there is also evidence that the created asset seeking efforts of developing country firms in the developed world often fail (Lautier 2001; SAPA 2003).

At the same time, there has been growing interest in South–South FDI, with considerable effort being invested in encouraging developing countries to forge economic relationships with each other (Sridharan 1998). FDI in other developing countries offers firms perhaps less of an opportunity to expand their capability base, but other developing countries do offer potentially more accessible markets. A now global player like SABMiller long focused only on developing countries, with substantial gains in global market share and profitability. This chapter attempts to provide a more general framework for understanding how developing countries' FDI in both developed and developing countries contributes to the competitiveness of their firms.

In order to understand the advantages firms gain from FDI, it is important to understand their initial (ownership) advantages. Another purpose of this chapter is therefore to investigate how investing companies are shaped by home country characteristics, and to relate that to the types and purpose of OFDI from developing countries. A number of rich studies document the relationship between country characteristics and the evolution of industries in the developed world (Chandler, Amatori and Hikino 1997; Mowery and Nelson 1999; Murmann 2003; Nelson 1993), but few studies focus specifically on how those patterns affect OFDI, or the pattern of the growth of industries in developing countries. The existing studies repeatedly highlight the role of the size of the domestic market – a large local market offers significant benefits as accessible outlet for innovations, provided that firms take advantage of it. Another often-mentioned dimension is the strength of the country's natural resource base in shaping the types of industries that evolve, and even for industries that are not necessarily regarded as resource-intensive, the way they develop. For example, the development of the internal combustion engine and chemical industry was shaped by the abundant supply of natural resources in the US (Mowery and Rosenberg 1998).

Tolentino (2000) explicitly studied how these two dimensions play out not only in the developed, but also in the developing world. She argued that the existence of a large resource base allows firms to develop and exploit abroad capabilities in natural resource extraction and related manufactures. In other words, she regarded natural resource-based industries as following a similar evolutionary path to any other type of industry. In contrast, Narula (1996) regarded natural resources as a 'starting point' or fundamental industry, and he argued that developing countries with a large natural resource base attract a relatively larger proportion of IFDI than countries at equivalent levels of development with a small resource base, that domestic firms therefore have more limited incentives to develop new ownership advantages, and that firms from resource-dominated economies therefore are relatively less likely to invest abroad. Both Narula and Tolentino agreed that developing countries with a small natural resource base need to invest abroad, whether to procure resources directly or to procure the foreign currency to fund resource purchases. For Tolentino, the need for international FDI and trade to support economies in resource-scarce countries results most importantly in the development of specialized service industries, an even more pronounced phenomenon in the smaller rather than larger countries.

Finally, these insights into how developing countries and their firms evolve need to be considered against the backdrop of a rise in globalization more widely, which is characterized by two closely related phenomena.

First is the fact that globalization has given rise simultaneously to the dispersal of some economic activities, but the concentration of others (Cantwell and Santangelo 2000; Narula 2003; Zaheer and Manrakhan 2001). Knowledge-based activities have become more fragmented or modularized, so locational concentration at the level of specific disaggregated fields of activity in appropriately specialized centers is matched by a tendency toward overall geographical dispersion in the aggregate. In particular, most knowledge-intensive activities are increasingly likely to be concentrated in locations with the most relevant expertise in any given field, such that the profile of national technological specialization has become more focused (Cantwell and Vertova 2004). Yet innovative activities in the aggregate have, on average, shifted since at least the early 1990s toward developing countries that are catching up technologically (Athreye and Cantwell 2007).

Second is the increasing recognition of path dependency in the development of capabilities. Because learning is cumulative and incremental (Cantwell 1991), the composition and scope of higher-valued added activities that they are able to attract may have far-reaching consequences for the potentially achievable growth paths of developing countries. As the leaders in any field benefit from an ongoing virtuous cycle of knowledge creation (Cantwell 1989; Nachum 2000), less-developed countries are potentially vulnerable to patterns of specialization that connect less well to knowledge development elsewhere and so leave their early efforts in innovation more isolated and confined.

The fact that industries evolve within the environment of certain socio-techno-economic paradigms represents a double-edged sword for industrial leaders, because the requirements for continuing success within a currently prevailing paradigm also often constrain the most firmly entrenched actors from fully exploiting the possibilities of a new paradigm. For example, the UK-based system of individual entrepreneurship and craftsmanship allowed it to dominate the first industrial (mechanical) revolution, but also constrained its ability to seize leadership during the emergence of science-based industry (chemicals, electrical equipment), for which a more systematic review of scientific opportunities was central, and in which a stronger organizational (rather than individual) focus on innovation was therefore needed (Murmann 2003). In other words, the economic leadership positions of countries are strongly influenced by the extent of any match between their pre-existing capabilities and the capability requirements of an era. This has not only led to different countries coming to prominence in different technological eras – with the UK leading the mechanical revolution, Germany and the US the chemical and electrical revolution and Japan and East Asia in the electronic era (Cantwell 1992); but because of the effects of path dependency, these are also the areas in which the countries retain a strong leadership role.

Even when countries struggle to develop capabilities outside of their areas of historical strength, there is generally a virtuous process of learning that supports capability development within the areas in which they have previously established technological leadership. Developing countries must find entry points for themselves in a world in which such technological and economic leadership positions are already well established. For their OFDI to contribute to their competitiveness, it must therefore reflect a strategic assessment of the role of established and emerging industries, the role of their own areas of economic strength, and the role of lead locations. This study investigates how developing country firms respond to that challenge.

5.2 THE IMPORTANCE OF FDI BY DEVELOPING COUNTRY FIRMS

Mergers and acquisitions (M&A) are an important indicator of the global competitiveness of firms. Whether as an attractive target or as the acquirer, a firm involved in a large deal can be assumed to be a successful firm with a significant human and capital resource base. In addition, M&A data capture this more than capital flows, and specifically indicate investment in the economic activity of a given industry in a given country. Because specific countries and industries can be identified, a more fine-grained analysis is possible than with just FDI data.

However, two concerns must be addressed when using M&A data. First, large M&As represent only the tip of the iceberg of the economic activity of developing-country firms. Much activity remains hidden from view. But although it cannot be concluded that M&A data capture all economic activity of the relevant firms, it is likely that such data are a reasonable proxy for the main cross-country and industry patterns of activity. Second, M&A data do not enable a distinction between correlation and causation in the mutual relationship between corporate competitiveness and OFDI. Developing-country firms that engage in large M&As have already achieved a significant degree of international competitiveness – and some initial level of competitiveness facilitates OFDI. In the usual sequence of events, an initial level of competitiveness facilitates OFDI, but OFDI also feeds back to enhance the competitiveness of firms. It is this connected process that makes for a continuing trend in some branches of OFDI – one without the other is more likely to be associated with some one-off or more intermittent series of increases in OFDI. Indeed, the macro-developmental models of FDI like the Investment Development Path and the flying geese model concur on the co-evolution of the competitiveness of home country firms and their OFDI.

Because the relationship between OFDI and firm competitiveness is interconnected, OFDI feeds back to enhance the competitiveness of firms. In other words, it is an evolutionary process, and a large M&A can be interpreted not only as evidence of an existing capability base, but also (if it is part of a continuing trend) as another step toward expanding the capability base of a firm. It is therefore instructive to examine where the M&As initiated by the firms of a given country and industry are located, how this fits with their evolving corporate strategy and where they are able to expand.

To determine the competitiveness of developing-country firms in a global context, data on all the M&As that have been recorded in the *World Investment Reports* from 1996 (for 1995) to 2005 (for 2004) were collated (UNCTAD 1996–2005) – the value of each M&A, and the country and main industry of both the acquired and the acquiring firm. The value of each was in excess of US$1 billion. The M&As involving developing country firms worth between US$100 million and US$1 billion from the 2005 *World Investment Report* were also recorded. Countries were designated as developed or developing, following the guidelines laid out by UNCTAD. However, UNCTAD identifies a firm's country of origin as the country in which it has its primary listing. In the few cases for which firm listings do not correspond to the country of ultimate ownership, for example, where firms are listed in well-known tax havens like Bermuda, the ultimate beneficiary country was identified and used instead.

In addition, the data were categorized according to the types of industries in which developing-country firms are active. To make more manageable the wide range of industries that were represented, the sample has been coded into the standard categories of research and development (R&D) intensity as used by Dunning (1996) and Lall (1998), expanded to include service industries. Table 5.1 records the categorization, based on the average R&D spending in each industry and recorded in the OECD Science, Technology and Industry Scoreboard (Pilat 2003). In coding the industries, there is clear evidence of specialization in certain types of industries, but virtually no evidence of the use of M&As to facilitate migration between industries. In the few cases in which there was backward or forward vertical integration, the research-intensity of the destination industry was coded.

Table 5.2 provides a descriptive overview of the extent of developing-country firms' M&As relative to total M&A activity. It is worth noting that developing-country firm acquisitions represent a small proportion of

Table 5.1   Categorization in terms of technological intensity (average R&D spending)

ISIC 2-digit Code	Industries included in each category
Resource-based firms	
01–02	Agriculture and forestry
05	Fishing
10–14	Mining
General service firms	
40–41	Provision of electricity, gas, water, sewerage etc.
45	Construction
50–52	Wholesale and retail trade
55	Hotels and restaurants
60–64	Transportation and storage
70–71	Real estate renting and business activities
Knowledge-intensive service firms	
65–67	Financial intermediation, banking, insurance and pension funding
72–74	Business services, computing, research and development
Low research-intensive manufacturing firms	
15–21	Food products, beverages, textiles, clothing, leather and leather-type products (e.g. footwear), wood and wood products, paper and paper products (e.g. printing)
36–39	Furniture and recycling
Medium research-intensive manufacturing firms	
23–29	Refined petroleum products, chemicals and chemical products, rubber and plastic products, building materials, basic metals and metal products
34	Motor vehicles and other transportation equipment
High research-intensive manufacturing firms	
30–33	Machinery and equipment, office, accounting and computing machinery, electrical machinery, communication equipment, medical, precision and optical instruments
35	Pharmaceuticals

global M&A activity, and that developing-country firms are the target rather than the acquirer for most of the M&As to which they are a party. However, as also indicated in Figure 5.1, their participation as buyers in global M&As is clearly rising. The next two sections investigate how that participation contributes to their competitiveness.

Table 5.2 *Developing countries' participation in M&As worth US$1 billion or more, 1995–2004*

Category	1995	1996	1997	1998	1999	2000	2001	2002	2003	2004
Number of all M&As worth more than US$1 billion (total US$)	35 (69.7)	45 (96.0)	58 (161.4)	88 (401.8)	109 (498.3)	175 (865.8)	113 (378.1)	81 (213.9)	56 (141.4)	75 (187.6)
Number of M&As involving less-developed countries (total US$)	4 (6.4)	5 (8.4)	13 (19.7)	12 (30.5)	11 (30.1)	22 (46.6)	15 (54.3)	15 (30.7)	12 (24.8)	18 (39.7)
Number of M&As with less-developed countries as buyers (total US$)	2 (3.9)	1 (1.4)	5 (7.2)	2 (6.2)	4 (8.6)	10 (17.3)	5 (18.1)	7 (15.4)	8 (19.6)	5 (16.4)
Number of M&As with both acquiring and acquired firm from less-developed countries (total US$)	2 (3.9)	- -	3 (4.4)	2 (6.2)	2 (2.1)	1 (1.4)	3 (8.5)	4 (6.6)	6 (14.9)	1 (1.5)
Number of M&As with acquiring firm from a more-developed and acquired firm from a less-developed country (total US$)	2 (2.5)	4 (7.0)	8 (12.5)	10 (24.3)	7 (21.5)	12 (29.3)	10 (36.2)	8 (15.3)	4 (5.2)	13 (23.3)
Number of M&As with acquiring firm from a less-developed and acquired firm from a more-developed country (total US$)	- -	1 (1.4)	2 (2.8)	- -	2 (6.5)	9 (15.9)	2 (9.6)	3 (8.8)	2 (4.7)	4 (14.9)

Table 5.2 (continued)

Category	1995	1996	1997	1998	1999	2000	2001	2002	2003	2004
Total number of M&As forging linkages between more- and less-developed countries, i.e. one firm from a more- and one from a less-developed country (total US$)	2 (2.5)	5 (8.4)	10 (15.3)	10 (24.3)	9 (28.0)	21 (45.2)	12 (45.8)	11 (24.1)	6 (9.9)	17 (38.2)
% of M&As with acquiring firm from a less-developed country relative to all M&As that forge linkages between more- and less-developed countries (% of total US$)	- -	20 (16.7)	20 (18.3)	- -	22.2 (23.2)	42.9 (35.2)	16.7 (21.0)	27.3 (36.5)	33.3 (47.5)	23.5 (39.0)

Source: UNCTAD, 1996–2005.

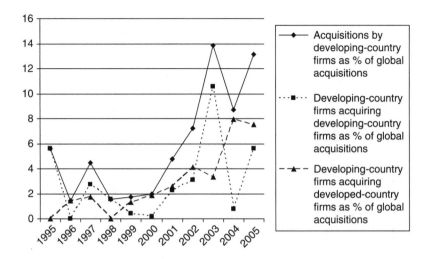

Source: UNCTAD, 1996–2005

Figure 5.1   *M&As with developing country firms as buyer as a proportion*
           of global M&As (in terms of US$ value of transactions),
           1995–2004 (%)

5.3   COMPETITIVENESS AND THE ORIGINATING LOCATION FOR FDI

Tolentino (2000) documented how the evolution of TNCs is influenced by two host country characteristics: the size of the home country, especially in terms of the market, and the extent to which TNCs can draw on a rich natural resource base. Using this as a basis, we divide developing-country firms into those that originate from small economies (for example, the island economies of Hong Kong (China), Singapore, Taiwan Province of China) and large countries (the Russian Federation and the even more populous developing countries of Brazil, India, Indonesia, China); we treat all other countries between these two extremes as medium-sized.

   We rely on the prior classification of Tolentino, on World Bank data for the sectoral composition of exports, and UNCTAD and CIA country overviews to categorize countries as resource-rich or resource-scarce. The Russian Federation and countries from Africa, the Middle East and Latin America rely heavily on resource extraction, whereas the Asian countries (not only the Asian Tigers, but also emerging economies like China and India) are relatively resource-scarce. No small resource-rich developing economies have engaged in global M&As, so a total of five country-types can be identified (Table 5.3).

Table 5.3   Concentration of large M&As in industrial categories by country type, 1995–2004 (US$b)

Category	Resource-based industry	General services	Knowledge-intensive services	Low research-intensive manufacturing	Medium research-intensive manufacturing	High research-intensive manufacturing	TOTAL
Small resource-scarce countries							
US$b value of transactions	0	**13.6**	**24.8**	0	0	4.1	42.5
as % of value of all transactions by small non-resource-based economies	0	**32%**	**58.35%**	0	0	0.09%	100%
as % of value of all transactions in category	0	**79%**	**55%**	0	0	100%	
Medium resource-scarce countries							
US$b value of transactions	1.8	2.5	5.6	1	1.1	0	12
as % of value of all transactions by medium non-resource-based economies	7.43%	20.83%	46.67%	8.33%	9.16%	0	100%
as % of value of all transactions in category	9.78%	14.53%	12.33%	4.87%	12.94%	0	
Large resource-scarce countries							
US$b value of transactions	3	0	0	0	1.5	0	4.5
as % of value of all transactions by large non-resource-based economies	66.70%	0	0	0	33.30%	0	100%

	(1)	(2)	(3)	(4)	(5)	(6)	Total
as % of value of all transactions in category	16.30%	0	0	0	17.64%	0	
Medium resource-rich countries							
US$b value of transactions	5	1.1	13.9	11.7	5.9	0	37.6
as % of value of all transactions by medium resource-based economies	19.68%	2.92%	36.97%	31.12%	15.69%	0	100%
as % of value of all transactions in category	27.17%	6.39%	30.62%	57.07%	69.41%	0	
Large resource-rich countries							
US$b value of transactions	8.6	0	1.1	7.8	0	0	17.5
as % of value of all transactions by large resource-based economies	49.14%	0	6.28%	44.57%	0	0	100%
as % of value of all transactions in category	46.74%	0	0.02%	38.04%	0	0	
TOTAL (US$b)	18.4	17.2	45.4	20.5	8.5	4.1	114.1

Source: UNCTAD, 1996–2005.

To determine the importance of a given category of economic activity for a given country type, we determine whether the FDI by that country type directed to that category has represented a sizable (20 per cent or more) proportion of the country's overall FDI and at the same time also represented a sizable (20 per cent or more) proportion of total FDI in that category. The rationale for this combination is that there has been a lot of activity in, for example, banking and telecommunications, knowledge-intensive services. A large proportion of the overall M&As of a specific country type may be in the category of knowledge-intensive services, but because there is so much M&A activity in that category, the total FDI of this particular country type in knowledge-intensive services may still be quite small. Table 5.3 shows the breakdown by country type and sectoral category using the US$ value of M&As as indicator, and Table 5.4 uses the total number of transactions as an indicator. The areas in which activity is relatively concentrated on the criteria above are indicated in bold.

As proposed by Tolentino (2000), most of the global M&A activity of large resource-rich developing countries is in resource-based industries, for example, Petrobras and BT Bumi from Brazil and Indonesia respectively. What is more noteworthy is the discrepancy between the value (Table 5.3) and number of transactions (Table 5.4) in resource-based industries. In terms of the simple number of transactions, there is a concentration in the number of resource-based M&As by medium-sized resource-rich economies and even the large resource-scarce economies, although this is not seen when focusing on the value of transactions.[1] This difference confirms that resource-based industries remain an important initial industry for developing countries, as suggested by Narula (1996). To the extent that transaction value reflects global competitiveness (rather than simply the incidence of economic activity), both the greater availability of natural resources and a historic FDI in natural resource extraction are necessary for global success.

In contrast, as also argued by Tolentino, the OFDI of small resource-scarce countries is clearly concentrated in the services sector, for example, Singapore's Neptune Orient Lines, or the retailing group A.S. Watson from Hong Kong (China). Small economies have completely dominated the historically better established general services category, but have also been very significant players in the emerging knowledge-intensive service industries, for example, with Asia Netcom (Hong Kong) and Singtel. Hong Kong's role as an entrepôt is well known (Lall, 1983), and some part of the importance of service industries can be explained by the historical role that many small economies played as intermediaries between local and colonial powers. The central purpose of service industries has been described as being to provide connections with other industries (Francois 1990; Nusbaumer 1987; Riddle

1986), and the strong presence of services in these countries is consistent with their long-established role as global intermediaries. Tolentino (2000, p. 428) pointed out:

> the scarcity of natural resources . . . and the consequent large dependence on international trade as both an engine and handmaiden of economic growth led to a common emergence of a domestically based infrastructure in support of trade – banks, shipping companies, marine insurance companies and, above all, trading companies – which emerged rapidly as MNCs [multinational corporations].

In addition, services differ from other industries in that the main inputs are human rather than physical. In short, a specialization in services can enable countries to overcome the constraints of physical resource availability.

It is telling that the international activities of firms from large countries are not at all concentrated in services. Services tend to be more localized than other industries, because production and consumption often happen at the same point (Boddewyn, Halbrich and Perry 1986) and service industries were therefore less internationalized until recently (Dunning 1989; UNCTAD 2004). Even though this is changing, for large developing countries the domestic market seems big enough and the costs of cross-border operation too high for their leading firms to expand abroad in the service industries. In general, as the total number of transactions indicate, large countries have been the least likely to engage in large M&As. This indicates that many developing countries use OFDI instead to overcome the constraints of a smaller, less wealthy domestic market rather than in search of (either natural or created) assets.

In contrast to the marked specialization of small resource-scarce countries, the medium and large resource-scarce countries have not exhibited such a clear pattern of specialization. Services have been relatively more important for the medium compared to the large resource-scarce countries, but in general their industrial profile is more widely distributed. This can be related to the fact that resource-scarce countries, given their relatively low state of development, have to develop some resource-based and low research-intensive industries, but that their resource scarcity simultaneously forces them also to explore other avenues of economic growth.

The migration into low research-intensive manufacturing from resource-based industries is evident from the concentration of low research-intensive manufacturing in (both medium-sized and large) resource-rich countries. In contrast, M&As in medium research-intensive manufacturing have been quite evenly spread across the large resource-scarce countries and medium-sized economies (whether resource-rich or not), but this industrial category does not seem to be an area of concentration for any country grouping. The

Table 5.4   Concentration of large M&As in industrial categories by country type, 1995–2004 (by number of transactions)

Category	Resource-based industry	General services	Knowledge-intensive services	Low research-intensive manufacturing	Medium research-intensive manufacturing	High research-intensive manufacturing	TOTAL
Small resource-scarce countries							
Number of transactions	0	7	7	0	0	2	16
as % of all transactions by small non-resource-based economies	0	**43.75%**	**43.75%**	0	0	12.25%	100%
as % of all transactions in category	0	70%	38.89%	0	0	100%	100%
Medium resource-scarce countries							
Number of transactions	1	**2**	3	1	1	0	8
as % of all transactions by medium non-resource-based economies	12.50%	25%	16.67%	16.67%	20.00%	0	100%
as % of all transactions in category	12.50%	20%	37.50%	12.50%	12.50%	0	
Large resource-scarce countries							
Number of transactions	**2**	0	0	0	**1**	0	3
as % of all transactions by large non-resource-based economies	**66.67%**	0	0	0	**33.3%**	0	100%
as % of all transactions in category	25%	0	0	0	20%	0	

Medium resource-rich countries

Number of transactions	3	1	7	4	3	0	18
as % of all transactions by medium resource-based economies	16.67%	5.56%	38.89%	22.22%	16.67%	0	100%
as % of all transactions in category	37.50%	10%	38.89%	66.67%	60%	0	
Large resource-rich countries							
Number of transactions	2	0	1	1	0	0	4
as % of all transactions by large resource-based economies	50%	0	25%	25%	0	0	100%
as % of all transactions in category	25%	0	0.05%	16.67%	0	0	
TOTAL	8	10	18	6	5	2	49

Source: UNCTAD, 1996–2005.

few high research-intensive manufacturing M&As that have occurred have been only in small non-resource-based economies. The dominance of economies like Singapore and Taiwan Province of China in those industries is well known, and although the contribution of high research-intensive manufacturing to the upgrading of those countries is familiar (Hobday 2000; Lall 1998), it is clear that this is not the only or indeed the main avenue for industrial upgrading.

In sum, globally competitive firms develop in different types of industries depending on both the resource intensity and market size of their home countries. For the most part, the patterns resemble those documented by Tolentino more than a decade ago, suggesting that increases in the OFDI of developing-country firms form part of an evolutionary process of development. The small island economies are concentrated in services, while large countries have been less active outbound investors overall, although the large resource-rich countries have dominated petroleum and minerals extraction. Whereas medium-sized resource-scarce economies have quite a diversified set of strong firms, firms from medium-sized resource-rich countries have been concentrated in the (historically well-established) low research-intensive manufacturing sector as well as in the (emerging) knowledge-intensive services sector.

Neither the countries' size nor their resource endowment by themselves would lead one to expect that economic activity would be concentrated in knowledge-intensive services. The firms in this sector also include a number of young players like Dimension Data (South Africa) and Movil (Mexico). In addition, the bulk of M&As by developing-country firms have been in knowledge-intensive services, suggesting that this sector reflects not only an evolutionary progression, but that it is playing a special role as a general engine of growth. The nature of this role can be further elucidated from the pattern of geographical concentration in this industry. The next section documents how firms' choice of FDI location also affects their competitiveness.

5.4   COMPETITIVENESS AND THE DESTINATION LOCATION FOR FDI

In section 5.2 we showed that, although M&As with developing-country firms as buyers still represent a small minority of M&As worldwide, the proportion of M&As in which developing country firms act as a buyer has been steadily increasing, both in terms of number of transactions and notably also the dollar value of transactions (Table 5.2). This increase is even more pronounced when considered relative to total M&A activity worldwide (Figure 5.1). Although there has been some increase in the rate at which developing-country firms have acquired other firms from both the developing and developed world, the fastest growth has been in the acquisition of firms from the developed world. In fact, when excluding M&As between firms that are both from developed countries and focusing only on M&As involving one firm from the developed and one from the developing world, in the most recent years for which data are available (2003 and 2004) acquisitions by developing-country firms accounted for more than 40 per cent of the US$ value of M&As. Increasingly, the connections between the developed and developing world – with the concomitant possibilities for knowledge transfer – are being initiated from both sides.

However, to the extent that the main economic agents worldwide benefit from an ongoing virtuous cycle of knowledge creation (Cantwell 1989; Nachum 2000), developing country firms have to be increasingly well interconnected with the main centers, and thus need to be sufficiently capable to thrive or even survive in developed locations. None of the 2004 M&As worth between US$100 million and US$1 billion involved developing-country firms acquiring firms from the developed world – although four M&As worth more than US$1 billion each did (UNCTAD 2005). To be successful in the developed world, increasingly sophisticated capabilities are needed – and they need to be continuously transformed, at a faster rate than most developing-country firms can generally manage in isolation. This would also suggest that a developing-country firm's decision to invest in the developed world carries greater implications for firm competitiveness than it did just one or two decades ago.

In this regard, it is interesting to compare the average value of M&As. Although the value of M&As with developing-country firms as acquirers has been on average smaller than it has for M&As between developed-country firms, this gap has been closing. Whether the value of transactions has been increasing because developing-country firms have been pursuing increasingly attractive targets, or because they have been willing to pay a premium for similar quality firms simply because they originate from the developed world, the trend confirms the increasing importance of the developed world as a host location for developing-country firms.

The pattern of specialization of OFDI in terms of industries also shows a geographical dimension to the principal direction of FDI movements. The industries from which developing-country firms tend to invest in the developed world are not the same as those from which developed-country firms tend to invest in the developing world. When looking at large M&As, whether the acquiring firm is itself a developing-country firm, or a firm from the developed world, developing-country firms are attractive targets especially for resource-based industries and for knowledge-intensive service industries (Table 5.5). The importance of resource-based industries in the developing world is well established, and that firms from developed and developing countries alike would decide to target resource bases in other lower wage countries rather than in more developed countries is in accord with the prior literature, such as the Investment Development Path or the flying geese model. The pattern for knowledge-intensive services is more complex, and will be discussed in more detail below.

However, a very different pattern emerges when looking at developing-country firms acquiring firms from the developed world. Developing-country firms have invested in the developed world especially in low research-intensive manufacturing and, to a lesser extent, medium research-intensive manufacturing. The M&As of low research-intensive firms are also the only M&As involving developing country firms (whether as target or acquirer) for which the average value of the transaction is higher than that paid by firms from developed countries. The importance of such Smithian (as opposed to Schumpeterian) industries in less-developed countries is well known (Lall 1998; Ozawa 1992; Wells 1983). Given that capability accumulation is cumulative, it is perhaps to be expected that the rate of capability accumulation of developing-country firms can keep up better with that of the developed world in this historically well-established range of industries than in the more science-based industries.

The types of developing-country firms found in the industries that are most prominent in OFDI in the developed world also raise important questions about the nature of firm learning. Firms in these industries – Cemex, the Mexican cement manufacturer, the Indian-controlled Mittal Steel and the South African beer producer SABMiller, to name some well-known firms – are characterized by capital-intensive production, scale economies and assembly-based mass production. In Pavitt's (1984) typology, they tend to follow supplier-dominated or scale-intensive technological trajectories. Formal R&D typically plays a relatively small role in the capability upgrading of such firms, while production learning and the inputs of suppliers play a much more important role. The increased competitiveness of those developing-country firms therefore results from learning-by-doing, responding to the bigger markets and increased competition of the developed world, and the increased proximity of many of their suppliers. Created asset seeking is not the central avenue for increasing competitiveness in this sector, and to the extent that it may be present it cannot be conceptualized narrowly in terms of the higher-grade categories of technological development measured by R&D or patenting.

A number of factors are evident when considering lower value M&As, the 2004 M&As with a value between US$100 million and US$1 billion in which developing countries acquired firms from other developing countries

Table 5.5   *Sectoral Breakdown of All M&As Worth US$1 Billion and More, 1995–2004*

Category	Acquiring firm from developing country investing in		Acquiring firm from developed country investing in		TOTAL
	developing countries	developed countries	developing countries	developed countries	
Resource-based industries					
Number of	6	2	7	45	60
M&As	0.72%	0.24%	0.84%	5.39%	7.19%
US$m	15	3.4	25.4	192.7	236.5
value	0.50%	0.11%	0.84%	6.39%	7.84%
General services					
Number of	4	6	17	202	229
M&As	0.48%	0.72%	2.04%	24.19%	27.43%
US$m	5.5	11.7	38.7	583.2	639.1
value	0.18%	0.39%	1.28%	19.35%	21.20%
Knowledge-intensive services					
Number of	11	7	40	234	292
M&As	1.32%	0.84%	4.79%	28.02%	34.97%
US$m	25.8	19.6	87.2	1153.5	1286.1
value	0.86%	0.65%	2.89%	38.27%	42.67%
Low research-intensive manufacturing					
Number of	2	4	5	62	73
M&As	0.24%	0.48%	0.60%	7.43%	8.75%
US$m	2.1	18.4	11.3	182.5	214.3
value	0.07%	0.61%	0.37%	6.06%	7.11%
Medium research-intensive manufacturing					
Number of	1	5	7	103	116
M&As	0.12%	0.60%	0.84%	12.34%	13.90%
US$m	1.1	10	10.9	365.2	387.2
value	0.04%	0.33%	0.36%	12.12%	12.85%
High research-intensive manufacturing					
Number of	0	1	2	62	65
M&As	0%	0.12%	0.24%	7.43%	8.00%
US$m	0	1.5	3.6	245.7	250.8
value	0%	0.05%	0.12%	8.15%	8.00%
Total					
Number of	24	25	78	708	835
M&As	2.88%	3.00%	9.35%	84.80%	100%
US$m	49.5	64.6	177.1	2722.8	3014
value	1.64%	2.14%	5.88%	90.34%	100%

Source: UNCTAD, 1996–2005.

(UNCTAD 2005). First, there have been no acquisitions of firms in the developed world under this heading, and almost no acquisitions of firms from extra-regional developing countries (Table 5.6). In keeping with Tolentino's (1993) argument that the greater the geographical and psychic distance of the FDI destination, the greater the capabilities that are required by the firm, more modest M&As by developing country firms have been focused almost exclusively in other developing countries in the region.

Even for M&As below US$1 billion in value, firms from developed countries acted as buyers in almost 60 per cent of the cases, and more if the financial value of transactions is considered. However, this difference is driven mostly by developed countries' more extensive FDI in manufacturing and resource-based industries. In service-based industries, there has been a much greater parity in the acquisitions of developed- and developing-country firms. Part of this parity can be explained by the fact that services, by their nature, tend to be 'location bound' (Boddewyn et al. 1986; Dunning 1989). Although in many service activities the advantages of required co-location are being eroded by the fact that service provision is becoming increasingly fragmented and tradable (UNCTAD 2004), geographically more proximate investors may well retain some advantage over more distant investors.

However, this still does not explain developing countries' much stronger performance in knowledge-intensive rather than in general services. Almost 50 per cent of all 2004 M&As in the developing world have been in this one category, and developing-country firms have been as likely to act as buyers as firms from the developed world. Although knowledge-intensive service firms from developing countries play a less prominent role in the developed world, there are also some examples of them having engaged in large M&As in developed countries (Table 5.4). Clearly, there is now a tremendous activity in the information technology, financial services and telecommunications industries of developing countries.

This focused FDI pattern is attributable to the emergent nature of many knowledge-intensive services, for example, software and telecommunications. Extensive M&A activity is evident in both the developed and developing world, as firms in these new and increasingly important sectors have consolidated their activity. But the active participation of developing-country firms cannot be simply attributed to consolidation, as they are (unusually) active and successful in knowledge-intensive service industries. Instead, the phenomenon can probably be explained by the fact that these industries have been central to a change in paradigm that has created opportunities for new players.

In contrast to established industries in which the current industrial leaders have become well-ensconced, in new and evolving fields, leadership

Table 5.6   *Sectoral breakdown of all 2004 M&As involving developing countries worth between US$100m and US$1b*

Category	Acquiring firm from developing country investing in			Acquiring firm from developed country investing in developing countries	TOTAL
	own developing region	other developing region	developed countries		
Resource-based industries					
Number of	1	2	0	8	11
M&As	0.96%	1.92%	0	7.69%	10.57%
US$m	105	302	0	3297	3704
value	0.38%	1.08%	0	11.83%	13.29%
General services					
Number of	9	0	0	12	21
M&As	8.65	0	0	11.54%	20.19%
US$m	1547	0	0	2891	4438
value	5.55%	0	0	10.37%	15.92%
Knowledge-intensive services					
Number of	24	1	0	25	50
M&As	23.08%	0.96%	0	24.04%	48.08%
US$m	6056	195	0	7367	13618
value	21.73%	0.70%	0	26.43%	48.86%
Low research-intensive manufacturing					
Number of	1	0	0	9	10
M&As	0.96%	0	0	8.65%	9.61%
US$m	102	0	0	2036	2138
value	0.37%	0	0	7.30%	7.67%
Medium research-intensive manufacturing					
Number of	3	0	0	3	6
M&As	2.88%	0	0	2.88%	5.76%
US$m	431	0	0	889	1320
value	1.55%	0	0	3.19%	4.74%
High research-intensive manufacturing					
Number of	1	0	0	5	6
M&As	0.96%	0	0	4.81%	5.77%
US$m	120	0	0	2536	2656
value	0.43%	0	0	9.10%	9.53%
Total					
Number of	39	3	0	62	104
M&As	37.50%	2.88%	0	59.62%	100%
US$m	8361	497	0	19016	27874
value	30.0%	1.78%	0	68.22%	100%

Source: UNCTAD, 2005.

positions have not yet been so cemented. For developing countries, industries that are still evolving with relatively fluid leadership positions especially offer a potential entry point into the global economy. Of course, developing countries suffer from a less advanced institutional, educational and economic infrastructure, and their firms are likely to be less competitive than knowledge-intensive service firms from the developed world across the full range of activity. But the gap between firms from more- and less-developed countries is likely to be smaller than in other fields, such as chemicals, and there are more niche positions that developing-country firms can occupy. The data suggest that, although the knowledge-intensive service firms from developing countries have still struggled to compete effectively in the developed world, they do seem to have been able to keep at bay competitors from the developed world in their own region. Intra-regional FDI has offered developing-country firms the advantage of geographic and cultural proximity – an advantage that they lose not only when investing in the developed world, but also in extra-regional South–South FDI. Intra-regional FDI in emerging industries like telecommunications and information technology services has therefore served as an important entry point for firms wishing to expand their capabilities and enter the global arena.

In contrast, relatively more FDI in the developed world has taken place in low research-intensive manufacturing, in what is sometimes termed 'sunset' industries (Tunzelmann and Acha 2005). Developing-country firms have dynamized their industries in areas of historical strength (commodity-type manufacturing) and have displaced incumbents in the developed world by innovating within mature industries, as in the case of Cemex's just-in-time delivery of mixed cement. The successful developing-country firms in this sector in the developed world have tended to be long-established in their home market (although with typically only one or two decades of international experience) and they have used FDI in the developed world to achieve a global leadership position in their respective industries.

CONCLUSION

In determining whether developing country firms benefit from investing abroad, a first point is that firms first need some initial ownership advantages to enable them to do so. In shaping the nature of these initial ownership advantages of developing-country firms, home country characteristics play an important role. The availability of a natural resource base – in both medium and large countries – allows firms to become global leaders not only in resource-based industries but also in low research-intensive manufacturing, whereas the absence of a natural resource base instead tends to be associated with outward FDI in the service industries. Services often evolved at first in order to procure natural resources, and have remained important because they rely on human rather than physical inputs, with the result that small resource-scarce countries have dominated FDI in services. In contrast, firms from large developing countries have been relatively less likely to invest abroad, probably because of their large domestic market.

Because even the most advanced developing country firms as a rule still lack the capabilities to spread their efforts widely enough to be able to construct meaningfully a portfolio of differentiated locational assets, their learning from their international operations is more isolated in specific targets, and from the parent company perspective is achieved through largely informal channels and through learning-by-doing. The nature of learning and benefits firms derive once abroad are therefore likely to differ across different specific types of host locations. There has been a marked split in terms of the types of industries investing in the more- and less-developed world, suggesting that OFDI to both more- and less-developed countries contributes to the competitiveness of developing-country firms, but in very different ways. FDI in the developed world seems to be the preserve of the most powerful developing-country firms, and those firms often engage in OFDI in order to assume global leadership positions in their respective industries. However, developing-country firms in the developed world operate mainly in low and medium research-intensive industries. These industries are defined as those with a relatively lower investment in R&D (OECD Science and Technology Scoreboard–Pilat 2003) and tend to rely heavily on capital-intensive processing. They are also the kinds of industries that most commonly have accounted for a higher share of activity in developing countries, and because of the commodity-like nature of these industries, they are more vulnerable to price fluctuations and economic cycles.

In contrast, most developing countries' M&A activity in the developing world, especially when looking at M&As with a value of less than US$1 billion, has been in knowledge-intensive services, such as telecommunications. Even within knowledge-intensive service firms, a hierarchy of more and less knowledge-intensive activities can be identified (Athreye 2005). Although it is not possible to identify how knowledge-intensive activities are distributed through different developing countries, firms' expansion and the local presence of competitors from the developed world have clearly triggered a process of evolution and capability development. By acting as a host location for smaller developing-country firms and firms in emerging industries, the developing world has enabled firms to expand their markets, develop expertise in doing business across national borders, and to remain 'in the game', although not (yet) as industry leaders. In other words, expansion to the developing world offers the opportunity for learning-by-doing in an environment that lacks the deterrent effect of the dominant local presence of major international competitors.

In sum, the simple answer to the question of whether developing-country firms increase their competitiveness by investing abroad is 'yes'. But the specifics of the answer are more nuanced, and suggest that there are more and less appropriate destinations for a firm's OFDI, given its existing ownership advantages and the industry in which the firm is positioned. The more- and less-developed worlds serve very different purposes for the OFDI of developing-country firms: the former allows firms to consolidate a position of strength, and the latter provides a somewhat less challenging 'learning laboratory'. The mechanism by which each environment enhances (or hinders) the increased competitiveness of developing-country firms is a topic that deserves additional research.

NOTE

1. Results are not statistically tested, but significance is assessed on the basis of whether it is simultaneously 20 per cent of total M&A in the category and 20 per cent of total M&A for the country.

REFERENCES

Akamatsu, K. (1962). 'A historical pattern of economic growth in developing countries', *The Developing Economies*, Preliminary Issue 1 (March–August), pp. 1–23.

Athreye, S. (2005). 'The Indian software industry and its evolving service capability', *Industrial and Corporate Change*, 14(3), pp. 393–418.

Athreye, S. and J.A. Cantwell (2007). 'Creating competition? Globalisation and the emergence of new technology producers', *Research Policy*, 36(2) pp. 209–226.

Boddewyn, J.J., M.B. Halbrich and A.C. Perry (1986). 'Service multinationals: conceptualization, measurement and theory', *Journal of International Business Studies*, 17(3), pp. 41–57.

Cantwell, J.A. (1989). 'A classical model of the impact of international trade and production on national industrial growth', in J. Cantwell, ed., *Technological Innovation and Multinational Corporations* (Oxford: Basil Blackwell), pp. 160–185.

Cantwell, J.A. (1991). 'The theory of technological competence and its application to international production', in D.G. McFetridge, ed., *Foreign Investment, Technology and Growth* (Calgary: University of Calgary Press), pp. 33–70.

Cantwell, J.A. (1992). 'Japan's industrial competitiveness and the technological capabilities of the leading Japanese firms', in T.S. Arrison et al., ed., *Japan's Growing Technological Capability: Implications for the US Economy* (Washington DC: National Research Council), pp. 165–188.

Cantwell, J.A. and L. Piscitello (2000). 'Accumulating technological competence: its changing impact on corporate diversification and internationalisation', *Industrial and Corporate Change*, 9(1), pp. 21–51.

Cantwell, J.A. and G.D. Santangelo (2000). 'Capitalism, profits and innovation in the new techno-economic paradigm', *Journal of Evolutionary Economics*, 10, pp. 131–157.

Cantwell, J.A. and G. Vertova (2004). 'Historical evolution of technological diversification', *Research Policy*, 33(3), pp. 511–529.

Chandler, A.D., F. Amatori and T. Hikino (1997). *Big Business and the Wealth of Nations* (Cambridge and New York: Cambridge University Press).

Chung, W. and J. Alcacer (2002). 'Knowledge seeking and location choice of foreign direct investment in the United States', *Management Science*, 48(12), pp. 1534–1554.

Dowling, M. and C.T. Cheang (2000). 'Shifting comparative advantage in Asia: new tests of the "flying geese" model', *Journal of Asian Economics*, 11, pp. 446–463.

Dunning, J.H. (1981). 'Explaining the international direct investment position of countries: towards a dynamic or developmental approach', *Weltwirtschaftliches Archiv*, 117(1), pp. 30–64.

Dunning, J.H. (1986). 'The investment development cycle revisited', *Weltwirtschaftliches Archiv*, 122(4), pp. 667–676.

Dunning, J.H. (1989). 'Multinational enterprises and the growth of services: some conceptual and theoretical issues', *The Service Industries Journal*, 9(1), pp. 5–39.

Dunning, J.H. (1996). 'The geographical sources of the competitiveness of firms: some results of a new survey', *Transnational Corporations*, 5(3), pp. 1–29.

Dunning, J.H. (1998). 'Location and the multinational enterprise: a neglected factor?' *Journal of International Business Studies*, 29(1), pp. 45–66.

Durán, J.J. and F. Úbeda (2001). 'The investment development path: a new empirical approach and some theoretical issues', *Transnational Corporations*, 10(2), pp. 1–38.

Durán, J.J. and F. Úbeda (2005). 'The investment development path of newly developed countries', *International Journal of the Economics of Business*, 12(1), pp. 123–137.

Francois, J. F. (1990). 'Producer services, scale and the division of labor', *Oxford Economic Papers*, 42(4), pp. 715–729.

Ginzberg, A. and A. Simonazzi (2005). 'Patterns of industrialization and the flying geese model: the case of electronics in East Asia', *Journal of Asian Economics*, 15, pp. 1051–1078.

Hobday, M. (2000). 'East versus Southeast Asian innovation systems: comparing OEM- and TNC-led growth in electronics', in L. Kim and R.R. Nelson, eds, *Technology, Learning, and Innovation* (Cambridge: Cambridge University Press), pp. 129–169.

Kim, L. (1998). 'Crisis construction and organizational learning: capability building in catching-up at Hyundai Motor Corporation', *Organization Science*, 9(4), pp. 506–521.

Kim, L. and R.R. Nelson, eds (2000). *Technology, Learning, and Innovation* (Cambridge: Cambridge University Press).

Kojima, K. (2000). 'The "flying geese" model of Asian economic development: origin, theoretical extensions, and regional policy implications', *Journal of Asian Economics*, 11, pp. 375–401.

Kuemmerle, W. (1999). 'The drivers of foreign direct investment into research and development: an empirical investigation', *Journal of International Business Studies*, 30(1), pp. 1–24.

Lall, S. (1983). *The New Multinationals: The Spread of Third World Enterprises* (Chichester and New York: Wiley).

Lall, S. (1998). 'Exports of manufactures by developing countries: emerging patterns of trade and location', *Oxford Review of Economic Policy*, 14(2), pp. 54–73.

Lautier, M. (2001). 'The international development of the Korean automobile industry', in F. Sachwald, ed., *Going Multinational: The Korean Experience of Direct Investment* (London: Routledge), pp. 207–273.

Lee, K.R. (2001). 'Technological catching-up through overseas direct investment: Samsung's camera business', in F. Sachwald, ed., *Going Multinational: The Korean Experience of Direct Investment* (London: Routledge), pp. 275–314.

Liu, X., T. Buck and C. Shu (2005). 'Chinese economic development, the next stage: outward FDI?' *International Business Review*, 14, pp. 97–115.

Mowery, D.C. and R.R. Nelson (1999). *Sources of Industrial Leadership* (Cambridge and New York: Cambridge University Press).

Mowery, D.C. and N. Rosenberg (1998). *Paths of Innovation: Technological Change in 20th-Century America* (Cambridge and New York: Cambridge University Press).

Murmann, J.P. (2003). *Knowledge and Competitive Advantage: The Coevolution of Firms, Technology, and Institutions* (Cambridge: Cambridge University Press).

Nachum, L. (2000). 'Economic geography and the location of TNCs: financial and professional service FDI to the USA', *Journal of International Business Studies*, 31(3), pp. 367–385.

Narula, R. (1996). *Multinational Investment and Economic Structure: Globalisation and Competitiveness* (London: Routledge).

Narula, R. (2003). *Globalization and Technology: Interdependence, Innovation Systems and Industrial Policy* (Cambridge: Polity Press).

Narula, R. and J.H. Dunning (2000). 'Industrial development, globalization and multinational enterprises: new realities for developing countries', *Oxford Development Studies*, 28(2), pp. 141–167.

Nelson, R.R. (1993). *National Innovation Systems: A Comparative Analysis* (New York: Oxford University Press).

Nusbaumer, J. (1987). *The Services Economy: Lever to Growth* (Boston MA: Kluwer Academic Publishers).

Ozawa, T. (1992). 'Foreign direct investment and economic development', *Transnational Corporations*, 1(1), pp. 27–54.

Pavitt, K. (1984). 'Sectoral patterns of technological change: towards a taxonomy and a theory', *Research Policy*, 13, pp. 343–373.

Pilat, D., ed. (2003). *OECD Science, Technology and Industry Scoreboard* (Paris: OECD).

Reynolds, C. (2001). 'A conceptual model of global business growth in Southeast Asia', *Journal of the Asia Pacific Economy*, 6(1), pp. 76–98.

Riddle, D.L. (1986). *Service-led Growth: The Role of the Service Sector in World Development* (New York: Praeger).

Sachwald, F. (2001). *Going Multinational: The Korean Experience of Direct Investment* (London: Routledge).

SAPA (2003). 'US, UK markets attract young SA firms', *Mail and Guardian* (Johannesburg), 27 May.

Sridharan, K. (1998). 'G-15 and South-South cooperation: promise and performance', *Third World Quarterly*, 19(3), pp. 357–373.

Tolentino, P.E. (1993). *Technological Innovation and Third World Multinationals* (London: Routledge).

Tolentino, P.E. (2000). *Multinational Corporations: Emergence and Evolution* (London: Routledge).

Tunzelmann, V. and V. Acha (2005). 'Innovation in "low-tech" industries', in J. Fagerberg, D.C. Mowery and R.R. Nelson, eds, *The Oxford Handbook of Innovation* (Oxford and New York: Oxford University Press), pp. 407–433.

UNCTAD (1996). *World Investment Report: Investment, Trade and International Policy Agreements* (New York and Geneva: United Nations).

UNCTAD (1997). *World Investment Report: Transnational Corporations, Market Structure and Competition Policy* (New York and Geneva: United Nations).

UNCTAD (1998). *World Investment Report: Trends and Determinants* (New York and Geneva: United Nations).

UNCTAD (1999). *World Investment Report: FDI and the Challenge of Development* (New York and Geneva: United Nations).

UNCTAD (2000). *World Investment Report: Cross-border M & A and Development* (New York and Geneva: United Nations).

UNCTAD (2001). *World Investment Report: Promoting Linkages* (New York and Geneva: United Nations).

UNCTAD (2002). *World Investment Report: Transnational Corporations and Export Competitiveness* (New York and Geneva: United Nations).

UNCTAD (2003). *World Investment Report: FDI Policies for Development: National and International Perspectives* (New York and Geneva: United Nations).

UNCTAD (2004). *World Investment Report: The Shift to Services* (New York and Geneva: United Nations).

UNCTAD (2005). *World Investment Report: Transnational Corporations and the Internationalization of R&D* (New York and Geneva: United Nations).

Wells, L.T., Jr (1983). *Third World Multinationals: The Rise of Foreign Investment from Developing Countries* (Cambridge, MA: MIT Press).

Zaheer, S. and S. Manrakhan (2001). 'Concentration and dispersion in global industries: remote electronic access and the location of economic activities', *Journal of International Business Studies*, 32(4), pp. 667–686.

6. How global are TNCs from emerging markets?

Alan Rugman

INTRODUCTION

The focus of this chapter is to identify and analyze the set of transnational corporations (TNCs) registered and based in the world's emerging markets. To do this, I take as the relevant population the world's 500 largest firms, ranked by total revenues, as compiled annually in the *Fortune* Global 500. This entire set of 500 firms (most of which are TNCs) was analyzed in Rugman (2005). In that study, the focus was on an examination of data on the regional sales of TNCs from the 'broad' triad markets of Europe, North America and the Asia Pacific, which account for nearly all of the 500 firms. The total number of TNCs from the 'core' triad of the EU, United States and Japan in 2001 was 428 of the 500. In this chapter, attention is paid to TNCs from emerging markets, which numbered 32 in 2001 (and 44 in 2004).

The chapter will first proceed to identify the set of 32 (or 44) TNCs from emerging markets. As most of these are from the Asia Pacific region, the substantive theoretical analysis of their performance will focus upon a set of Chinese TNCs. The 16 Chinese TNCs already in the 2004 list of the world's 500 largest firms provide perhaps the most interesting challenge to theories of international business, international economics and explanations of foreign direct investment. In order to apply the relevant theory, I shall adapt the basic firm and country level matrix (Rugman 1981) to analyze the performance of China's TNCs.

China is the home to a set of large firms which can now be classified as TNCs, that is, firms with some foreign sales and some foreign production, usually 10 per cent or more. The foreign production takes place in a wholly-owned foreign subsidiary, and a TNC is also defined as having a foreign affiliate in three or more countries (Rugman 1981). Using these definitions, basically all of the firms in the *Fortune* Global 500 qualify as TNCs. In the list of the world's largest 500 companies, ranked by sales for 2001, Rugman (2005) found that there were 11 Chinese TNCs. In 2004, there were 16 Chinese firms in this list. These large TNCs are discussed here as the basic

Table 6.1   Intra-regional sales of the largest 500 firms, 2001 (US$b, %)

Region	Number of TNCs	Average Revenue	Intra-regional Sales (%)
Total	379 (500)	29 (28)	75
North America	186 (219)	29 (29)	79
Europe	118 (159)	31 (29)	66
Asia	75 (122)	27 (26)	78
Emerging markets	5 (34)	23 (22)	70

Note: Values in parentheses are for the entire set of the largest 500 TNCs in 2001. Only 379 TNCs' intra-regional sales can be identified. The emerging economies include only Brazil, China, Malaysia, Mexico, Republic of Korea, Russia, Singapore and Venezuela.

Source: the author's calculations, based on Rugman (2005).

set of firms that will determine the success of China in developing TNCs. This theory and analysis can be generalized to all TNCs from emerging markets.

6.1   THE REGIONAL PERFORMANCE OF TNCs

The performance of the world's 500 largest TNCs has been examined in Rugman (2005). These firms, ranked by revenues, account for approximately 90 per cent of the world's stock of FDI. They also account for over half of the world's trade (Rugman 2000). Recent research has shown that the vast majority of these large TNCs operate on an intra-regional basis. This information is summarized in Table 6.1. The geographic basis for the broad regions of the triad are developed and explained in Rugman (2005). Of the world's largest 500 firms, a total of 379 provide data on the geographic dispersion of their sales across the three broad regions of the triad. As shown in Table 6.1, the 75 TNCs from Asia have an average of nearly 80 per cent of their sales in their home region. This is somewhat above the average for the 379 TNCs, which have 75 per cent of their sales in home regions. Otherwise, the 75 Asian TNCs have an average revenue of $27 billion, which is only slightly less than the average $29 billion for North American TNCs and the $31 billion for the European TNCs. In summary, the regional performance of Asian TNCs parallels that of the regional nature of business of their competitor TNCs from North America and Europe.

The asymmetric pattern of classifications reported in Table 6.1 is based on the data for year 2001, in Rugman (2005). Some criticism of this book has been advanced to the effect that these data present a snapshot and do not reveal a trend toward regionalization. In fact, in Rugman (2005), it was demonstrated that these data were consistent over the time period for which firms reported their geographic distribution of sales, basically starting with fewer than 200 of the largest 500 in the late 1990s. Indeed, for 2002 data, the same pattern emerged as for 2001. To further address the nature of the longitudinal data, consider Table 6.2.

This table reports data for the world's 500 largest firms in years 2001, 2003 and 2004. In the most recent years, more firms report the geographic dispersion of their sales. For example, back in 1998, less than 200 firms reported such data, so the set of firms in Table 6.2 for year 2001 differs from the set in Table 6.1, as fewer of these remained in years 2003 and 2004. More specifically, Table 6.2 is based on the data for year 2004 instead of 2001, as in Table 6.1. The reason we take 2004 is that this is the year with most firms reporting data on geographical sales. Based on the set of firms with 2004 data, we then find the regional sales of the firms for three years. Thus only 291 firms are present in this data set for 2001, based on the 2004 listing (as some firms had left the 2001 list by 2004).

It can be seen from Table 6.2 that, in the year 2001, data on geographic sales were available from 291 firms. Of these, only eight can be classified as global, with over 20 per cent of sales in each region of the triad. Another 33 are bi-regional (of which six are host-region oriented). The remaining 250 firms are home-region based. These firms average 77 per cent of their sales in their home region. Basically, the same data apply in year 2003. There are eight global firms and 41 bi-regional firms (of which eight are

Table 6.2   The regional sales of the largest 500 firms, 2001, 2003, 2004

Year	Total	Home region		Bi-regional		Host region		Global	
		No. of firms	% intra-regional sales	No. of firms	% intra-regional sales	No. of firms	% intra-regional sales	No. of firms	% intra-regional sales
2001	291	250	77	27	42	6	24	8	34
2003	337	288	77	33	43	8	29	8	33
2004	311	271	77	26	41	7	29	7	34

Note: Among the 500 largest firms, data for 350 firms are available for 2003, but data for only 337 firms are sufficient to find their regional category. The number of firms whose data are insufficient to include in these tables are: 21 for 2001, 13 for 2003 and 18 for 2004. Of the 350 firms for year 2003, 312 firms and 329 firms are listed in the *Fortune* Global 500 for 2002 and 2005 respectively.

Source: The data for 2001 and the methodology for this table are based on Rugman (2005). Other data come from *Fortune* Global 500, 2004.

host-region oriented). Again, 288 of the 337 firms for year 2003 are home-region oriented. These 288 firms also average 77 per cent of their sales in their home region. Finally, for year 2004, there are seven global firms and 33 bi-regional firms (of which seven are host-region oriented). The vast majority (271) of the 311 firms for year 2004 are home-region oriented. Of these 271 firms, their average home-region sales are again 77 per cent. The conclusion to be drawn from Table 6.2 is that the world's largest 500 firms operate predominately on an intra-regional basis, not globally, and that this picture is consistent over time.

6.2   TNCs FROM EMERGING MARKETS

In this section, data are reported on TNCs from emerging markets. Table 6.3 lists 32 such TNCs for the year 2001. Table 6.4 lists 44 TNCs from emerging markets for 2004. In Table 6.3, the 32 TNCs from emerging markets are mainly from Asia Pacific. Only two are from Europe, the Russian firms (Gazpron, Lukoil). Another three are from the Americas (Pemex and Carso Global Telecom from Mexico and one oil firm from Venezuela). In contrast, there are 12 firms from the Republic of Korea. Another 12 are from China, with another two from Taiwan Province of China, one from Singapore and one from Malaysia.

Relatively few of the set of 32 TNCs from emerging economies in year 2001 provide data on the geographic dispersion of their sales. Using the 2001 data and the methodology in Rugman (2005), the following facts emerge. First, five South Korean firms provide data which show that all of them are home-region oriented. For example, POSCO has 92 per cent of its sales in Asia Pacific, while Hyundai Motor has 81 per cent of its sales in Asia Pacific and 18 per cent in North America. The remaining three Korean firms are close to being bi-regional, but need to be classified as home-region based since more than 50 per cent of their sales are in Asia Pacific. These include Samsung Electronics, which has 61 per cent of its sales in Asia Pacific, 20.8 per cent in North America and 18.3 per cent in Europe. Then LG Electronics has 60 per cent of its sales in Asia Pacific, 24 per cent in North America and 12 per cent in Europe. Finally, Hyundai (different from Hyundai Motor) has 56 per cent of its sales in Asia Pacific, 24 per cent in North America and 10 per cent in Europe. Only one of the 34 TNCs from emerging markets is a global firm. This is Flextronics of Singapore. It has only 20 per cent of its sales in its home region, but 44 per cent in North America and 36 per cent in Europe. This firm is clearly an exception. In contrast, all other TNCs from emerging economies reporting data on regional sales are home-region based. Some of the most extreme examples come

Table 6.3   The world's 32 largest TNCs in emerging markets, 2001 (US$b)

Company name	Industry	Economy	Revenue	North America	Europe	Asia-Pacific
State Power	Electricity	China	48	-	-	-
PDVSA	Gas	Venezuela	46	-	-	-
China National Petroleum	Gas	China	42	-	-	-
Sinopec	Gas	China	40	-	-	>90
Pemex (q)	Gas	Mexico	39	92	4	-
Samsung Electronics	Electronic	Korea	36	21	18	61
Samsung	Trading	Korea	33	-	-	-
SK	Gas	Korea	33	-	-	-
Hyundai Motor	Motor	Korea	31	18	0	81
LG Electronics	Electronic	Korea	23	24	12	60
China Telecommunications	Telecom	China	22	-	-	100
Hyundai	Motor	Korea	22	24	10	56
Gazprom	Gas	Russia	20	-	-	-
Ind. & Comm. Bank of China	Bank	China	20	-	-	-
LG International	Trading	Korea	20	-	-	-
Bank of China	Bank	China	18	-	-	-
Petronas	Gas	Malaysia	18	-	-	-
Samsung Life Insurance	Insurance	Korea	18	-	-	-
China Mobile Communications	Telecom	China	17	-	-	-
SK Global	Trading	Korea	17	-	-	-
Sinochem	Chemical	China	16	-	-	-
Korea Electric Power	Electricity	Korea	16	-	-	-
Flextronics International	Electronic	Singapore	13	44	36	20
China Construction Bank	Bank	China	13	-	-	-
COFCO	Food, cereal	China	13	-	-	-
KT	Telecom	Korea	12	-	-	-
Lukoil	Gas	Russia	12	-	36	-
Carso Global Telecom	Telecom	Mexico	12	-	-	>90
Cathay Life	Insurance	Taiwan Pr. of China	12	-	-	100
Chinese Petroleum	Gas	Taiwan Pr. of China	11	-	-	-
Agricultural Bank of China	Bank	China	11	-	-	-
POSCO	Steel	Korea	10	3	-	92

Source: the author's calculations, based on Rugman (2005).

from China, although the data are sketchy. China Telecommunications has 100 per cent of its sales at home. The Bank of China has 98 per cent of its sales in Asia Pacific, and Sinopec has 90 per cent or more in the Asia Pacific region. A related firm, Cathay Life, from Taiwan Province of China has 100 per cent of its sales in its home region. The pattern of dependence on sales in the home region for Asian TNCs is followed by Pemex of Mexico, which has 92 per cent of its sales in North America.

Table 6.4 updates the TNCs from emerging markets for year 2004. The number has increased to a total of 44. There are now three from Russia, one from Turkey and another from Saudi Arabia. There are still two from Mexico. Otherwise the TNCs from emerging markets are all from the Asia Pacific region, including India. There are 16 from China, and again two from Taiwan Province of China, one from Singapore and one from Malaysia. There are 11 from the Republic of Korea. In addition, there are now five firms from India, which we will include in the Asia Pacific category. Data on the regional sales of these TNCs for 2004 have not yet been compiled, but it is highly unlikely to be any different from that of 2001. Due to the emergence of a large number of TNCs from China in recent years, the remainder of the chapter will focus on this group.

The data on the regional sales of these 44 TNCs from emerging markets for year 2004 in Table 6.4 shows much the same picture as the 2001 data in Table 6.3. There are now 25 firms providing some evidence that they are home-region based. Only five firms are bi-regional (mostly the Korean firms, plus Flextronics). However, Flextronics is no longer a global firm, as its sales to North America have fallen to 14 per cent. It is now like Samsung Electronics, which is a bi-regional firm, with over 20 per cent of its sales in each broad-triad region, but over 50 per cent in its home region. Overall, the data show that the firms from emerging markets are mainly home-region based.

Before exploring the data on China's TNCs, the next section reviews the relevant theory needed to analyze TNCs from such emerging markets.

6.3 THEORY: THE FIRM-SPECIFIC/COUNTRY-SPECIFIC ADVANTAGE MATRIX OF TNCs

The literature in international business analyzes the growth and foreign expansion phase of TNCs. The starting point of this theory of TNCs (Rugman 1981, 1996) is the proposition that a TNC goes abroad to expand further on its firm-specific advantage. These firm-specific advantages are proprietary to a firm; they can be technology-based or knowledge-based or they can reflect managerial and/or marketing skills (Rugman and Verbeke

Table 6.4   The world's 44 largest TNCs in emerging markets, 2004 (US$b)

Company name	Industry	Country	Revenue	North America	Europe	Asia-Pacific
Sinopec	Gas	China	75	-	-	>90
Samsung Electronics	Electronic	Korea	72	23	22	55
State Grid	Electricity	China	71	-	-	>90
China National Petroleum	Gas	China	68	-	-	-
Pemex	Gas	Mexico	64	>58	-	-
Hyundai Motor	Motor	Korea	46	25	12	63
LG Electronics	Electronic	Korea	38	25	16	51
SK	Gas	Korea	38	-	-	-
Petronas	Gas	Malaysia	36	-	-	>90
OAO Gazprom	Gas	Russia	35	0	100	0
Indian Oil	Gas	India	30	-	-	96
Lukoil	Gas	Russia	29	-	>22	-
China Life Insurance	Insurance	China	25	-	-	-
China Mobile Comm.	Telecom	China	24	-	-	-
Ind. & Comm. Bank of China	Bank	China	23	-	-	-
UES of Russia	Electricity	Russia	23	-	>99	-
Samsung Life Insurance	Insurance	Korea	22	-	-	-
China Telecommunications	Telecom	China	22	0	0	100
POSCO	Steel	Korea	21	2	-	94
Korea Electric Power	Electricity	Korea	21	-	-	-
Sinochem	Chemical	China	20	-	-	>90
Shanghai Baosteel Group	Steel	China	20	-	-	>90
China Construction Bank	Bank	China	19	-	-	-
China Southern Power Grid	Electricity	China	19	-	-	100
Sabic	Chemical	Saudi Arabia	18	-	-	-
Bank of China	Bank	China	18	-	-	>98
Hutchison Whampoa	Telecom	China	17	14	34	52
Hon Hai Precision Industry	Electronic	Taiwan Pr. of China	16	-	-	-
PTT	Gas	Thailand	16	-	-	>90
Flextronics International	Electronic	Singapore	16	14	41	45

Table 6.4 (continued)

Company name	Industry	Country	Revenue	North America	Europe	Asia-Pacific
Koc Holding	Manufacturing	Turkey	16	-	-	-
Hanwha	Chemical	Korea	15	-	-	-
Agricultural Bank of China	Bank	China	15	-	-	>90
Chinese Petroleum	Gas	Taiwan Pr. of China	15	-	-	-
KT	Telecom	Korea	15	-	-	-
Reliance Industries	Gas	India	15	-	-	>78
CFE	Electricity	Mexico	15	-	-	-
Bharat Petroleum	Gas	India	14	0	0	100
COFCO	Food, cereal	China	14	-	-	>90
Hindustan Petroleum	Gas	India	14	0	0	100
Samsung	Trading	Korea	14	3	4	93
SK Networks	Telecom	Korea	14	-	-	>82
China First Automotive Works	Motor	China	14	-	-	>90
Oil & Natural Gas	Gas	India	14	-	-	>91

Source: the author's calculations, based on *Fortune* Global 500.

2003). Further, large TNCs often serve as 'flagship' firms at the hub of large business networks where key suppliers, distributors and businesses in the non-government infrastructure all come together in a cluster to help promote foreign sales (Rugman and D'Cruz 2000).

There are two building blocks in the basic matrix used in international business to analyze the nature, performance and strategies of TNCs (Rugman 1981, 1996). First, there is a set of firm-specific factors that determine the competitive advantage of an organization. We call these firm-specific advantages, defined as a unique capability proprietary to the organization which may be built upon product or process technology, marketing or distributional skills. Second, there are country factors, unique to the business in each country. They can lead to country-specific advantages, which can be based on natural resource endowments (minerals, energy, forests) or on the labor force and associated cultural factors.

Managers of most TNCs use strategies that build upon the interactions of country-specific and firm-specific advantages so that they can be positioned in a unique strategic space. The country-specific advantages represent the natural factor endowments of a nation; they are based on the key variables in its aggregate production function. For example, country-specific advantages can consist of the quantity, quality and cost of the major factor endowment, namely resources.

The firm-specific advantages possessed by a firm are based ultimately on its internalization of an asset, such as production knowledge or manager-ial or marketing capabilities over which the firm has proprietary control. Firm-specific advantages are thus related to a firm's ability to coordinate the use of the advantage in production, marketing or the customization of services (Rugman 1981).

Using Porter's terminology, the country-specific advantages form the basis of the global platform from which a TNC derives a home-base 'diamond' advantage in global competition (Porter 1990). Tariff and non-tariff barriers to trade and government regulations also influence country-specific advantages; building on them, a firm makes decisions about the efficient global configuration and coordination between segments of its value chain (operations, marketing, R&D, logistics). The skill in making such decisions represents a strong, managerial, firm-specific advantage.

To help formulate the strategic options of TNCs, it is useful to identify the relative strengths and weaknesses of the country-specific and firm-specific advantages that they possess. Figure 6.1, the country-specific/firm-specific advantage matrix, provides a useful framework for discussion of these issues. In this figure, quadrants 1, 2 and 3 can incorporate the three generic strategies suggested by Porter (1980): cost leadership, differentiation and focus. Quadrant 1 firms are generally the cost leadership ones; they are generally resource-based and/or mature, internationally-oriented firms producing a commodity-type product. Given their late stage in the product life cycle, production firm-specific advantages flowing from

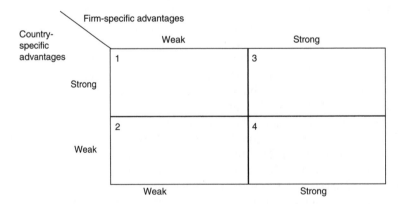

Figure 6.1   The country-specific/firm-specific advantage matrix

the possession of intangible skills are less important than the country-specific advantages of location and energy costs, which are the main sources of the firm's competitive advantage. Quadrant 2 firms represent inefficient, floundering firms with neither consistent strategy nor any intrinsic country-specific or firm-specific advantages. These firms are preparing to exit or to restructure. Quadrant 2 can also represent domestic small and medium-sized firms with little global exposure. Firms in quadrant 4 are generally differentiated firms with strong firm-specific advantages in marketing and customization. These firms usually have strong brands. In quadrant 4, firm-specific advantages dominate, so in world markets, the home-country advantages are not essential in the long run. Quadrant 3 firms generally can choose to follow any of the strategies listed above because of the strength of both their country-specific and firm-specific advantages.

It is useful to note the following two points. First, if a firm has a conglomerate structure, it should be more useful to situate each division or product line individually, recognizing that different units of a diversified firm would use different generic strategies. Second, changes in the trading environment, such as the EU 1992 single-market measures, or the EU 1999 single currency, or the United States–Canada Free Trade Agreement and NAFTA, will affect the relative country-specific advantages of a firm. To the extent that country-specific advantages are improved, firms will tend to move to quadrant 3, and, to the extent that the country-specific advantages are hampered, a firm or some of its product lines may move to exit, as in quadrant 2.

6.4 THE THEORY OF TNCs IN A CHINESE CONTEXT

One of the unresolved problems facing a TNC in a foreign country is that it suffers from a liability of foreignness. From the viewpoint of a TNC's managers, foreign markets present risks as there are social, political and economic costs associated with entry to unfamiliar markets. The liability-of-foreignness literature suggests that a TNC has to make an investment in learning about foreign markets. In general, this follows a process of internationalization as a TNC goes to nearby countries. The liability-of-foreignness is thereby consistent with the empirical finding that the great majority of international business is conducted by TNCs in their home region.

The new insight that comes from this literature is that we cannot analyze the role of TNCs in a purely global sense. Instead, they need to be analyzed regionally. We need to analyze the impact of Asian TNCs, primarily

Japanese ones (66 of the 75 largest TNCs in Asia are Japanese) on the rest of Asia. Likewise, we can analyze the role of Chinese TNCs themselves; we follow this approach in the next section. We need to remember that, out of the 380 of the world's largest 500 TNCs for which data are available, 320 have an average of 80 per cent of their sales in their home region (Rugman 2005). Their distribution of foreign assets is even more regionalized. We conclude that analysis of Chinese TNCs is actually about their regional sales in Asia.

A case can be made that the recent economic development of China is almost entirely due to FDI. The opening of the Chinese economy to foreign TNCs, first in the Special Economic Zones in the 1980s, followed by the opening of most coastal cities in the 1990s, has introduced some market-based efficiency to a previously totally command economy. While China is still dominated by state-owned enterprises and collectives, by 2005, foreign affiliates accounted for one-third of production and 50 per cent of exports (Thun 2005). The foreign TNCs operate on a world-class basis of compe-tition, and they have developed efficient supply networks. Much of the pri-vatized sector of small and medium-sized enterprises (SMEs) in China is affiliated to TNCs. Together, TNCs and SMEs are now driving forward the economic development of China. The inefficient and protected state-owned enterprises are beginning to reform and are starting to adopt more market-based strategies in the face of this new type of TNC-led domestic compe-tition. Through this process, efficiency-based thinking is spreading from the coastal cities throughout China. In this sense, foreign TNCs are the agents of economic development for China.

This raises the following question: when will China generate its own TNCs? The answer is – not for another 10 to 20 years. While 11 Chinese firms are in the *Fortune* top global 500, the evidence suggests that none of them are truly internationalized. Indeed, these large Chinese firms are mainly state-owned enterprises and they have well over 95 per cent of their sales within China (although only partial data are available for eight firms). They are still largely in the protected banking, natural resources and telecom industries; they show few signs of developing any proprietary firm-specific advantages that would allow them to compete internationally even on an intra-regional basis.

When Chinese state-owned enterprises do go abroad, they build on country-specific advantages in natural resources or they try to acquire tech-nology. However, they are not doing well through acquisition. Lenovo bought an obsolete IBM line of business; Baosteel bought up iron ore sup-plies in Brazil; Shanghai Motors bought the technologically laggard Rover of the UK; and Haier bought Thomson TV and has found it difficult to upgrade it. Overall, all of these Chinese acquisitions reveal a search for the technology, management and strategy skills missing in Chinese state-owned enterprises. The objectives appear to be to secure natural resources and market access, but in fact, no useful technologies have been acquired. Chinese TNCs still lack the internal managerial capabilities to integrate foreign acquisitions to develop anything resembling dynamic capabilities. They suffer from a Penrose effect of a lack of top management talent. This competitive disadvantage in management will take about a decade to remedy, before Chinese state-owned enterprises are competitive with Western TNCs.

Related work by Nolan (2004) found that Chinese firms have failed to develop firm-specific advantages and are lagging well behind Western firms, especially in their lack of technology. Nolan found no evidence that Chinese firms can develop knowledge of the systems integration skills that characterize successful Western TNCs. The Chinese firms are protected, resource-based, labor-intensive, low-technology and inefficient firms. Potentially efficient SMEs are now linking to foreign TNCs, rather than to the inefficient and uncompetitive Chinese state-owned enterprises. Japanese and Korean TNCs have developed firm-specific advantages whereas Chinese firms have not. Basically there are no Chinese TNCs; there are just Chinese home firms.

6.5 THE LITERATURE ON FIRM-SPECIFIC AND COUNTRY-SPECIFIC ADVANTAGES IN AN ASIAN CONTEXT

The World Bank (1993) categorized eight Asian countries into three groups: first, Japan; second, the first-generation, newly industrialized economies (Hong Kong, Republic of Korea, Singapore, Taiwan Province of China); and third, the second-generation, newly industrializing countries (Indonesia, Malaysia, Thailand). Even though these Asian economies have experienced fast and export-oriented economic growth, they have different TNCs based on country-specific advantages.

Debrah, McGovern and Budhwar (2000) showed that Singapore's country-specific advantages lie in skilled labor, advanced technology, advanced physical infrastructure and advanced commercial infrastructure, while Indonesia and Malaysia have advantages in cheap (unskilled) labor and natural resources. The three other first-generation countries (and Japan) have similar advantages to Singapore.

Nelson and Pack (1999) explained the successful growth of the Republic of Korea and Taiwan Province of China by using technology assimilation. They argued that individual firms had strong incentives to improve their firm-specific advantages in efficiency to enable them to export rather than to engage in rent seeking in the domestic market. Brouthers, O'Donnell and Hadjimarcou (2005) showed that emerging market firms achieve a higher level of export performance when they mimic the product strategies of Western TNCs in triad markets rather than when they enter emerging markets or develop other product strategies in triad markets.

Due to geographical, cultural, institutional and historical similarities, the internationally successful Korean and Japanese firms can be models for Chinese firms. For example, as discussed earlier for Chinese firms (Haier, Lenovo and so on), Korean TNCs have acquired foreign technologies (but not really strong firm-specific advantages) by acquisition; for example, Samsung Electronics acquired Harris Microwave Semiconductor in 1993, and LG Electronics purchased 57.7 per cent of the stock of Zenith Electronics in 1995.

Japanese firms are linked to firms in the newly industrialized Asian economies as markets for final electrical and electronic products and as customers for Japanese-made components. The first-generation newly industrialized economies developed their technological capabilities relying on Japanese firms' firm-specific advantages. Korea and Taiwan Province of China electronic firms acquired technology mainly through licensing and contracting arrangements with Japanese firms such as Sony, Sanyo and Matsushita in 1970–1980 (Hobday 1995).

6.6   DATA ON ASIA'S AND CHINA'S TNCs

In Table 6.5 we identify the country home base of the 45 Asian TNCs providing data on their sales in each region of the triad. This list is dominated by the 37 TNCs from Japan, which average 75 per cent of their sales in Asia, 15 per cent in North America, and 7 per cent in Europe. While there are 11 Chinese TNCs in the dataset analyzed by Rugman (2005), none of them report their geographic sales across each region of the triad. The only firm from Taiwan Province of China reporting has 100 per cent of its sales in Asia. I would anticipate that the other 11 TNCs from China would also have close to 100 per cent of their sales in Asia.

Table 6.6 lists the 11 Chinese firms in the top 500 for 2001, arranged by industry group. We also show the 16 Chinese firms for 2004. In order to explore this, Table 6.7 reports data on the regional sales of the eight Chinese TNCs providing some data on the geographic dispersion of their sales in 2004. In this table, we can see that China Telecom and China Southern Power have 100 per cent of their sales in Asia (indeed, virtually all of these within China itself). The Bank of China has at least 98 per cent of its sales

Table 6.5   Regional sales of Asian TNCs, 2001 (US$b, %)

Economy	Number of TNCs	Average revenue	Regional sales			
			North America	Europe	Asia	Unidentified
Total	45 (112)	32 (26)	16	8	73	3
Australia	4 (6)	14 (14)	22	7	69	2
Japan	37 (88)	36 (28)	15	7	75	3
Korea	2 (12)	26 (21)	21	5	69	5
Malaysia	0 (1)	- (18)	-	-	-	-
Singapore	1 (1)	13 (13)	46	31	22	0
Taiwan Pr. of China	1 (2)	12 (11)	0	0	100	0
China	0 (11)	- (25)	-	-	-	-

Note: Values in parentheses are for the entire set of the largest 500 TNCs in 2001.

Source: the author's calculations, based on Rugman (2005).

in Asia. Four of the other five Chinese firms have over 90 per cent of their sales in Asia. Overall, these eight large Chinese firms, most of which have the potential of being classified as TNCs, average 93 per cent of their sales in Asia. I do not foresee that this number will fall below 90 per cent for many years. Indeed, it is likely to be at least 10 to 15 years before the largest 15 Chinese firms have intra-regional sales close to the world average of about 75 per cent. Until then, the Chinese TNCs will continue to experience strong sales within China itself, with a gradual increase in foreign sales, but mostly within the Asian region.

6.7   COUNTRY-LEVEL DATA ON TRADE AND FDI PERFORMANCE

Table 6.8 reports ratios of trade and FDI stock to GDP across the three broad regions of the triad. The overall interpretation of this table is that Asian economies are more heavily involved in the international economy through their trade performance rather than through their FDI performance. While Asia is very close to the overall average ratio of 24 per cent trade to GDP, it is considerably below the average ratio of FDI stock to GDP. As can be seen in Table 6.8, Asia averages 12 per cent as against the overall total average of 20 per cent – these data refer to inward FDI stocks. In a similar manner, the Asian outward FDI stock to GDP is 10 per cent,

Table 6.6   List of Chinese TNCs in the world's largest 500 firms, 2001, 2004

Industry	Company name	Revenue (US$b)
Year 2001		
Banking (4)	Industrial & Commercial Bank of China	20
	Bank of China	18
	China Construction Bank	13
	Agricultural Bank of China	11
Utilities (3)	State Power	48
	China Telecommunications	22
	China Mobile Telecommunications	17
Natural resource	China National Petroleum	42
manufacturing (2)	Sinopec	20
Other	Sinochem	16
manufacturing (2)	COFCO	13
Total (11)		
Average		22
Year 2004		
Banking and	China Life Insurance	25
insurance (5)	Industrial & Commercial Bank of China	23
	China Construction Bank	19
	Bank of China	18
	Agricultural Bank of China	15
Utilities (4)	State Grid	71
	China Mobile Telecommunications	24
	China Telecommunications	22
	China Southern Power Grid	19
Natural resource	Sinopec	75
manufacturing (3)	China National Petroleum	68
	Shanghai Baosteel Group	20
Other	Sinochem	20
manufacturing (3)	COFCO	14
	China First Automotive Works	14
Other (1)	Hutchison Whampoa	17
Total (16)		
Average		29

Source: the author, based on Rugman (2005).

Table 6.7   Regional sales of eight Chinese TNCs, 2004 (US$b)

Company name	Revenue	Regional Sales			
		N. America	Europe	Asia	Unidentified
Sinopec	75	-	-	>90	<10
China Telecom	22	-	-	100	0
Sinochem	20	-	-	>90	<10
China Const. Bank	19	-	-	>90	<10
China Southern Power	19	-	-	100	0
Bank of China	18	-	-	>98	<2
Hutchison Whampoa	17	14	33	53	0
Agri. Bank of China	15	-	-	>90	<10
Average	20 (29)	-	-	93	5

Notes:
1. Sinopec – annual report notes that Sinopec has less than 10% of sales and investment in foreign areas, and it does not need to report its geographic sales following international financial reporting standards (IFRS).
2. China Telecommunications – annual report shows all the group's operating activities are carried out in China.
3. Sinochem – based on Sinochem's sales composition, exports make up 10%. Sinochem's regional sales would be larger than 10%.
4. China Construction Bank – annual report explains that the company follows IFRS, but it does not specify geographic segment data. It is possible to presume that China Construction Bank has less than 10% of foreign sales and assets.
5. China Southern Power – the website of China Southern Power shows that the company covers Guangdong, Guangxi, Guizhou, Yunnan and Hainan, which is also connected with the power grid in middle China, Hong Kong (China) and Macao. It is possible to presume that the portion of home region sales and assets are 100%.
6. Bank of China – annual report explicitly shows that the portion of sales from China, Hong Kong and Macau is 98% and that of assets is 95%.
7. Hutchison Whampoa – annual report shows the value of geographic sales.
8. Agricultural Bank of China – the values are not explicitly noted in the annual report, but it is possible to judge that the domestic sales would be larger than 90% from the geographic data on deposit, borrowing, etc.

Source: the author, based on 2005 annual report for each company. Value in parenthesis is for all 16 Chinese TNCs in the largest 500 TNCs in 2004. Only six of them report their regional sales. If values are larger than 90%, 90% is used for the calculation.

under half that of the overall average of 22 per cent. For the outward trade ratios, again the Asian performance, at 22 per cent, is close to the overall average of 24 per cent. Perhaps the most significant point in Table 6.8 is that the outward FDI stock performance of Asian countries is significantly below that of North American and European countries. This particular statistic is unlikely to improve in the near future (three to five years) because it generally takes a long time to increase FDI stock.

Table 6.8   Inward and outward FDI stocks and trade as a percentage of GDP, 2002

Region	Inward		Outward	
	FDI (Stock) (% of GDP)	**Trade (% of GDP)**	**FDI (Stock) (% of GDP)**	**Trade (% of GDP)**
America	16	13	16	16
North America	15	13	16	16
South America	31	22	11	19
Asia-Pacific	13	24	11	23
Asia	12	25	10	22
Oceania	35	21	21	23
Europe, Africa, and Middle East	30	36	37	34
Africa-Middle East	19	34	5	32
Europe	31	36	41	34
Total (Average)	20	24	22	24

Note: Central America countries are included in North America; Caribbean countries are included in South America.

Sources: the author. FDI data are from UNCTAD (2004). Trade and GDP data are from The World Bank (2005).

Table 6.9 shows that developed countries provide over 90 per cent of the outward stock of the world's FDI but that they receive considerably less of the inward stock at 75 per cent. In contrast, less-developed countries (which include China) receive nearly one-quarter of the world's inward FDI stock, but contribute under 10 per cent of the world's outward stock. China is a microcosm of less-developed countries in this respect: it receives much more inward FDI than it generates outward FDI.

CONCLUSION

The main conclusion of this chapter is that TNCs from emerging markets are not operating globally; instead they are home-region-based firms, like most of the world's other TNCs. Nor is there any evidence that there is a trend toward globalization for either TNCs from emerging economies, or for TNCs in general. With reference to TNCs from China, based on the foregoing theoretical and empirical analysis, the following three major conclusions can be drawn about the nature, extent and future of outward FDI by Chinese TNCs.

Table 6.9   Stock and flows of inward and outward FDI, 2002 (US$b)

Panel A. Inward FDI

Country group	Inward stock		Inward flows	
	Value	**Percent of total**	**Value**	**Percent of total**
Developed countries	7215	75	566	81
Less-developed countries	2289	24	130	19
Least-developed countries	139	1	5	1
Total	9641	100	701	100

Panel B. Outward FDI

	Outward stock		Outward flows	
	Value	**Percent of total**	**Value**	**Percent of total**
Developed countries	6416	91	603	94
Less-developed countries	650	9	40	6
Least-developed countries	2	0	0	0
Total	7069	100	643	100

Note: In this table, Mexico, the Republic of Korea and Turkey are moved from the UNCTAD 'less developed' category to the 'developed' category. There are 33 developed countries, 82 less developed countries and 31 least developed countries.

Sources: Data are from UNCTAD (2004) and UNCTAD (2002).

First, the theoretical literature indicates that TNCs expand abroad based upon a complex interaction between firm-specific advantages and country-specific advantages. Successful TNCs from North America, Europe and Japan, in general (this is somewhat of a simplification) expand abroad in order to exploit firm-specific advantages that they have developed in their large internal home markets. The activities of their foreign subsidiaries, to an overwhelming degree, tend to replicate for local distribution the firm-specific advantages developed in the home market. This explanation of TNCs was developed in Rugman (1981), and is still true today on the twenty-fifth anniversary re-publication of that book in 2006. Only to a minor extent do TNCs go abroad to gain access to knowledge and technology. A few Japanese TNCs engaged in asset-seeking FDI in North America are the main exceptions to the rule; in those cases, knowledge and technology is usually developed in the home market. Similarly, only a small set of Western TNCs go abroad to exploit natural resources. These are TNCs in the energy, mining and forestry industries, which go abroad to exploit host country-specific advantages, but they retain proprietary control over managerial and marketing firm-specific advantages, where the latter are identified with their home countries. The implication of this for China is that its TNCs are likely to develop by exploiting China's country-specific advantages in cheap, unskilled and skilled labor. It is highly unlikely that Chinese TNCs will go abroad in any significant numbers over the next five to ten years on the basis of firm-specific advantages. In general, China lacks firms with firm-specific advantages in knowledge and systems integration, especially in comparison to Western TNCs in the world's top 500.

Second, as Chinese TNCs develop and go abroad, their primary geographic focus will be within the Asia Pacific region. Here, their main competitors will be from other Asia-Pacific TNCs based in Japan, Australia, the Republic of Korea, Singapore and other Asian Tigers. The empirical evidence on the performance on the world's largest 500 TNCs, as summarized in Rugman (2005), shows that the great majority of these firms operate on an intra-regional basis. Of the 380 firms providing data on geographic sales, the largest set of 320 average 80 per cent of their sales in their home region. These firms have an even higher proportion of their foreign assets in their home region. There are extremely few 'global' firms, and only three dozen bi-regional firms. The Chinese TNCs are highly unlikely to become global or bi-regional firms in the next ten to twenty years. However, this is not a problem since there is no evidence showing that global and bi-regional firms are more profitable than home-region TNCs.

Third, the major impact of the growth of Chinese outward FDI, and the development of Chinese-based TNCs, will be to enhance the internal efficiency of the Chinese economy. Only the best Chinese firms will succeed abroad. Thus, a prerequisite for international success is domestic efficiency. As the Government of China has supported the establishment and improvement of domestic markets, so economic efficiency within China has improved. The key agent for change in China has been the unrestricted entry of foreign direct investment. Over the past ten years, Western TNCs have greatly improved the efficiency of the Chinese economy. They have established clusters and business networks with links to new and regenerated Chinese businesses. Indeed, many small to medium-sized Chinese firms are now affiliated in business networks with TNCs. In contrast, the old state-owned enterprises have been slower to engage in the realities of market-driven efficiency. Consequently, many of these state-owned enterprises are poor candidates for internationalization. As they go abroad, their domestic monopoly protection, with its resulting inefficiency, will serve them badly in competitive foreign markets. Only the newer and more entrepreneurial firms in China will succeed internationally. The role of the Government of China is to facilitate continuous improvements in the domestic market system. The Government should continue to improve basic infrastructure, but a faster pace of liberalization in the services sector, especially financial services, is required to develop a competitive Chinese business system. As China's economy improves, the most efficient firms will be able to expand abroad. Initially, they will build on China's country-specific advantages, but eventually they will start to generate home-grown firm-specific advantages in knowledge and technology. Then Chinese TNCs will be on an equal footing with foreign TNCs in the world's list of the 500 largest firms.

ACKNOWLEDGEMENTS

The author is pleased to acknowledge the excellent research assistance, in the preparation of data for many of the tables, of Chang Hoon Oh of the Kelley School of Business, Indiana University. The author also thanks several anonymous reviewers and *The Rise of TNCs from Emerging Markets: Threat or Opportunity?* Conference participants for helpful comments.

REFERENCES

Brouthers, L.E., E. O'Donnell and J. Hadjimarcou (2005). 'Generic product strategies for emerging market exports into triad nation markets: a mimetic isomorphism approach', *Journal of Management Studies*, 42(1), pp. 225–245.
Debrah, Y.A., I. McGovern and P. Budhwar (2000). 'Complementarity or competition; the development of human resources in a South-East Asian growth triangle: Indonesia, Malaysia and Singapore', *International Journal of Human Resource Management*, 11(2), pp. 314–335.
Fortune Global 500, *Fortune, available at* http://money.cnn.com/magazines/fortune/global500/2006/ (last visited 4 December 2006).
Hobday, M. (1995). 'East Asian latecomer firms: learning the technology of electronics', *World Development*, 23(7), pp. 1171–1193.
Nelson, R.R. and H. Pack (1999). 'The Asian miracle and modern growth theory', *The Economic Journal*, 109, pp. 416–436.
Nolan, P. (2004). *China at the Crossroads* (Cambridge: Polity Press).
Porter, M.E. (1980). *Competitive Strategy: Techniques for Analyzing Industries and Competitors* (New York: Free Press).
Porter, M.E. (1990). *The Competitive Advantage of Nations* (New York: Free Press, Macmillan).
Rugman, A.M. (1981). *Inside the Multinationals: The Economics of Internal Markets* (New York: Columbia University Press; New York: Palgrave Macmillan).
Rugman, A.M. (1996). *The Theory of Multinational Enterprises* (Cheltenham: Edward Elgar).

Rugman, A.M. (2000). *The End of Globalization* (London: Random House).

Rugman, A.M. (2005). *The Regional Multinationals* (Cambridge: Cambridge University Press).

Rugman, A.M. (2006). *Inside the Multinationals,* 25th anniversary edition (New York: Palgrave Macmillan).

Rugman, A.M. and J. D'Cruz (2000). *Multinational as Flagship Firms: Regional Business Networks* (New York: Oxford University Press).

Rugman, A.M. and A. Verbeke (2003). 'Extending the theory of the multinational enterprise: internalization and strategic management perspectives', *Journal of International Business Studies,* 34, pp. 125–137.

Thun, E. (2005). *Changing Lanes in China: Foreign Direct Investment* (Cambridge: Cambridge University Press).

United Nations Conference on Trade and Development (2004). *The Least Developed Countries Report: Escaping the Poverty Trap* (Geneva: United Nations).

United Nations Conference on Trade and Development (2004) *World Investment Report: The Shift Toward Services* (Geneva: United Nations).

World Bank (1993). *The East Asian Miracle: Economic Growth and Public Policy* (New York: Oxford University Press).

World Bank (2005). *World Development Indicator* (Washington, DC: The World Bank).

7. Explaining China's outward FDI: an institutional perspective

**Peter J. Buckley, Jeremy L. Clegg,
Adam R. Cross, Hinrich Voss, Mark Rhodes
and Ping Zheng**

State-owned Chinese firms are busily seeking resources abroad, often with the
support of Beijing, which courts supplier states by cultivating bilateral relations
and providing aid and other forms of development assistance. The Commerce
Ministry and the National Development and Reform Commission have published a list of countries and resources in which investment is eligible for state
subsidies. In addition to reinforcing the nexus between the Chinese government
and the business sector, this strategy has solidified China's relations with many
developing countries (Zweig and Bi 2005, p. 27).

INTRODUCTION

China has evolved to become an important outward investor country over
the past decade.[1] Annual outward foreign direct investment (OFDI) flows
from China grew from US$0.8 billion in 1990 to more than US$12 billion
in 2005. This has culminated in Chinese enterprises owning an OFDI stock
of about US$52 billion in 2005 (MOFCOM 2006; UNCTAD 2005a).
Chinese OFDI is now distributed across more than 160 countries.

A variety of explanations have been advanced to account for the
growing international presence of Chinese transnational corporations
(TNCs) and their global economic and political impact. One reason put
forward is the highly prominent role played by the Government of China
in nurturing and fostering Chinese international enterprise (Sauvant
2005). Government intervention in China's OFDI can be seen in four
aspects: (1) the high number of state-owned enterprises now undertaking
overseas investment projects; (2) the Government-led quest for natural
resources in short supply at home; (3) the general political framework in
China; and (4) the high degree of regulation and control of Chinese
OFDI since the early 1980s (the ultimate aim of which has been to fulfil
certain economic development objectives and ideological imperatives) (for

example, Deutsche Bank 2006a; Ma and Andrews-Speed 2006; Scott 2002; Zhang 2003).

Historically, empirical research on Chinese OFDI has generally relied on case studies of a small selection of high profile international Chinese investing firms (for example, Zhang 2003) or descriptive analyses of aggregate Chinese OFDI data (Buckley *et al.* 2006; Deng 2003). More recently, a small number of econometric studies have sought formally to model and analyze patterns of Chinese OFDI. In particular, Liu *et al.* (2005) used Dunning's investment development path approach to analyze a narrow set of data on Chinese OFDI published by the Ministry of Commerce (MOFCOM). Cross *et al.* (2007) analyzed the locational determinants of Chinese OFDI using MOFCOM data on Chinese OFDI as the dependent variable, while Buckley *et al.* (2007) used instead project level data collected by the State Administration of Foreign Exchange (SAFE) – the agency responsible for approving the amounts of foreign exchange to be committed abroad, and hence a key player in the formal investment approval process. Buckley *et al.* (2007) assessed the degree of 'home country embeddedness' and, in particular, the capital market imperfections that Chinese TNCs leverage to assist them with their transnationalization efforts. They found that Chinese OFDI is associated particularly with those foreign countries that exhibit high levels of country risk (as measured by the familiar risk index, the International Country Risk Guide). Buckley *et al.* (2007) argued that domestic capital market imperfections have led Chinese TNCs to demonstrate a perverse and pervasive attitude toward country risk in comparison to industrialized country TNCs.

In this chapter, we argue that one shortcoming of these studies is that they failed to capture properly the determining role of institutions (Voss 2007). We build upon this existing work by taking greater account of the national and supranational institutional framework that confronts the investing Chinese firm and by empirically testing various elements of it as determinants of Chinese OFDI patterns. Our time frame is the period from 1991 to 2003, which further extends that covered by existing work.

Our analysis incorporates two major aspects of the investment behavior of Chinese TNCs, namely: (1) the motivation underpinning their outward investment decisions; and (2) how these decisions are influenced by the institutional framework within which they take place. First, we take the conventional motivations of FDI identified by Dunning (1993) for industrialized country TNCs and test their applicability to Chinese TNCs. This allows us to relate our findings to, and comment on, those of Buckley *et al.* (2007) and Cross *et al.* (2007). We then go on to analyze the effect of eight institutional factors – two that are domestic (endogenous to China) and six that are supranational (exogenous to China) – which both theory and observation suggest may impinge on the decision making of Chinese TNCs. To our knowledge, none of the institutional factors we consider have been investigated previously in the context of Chinese OFDI (or for that matter, in that of transition and emerging countries in general).

In the following section, we discuss key concepts and definitions of the institutional framework of OFDI using a 'new institutional theory' perspective. We then review in section 7.2 a body of literature that characterizes the recent development of Chinese OFDI. In section 7.3, we develop three sets of hypotheses that relate to (1) the investment motivations of Chinese firms; (2) the institutional explanations of Chinese OFDI; and (3) a number of control variables that we derive from standard empirical research on FDI flows. We then present the model used to test the hypotheses and describe our data sources (section 7.4). Our dependent variable is the amount of approved outward FDI per annum as published by the Chinese Ministry of Commerce (MOFCOM) in the *Almanac of China's Foreign Economic Relation and Trade* and the *China Commerce Yearbook*. In section 7.5, the model is tested using panel data and both pooled ordinary least squares and random effects estimators. We discuss our findings and draw implications for theory development in the concluding section.

7.1 THE INSTITUTIONAL FRAMEWORK OF OFDI: CONCEPTS AND DEFINITIONS

First, it is important to explain what the institutional framework of OFDI means. We do this using an institutional theory perspective. The basic thrust of the institution-based view of firm strategy, or 'institutional theory' for short, is that decision making within a TNC is constrained by conditions set by the home country, host country and supranational institutional environment or, more colloquially, by the 'rules of the game' (Buckley *et al.* 2006; Meyer 2004; North 1990; Peng 2002; Ramamurti 2001; Wright *et al.* 2005). Formal rules are implemented and policed mainly by governments and their agencies. Therefore, the institutional setting determines the pace and scope of a country's economic development as a consequence of the constraints and resources provided by a government to local and foreign firms: path dependencies are created (North 1990). However, the concept of 'institution' is fuzzy (Markusen 2003). This is because it can be said to comprise a wide range of elements, including customs and beliefs, religious and other norms, the legislature, judiciary and bureaucracy, government structures and market mechanisms (Williamson 2000), many of which are difficult to measure and are therefore difficult to model. In this chapter, we assert that the institutional environment that confronts Chinese firms is likely to have the potential to explain at least a portion of the distinctiveness evident in patterns of Chinese OFDI observed in previous research (Buckley *et al.* 2007; Cross *et al.* 2007).

We recognize that the institutional setting within which Chinese TNCs operate – which henceforth we term the 'Chinese OFDI regime' – has both a national and supranational character. Its national features (the endogenous institutional factors) include those formal structures and outcomes of the Government of China that pertain to OFDI. This comprises the policies and regulations of agencies such as the Chinese Ministry of Commerce, SAFE, the National Development and Reform Commission, the Ministry of Finance, the Ministry for Foreign Affairs and the People's Bank of China (Liu 2007). Also important are the legislature, judiciary and bureaucracy. Although these are formal institutions, their sphere of action and influence may reach into informal areas – for example, in instances in which laws and regulations are interpreted and applied in a discretionary way by certain actors in society.

Of the supranational features of the Chinese OFDI regime (the exogenous institutional factors) we recognize both formal and informal elements that might impact on Chinese firms. With regards to the formal elements, most countries are now embedded in a nexus of multilateral and, increasingly today, bilateral agreements that are administered and managed both by supranational agencies such as the World Trade Organization (WTO), the World Intellectual Property Organization (WIPO) and individual governments (Ramamurti 2001). Ultimately, these have the potential to influence greatly the behavior of TNCs. It is also the case for Chinese firms: China has entered into a number of bilateral investment treaties and agreements (for example, double taxation agreements) with potential and current host countries. China also participates increasingly in multilateral agreements and treaties administered by multilateral bodies such as the WTO. Collectively, these agreements and treaties have the potential to shape direct investment and trade flows between China and other countries, with trade often serving as a precursor for FDI.

In addition to these formal elements, informal, supranational features of the Chinese OFDI regime can also be recognized. Such elements might include international state visits by leading politicians to and from the countries concerned, which may be followed by informal arrangements between governments that influence the behaviour of state-owned Chinese firms. It also includes those factors that are not directly linked to China but may have a signaling effect for Chinese companies. These include those investment and trade treaties signed between a particular host country and a third country which, for example, might strengthen the reputation of the former as an upholder of the rights of foreign investors. The informal exogenous element of the Chinese OFDI regime also includes those social and ethnic networks that have been established within and between the Chinese diaspora and the mainland, since these also have the potential to facilitate investment flows among countries. To illustrate, Buckley *et al.* (2007) found a strong and positive relationship between the proportion of the host country population that is ethnically Chinese and the propensity for that country to attract Chinese OFDI.

This short overview suggests, therefore, that there are both formal and informal endogenous and exogenous factors that may combine to influence the transnationalization decisions of Chinese TNCs. In this chapter, we contribute to the understanding of institutional theory in international business by investigating the effect of these factors on the OFDI behavior of Chinese TNCs using the synthesizing concept of the Chinese OFDI regime. Before we assess how the Government of China has helped to shape the Chinese OFDI regime over the period from 1991 to 2003, when Chinese OFDI accelerated rapidly, we first review some contributions to the literature that seek to account for this growth.

7.2   LITERATURE REVIEW

The surge in Chinese OFDI since the mid-1990s (Table A7.1 in the Appendix to this chapter) has attracted growing attention from international business scholars. Contributors to the discussion of its causes have tended to argue for the primacy of either Dunning's eclectic paradigm (for example, Deng 2004; Erdener and Shapiro 2005; Warner *et al.* 2004; Wu and Sia 2002) or the resource-based view of the firm (for example, Deng 2007). By emphasizing the potential of an institutional theory explanation, we offer an alternative standpoint.

Since the early 1980s, a significant body of literature has grown on the transnationalization of firms from other Asian developing countries (Bartlett and Ghoshal 2000; Buckley and Mirza 1999; Chen 2003; Chen and Chen 1998; Cho *et al.* 1998; Ghymn 1980; Kumar and Kim 1984; Lall 1991; Lee and Chen 2003; Makino *et al.* 2002; Mathews 2006; Sim 2006; Sim and Pandian 2002; Tallman and Shenkar 1990; Ulgado *et al.* 1994; van Hoesel 1997; Yeung 1994). One of the main strands of this literature places particular importance on the determining role played by state engagement in the business affairs of domestic TNCs, either through direct ownership of productive assets or indirectly through various kinds of regulatory control. Of course, for much of its recent past this has also been the case for China (Sauvant 2005). To illustrate, extant literature generally asserts that Chinese firms transnationalized prior to the mid-1990s in order to

pursue certain national and provincial economic goals and policy objectives, in particular to: (1) support the export function of state-owned manufacturers; (2) help stabilize the supply of domestically-scarce natural
resources; and (3) acquire information and learning about operating
abroad for the benefit of other domestic enterprises (Lu 2002; Ye 1992;
Zhan 1995).

More recently, Chinese firms have been portrayed as transnationalizing
in order to: (4) achieve improved access to foreign proprietary technology,
immobile strategic assets and capabilities; (5) exploit new markets for
products and services; and (6) enhance competitiveness through the
diversification of business activity (for example, Beebe 2006; Child and
Rodrigues 2005; Deng 2003, 2004; Pei and Wang 2001; Sauvant 2005;
Taylor 2002; Warner *et al.* 2004; Zhang 2003; Zhang 2005). Ostensibly,
these latter three motivations can be attributed as much to market forces,
industry dynamics and discretionary managerial decision making as to
government intervention and fiat. Concomitantly, state control over the
international activities of Chinese firms has been relaxed in recent years,
partly in response to the marketization of the Chinese economy and the
country's WTO accession commitments (Sauvant 2005). This disengagement has been formally articulated with the introduction in 1999 of China's
'Go Global' (*zou chu qu*) policies, which were established in China's tenth
five-year plan and reinforced in its eleventh. The objective of these policies
is to encourage OFDI. Nevertheless, the presumption seemingly held by
some researchers is that the Chinese authorities continue to exert substantial influence over the OFDI activities of Chinese firms (for example, Deng
2003; Deutsche Bank Research 2006a; Sauvant 2005). In this somewhat
paradoxical context, an interesting research agenda is emerging on the
extent to which the engagement and disengagement of various levels of
government has shaped and continues to shape the transnationalization
decision of Chinese firms.

7.3   HYPOTHESES DEVELOPMENT

In this section, we develop our hypotheses in two parts. The first considers
what we describe as 'traditional' explanations of Chinese OFDI and the
second, our 'institutional' explanations.

7.3.1   Traditional Explanations for Chinese OFDI

First, we evaluate whether or not the traditional explanations derived from
work on OFDI from the industrialized countries have explanatory power.

Typically, such FDI is explained by at least one of the following four motivations that underpin the decision to produce abroad, namely market-seeking, resource-seeking, strategic asset-seeking and efficiency-seeking motives (Dunning 1993).

Market-seeking FDI

Market-seeking FDI is generally undertaken by firms in response to opportunities presented by market size and growth of a host country. It occurs as companies seek to strengthen existing markets or to develop and explore new markets. Market-seeking FDI can thus be undertaken for trade-supporting reasons (that is, to facilitate the exports of domestic producers) or for trade-substituting reasons (for example, in response to restrictive and costly import procedures and regulations or other trade barriers imposed by the host country).

Developing-country firms typically invest in other developing countries where they enjoy lower 'costs of foreignness' (Hymer 1960, 1976) and where they can exploit their home-country embeddedness for competitive advantage (Cross *et al.* 2007). This is because such firms can leverage in other developing markets their experience of operating in a domestic environment characterized by regulatory constraints, bureaucratic hurdles, high barriers to entry, market volatility and so forth (Cross *et al.* 2007; Lall 1983; Lau 2003). They may also be better able (than industrialized country firms) to meet the specific demand conditions and price expectations of lower income customers (Lau 2003; Lecraw 1977; Monkiewicz 1986). This can be accomplished, for example, by simplifying or substituting local inputs, or by increasing the labor intensity of production (Cross *et al.* 2007; Shenkar and Luo 2004). Therefore, although empirical studies show that FDI flows and market size are correlated positively for industrialized countries (Chakrabarti 2001), the presumption that Chinese investors will be attracted toward larger markets is challengeable. Our discussion suggests that Chinese TNCs are likely to have ownership advantages that fit better the industrial structure of a developing and not a developed country. Thus:

Hypothesis 1:   The relative market size of a host country is negatively associated with Chinese OFDI flows.

Recent work points to the growing importance of market-seeking FDI by Chinese TNCs in both developing and developed host countries in response to policy liberalization in China (Cross *et al.* 2007; Deng 2004; Taylor 2002; Zhang 2003). To explore this, we use a structural break in our model for 1999, the year in which China's 'Go Global' policy was introduced.

Natural resource-seeking FDI

Natural resource-seeking FDI relates to investment that exploits immobile natural factor endowments abroad such as oil, minerals and other raw materials. This type of investment is commonly undertaken by developing country firms to secure the supply of raw materials for national economic development purposes (that is, to fulfill a national policy agenda). This has been the case for China for many years (Ye 1992; Zhan 1995), as evidenced by the recent flurry of successful and aborted acquisitions of western companies in the extractive industries, for example (Buckley *et al.* 2006). This activity has been supported, both directly and indirectly, at a governmental level by numerous state visits to resource-rich countries across Africa, Latin America and beyond (*Financial Times* 2006; Jubany and Poon 2006; *Latin Business Chronicle* 2006). Limited resource endowments in China, rapid domestic economic growth rates and high commodity prices are key drivers (for example, Deutsche Bank Research 2006b). To capture the natural resource-seeking FDI activities of Chinese TNCs, we incorporate a variable that measures the exports of host countries of crude petroleum and natural liquified gas, which are arguably the most important natural resources sought by China today (for example, Deutsche Bank Research 2006b).

> **Hypothesis 2:** The level of natural resource endowments of a host country is associated positively with Chinese OFDI flows.

Strategic asset-seeking FDI

Strategic asset-seeking FDI occurs when firms transnationalize in order to create, sustain or maintain their competitive position, often by acquiring, in whole or in part, the proprietary assets of another, foreign company (Dunning 1993). Technology-seeking investment is conducted in areas such as R&D and design facilities. The objective of investing firms is to tap into existing knowledge stocks and expertise, and to participate more fully in new product development and standard setting in order to maximize their competitive position. The investor normally intends to benefit from spillover effects deriving from agglomerations of similar minded companies and from complementary industries in the host country. Strategic asset-seeking FDI also occurs when access to (internationally) recognized brand names, local distribution systems and managerial practice and expertise is improved, either through direct purchase or through proximity of operations (which in turn gives rise to demonstration effects and spillover benefits). While Dunning's (1977) eclectic paradigm proposes that companies seek to exploit ownership advantages in host countries, the strategic asset-seeking motivation gives leeway to allow for asset-augmenting investments. These are investments conducted by companies that have few, if any, ownership advantages themselves (outside of their domestic market) and which therefore invest internationally to acquire such advantage. This type of behavior is said to be an essential component of the transnationalization strategy of developing country firms (Bartlett and Ghoshal 2000; Dunning *et al*. 1998; Dunning 2001; Makino *et al*. 2002). There is also evidence to suggest that Chinese companies are increasingly extending their international activities to acquire advanced technology and manufacturing know-how (Buckley *et al*. 2007; Cross *et al*. 2007; Sigurdson 2005). In this chapter, we measure the attractiveness of a country for strategic asset-seeking FDI by using the total number of patents it has granted.

Hypothesis 3:   The number of granted patents in a host country is positively associated with Chinese OFDI flows.

Efficiency-seeking FDI
Efficiency-seeking FDI occurs when outward investors seek lower cost locations for their operations and production activities, especially in relation to manufacturing, R&D, labor, communication, administrative and distribution costs. Given domestic market conditions, this type of investment behavior is likely to be of reduced importance to Chinese companies because they can presently rely on a steady and cheap supply of migrant workers, especially when production takes place in China's central and western provinces. Consequently, we do not incorporate efficiency-seeking motives in our model. However, we note that, as Chinese firms increasingly extend their operations into international markets, as they seek to gain advantage from regional integration in South-East Asia and elsewhere, and as they confront rising production costs at home (especially in the coastal regions), efficiency-seeking motives may become much more important in future.

The preceding three hypotheses largely derive from current understanding of the motives that underpin Chinese OFDI. However, it is clear from our earlier discussion that institutional theory explanations are likely to have an important contributory effect and we consider these in more detail below.

7.3.2   Institutional Explanations for Chinese OFDI

The general theory of FDI stipulates that companies invest internationally to internalize markets for intermediate goods and knowledge and to leverage existing market imperfections in the host country (Buckley and Casson 1976; Rugman 1999). Companies incorporate markets into their organizational hierarchies and across national boundaries, until the marginal costs of so doing exceed the marginal benefit – that is, when it is cheaper and more effective to organize business activities at arm's length through the market (Buckley and Casson 1976).

In their study of the determinants of Chinese OFDI, Buckley *et al.* (2007) extended internalization theory to incorporate domestic capital market imperfections. Under this thesis, domestic capital market imperfections provide Chinese TNCs, especially state-owned ones, with the necessary investment funds in the form of: (1) capital provided to them at below market rates; (2) soft loans made available by China's inefficient banking system, either as policy or through inefficiency (many of which are now identified as non-performing loans); (3) intra-company subsidies; and, (4) privileged access to cheap capital provided by family members and through other relationships (a benefit that may be of particular importance to privately-owned Chinese TNCs) (Buckley *et al.* 2007). Buckley *et al.* attributed the positive relationship they found between Chinese OFDI and rising levels of host country risk to capital market imperfections in China.

Both the internalization and capital market imperfections approaches of Buckley *et al.* (2007) contain an implicit acknowledgement of the importance of the national institutional elements of the OFDI regime. They did not elaborate upon or develop this dimension fully. However, market imperfections are often not accidental but are created and promoted by home country institutions and the constraints that are imposed are intentional (North 1990). This is certainly the case for China, as evidenced by the following quotation from Scott (2002, p. 65)

> the Chinese state is constituted to act . . . as an active player, promoting and controlling economic development. The norms governing state actors and citizens clearly differ: Chinese officials are more likely to presume that they, rather than any subordinate constituency, are obliged to decide and act for the common good.

Of course, the influence of institutions is not restricted to the domestic realm but also plays a crucial role, both positively and negatively, in the transnationalization of domestic companies. Expressed another way, the behavior and decisions of a country's domestic institutions may lead to market imperfections that then impact on the decision making of its TNCs (Brewer 1993).

For China, as with many developing countries, the control and, effectively, the restriction of OFDI has been a major strand of economic policy, with the maintenance of domestic investment levels and the bolstering of foreign exchange levels being prime objectives (Sauvant 2005). The institutional framework is therefore likely to have determined, to a considerable degree, the ability and will of domestic firms to invest abroad (Buckley *et al*. 2007). Because of the central role played by the Government of China, especially before 2003 (when major reforms to the Chinese OFDI regime took place, including allowing private firms to invest abroad), institutional theory has the potential to explain a great deal of Chinese OFDI. On the one hand, the Government of China has imposed the legal, regulatory and financial components of the Chinese OFDI regime, either directly, by administrative fiat (via the OFDI approval process and foreign exchange controls), or indirectly, using economic policy implementation and other measures (Buckley *et al*. 2006). On the other, as the ultimate owner of state-owned enterprises (which dominated Chinese OFDI prior to 2003), the Government has also effectively been the key operational decision maker in many investment projects (Buckley *et al*. 2006). The endogenous (or national) element of the Chinese OFDI regime will therefore shape outward investment behavior. While domestic capital market imperfections may supply companies with sufficient funds to operate internationally (Buckley *et al*. 2007), it may also inhibit the development of internationally competitive companies. Similarly, overly restrictive foreign exchange policy and outward investment approval procedures may restrict or even prevent OFDI from happening. It is clear, therefore, that the picture is complex and the challenge for research, including that of the present study, is to disentangle the role of institutional factors from other influences, such as demand conditions and competition levels, on the investment behavior of Chinese firms.

At the supranational level (that is, extending beyond national boundaries and including at least two countries), the concept of 'institution' comprises a set of 'soft' (or informal) factors and 'hard' (or formal) factors. In the context of a country's OFDI regime, the former includes state visits and foreign policy initiatives while the latter includes concluded bilateral investment treaties (BITs) and membership in free trade areas and customs unions, for example. Although separate, these two factors are also interlinked. State visits commonly pave the way for more formal arrangements and relationships as the terms and conditions of bilateral agreements and accession to a free trade area are negotiated and implemented. These elements can support and strengthen the stance of a country's TNCs abroad (Ramamurti 2001). Of interest here are three supranational elements of the Chinese OFDI regime that have the potential to influence Chinese FDI flows and which have each become increasingly prevalent over the past two decades, namely BITs, double taxation treaties (DTTs) and membership in the WTO/General Agreement on Tariffs and Trade (GATT). BITs and DTTs are often seen as policy instruments that countries can introduce to improve their locational attractiveness to TNCs (Mallampally and Sauvant 1999). We now discuss in more detail the hypothesized effects of these endogenous and exogenous institutional factors on Chinese OFDI.

Foreign exchange control and liberalization

One area of government anxiety over the economic impact of OFDI concerns the issue of foreign exchange. Foreign exchange accumulation has been a central plank of Chinese macroeconomic policy since the 1970s.[2] In 1989, the Chinese State Administration for Foreign Exchange was charged with managing foreign exchange for outward investment. On the one hand, China's (now substantial) foreign exchange reserves have been available, in theory at least, to finance the purchase of overseas assets.[3] However, for many years, the Government has been keen to restrict this type of use, preferring instead for firms to make investments 'in kind', in the form of physical equipment, know-how, raw materials and the like (Liu 2007). The Government of China has also reserved for itself priority in the use of foreign exchange. Overseas projects considered of strategic national importance have normally enjoyed foreign exchange-related privileges, and qualifying Chinese firms have been able to purchase readily foreign exchange and receive loans denominated in foreign currency from domestic financial institutions, even during periods of tight foreign exchange control. Priority activities like natural resource exploration and overseas processing and assembly projects have been allowed to be financed in whole or in part with foreign exchange (the former to 100 per cent, the latter up to 40 per cent).

Prior to 1994, only Chinese companies that had been granted international trade rights could earn foreign currencies and use this to fund OFDI projects. Companies without international trading rights could not earn foreign currency and were thus highly restricted in their international investment activities (Lin and Schramm 2004; Zhang 1999; Zhang 2003). Therefore, the number of potential Chinese international investors was artificially restricted to a small club of (successful) international traders. However, in 1994 the Government significantly liberalized its foreign exchange regime and moved from an 'earning-to-use' to a 'buying-to-use' foreign exchange policy. This was a crucial development in the evolution of the Chinese OFDI regime, since the Chinese outward investment approval procedure generally begins with an investigation of the foreign currency involved. From 1994 onwards, foreign exchange could be bought from the State Administration for Foreign Exchange to finance OFDI projects regardless of whether or not the applicant had previously generated foreign exchange earnings. It is likely that liberalization enabled more Chinese companies to finance international investments by converting domestically earned yuan into foreign currency. Consequently, as the number of Chinese companies eligible for OFDI increases, China's OFDI may likewise have increased. Hence:

Hypothesis 4: China's OFDI flow is positively associated with the liberalization of foreign exchange controls in 1994.

The 'Go Global' strategy and Chinese OFDI

The commitment of China's leadership to see greater involvement of Chinese firms in the global economy has been articulated regularly since the beginning of the 'open-door policy' in 1978 (Zhang 2003). However, the 'Go Global' policy was given substance when it was officially expressed by the former Chinese President Jiang Zemin and the former Chinese Premier Zhu Rongji (Zhu 2001) and when it was formally written into China's 10th and 11th five-year plans (2001–2005 and 2006–2010, respectively) for national economic and social development and restructuring (Wang 2001; Zhao 2000). In the long run, the policy of creating favorable conditions for domestic enterprises should see increasing numbers of Chinese firms locate productive activity abroad. The response of relevant government agencies has been to provide greater support for, and promotion of, OFDI by offering favorable policies and procedures to investors in many areas, such as in finance, insurance, foreign exchange, taxation, human resources, law and regulation, the provision of information services, training courses on international business, and language training. Key OFDI-promoting measures introduced recently include improvements to the availability of commercial loans, finance from the Export-Import Bank of China (using China's extensive foreign exchange reserves) and preferential arrangements concerning foreign exchange and corporate income tax exemptions for qualifying firms and projects. Arguably, many of these developments constitute additional soft budget constraints enjoyed by Chinese TNCs. The intention of the Government is to improve the quality of service by further devolving decision making on outward investment approvals to local governments. It also intends to minimize unfair competition among Chinese companies (Wang 2001) and to introduce measures to coordinate investment in a way that prevents OFDI in the same industries in the same countries, because this might lead to market cannibalism among Chinese firms. The Government is also active at the supranational level in further supporting and strengthening the outward orientation of Chinese companies. It intends to conclude more BITs and DTTs to protect Chinese investors (Wang 2001). In sum, and following full implementation of China's WTO commitments (for example, concerning equal treatment of firms and most-favored-nation clauses), China is likely to further deregulate and liberalize OFDI-restricting measures, with indirect, hands-off economic policies increasingly substituting for direct, hands-on administrative methods of management (Buckley *et al.* 2006; Sauvant 2005). In the current study, we capture the effects of the 'Go Global' policy by introducing a structural break to our model for the year 1999.

BITs and Chinese OFDI

BITs are concluded between two countries in order to protect and promote bilateral investment flows (UNCTAD 2000, 2005b). Prior to 1979, a total of 165 BITs had been concluded between countries, a figure that stood at 2392 in 2004 (UNCTAD 2005b). Of these, almost 1600 were agreed in the 1990s, which highlights their growing importance in the international political economy (UNCTAD 2000). China is now second only to Germany as a participant nation, with 112 BITs concluded by 2004, of which 63 were agreed with other developing countries (UNCTAD 2005a, 2005b).

A BIT provides a legally binding situation in which the foreign investor enjoys greater investment protection than domestic laws might otherwise allow. BITs generally reflect a progressive and positive attitude toward economic liberalism by the contracting parties (Vandervelde 1998). Typically, a BIT includes the following elements: national treatment of foreign investors, most favored nation treatment, fair and equitable treatment of foreign investors, abolishment of discriminatory treatment of foreign investors (that is, it provides for equal treatment), compensation for expropriated property, and the repatriation of profits and capital (Neumayer and Spess 2005; Ramamurti 2001). It may also involve the removal of restrictions on FDI. Normally, this applies equally to outbound and inbound investments (UNCTAD 2000). In addition to these direct benefits, greater transparency, an improved institutional framework and the removal of FDI restrictions in signatory countries may work as a trigger for FDI since overall investment costs and risks are decreased and business opportunities are widened (Egger and Pfaffermayr 2004; Ramamurti 2001). BITs have therefore become an important policy tool for international organizations such as UNCTAD, which actively helps developing countries to negotiate, sign and ratify BITs and DTTs (UNCTAD 2000). Moreover, a concluded BIT may also provide a signaling effect to potential investors from third countries outside of the agreement because of the stable, transparent and predictable investment environment presented by signatory countries (UNCTAD 2005b; Neumayer and Spess 2005). However, any such signaling effect may gradually deteriorate over time (Neumayer and Spess 2005).

The empirical evidence concerning the effect of BITs on the investment behavior of TNCs is ambiguous. Some research found empirical support for the positive impact of BITs on FDI (for example, Egger and Pfaffermayr 2004; Grosse and Trevino 2005; Neumayer and Spess 2005;

Salacuse and Sullivan 2005). One of the more comprehensive studies, that by Neumayer and Spess (2005), found that BITs signed between developing and OECD countries have had a strong positive and robust effect on IFDI flows to developing countries over the period 1970 to 2001. They also found evidence that BITs signed with third countries have a positive signaling effect on FDI inflows from other countries. Egger and Pfaffermayr (2004) revealed that implemented treaties have a stronger positive effect than ones that have merely been signed. However, they found limited evidence that signaling effects are at work in third countries. They also found little pattern of significance depending on the level of development of the countries involved. Grosse and Trevino (2005), in a study of the determinants of FDI to Central and Eastern Europe, reported a strong positive relationship between the total numbers of BITs concluded by a country and IFDI flows.

Other research yielded contrasting results, however. For example, Tobin and Rose-Ackerman (2005) argued that the effect of a BIT on FDI is mitigated by country risk levels. They found that, of the developing countries that have concluded a high number of BITs, those with high levels of country risk attract less IFDI, while the converse is found for low risk countries. One interpretation is that investing firms are more influenced by risk conditions than by the nature of supranational investment relations between home and host country. Hallward-Driemeier (2003) also found that the existence of a BIT has little to no effect upon the flow of FDI from OECD to developing countries. Rather, she argued that a BIT may have an institution-complementing effect instead of providing a better institutional setting, a finding that supports the work of Tobin and Rose-Ackerman (2005). This accords with Ginsburg (2005), who argued that BITs can have a counterproductive effect on the development of sound institutions in developing countries if the country concerned relies on supranational bodies for dispute settlement and so forth. The lack of institutional development may also serve to lower both investor confidence and FDI inflows in the long run. To our knowledge, the effect of BITs on Chinese investment behavior has not been researched. However, given the number of BITs that China has concluded, the weight of evidence suggests that there is likely to be a positive relationship between Chinese OFDI and whether or not a host country is signatory to a BIT with China. Thus:

Hypothesis 5a: A host country's propensity to attract Chinese OFDI flows is positively associated with the conclusion of a BIT with China.

In addition to the direct influence on firms domiciled in the signatory countries, BITs can also have a signaling effect, as discussed above. In effect, a treaty signed between two countries may attract to them investment from a third country because of the investor protection which the signatory countries are seeking to implement (Neumayer and Spess 2005). This signaling effect is captured as follows:

Hypothesis 5b: A host country's propensity to attract Chinese OFDI flows is positively associated with the total number of BITs it has concluded.

DTTs and Chinese OFDI

The increasing importance of DTTs is reflected in the growing number of agreements signed over the past two decades. The number of DTTs concluded worldwide doubled from 1990 to reach 2559 in 2004 (UNCTAD 2005b). DTTs are normally concluded between two countries to avoid the double taxation of companies operating in both countries. Country attractiveness is increased because future tax rates on (profitable) foreign affiliates are made more predictable for the investing parent company (Davies 2004). DTTs also reduce the opportunities for tax avoidance by TNCs, and this may be an investment disincentive (Davies 2004; Egger *et al.* 2006). Moreover, DTTs may be less important than other locational determinants, especially in the developing world. For example, investors in Africa ranked DTTs in eighteenth position behind other locational factors such as economic and political stability (UNIDO 2006). This suggests that DTTs have some merit in the investment package, but may not be as important as other FDI determinants.

To date, empirical studies have found either zero effect or a negative effect of DTTs on FDI flows and stocks (Davies 2004; Egger *et al.* 2006). For example, Egger *et al.* (2006) found a significant negative impact of newly implemented DTTs on OFDI stock from OECD countries. In other words, DTTs (with and without in-built mechanisms to minimize tax avoidance) decrease FDI. One explanation is that the smaller public budgets that result from the enactment of DTT principles mean that governments have fewer resources to build the physical, commercial and social infrastructure necessary to attract and support FDI. Blonigen and Davies (2004) also found significant and negative effects of new DTTs on FDI, although old treaties are found to have a positive and significant effect. Ambiguities in this work may be a consequence of noisy data and the inclusion of political and economical risk variables that mask certain interactions (Blonigen and Davies 2004; Davies 2004). Again, to our knowledge, the effect of DTTs on Chinese investment behavior has not been researched before. However, from the discussion above, we assume that the overall effect will be positive, thus:

Hypothesis 6a: A host country's propensity to attract Chinese OFDI flows is positively associated with the conclusion of a DTT with China.

And, to capture signaling effects:

Hypothesis 6b: A host country's propensity to attract Chinese OFDI flows is positively associated with the total number of DTTs it has concluded.

WTO/GATT membership

Membership of a host country in the WTO is also incorporated into our model as a formal, exogenous element of the Chinese OFDI regime. The WTO is responsible for administering approximately 30 international treaties and agreements, such as the GATT, the Agreement on Trade-Related Intellectual Property Rights (TRIPs) and the Agreement on Trade-Related Investment Measures (TRIMs). These Agreements provide much of the framework for international trade (via most-favored-nation treatment clauses and equal treatment of domestic and foreign firms, trade dispute resolution, market access, reductions in preferential trading arrangements and so forth). Membership of the WTO may signal to foreign firms that a country will conform to its strictures and obligations with respect to international trade and investment. The WTO thus constitutes an important supranational component of the institutional framework within which TNCs operate, and by extension, this is likely also to be the case for the Chinese OFDI regime. Thus we include a variable for WTO membership status. Our expectation is that WTO membership will be viewed favorably by potential Chinese investors, although lack of prior research on this point prevents us from providing further empirical support.

Hypothesis 7:   Countries that are members of the WTO attract higher Chinese OFDI flows.

Cultural proximity

We regard the development of international business networks to be an important informal element of the Chinese OFDI regime, and hence, we incorporate it in our model. This is because the overseas Chinese in Asia (the Chinese diaspora) are acknowledged to have contributed appreciably to the integration of China into the world economy, especially by investing heavily in mainland China (Henley *et al*. 1999; Ng and Tuan 2002; Yeung 1999, 2000). Strong economic connections between the mainland and the overseas Chinese, and the importance of *guanxi* in Chinese business dealings, may also have had an influence on patterns of Chinese OFDI (Buckley *et al.* 2007; Luo 1997; Standifird and Marshall 2000; Tong 2003). For example, it is maintained that the Government of China has used the extensive network of overseas Chinese to promote the sales of Chinese goods worldwide (Barabantseva 2005). This could be a manifestation of early steps by the Government to encourage the overseas Chinese to support OFDI. Chinese companies may benefit from, and even accelerate, their transnationalization through the international business and social networks that overseas Chinese have already established (Johanson and Vahlne 2003; Oviatt and McDougall 2005). Networks are a 'set of high-trust relationships which either directly or indirectly link together everyone in a social group' for the recursive exchange of information (Casson 1997, p. 813).

Business and social networks can help companies to transnationalize because they: (1) allow for the dissemination among actors of information that was previously unknown to them; (2) lower transaction costs (especially business opportunity search costs); and (3) mitigate perceptions of risk (Aharoni 1999; Johanson and Vahlne 2003, 2006). Access to such networks may be construed as an intangible asset for a company, something which Dunning (2002) defines as a 'relational asset'. A number of scholars assert that ethnic and family networks constitute a firm-specific advantage for Chinese TNCs for these reasons (Braeutigam 2003; Erdener and Shapiro 2005; Sung 1996; Zhan 1995). An established and trustworthy network may also compensate Chinese TNCs for their relatively late entry into international markets (Li 2003). Consequently, privileged access to relevant, ethnically-derived relational assets can constitute a special ownership advantage for Chinese firms in particular contexts. This argument suggests that Chinese firms may reveal a propensity to invest in countries where a large population of ethnic Chinese resides and where *guanxi* and familial networks can be readily exploited or established. Indeed, Buckley *et al.* (2007) found a positive and significant relationship between Chinese OFDI to a country and the proportion of ethnic Chinese that makes up its population.[4] Thus:

Hypothesis 8:   China's OFDI is positively associated with a greater proportion of ethnic Chinese people in a host country's population.

Geographic distance between China and the host country
Internalization theory predicts that market-seeking firms are more likely to serve geographically proximate countries through exports and more distant markets via FDI (Buckley and Casson 1981). This suggests a substitution of FDI for other modes as geographic distance increases. However, the

stages theory of internationalization suggests that firms engage first in more geographically proximate locations and that, by implication, FDI will first occur in such markets. Work that applies gravity approaches to the understanding of the spatial distribution of international business confirms this view. Research on the role of geographic distance on Chinese OFDI patterns is somewhat ambiguous, however. Buckley *et al.* (2007) found that aggregate Chinese OFDI is negatively correlated with geographic distance. In a second study, Cross *et al.* (2007) found that, when examining differences by host country development level, Chinese OFDI is positively and significantly associated with distance, but for OECD countries only. They attributed this finding to greater market-seeking and resource-seeking investment by Chinese firms in developed markets that are spatially distant from mainland China. For the period from 1984 to 1991, Cross *et al.* (2007) reported that Chinese OFDI is significantly associated, but negatively, with spatial distance. They concluded that this reflects the relative inexperience of Chinese TNCs prior to 1991, when many invested in proximate markets. In the current study, we update the work of Cross *et al.* by examining more recent years (up to 2003). We assume that greater market-seeking and resource-seeking FDI is now occurring in more distant countries and therefore that:

Hypothesis 9: Geographic distance of the host country's capital from Beijing is positively associated with Chinese OFDI flow.

We note, of course, that geographic distance is not an institutional-related factor per se. However, we include it here under institutional explanations of Chinese OFDI since it bears upon transaction costs, which themselves arise from the institutional environment within which transactions take place.

7.3.3   Control Variables

Following Buckley *et al.* (2007), we introduce a set of conventional (control) variables from standard theory to specify correctly the estimated equation. We now hypothesize on the effect of these control variables.

Political risk
Internalization theory predicts that, in countries with high levels of political risk, market-oriented firms will tend to substitute arm's length servicing modes (exporting or licensing) for directly owned local production, and that resource-oriented firms will be discouraged from investing substantial sunk costs in FDI projects (Buckley and Casson 1981, 1999). Thus, high

political risk is generally associated with low values of FDI inflow, *ceteris paribus* (Chakrabarti 2001). Our measure of political risk assigns higher values to greater political stability. Therefore, the general theory of FDI predicts a positive relationship between the dependent and the control variable, thus:

> **Hypothesis 10:**   High levels of host country political risk are associated with lower Chinese OFDI flows.

Purchasing power parity
We control for changes relative to purchasing power parity (PPP) in order to capture variation in domestic prices that are not fully reflected in the exchange rate (see Hypothesis 12 below). As prices become cheaper in a host country, we would expect market-seeking Chinese FDI to be encouraged. Therefore:

> **Hypothesis 11:**   A relative decrease in PPP in a host country is positively associated with Chinese OFDI flows.

Exchange rate
Theory posits that a low or undervalued exchange rate encourages exports but discourages outward FDI (Kohlhagen 1977; Logue and Willet 1977; Stevens 1993). As the home country exchange rate appreciates, more profitable opportunities for OFDI will occur because foreign currency denominated assets become cheaper. An appreciation of the home country's currency vis-à-vis other countries should increase OFDI into the latter, as it is effectively a depreciation in the host country's currency (Clegg and Scott-Green 1999). In the case of China, the yuan was *de facto* pegged to the US dollar at a constant nominal level over the period under study (Hall 2004; Roberts and Tyers 2003). However, this allowed for revaluation of the yuan against other currencies (Hall 2004). Following Cross *et al.* (2007), exchange rate movements may influence patterns of Chinese FDI flows and we therefore control for this, as follows:

> **Hypothesis 12:**   A relative depreciation of the host country's currency is positively associated with Chinese OFDI flows.

Host inflation rate
Volatile and unpredictable inflation rates in a host country impede market-seeking FDI because this creates uncertainty and renders problematic certain aspects of long-term corporate planning, not least in respect of

price setting and profit forecasting (Buckley *et al.* 2007; Cross *et al.* 2007). High rates of inflation may also lead to domestic currency devaluations, which in turn reduce the real value of earnings in local currency for market-seeking inward investing firms. High inflation rates may lead to rising prices for locally sourced inputs, and this may constrain the export performance of domestic and foreign investors, which in turn discourages export-oriented FDI. We therefore expect a negative association between Chinese OFDI and host country inflation.

Hypothesis 13: Host country inflation has an inverse relationship with Chinese OFDI flows.

Trade

Exports and imports between a home country and a host country capture the intensity of trade relations. Exports from China proxy a key aspect of the intensity of trade relations between home and host country by capturing market-seeking motives of Chinese firms. During the 1980s and 1990s, Chinese OFDI was explicitly encouraged to support Chinese exporters and to promote hard currency earnings (Guo 1984). China is now increasingly investing abroad to secure the supply of raw materials and natural resources such as oil, minerals and timber. We would therefore expect China's imports to be positively associated with OFDI. This generates the following two hypotheses:

Hypothesis 14: Levels of exports from China to a host country are positively associated with Chinese OFDI flows.

Hypothesis 15: Levels of imports from a host country to China are positively associated with Chinese OFDI flows.

Market openness to inward FDI

The openness of a country to foreign investors is a measurement of the country's attitude toward liberalization and overall attractiveness and stability. To account for country size differences, we use the ratio of inward FDI to GDP as a proxy for market openness, thus:

Hypothesis 16: The level of openness towards inward FDI of a host country is positively associated with Chinese OFDI flows.

In Table A7.1, in the Appendix to this chapter, we recapitulate the hypotheses, the expected signs and the variables that we use to test them.

7.4   THE MODEL, DATA SOURCES AND METHODOLOGY

7.4.1   The Model

Our discussions suggest that a well-specified model for the explanation of Chinese OFDI using variables derived from theory can be constructed as follows:

FDI = f(market-seeking FDI, resource-seeking FDI, asset-seeking FDI, foreign exchange liberalization in 1994, BIT with China, accumulated BITs, DTT with China, accumulated DTTs, WTO membership, cultural proximity, geographic distance, political risk, PPP, exchange rate, inflation, China's exports, China's imports, openness to FDI).

$$\begin{aligned} LFDI = {} & \alpha + \beta_1 LGDPPC + \beta_2 LOIL + \beta_3 LPATENT + \beta_4 TD94 + \beta_5 BIT \\ & + \beta_6 LACBIT + \beta_7 DTT + \beta_8 LACDTT + \beta_9 WTO + \beta_{10} CP \\ & + \beta_{11} LDIS + \beta_{12} LRISK + \beta_{13} LPPP + \beta_{14} LERATE + \beta_{15} LINF \\ & + \beta_{16} LEXP + \beta_{17} LIMP + \beta_{18} LINFDI + \varepsilon_{it}. \end{aligned} \tag{7.1}$$

7.4.2   Data Sources

The dependent variable is calculated for the years 1991 to 2003 from the following annual MOFCOM publications: the *Almanac of China's Foreign Economic Relations and Trade* and the *China Commerce Yearbook*. Proxies for market-seeking and resource-seeking FDI are obtained as follows. For market-seeking FDI, GDP per capita data (LGDPPC) are taken from the *World Development Indicators* (WDI) for April 2005 and 2006 (World Bank 2006). To proxy for resource-seeking FDI, data on crude oil and natural liquified gas (NLG) exports and petroleum product exports (LOIL) for the host countries are taken from the *Oil Information 2006* (International Energy Agency). The *WDI* and *Oil Information* databases were accessed using ESDS International. Asset-seeking FDI (LPATENT) is proxied by total annual patent grants (residents plus non-residents) by an economy as published by the World Intellectual Property Organisation (2006).

The second part of the chapter focuses on the impact of institutional factors on China's OFDI. Thus our explanatory variables comprise endogenous and exogenous Chinese OFDI regime factors. Our single endogenous institutional factor is the liberalization of foreign exchange control in China (TD94, 1994–2003 = 1; otherwise 0) as derived from the above discussion. The five formal exogenous institutional factors are: (1) the number of BITs a country has concluded with China (BIT); (2) the total number of BITs a country has concluded, including with China (LACBIT); (3) the number of DTTs a country has concluded with China (DTT); (4) the total number of DTTs a country has concluded, including with China (LACDTT); and (5) membership of a country in the WTO/GATT (WTO). We also introduce an informal exogenous institutional factor, namely cultural proximity to China (CP). To account for the spatial costs of international business, we incorporate a measure for geographic distance from China (LDIS). Data on BITs and DTTs were obtained from UNCTAD. WTO/GATT membership status of a country was obtained from the WTO website. Cultural distance is obtained by using a dummy variable (1 = ethnic Chinese >1 per cent of total population; 0 otherwise). Estimates for the share of ethnic Chinese people in the total population were calculated using the WDI total population figure and overseas Chinese data for each country obtained for the year 1997 (or nearest year) from various sources, including the Ohio Library (2006), the Overseas Chinese Affairs Commission (2005), and from Ma (2003) and Kent (2003). The figure for Ukraine was taken from census data, and the Chinese Embassy in Croatia sent us directly a country estimate. Geographical distance was calculated from Beijing to the host country capital using the distance tool found at www.geobytes.com.[5] Finally, a further endogenous Chinese OFDI regime factor is captured by the structural break we introduce for the year 1999 to account for the change in policy direction initiated by China's 'Go Global' promotion measures.

For our control variables, we use political risk (LRISK), calculated from risk components provided by the *International Country Risk Guide* (ICRG) (Political Risk Services 2005); purchasing power parity (PPP) (calculated using the difference in the inflation rate between host country and China plus the percentage appreciation of the host country currency against the renminbi); exchange rate (LERATE) (*World Development Indicators* – World Bank 2006); inflation (LINF) (annual inflation rate of the host country obtained from the *World Economic Outlook Database* – International Monetary Fund 2005); exports (from China; LEXP) and imports (to China; LIMP) (obtained from China's annually published *Statistical Yearbook*); and market openness (LINFDI) which is the ratio of inward FDI to GDP published by UNCTAD (2006). All monetary figures were obtained either in constant 2000 prices or were transformed into 2000 constant prices.

7.4.3 Methodology

We employ a panel of data on 55 countries for the 13 years from 1991 to 2003. Pooled ordinary least squares (POLS) and one-way random effects (RE) estimators were applied to estimate the above equation (7.1). A fixed effects estimator cannot be used since equation (7.1) includes dummy variables that are invariant with respect to time for the country concerned. A Lagrangian multiplier (LM) test was conducted to identify whether POLS or RE furnished the better model for the full sample period and the sub-samples under investigation. The LM test values were significantly different from zero in five of nine cases. Table A7.3 in the appendix to this chapter presents the results and indicates if the POLS or RE results are preferred and are hence discussed. We also explore differences by level of development of the host country by separating our results for OECD and non-OECD member countries. The correlation table (Table A7.4) indicates no major problem of collinearity.

7.5   STATISTICAL RESULTS AND DISCUSSION

First, we discuss the results for the RE model for the entire time period (1991–2003) (column 1, Table A7.3). We then compare and discuss our findings using several structural breaks. Since our discussions suggest that Chinese OFDI might be influenced by different factors over time, we consider separately results for the full sample for the periods 1991 to 1998 (column 2) and 1999 to 2003 (column 3). To see if the determinants of Chinese OFDI vary with the level of development of the host country, we then examine results separately depending on the OECD membership status of the host country, namely members (columns 4–6) and non-members (columns 7–9). Again, since changes in the determinants of Chinese OFDI over time may differ depending on the development level of the host country, we re-apply the temporal structural break at the year 1999 to OECD (columns 5 and 6) and non-OECD (columns 8 and 9) countries separately and compare findings.

7.5.1   Findings for the Full Time Period and All Countries (column 1)

The following main independent variables were significant and had coefficients of the expected sign, namely relative market size (LGDPPC); WTO membership status of the host country (WTO); and cultural proximity (CP). Thus, we find support for Hypotheses H1, H7 and H8.

Chinese TNCs are revealed to invest preferentially in countries that register relatively low GDP per capita levels; that is, they invest in other developing countries. One interpretation is that market-seeking Chinese firms seek investment opportunities in countries that are at a similar stage of development to China and where they enjoy a competitive advantage over local and foreign firms, perhaps as a consequence of home-country embeddedness (that is, their prior experience of operating in a developing country context gained in China). This finding contrasts with that of Cross *et al.* (2007), who reported no significance for this variable. However, it is in line with the body of literature that asserts that developing country TNCs tend to invest preferentially in other developing countries (for example, Lall 1983; Lecraw 1977; Monkiewicz 1986). We also find some support for the importance of both formal and informal exogenous supranational elements of the Chinese OFDI regime. Of the formal element, we find that host country membership of the WTO is positively associated with greater inflows of Chinese OFDI. This we attribute in part to the locational advantages derived from compliance of a host country with international trade and investment rules and frameworks that are attractive to Chinese TNCs. Market-seeking Chinese firms that engage in export-platform FDI to serve third markets may also benefit from tariff reductions and GATT-imposed trade regimes by investing in a WTO member state. We also find some support for the role played by one aspect of the informal exogenous element of the Chinese OFDI regime, namely cultural proximity. This substitutes for the existence of business and social networks (*guanxi* relationships). The presence of an appreciable Chinese population in a host country is positively associated with inbound Chinese OFDI flows. This suggests strongly that relational assets are important to the transnationalization of Chinese firms. This is a robust finding for studies of this type. For example, Buckley *et al.* (2007) also reported a positive association between cultural proximity and Chinese OFDI in their full model (1984–2001) and various sub-periods they examined (divided at 1991). Given that Chinese TNCs in the period under study were almost entirely state-owned, this finding might be regarded as surprising. However, it is clear from this and other studies that relational assets are an enduring source of competitive advantage for Chinese firms. This provides partial support for the conclusions drawn on this issue made in previous work on Chinese firms (for example, Dunning 2002; Erdener and Shapiro 2005).

The time dummy for our measure of the formal endogenous element of the Chinese OFDI regime, namely policy change in 1994 (TD94) (relaxation of foreign currency controls by SAFE), is statistically significant but with a sign contrary to expectation. Thus, Hypothesis 4 is not confirmed. Chinese OFDI is negatively associated with the liberalization of foreign exchange controls in 1994. This result is surprising but may provide some evidence of an idiosyncratic approach to decision making on international business matters by Chinese TNCs. Buckley *et al.* (2007) offered persuasive evidence that Chinese TNCs demonstrate a perverse attitude toward risk (by comparison to industrialized country firms) in that they reveal a propensity to invest in higher risk countries (as measured using a country risk index developed in the west). The authors related this phenomenon to capital market imperfections enjoyed by Chinese TNCs. One interpretation for the reduction in Chinese OFDI after 1994 is that foreign exchange liberalization provided Chinese firms with greater access to hard currencies from domestic sources, and this reduced the need to invest abroad. However, further research on this point is required.

Of the remaining main variables, we find no significant relationship between Chinese OFDI and the following motivation- and institution-related variables: the host country's exports of oil and NLG (LOIL); patents granted (LPATENT); the conclusion of a BIT or a DTT with China (BIT and DTT respectively); the signaling effect of total BITs and DTTs concluded by a country (LACBIT and LACDTT respectively); and geographic distance from Beijing. Thus, hypotheses H2, H3, H5a, H5b, H6a, H6b and H9 are not supported.

With respect to the FDI motivations of Chinese firms, we find no evidence to support either natural resource-seeking or asset-seeking behavior of Chinese TNCs. In the case of strategic-asset seeking FDI, our finding concurs with that of Buckley *et al.* (2007) and supports the view that Chinese TNCs have only recently begun their international quest for improved access to foreign-held knowledge, technology and skills (see also Buckley *et al.* 2006). Our finding that the proxy for natural resource FDI is insignificant contrasts with that of Buckley *et al.* (2006, 2007), who found a positive and significant effect for resource endowments for the latter period under consideration (1992–2001) in both of their studies, and when confined to developed-country markets only in their third study (2007a). However, we note that these studies employed a different measure of host country resources endowments (namely metals and minerals exports) than that used here. Our finding offers support for the contention of Ma and Andrew-Speed (2006) that the internationalization of Chinese oil companies was at an infancy stage in the mid-1990s.

With respect to the Chinese OFDI regime-related variables, we find no evidence to support the view that formal supranational agreements have influenced the volume and direction of Chinese OFDI. By itself, this does not necessarily discount the fact that the institutional regime has an effect, but rather that Chinese firms may have responded to the OFDI facilitation characteristics associated with supranational agreements in an idiosyncratic way. In other words, Chinese firms may not place much importance on the investment and financial risk-reducing features of international treaties such as BITs and DTTs. There are a number of explanations. One is that capital market imperfections in China, identified as an important determinant of investment behavior for Chinese TNCs as we discuss above (Buckley *et al.* 2007), give rise to perverse attitudes toward risk and profit maximization. Simply, the benefits of international trade and investment agreements may be irrelevant to, or are disregarded by Chinese TNCs. Second, the Government of China might conclude BITs as a sign of friendship and political support for the host countries in question, but this does little to attract Chinese TNCs. Third, and in similar vein, although such treaties may nominally be bilateral, in effect they may be concluded more to provide greater access to and protection of foreign investment in China rather than of Chinese FDI elsewhere.

Finally, our finding for geographic distance is also not significant for the full sample. Again, this is in contrast to the work of Buckley *et al.* (2007) and Cross *et al.* (2007), who reported a significant and negative association between distance and Chinese OFDI volumes.

With respect to our control variables, we find statistically significant results and positive coefficients for exchange rate (LERATE), China's exports (LEXP), China's imports (LIMP) and openness to FDI (LINFDI). Also, there is a significant result and a negative coefficient for host country inflation rates (LINF). Thus, hypotheses H12, H13, H14, H15 and H16 are confirmed. Hypothesis 10 concerning host country risk (LRISK) is not confirmed.

7.5.2 Findings for the Time Period 1991 to 1998 and All Countries (column 2)

We now examine whether or not the introduction of a structural break has any effect on these key findings. For the period 1991 to 1998 (before the 'Go Global' policy was introduced) we find no change in our results for market-seeking FDI behavior (H1), the time dummy for 1994 (H4) and cultural proximity (H8). Thus, Hypotheses H1, H4 and H8 are supported for this time period. However, we find that the result for WTO membership (H7) is no longer significant. By contrast, geographic distance now attains significance and has a positive coefficient. This provides support for Hypothesis H9, but only in the earlier years of Chinese firms' transnationalization. These findings suggest that some aspects of the transnationalization of Chinese firms are predictable by general theory, which asserts that firms substitute FDI for exports when serving more distant markets (Buckley and Casson 1981). Of the control variables, we find that the measures for China's imports (LIMP) and market openness (LINFDI) lose their significance, but that the other variables continue to be significant.

7.5.3 Findings for the Time Period 1999 to 2003 and All Countries (column 3)

For the second time period (1999 to 2003), we also detect a number of differences compared to our main findings. In particular, the coefficient for crude oil and NLG exports (LOIL) is now significant and positive. We therefore find support for H2, but only for the latter time period. This lends further weight to the contention of Ma and Andrews-Speed (2006) that the transnationalization of Chinese oil companies accelerated only in the late 1990s. In contrast, our measures of cultural proximity (CP) and geographic distance (LDIS) lose their significance, as do the control variables of exchange rate (LERATE) and inflation (LINF). Viewed together, the findings for cultural proximity across the two sub-periods may reflect growing confidence in the ability of state-owned firms to conduct international business independently of local ethnic and social business networks. However, the advantages of cultural proximity may become significant again in the future, as greater amounts of Chinese FDI are accounted for by private, and not state-owned, Chinese TNCs. (We note that the contribution of private TNCs to total Chinese OFDI is likely to have increased since 2003 when the Chinese OFDI regime was liberalized to allow for FDI to be conducted legally by such firms). Our finding for geographic distance may reflect a wider spatial distribution of Chinese OFDI in more recent years (see also Table A7.1). This might be in response to Government policy (Buckley *et al.* 2006) or to greater influence of market forces and discretionary decision making by Chinese TNCs. Further work on this issue is required. We now turn to key differences between our main findings and those for various sub-samples of our data set.

7.5.4 Findings for the Full Time Period and Split by OECD and Non-OECD Countries (columns 4 and 7)

In order to assess whether or not the level of development of a host country influences our findings, the model was run separately for OECD and non-OECD countries. We find continued support for H1 (relative market size, LGDPPC), but only for the non-OECD country sub-sample. We no longer find support for H7 (WTO membership) or H8 (cultural proximity) when individual country sub-samples are considered. This suggests that there is greater variance for these two variables between rather than within country groupings. The measure we use to test H4 (the policy time dummy TD94) continues to be significant and is positively signed, but only for the OECD country sub-sample; we find no support for H4 when the non-OECD country sub-sample is examined separately. We do find, however, that the variable LPATENT attains significance for the non-OECD countries alone, but with a negatively signed coefficient, contrary to expectation for the full sample. This is our proxy to capture the strategic asset-seeking behavior of Chinese TNCs under H3. This finding reveals a propensity for Chinese

TNCs to invest in countries with relatively lower technology asset stocks, but only when non-OECD countries are concerned. This may reflect improved competitiveness of Chinese TNCs in such contexts, as well as complementarities between their offering and local demand conditions. Of our control variables, we find that Chinese FDI in the OECD countries is statistically significant and positively associated with purchasing power parity (PPP), exchange rate (LERATE), trade intensity (LEXP and LIMP), and openness to inward investment (LINFDI). Thus, we find support for Hypotheses H11, H12, H14, H15 and H16. We find no support for H10 (LRISU). With the exception of our finding for PPP, the results for the OECD country sub-sample mirror those for the full sample, as do our results for the control variables for non-OECD countries. Our measures of the level of trade intensity with the host country (LEXP and LIMP) and openness to inward investment of the host country (LINFDI) are statistically significant and positively related to Chinese OFDI. Again, Hypotheses H14, H15 and H16 are supported.

7.5.5 Findings for OECD Countries for the Two Sub-Periods (columns 5 and 6)

When we re-invoke the structural break for 1999 for the OECD countries alone, we find that our measure of the resources endowments of the host country (LOIL) attains significance for the later but not the earlier sub-period, and has the expected sign. Thus, we find evidence to support H2 for OECD countries, but only for more recent years. This finding seems to capture the growth in natural resource-seeking behavior by Chinese TNCs observed in the full sample (Ma and Andrews-Speed 2006), which is increasingly being directed to the industrialized countries. Similarly, our finding for LPATENT in the earlier period (1991–1998), which is significant and positively signed (as expected), provides the only support for H3 in our model. This finding indicates that Chinese TNCs have been attracted to countries with higher levels of technology stocks, but only when that country is an industrialized country and only in the earlier period of international expansion of Chinese OFDI under study. This finding is at odds with some aspects of the received wisdom concerning the transnationalization of Chinese firms in the 1990s, which indicates that information gathering and support of the export process historically were key drivers for Chinese OFDI and that technology-seeking motivations have only become significant in more recent years. Examination of the sub-time periods for OECD countries also reveals the statistical significance of LACBIT, one of our measures of the formal, exogenous component of the Chinese OFDI regime, which only attains significance for the period

1991–1998. However, the negative sign on the coefficient is contrary to expectation. This finding reveals that Chinese TNCs tend to invest preferentially in OECD countries that have concluded fewer BITs. One interpretation is that the decision-making of Chinese TNCs is unaffected by the positive signaling effects associated with the conclusion of BITs by host countries.

7.5.6   Findings for Non-OECD Countries for the Two Sub-Periods (columns 8 and 9)

When we re-invoke the structural break for 1998 for the non-OECD countries, we find that, as for the full sample, our measures of cultural proximity (CP) and geographic distance (LDIS) are significant and with the expected sign, but for the earlier period (1991–1998) only. This provides support for H8 and H9, and therefore for the informal, exogenous institutional component of the framework, but only for developing host countries and in the early years of Chinese OFDI expansion. We note that our findings for LGDPPC is unchanged across both time periods for non-OECD countries. This indicates that market-seeking behavior by Chinese TNCs is a key determinant of Chinese FDI in less-developed countries for the full period under study.

CONCLUSION

In this chapter, we address a gap in the literature by presenting a conceptual framework that models the institutional environment within which international investment decision making by Chinese TNCs occurs. This framework provides a major extension to previous research on Chinese TNCs, which generally focuses on the underlying motivations of OFDI. Like Buckley *et al.* (2007) and Cross *et al.* (2007), we find that Chinese OFDI has both a general and an idiosyncratic nature.

Our analysis of investment motivations and the potential influence of endogenous and exogenous institutional factors on the decision making of Chinese TNCs yields a number of interesting findings. As with other studies, we find that general market-seeking motives underpin much Chinese investment behavior, but that this is associated with investment in developing rather than developed countries over the period under investigation. This finding suggests that home-country embeddedness is at least part of the story and that Chinese firms may be able to exploit in other developing countries their ability to cope with challenging conditions at home. We find that natural resource-seeking motives are also important, but only for Chinese OFDI that occurred in the later time period investigated (1999 to 2003) for both the full country sample and the developed country sub-sample. This is likely to be a consequence of government policy on energy security and increased domestic demand. We find that strategic asset-seeking FDI by Chinese companies has occurred in the OECD countries, as one might expect, but that this is associated only with the period 1991 to 1998, somewhat earlier than previous research suggests. It may reflect government-induced investment by state-owned enterprises for asset-augmenting purposes.

With regard to our Chinese OFDI regime framework, we find only partial support for the notion that formal and informal, endogenous and exogenous elements have had determinant effects on the investment behavior of Chinese TNCs. With respect to the endogenous components and contrary to expectation, we find that foreign exchange policy liberalization in 1994 (one formal endogenous institutional factor) had a negative effect on Chinese OFDI for the full country sample and most sub-samples. The second formal endogenous institutional factor in our model is the 'Go Global' policy introduced in 1999. We find that two variables that attained significance before its introduction lose this significance afterwards, namely cultural proximity and geographical distance. We therefore find support for the inclusion of this institutional factor in our Chinese OFDI regime framework.

We also find mixed results for the exogenous factors of the Chinese OFDI regime framework. Cultural proximity (an informal exogenous factor), host country membership of the WTO (a formal exogenous factor) and geographical distance are important determinants for the full sample, again lending support for their inclusion in our framework. However, this significance is mostly lost when various sub-samples of the data set are analyzed (with the exception of cultural proximity and geographical distance for non-OECD countries in the sub-period 1991 to 1998). Our finding for cultural proximity provides further confirmation of the importance of lower information costs, transaction costs and perceptions of risk for Chinese TNCs that derive from the presence of a significant ethnic Chinese population in the host country, as revealed previously by Buckley *et al.* (2007). So far as we are aware, our finding concerning the role of WTO membership in shaping Chinese OFDI is previously unreported, and may reflect the response of Chinese firms to the enhanced trade and investment conditions of member countries.

We find that other formal exogenous components of the Chinese OFDI regime framework, namely the number of BITs and DTTs concluded between host countries and China, and in total have little measurable effect on the decision making of Chinese TNCs. One interpretation is that domestic capital market imperfections cause Chinese firms to dismiss or discount the advantages that such agreements and treaties bring. Another explanation is that other location-specific factors (such as demand conditions, factor input costs or infrastructure quality) exert greater effect on the decision making of Chinese firms than do supranational arrangements with a host country. It may also be the case that Chinese companies are simply unaware of the existence and potential benefits of such agreements, an argument that has been advanced by the World Bank (2005) for developing country TNCs in general. Our findings lend some weight, therefore, to the argument that BITs and DTTs serve little to promote FDI outflows from developing countries or enhance their locational advantages (Hallward-Driemeier 2003). Clearly, however, more fine-grained research is needed to assess fully the effect of this particular aspect of a country's OFDI regime on outward investment trends.

In sum, our broad finding that the OFDI regime of China has had only a modest detectable effect on patterns of Chinese OFDI (when viewed in aggregate) is perhaps somewhat paradoxical given the high levels of Government engagement that is reported in numerous other studies (for example, Buckley *et al.* 2006; Sauvant 2005; Zhang 2003; Zweig and Bi 2005). However, the majority of this work relies on case studies and descriptive analysis of Chinese OFDI trends. An interesting research agenda is now emerging on the extent to which the transnationalization decisions of Chinese firms have been, and continue to be, influenced by the intervention of government and its agencies. Future work should employ more carefully crafted measures of those formal and informal, endogenous and exogenous elements of the Chinese OFDI regime we identify here, as well as broadening its scope, in order to account more fully for the nuances and changes in those policies, rules, attitudes and norms that it comprises. The OFDI regime framework we develop here should also be extended to other countries, generating the potential for comparative work. This would further refine our understanding of how the institutional framework of countries impacts on the outward investment decisions of domestic firms.

ACKNOWLEDGEMENTS

The authors would like to thank James X. Zhan and Amare Bekele, both of UNCTAD, for their very supportive work and Leeds University Business School for its administrative assistance.

NOTES

1. In this study and in related work (for example, Buckley *et al.* 2007a, 2007b), the terms 'China' and 'Mainland China' are used interchangeably to refer to the People's Republic of China (PRC). For our purposes, the PRC excludes the special autonomous regions of Hong Kong (China) and Macau unless specifically stated. Taiwan Province of China is treated as a separate economy. All our statistics and figures respect these distinctions. Regions with disputed borders (for example, the Spratly Islands) are excluded from our definition of the PRC, as are associated economic activities.
2. See Liew (2004) for an extensive survey of China's ensnared foreign exchange rate policy making.
3. China's foreign exchange reserves stood at nearly US$ 1000 billion in September 2006, the largest in the world (McGregor 2006).
4. However, it is also important to recognize that the importance of social and ethnic networks may vary depending on the governance structure of the Chinese firm.
5. www.geobytes.com/citydistancetool.htm

REFERENCES

Aharoni, Yair (1999). 'The foreign investment process', in Peter J. Buckley and Pervez N. Ghauri, eds, *The Internationalization of the Firm: A Reader* (2nd ed., London: International Thomson Business), pp. 3–13.

Barabantseva, Elena (2005). 'Trans-nationalising Chineseness: overseas Chinese policies of the PRC's Central Government', *Asien*, 96, pp. 7–28.

Bartlett, Christopher A. and Sumantra Ghoshal (2000). 'Going global: lessons from late movers', *Harvard Business Review*, 78, pp. 132–142.

Beebe, Alan (2006). 'Going global: prospects and challenges for Chinese companies on the world stage', *IBM Business Consulting Services* (Beijing: IBM Institute for Business Value).

Blonigen, Bruce A. and Ronald B. Davies (2004). 'The effects of bilateral tax treaties on U.S. FDI activity', International Tax and Public Finance, 11, pp. 601–622.

Braeutigam, Deborah (2003). 'Close encounters: Chinese business networks as industrial catalysts in sub-Saharan Africa', *African Affairs*, 102, pp. 447–467.

Brewer, Thomas L. (1993). 'Government policies, market imperfections, and foreign direct investments', *Journal of International Business Studies*, 24(1), pp. 101–120.

Buckley, Peter J. and Mark C. Casson (1976). *The Future of the Multinational Enterprise* (Houndsmill: Palgrave).

Buckley, Peter J. and Mark C. Casson (1981). 'The optimal timing of a foreign direct investment', *Economic Journal*, 91, pp. 75–87.

Buckley, Peter J. and Mark C. Casson (1999). 'A theory of international operations', in Peter J. Buckley and Pervez N. Ghauri, eds, *The Internationalization Process of the Firm: A Reader* (2nd ed., London: International Business Thomson), pp. 55–60.

Buckley, Peter J., Adam R. Cross, Hui Tan, Xin Liu and Hinrich Voss (2006). *An Examination of Recent Trends in China's OFDI Position*, CIBUL Working Paper (Leeds: University of Leeds, CIBUL), mimeo.

Buckley, Peter J., L.J. Clagg, A.R. Cross, Xin Liu, H. Voss and Ping Zheng (2007). 'The determinants of Chinese outward foreign direct investment', *Journal of International Business Studies*, 38(4), pp. 499–518.

Buckley, Peter J. and Hafiz Mirza (1999). 'The strategy of Pacific Asian multi-nationals', in Peter J. Buckley and Pervez N. Ghauri, eds, *The Global Challenge for Multinational Enterprises: Managing Increasing Interdependence* (Amsterdam: Pergamon), pp. 318–338.

Casson, Mark C. (1997). 'Entrepreneurial networks in international business', *Business and Economic History*, 26, pp. 811–823.

Chakrabarti, Avik (2001). 'The determinants of foreign direct investment: sensitivity analysis of cross-country regressions', *Kyklos*, 54, pp. 89–114.

Chen, Homin and Tain-Jy Chen (1998). 'Network linkages and location choice in foreign direct investment', *Journal of International Business Studies*, 29, pp. 445–468.

Chen, Tain-Jy (2003). 'Network resources for internationalization: the case of Taiwan's electronics firms', *Journal of Management Studies*, 40, pp. 1107–1130.

Child, John and Suzana B. Rodrigues (2005). 'The internationalization of Chinese firms: a case for theoretical extension?' *Management and Organization Review*, 1, pp. 381–410.

Cho, Dong-Sung, Dong-Jae Kim and Dong Kee Rhee (1998). 'Latecomer strategies: evidence from the semiconductor industry in Japan and Korea', *Organization Science*, 9, pp. 489–506.

Clegg, L. Jeremy and Susan Scott-Green (1999). 'The determinants of new FDI capital flows into the EC: a statistical comparison of the USA and Japan', *Journal of Common Market Studies*, 37, pp. 597–616.

Cross, Adam R., Peter J. Buckley, L. Jeremy Clegg, Hinrich Voss, Mark Rhodes, Ping Zheng and Xin Liu (2007). 'An econometric investigation of Chinese OFDI', in John H. Dunning and Tsai-Mei Lin, eds, *Multinational Enterprises and Challenges in the 21st Century* (Cheltenham, UK and Northampton, MA, USA: Edward Elgar).

Davies, Ronald B. (2004). 'Tax treaties and foreign direct investment: potential versus performance', *International Tax and Public Finance*, 11, pp. 775–802.

Deng, Ping (2003). 'Foreign direct investment by transnationals from emerging countries: the case of China', *Journal of Leadership and Organizational Studies*, 10(2), pp. 113–124.

Deng, Ping (2004). 'Outward investment by Chinese MNCs: motivations and implications', *Business Horizons*, 47, pp. 8–16.

Deng, Ping (2007). 'Investing for strategic resources and its rationale: the case of outward FDI from Chinese companies', *Business Horizons*, 50, pp. 71–81.

Deutsche Bank Research (2006a). 'Global champions in waiting: perspectives on China's overseas direct investment', *Deutsche Bank Research China Special*, 4 August.

Deutsche Bank Research (2006b). 'China's commodity hunger: implications for Africa and Latin America', *Deutsche Bank Research China Special*, 13 June.

Dunning, John H. (1977). 'Trade, location of economic activity and the TNC: a search for an eclectic approach', in B. Ohlin, P.O. Hesselborn and P.M. Wijkmon, eds, *The International Location of Economic Activity* (London: Macmillan), pp. 395–418.

Dunning, John H. (1993). *Multinational Enterprises and the Global Economy* (Boston MA: Addison Wesley).

Dunning, John H. (2001). 'The eclectic (OLI) paradigm of international production: past, present and future', *International Journal of the Economics of Business*, 8, pp. 173–190.

Dunning, John H. (2002). 'Relational assets, networks, and international business activities', in Farok J. Contractor and Peter Lorange, eds, *Cooperative Strategies and Alliances* (Amsterdam: Pergamon), pp. 569–593.

Dunning, John H., Roger van Hoesel and Rajneesh Narula (1998). 'Third World multinationals revisited: new developments and theoretical implications', in John H. Dunning, ed., *Globalization, Trade, and Foreign Direct Investment* (Amsterdam and Oxford: Elsevier), pp. 255–285.

Egger, Peter, M. Larch, M. Pfaffermayr and H. Winner (2006). 'The impact of endogenous tax treaties on foreign direct investment: theory and evidence', *Canadian Journal of Economics/Revue Canadienne d'Economique*, 39, pp. 901–931.

Egger, Peter and Michael Pfaffermayr (2004). 'The impact of bilateral investment treaties on foreign direct investment', *Journal of Comparative Economics*, 32, pp. 788–804.

Erdener, Carolyn and Daniel M. Shapiro (2005). 'The internationalization of Chinese family enterprises and Dunning's eclectic TNC paradigm', *Management and Organization Review*, 1, pp. 411–436.

Financial Times (2006). 'Friend or forager? How China is winning the resources and the loyalties of Africa', *Financial Times*, 23 February, p. 15.

Ghymn, Kyung-il (1980). 'Multinational enterprises from the Third World', *Journal of International Business Studies*, 11, pp. 118–122.

Ginsberg, Tom (2005). 'International substitutes for domestic institutions: bilateral investment treaties and governance', *International Review of Law and Economics*, 25, pp. 107–123.

Grosse, Robert and Len J. Trevino (2005). 'New institutional economics and FDI location in Central and Eastern Europe', *Management International Review*, 45, pp. 123–145.

Guo, Hanbin (1984). 'On establishment of joint ventures abroad', in *Almanac of China's Foreign Economic Relations and Trade* (Beijing: Ministry of Commerce [MOFCOM]), pp. 652–654.

Hall, Thomas (2004). 'Controlling for risk: an analysis of China's system of foreign exchange and exchange rate management', *Columbia Journal of Asian Law*, 17, pp. 433–481.

Hallward-Driemeier, Mary (2003). *Do Bilateral Investment Treaties Attract FDI? Only a Bit. . . and They Could Bite*, World Bank Policy Research Paper WPS 3121 (Washington DC: World Bank), mimeo.

Henley, John, Colin Kirkpatrick and Georgina Wilde (1999). 'Foreign direct investment in China: recent trends and current policy issues', *The World Economy*, 22, pp. 223–243.

Hymer, Stephen H. (1960). *The International Operations of National Firms: A Study of Direct Foreign Investment* (unpublished PhD thesis, MIT).

Hymer, Stephen H. (1976). *The International Operations of National Firms: a Study of Direct Foreign Investment* (Cambridge, MA: MIT Press).

International Energy Agency (IEA) (2006). *Oil Information 2006* (with 2005 data), ESDS International, (MIMAS) University of Manchester.

International Monetary Fund (IMF) (2005). *World Economic Outlook Database*, *available at* http://www.imf.org/external/pubs/ft/weo/2005/01/data/dbcsubm.cfm (last visited 26 September 2006).

Johanson, Jan and Jan-Erik Vahlne (2003). 'Business relationship learning and commitment in the internationalisation process', *Journal of International Entrepreneurship*, 1, pp. 83–101.

Johanson, Jan and Jan-Erik Vahlne (2006). 'Commitment and opportunity development in the internationalization process: a note on the Uppsala Internationalization Process Model', *Management International Review*, 46, pp. 165–178.

Jubany, F. and D. Poon (2006). 'China and Latin America: historic opportunity', *Latin Business Chronicle*, 1 March, available at www.latinbusinesschronicle.com/app/article.aspx?id=224, (last visited 14 September 2006).

Kent, Robert B. (2003). 'A diaspora of Chinese settlement in Latin America and the Caribbean', in Laurence J.C. Ma and Carolyn Cartier, eds, *The Chinese Diaspora: Space, Place, Mobility, and Identity* (Lanham: Rowman and Littlefield), pp. 117–138.

Kohlhagen, Stephen W. (1977). 'The effects of exchange-rate adjustments on international investment: comment', in Peter B. Clark, Dennis E. Logue and Richard Sweeney, eds, *The Effects of Exchange Rate Adjustments* (Washington DC: US Government Printing Office), pp. 194–197.

Kumar, Krishna and Kee Y. Kim (1984). 'The Korean manufacturing multinationals', *Journal of International Business Studies*, 15, pp. 45–61.

Lall, Sanjaya (1983). 'The rise of multinationals from the Third World', *Third World Quarterly*, 5, pp. 618–626.

Lall, Sanjaya (1991). 'Asia's emerging sources of foreign investment: Hong Kong, Singapore, Taiwan, Korea', *East Asian Executive Reports*, 13, pp. 7–25.

Latin Business Chronicle (2006). 'China Doubles Latin FDI', *Latin Business Chronicle*, 24 April.

Lau, Ho-Fuk (2003). 'Industry evolution and internationalization processes of firms from a newly industrialized economy', *Journal of Business Research*, 56, pp. 847–852.

Lecraw, Donald J. (1977). 'Direct investment by firms from less developed countries', *Oxford Economic Papers*, 29, pp. 442–457.

Lee, Ji-Ren and Jen-Shyang Chen (2003). 'Internationalization, local adaptation, and subsidiary's entrepreneurship: an exploratory study on Taiwanese manufacturing firms in Indonesia and Malaysia', *Asia Pacific Journal of Management*, 20, pp. 51–72.

Li, Peter P. (2003). 'Toward a geocentric theory of multinational evolution: the implications from the Asian TNCs as latecomers', *Asia Pacific Journal of Management*, 20, pp. 217–242.

Liew, Leong H. (2004). 'Policy elites in the political economy of China's exchange rate policymaking', *Journal of Contemporary China*, 13, pp. 21–51.

Lin, Guijun and Ronald M. Schramm (2004). 'China's progression toward currency convertibility', *The Chinese Economy*, 37, pp. 78–100.

Liu, Xiaohui, Trevor Buck and Chang Shu (2005). 'Chinese economic development, next stage: outward FDI?' *International Business Review*, 14, pp. 97–115.

Liu, Xin (2007). *The Outward Direct Investment Strategies of Chinese Firms* (unpublished PhD thesis, University of Leeds).

Logue, Dennis E. and Thomas D. Willet (1977). 'The effects of exchange-rate adjustments on international investment', in Peter B. Clark, Dennis E. Logue and Richard Sweeney, eds, *The Effects of Exchange Rate Adjustments* (Washington DC: US Government Printing Office), pp. 137–150.

Lu, T. (2002). *The International Corporation of Chinese MNCs: An Empirical Study on Chinese MNCs in UK* (Beijing: The People's Press), in Chinese.

Luo, Yadong (1997). 'Guanxi: principles, philosophies, and implications', *Human Systems Management*, 16(1), pp. 43–51.

Ma, Laurence J.C. (2003). 'Space, place, and transnationalism in the Chinese diaspora', in Laurence J.C. Ma and Carolyn Cartier, eds, *The Chinese Diaspora: Space, Place, Mobility, and Identity* (Lanham: Rowman and Littlefield), pp. 1–4.

Ma, Xin and Philip Andrew-Speed (2006). 'The overseas activities of China's national oil companies: rationale and outlook', *Minerals and Energy*, 21, pp. 17–30.

Makino, Shige, Chung-Ming Lau and Rhy-Song Leh (2002). 'Asset-exploitation versus asset-seeking: implications for location choice of foreign direct investment from newly industrialized economies', *Journal of International Business Studies*, 33, pp. 403–422.

Mallampally, P. and Karl P. Sauvant (1999). 'Foreign direct investment in developing countries', *Finance and Development*, 36, available at www.imf.org/external/pubs/ft/fandd/1999/03/mallampa.htm (last visited 3 October 2006).

Markusen, Ann (2003). 'Fuzzy concepts, scanty evidence, policy distance: the case for rigour and policy relevance in critical regional studies', *Regional Studies*, 37, pp. 701–717.

Mathews, John (2006). 'Dragon multinationals: new players in 21st century globalization', *Asia Pacific Journal of Management*, 23, pp. 5–27.

McGregor, Richard (2006). 'The trillion dollar question: China is grappling with how to deploy its foreign exchange riches', *Financial Times*, 25 September, p. 15.

Meyer, Klaus E. (2004). 'Perspectives on multinational enterprises in emerging economies', *Journal of International Business Studies*, 35(4), pp. 259–277.

MOFCOM (2006). 'Statistical Bulletin on Direct Overseas Investment of China 2005 jointly issued by MOFCOM and NBS', 6 September, available at http://english.mofcom.gov.cn/aarticle/newsrelease/significantnews/200609/20060903072019.html, (last visited 2 October 2006).

Monkiewicz, Jan (1986). 'Multinational enterprises of developing countries: some emerging characteristics', *Management International Review*, 26, pp. 67–79.

Neumayer, Eric and Laura Spess (2005). 'Do bilateral investment treaties increase foreign direct investment to developing countries?' *World Development*, 33, pp. 1567–1585.

Ng, Linda F.Y. and Chyau Tuan (2002). 'Building a favourable investment environment: evidence for the facilitation of FDI in China', *The World Economy*, 25, pp. 1095–1114.

North, Douglass C. (1990). *Institutions, Institutional Change and Economic Performance* (Cambridge: Cambridge University Press).

Ohio University (2006). *Distribution of the Ethnic Chinese Population Around the World*, (University Libraries, Ohio University) available at http://cicdatabank.library. ohiou.edu/opac/population.php, (last visited 17 May 2006).

Oviatt, Benjamin M. and Patricia P. McDougall (2005). 'Defining international entrepreneurship and modeling the speed of internationalization', *Entrepreneurship Theory and Practice*, 29, pp. 537–553.

Pei, Chang-Hong and Lei Wang (2001). 'Chinese corporate investment in the United States', *China and World Economy*, 5, pp. 17–22.

Peng, Mike W. (2002). 'Towards an institution-based view of business strategy', *Asia Pacific Journal of Management*, 19, pp. 251–267.

Political Risk Services (PRS) (2005). *International Country Risk Guide (ICRG)*, available at www.prsgroup.com/icrg/icrg.html, (by subscription, last visited April 2005).

Ramamurti, Ravi (2001). ' "The obsolescing bargaining model?" MNC-host developing country relations revisited', *Journal of International Business Studies*, 32, pp. 23–39.

Overseas Chinese Affairs Commission (2005). *Huaqiao Jingji Nianjian* (Overseas Chinese Economy Yearbook), (Taipei: Committee for Overseas Chinese Affairs).

Roberts, Ivan and Rod Tyers (2003). 'China's exchange rate policy: the case for greater flexibility', *Asian Economic Journal*, 17, pp. 155–184.

Rugman, Alan M. (1999). 'Forty years of the theory of the transnational corporation', *Transnational Corporations*, 8, pp. 51–70.

Salacuse, Jeswald W. and Nicholas P. Sullivan (2005). 'Do BITs really work? An evaluation of bilateral investment treaties and their grand bargain', *Harvard International Law Journal*, 46, pp. 67–130.

Sauvant, Karl P. (2005). 'New sources of FDI: the BRICs. Outward FDI from Brazil, Russia, India and China', *Journal of World Investment and Trade*, 6, pp. 639–709.

Scott, W. Richard (2002). 'The changing world of Chinese enterprises: an institutional perspective', in Anne S. Tsui and Chung-Ming Lau, eds, *Management of Enterprises in the People's Republic of China* (Boston MA: Kluwer Academic Press), pp. 59–78.

Shenkar, Oded and Yadong Luo (2004). *International Business* (Hoboken, NJ: John Wiley and Sons).

Sigurdson, Jon (2005). *Technological Superpower China* (Cheltenham, UK: Edward Elgar).

Sim, Ah Ba (2006). 'Internationalization strategies of emerging Asian TNCs: case study evidence on Singaporean and Malaysian firms', *Asia Pacific Business Review*, 12, pp. 487–505.

Sim, Ah Ba and J. Rajendran Pandian (2002). 'Internationalization strategies of emerging Asian TNCs: cases study evidence on Taiwanese firms', *Journal of Asian Business*, 18(1), pp. 67–80.

Standifird, Stephen S. and Scott R. Marshall (2000). 'The transaction cost advantage of guanxi-based business practices', *Journal of World Business*, 35, pp. 21–42.

Stevens, Guy V.G. (1993). *Exchange Rates and Foreign Direct Investment: A Note*, International Finance Discussion Papers, No. 444 (Washington DC: Board of Governors of the Federal Reserve System).

Sung, Yun-Wing (1996). *Chinese Outward Investment in Hong Kong: Trends, Prospects and Policy Implications*, OECD Development Centre Technical Papers No 113 (Paris: OECD), mimeo.

Tallman, Stephen B. and Oded Shenkar (1990). 'International cooperative venture strategies: outward investment and small firms from NICs', *Management International Review*, 30 (Fourth Quarter), pp. 299–315.

Taylor, Robert (2002). 'Globalization strategies of Chinese companies: current developments and future prospects', *Asian Business and Management*, 1, pp. 209–225.

Tobin, Jennifer and Susan Rose-Ackerman (2005). *Foreign Direct Investment and the Business Environment in Developing Countries: The Impact of Bilateral Investment Treaties*, Economics and Public Policy Research Paper No. 293 (Yale Law School), mimeo.

Tong, Sarah Y. (2003). *Ethnic Chinese Networking in Cross-Border Investment: The Impact of Economic and Institutional Development*, HIEBS Working Paper

No. 1024 (Hong Kong: Hong Kong Institute of Economics and Business Strategy), mimeo.

Ulgado, Francis M., Chwo-Ming J. Yu and Anant R. Negandhi (1994). 'Multinational enterprises from Asian developing countries: management and organizational characteristics', *International Business Review*, 3, pp. 123–133.

UNCTAD (2000). *Bilateral Investment Treaties 1959–1999* (New York and Geneva: United Nations).

UNCTAD (2003). World Investment Report 2003: FDI Policies for Development – National and International Perspectives (New York and Geneva: United Nations).

UNCTAD (2005a). *World Investment Report 2005: Transnational Corporations and the Internationalization of R&D* (New York and Geneva: United Nations).

UNCTAD (2005b). *South-South Cooperation in International Investment Arrangements* (New York and Geneva: United Nations).

UNCTAD (2006). *FDI/TNC Database*, available at http://stats.unctad.org/fdi (last visited 1 October 2006).

UNIDO (2006). Africa Foreign Investor Survey 2005: Understanding the Contribution of Different Investor Categories to Development – Implications for Targeting Strategies (Vienna: United Nations Industrial Development Organisation).

van Hoesel, Roger (1997). 'The emergence of Korean and Taiwanese multinationals in Europe: prospects and limitations', *Asia Pacific Business Review*, 4, pp. 109–129.

Vandervelde, Kenneth J. (1998). 'The political economy of a bilateral investment treaty', *The American Journal of International Law*, 92, pp. 621–641.

Voss, Hinrich (2007). *The foreign direct investment behaviour of Chinese firms: does the 'new institutional theory' approach offer explanatory power?* (unpublished PhD thesis, University of Leeds).

Wang, H. (2001). 'Implementing vigorously the opening strategy of "going global"', in *Almanac of China's Foreign Economic Relations and Trade 2001* (Beijing: MOFCOM), pp. 94–95.

Warner, Malcolm, Ng S. Hong and Xiaojun Xu (2004). 'Late development experience and the evolution of transnational firms in the People's Republic of China', *Asia Pacific Business Review*, 10, pp. 324–345.

Williamson, Oliver E. (2000). 'The new institutional economics: taking stock, looking ahead', *Journal of Economic Literature*, 38, pp. 595–613.

Wong, John and Sarah Chan (2003). 'China's OFDI: expanding worldwide', *China: An International Journal*, 1, pp. 273–301.

World Bank (2005). *World Development Report 2005: A Better Investment Climate for Everyone* (Washington DC: World Bank).

World Bank (2006). *World Development Indicators (WDI)*, ESDS International, (MIMAS) University of Manchester.

World Intellectual Property Organisation (WIPO) (2006). *Patents and PCT Statistics*, available at www.wipo.int/ipstats/en/statistics/patents/ (last visited 26 September 2006).

Wright, Mike, I. Filatotcher, R.E. Hoskisson and M.W. Peng (2005). 'Strategy research in emerging economies: challenging the conventional wisdom', *Journal of Management Studies*, 42, pp. 1–33.

Wu, Friedrich and Yeo H. Sia (2002). 'China's rising investment in Southeast Asia: trends and outlook', *Journal of Asian Business*, 18(2), pp. 41–61.

Ye, Gang (1992). 'Chinese transnational corporations', *Transnational Corporations*, 1, pp. 125–133.

Yeung, Henry W.-C. (1994). 'Transnational corporations from Asian developing countries: their characteristics and competitive edge', *Journal of Asian Business*, 10(4), pp. 17–60.

Yeung, Henry W.-C. (1999). 'The internationalization of ethnic Chinese business firms from Southeast Asia: strategies, processes and competitive advantage', *International Journal of Urban and Regional Research*, 23, pp. 103–127.

Zhan, James X. (1995). 'Transnationalization and outward investment: the case of Chinese firms', *Transnational Corporations*, 4, pp. 67–100.

Zhang, Jianhong (2005). 'An explanatory study of bilateral FDI relations: the case of China', *Journal of Chinese Economic and Business Studies*, 3, pp. 133–150.

Zhang, Yongjin (2003). *China's Emerging Global Businesses: Political Economy and Institutional Investigations* (New York: Palgrave Macmillan).

Zhao, Chuang (2000). 'Developing overseas investments with overseas processing trade as the new starting point', in *Almanac of China's Foreign Economic Relations and Trade 2000* (Beijing: MOFCOM), pp. 45–46.

Zhu, Rongji (2001). 'Report on the outline of the Tenth Five-Year Plan for National Economic and Social Development (Excerpts)', in *Almanac of China's Foreign Economic Relations and Trade 2001* (Beijing: MOFCOM), pp. 31–44.

Zweig, David and Bi, Jianhai (2005). 'China's global hunt for energy', *Foreign Affairs*, 84, pp. 25–38.

Table A7.1 Approved Chinese FDI outflows, by host region and economy, 1990–2003 (US$10 000 and %)

Destination economy/region	Percentage annual average stock (No. of investment projects)				
	1990–1992	1993–1995	1996–1998	1999–2001	2002–2003
Total Chinese outward FDI	133 847.53 (1057)	176 010.77 (1765)	235 466.77 (2173)	377 761.70 (2855)	1 038 208.76 (7214)
Percentage distribution by area:					
Developed countries	69.44 (384)	64.12 (574)	49.95 (652)	36.11 (759)	22.60 (1818)
Western Europe	2.62 (81)	2.63 (108)	2.21 (122)	1.72 (141)	4.15 (430)
European Union (15 countries)	2.29 (71)	2.38 (97)	2.01 (110)	1.58 (129)	4.08 (412)
Denmark	0.02 (2)	0.02 (2)	0.01 (2)	0.01 (2)	2.22 (3)
Germany	0.52 (21)	0.48 (27)	0.42 (30)	0.36 (35)	0.61 (159)
France	0.58 (8)	0.52 (12)	0.41 (14)	0.26 (16)	0.32 (54)
Italy	0.22 (6)	0.17 (6)	0.13 (6)	0.22 (9)	0.25 (32)
UK	0.33 (6)	0.33 (8)	0.29 (10)	0.22 (13)	0.24 (55)
Other Western Europe (3 countries)	0.33 (11)	0.25 (11)	0.20 (12)	0.14 (12)	0.07 (18)
North America	41.59 (186)	39.86 (291)	31.25 (335)	23.67 (401)	12.82 (894)
USA	22.19 (137)	18.87 (217)	15.98 (256)	13.65 (311)	8.58 (745)
Canada	19.40 (49)	20.98 (74)	15.27 (79)	10.03 (90)	4.24 (150)
Other developed countries (4 countries)	25.22 (117)	21.63 (174)	16.49 (194)	10.71 (217)	5.62 (494)
Australia	23.34 (56)	18.39 (85)	13.93 (95)	9.03 (110)	4.31 (220)
Japan	0.71 (56)	0.78 (77)	0.68 (85)	0.46 (90)	0.83 (243)
New Zealand	1.18 (5)	2.46 (11)	1.88 (14)	1.22 (16)	0.47 (27)
Developing countries	30.56 (673)	35.88 (1191)	50.05 (1521)	63.89 (2096)	77.40 (5397)
Africa	4.03 (111)	5.18 (173)	11.02 (259)	16.07 (401)	8.40 (612)
North Africa (6 countries)	0.20 (10)	0.19 (16)	0.76 (24)	1.13 (43)	0.85 (88)
Egypt	0.14 (3)	0.10 (3)	0.37 (5)	0.70 (15)	0.50 (30)

Destination economy/region	Percentage annual average stock (No. of investment projects)					
	1990–1992	1993–1995	1996–1998	1999–2001	2002–2003
Morocco	0.03 (5)	0.05 (10)	0.04 (10)	0.07 (14)	0.07 (24)
Sudan	0.00 (0)	0.01 (1)	0.32 (6)	0.30 (8)	0.20 (14)
Other Africa (46 countries)	3.83 (101)	4.99 (156)	10.27 (235)	14.93 (358)	7.55 (524)
Zambia	0.24 (3)	0.20 (4)	0.91 (8)	2.77 (15)	1.29 (18)
South Africa	0.02 (1)	0.45 (14)	1.95 (39)	2.44 (76)	1.18 (103)
Mali	0.00 (1)	0.42 (2)	1.20 (3)	1.29 (5)	0.56 (5)
Nigeria	0.51 (11)	0.68 (18)	0.65 (21)	0.69 (27)	0.48 (56)
Tanzania	0.15 (2)	0.19 (6)	0.69 (9)	1.02 (13)	0.40 (20)
Zimbabwe	0.19 (1)	0.14 (1)	0.88 (4)	0.85 (9)	0.34 (15)
Latin America & the Caribbean	4.87 (72)	4.96 (121)	10.04 (147)	13.83 (207)	7.13 (372)
South America (12 countries)	3.64 (45)	3.19 (70)	8.40 (85)	8.89 (109)	4.18 (203)
Peru	0.06 (2)	0.14 (6)	5.12 (8)	5.23 (11)	1.94 (22)
Brazil	0.83 (10)	0.72 (15)	1.38 (21)	1.78 (27)	1.20 (70)
Chile	1.60 (4)	1.24 (5)	0.93 (6)	0.55 (6)	0.24 (19)
Argentina	0.03 (6)	0.11 (10)	0.16 (13)	0.20 (18)	0.11 (28)
Other Latin America & Caribbean (18 countries)	1.23 (27)	1.78 (52)	1.64 (62)	4.94 (98)	2.95 (169)
Mexico	0.38 (9)	0.92 (27)	0.83 (30)	3.60 (35)	1.61 (46)
British Virgin Islands	(0)	(0)	(0)	(17)	(45)
Bermuda	0.37 (2)	0.28 (2)	0.33 (3)	0.36 (8)	0.78 (11)
Cuba	0.00 (0)	0.00 (0)	0.00 (0)	0.35 (3)	0.16 (9)
Honduras	0.00 (0)	0.06 (1)	0.06 (1)	0.30 (4)	0.16 (5)
Central & Eastern Europe (18 countries)	4.17 (114)	5.76 (251)	4.85 (280)	4.44 (344)	4.62 (690)

Russian Federation	4.09 (106)	5.43 (224)	4.14 (240)	3.09 (284)	3.63 (503)
Czech Republic	(2)		(3)	(4)	(14)
Georgia	0.00 (0)	0.00 (0)	0.01 (1)	0.24 (2)	0.25 (5)
Asia	16.61 (358)	18.71 (606)	22.22 (790)	27.87 (1090)	56.60 (3662)
West Asia (Middle East) (12 countries)	1.09 (35)	1.17 (47)	0.98 (51)	1.61 (67)	1.46 (137)
United Arab Emirates	0.32 (12)	0.38 (16)	0.33 (19)	0.44 (25)	0.47 (74)
Yemen	0.24 (7)	0.22 (8)	0.18 (8)	0.49 (9)	0.35 (10)
Central Asia (8 countries)	0.09 (5)	0.26 (19)	0.49 (34)	1.50 (75)	0.91 (132)
Kazakhstan	0.01 (2)	0.08 (12)	0.16 (17)	0.80 (36)	0.40 (55)
Kyrgyzstan	0.02 (1)	0.06 (4)	0.16 (8)	0.46 (19)	0.29 (32)
Uzbekistan	0.04 (2)	0.09 (2)	0.12 (6)	0.17 (15)	0.17 (32)
South, East and SE Asia (20 countries)	15.42 (319)	17.28 (540)	20.74 (705)	24.75 (948)	54.22 (3393)
Hong Kong (China)	8.12 (116)	8.08 (146)	9.35 (176)	8.83 (240)	40.53 (2062)
Thailand	2.94 (76)	3.15 (120)	2.83 (135)	2.96 (146)	2.30 (240)
Korea, Republic	0.23 (2)	0.39 (9)	0.39 (17)	0.35 (23)	1.98 (67)
Macao (China SAR)	1.19 (24)	1.02 (26)	2.11 (40)	1.55 (57)	1.92 (234)
Cambodia	0.00 (0)	0.11 (4)	1.17 (21)	2.40 (47)	1.37 (63)
Indonesia	0.16 (4)	0.78 (27)	0.96 (37)	1.45 (43)	1.12 (62)
Viet Nam	0.00 (0)	0.03 (2)	0.14 (8)	0.86 (27)	0.86 (82)
Singapore	0.65 (26)	0.81 (49)	0.87 (69)	0.86 (90)	0.82 (180)
The Pacific (9 countries)	0.88 (18)	1.27 (41)	1.92 (46)	1.69 (55)	0.67 (62)
Papua New Guinea	0.45 (5)	0.56 (9)	1.31 (12)	1.16 (17)	0.43 (20)
Fiji	0.21 (6)	0.29 (11)	0.26 (13)	0.24 (14)	0.10 (16)

Note: The principal host countries of Chinese FDI are listed for each region. The total number of recipients of Chinese FDI is shown in the region heading. Regions are as listed in UNCTAD (2003). Countries are in declining rank order for the period 2002–2003.

Source: Calculated from MOFCOM, *Almanac of China's Economic Foreign Relations and Trade 1991–2003* and *Yearbook of Commerce 2004.*

Table A7.2   Summary of hypotheses, data sources and theoretical justification

Hypothesis	Variable	Proxy	Measurement	Source	Theoretical justification	M/C[1]	Expected sign
H1	FDI (dependent variable)	Annual outflow of Chinese FDI	Constant (2000) US$m	MOFCOM			
	Host market characteristics – Market-seeking FDI	LGDPPC: Host country GDP per capita	Constant (2000) US$	World Bank *World Development Indicators* (WDI)	Market seeking	M	–
H2	Host market characteristics – Natural resource seeking FDI	LOIL: Exports of crude oil and natural liquid gas (NLG)	1000 tonnes	IEA Oil information	Natural resource seeking	M	+
H3	Host market characteristics – Asset seeking FDI	LPATENT: Total (resident plus non-resident) annual patent registrations in host country	Annual cumulative figures	WIPO	Strategic asset seeking	M	+
H4	Foreign exchange policy liberalisation	TD94: For 1994, to capture the impact of the foreign currency account policy change	Time dummy for the whole period after 1994	Diverse sources	Endogenous institutional factor	M	+
H5a	Bilateral Investment Treaty (BITs)	BIT: Existence of a BIT between China and the host country	Binary: 1=treaty; 0=no treaty	UNCTAD	Formal exogenous institutional factor	M	+

H5b	Accumulated BITs	LACBIT: Accumulated number of BITs concluded by a country	Summed number of signed treaties from 1980 onwards	UNCTAD	Formal exogenous institutional factor	M	+
H6a	Double Taxation Treaty (DTTs)	DTT: Existence of a DTT between China and the host country	Binary: 1=treaty; 0=no treaty	UNCTAD	Formal exogenous institutional factor	M	+
H6b	Accumulated DTTs	LACDTT: Accumulated number of DTTs concluded by a country	Summed number of signed treaties from 1980 onwards	UNCTAD	Formal exogenous institutional factor	M	+
H7	WTO/GATT membership	WTO: the host country is member of WTO/GATT	Binary: 1=agreement; 0= no agreement	WTO	Formal exogenous institutional factor	M	+
H8	Cultural proximity to China	CP: to capture international social and ethnic links with China and the host country	1 when percentage of ethnic Chinese in total population is >1%	Diverse sources	Informal exogenous institutional factor	M	+
H9	Geographic distance from China	LDIS: Geographic distance between host country capital and Beijing.	km	City distance tool[2]	Spatial costs	M	+
H10	Political risk	LRISK: Host country's political risk rating (higher values indicate greater stability).	Scale of 0 to 100: 0=very high risk and 100=very low risk	International Country Risk Guide (ICRG)	Transaction costs	C	+

Table A7.2 (continued)

Hypothesis	Variable	Proxy	Measurement	Source	Theoretical justification	M/C[1]	Expected sign
H11	Purchasing power parity	PPP	See text	Author's calculation	Macroeconomic conditions	C	−
H12	Exchange rate	LERATE: Host country official annual average exchange rate against RMB (fixed to dollar)	LCU, period average	World Bank WDI	Macroeconomic conditions	C	+
H13	Host country inflation rate	LINF: Host country annual inflation rate	%	World Bank WDI	Macroeconomic conditions	C	−
H14	China's exports	LEXP: China's exports to the host country	Constant (2000) US$m	China National Bureau of Statistics	Market seeking	C	+
H15	China's imports	LIMP: China's imports from the host country	Constant (2000) US$m	China National Bureau of Statistics	Trade intensity	C	+
H16	Host country's openness to FDI	LINFDI: Ratio of inward FDI stock to GDP of host country	%	UNCTAD	Trade and investment policy	C	+

Notes:
1. M = Main; C= Control.
2. www.geobytes.com/citydistancetool.htm.

Table A7.3 Results of the determinants of Chinese OFDI

Hypothesis	Estimation technique	All host countries				OECD host countries only			Non-OECD host countries only		
		OLS 1991–2003 (1)	RE 1991–2003	RE 1991–1998 (2)	RE 1999–2003 (3)	OLS 1991–2003 (4)	OLS 1991–1998 (5)	RE 1999–2003 (6)	OLS 1991–2003 (7)	OLS 1991–1998 (8)	RE 1999–2003 (9)
H1	Log GDP per capita (LGDPPC)	−1.591 (0.270)***	−1.409 (0.425)***	−1.426 (0.479)***	−1.794 (0.631)***	−0.773 (0.675)	−0.942 (0.904)	0.234 (1.146)	−1.696 (0.338)***	−1.527 (0.429)***	−2.079 (0.922)**
H2	Log crude oil/NLG export (LOIL)	0.086 (0.065)	0.044 (0.090)	0.038 (0.112)	0.238 (0.142)*	0.166 (0.120)	−0.136 (0.159)	0.360 (0.208)*	0.243 (0.080)	−0.173 (0.103)	0.193 (0.211)
H3	Log patent (LPATENT)	−0.029 (0.083)	−0.065 (0.093)	−0.017 (0.124)	0.013 (0.140)	0.248 (0.189)	0.468 (0.247)*	0.145 (0.325)	−0.171 (0.103)*	−0.135 (0.141)	−0.768 (0.153)
H4	Policy time dummy 1994 (TD94)	−1.750 (0.655)***	−2.852 (0.671)***	−2.999 (0.689)***	—	−3.835 (1.002)***	−4.959 (1.057)***	—	−0.650 (0.908)	−0.900 (0.969)	—
H5a	Bilateral investment treaty with China (BIT)	−0.900 (0.657)	−1.064 (0.814)	−1.025 (0.964)	−1.046 (1.437)	−2.254 (1.533)	−2.326 (1.732)	−1.464 (3.790)	−0.526 (0.892)	−1.009 (1.163)	0.380 (1.846)
H5b	Log accumulated BITs (LACBIT)	−0.670 (0.353)*	0.021 (0.460)	−0.335 (0.511)	−0.968 (1.027)	−0.341 (0.655)	−1.307 (0.738)*	2.769 (1.821)	−0.465 (0.530)	−0.263 (0.648)	−2.525 (1.560)

Table A7.3 (continued)

Hypothesis	Estimation technique	All host countries				OECD host countries only			Non-OECD host countries only		
		OLS 1991–2003	RE 1991–2003 (1)	RE 1991–1998 (2)	RE 1999–2003 (3)	OLS 1991–2003 (4)	OLS 1991–1998 (5)	RE 1999–2003 (6)	OLS 1991–2003 (7)	OLS 1991–1998 (8)	RE 1999–2003 (9)
H6a	Double taxation treaty with China (DTT)	0.816 (0.684)	0.894 (0.836)	1.420 (1.039)	−0.300 (1.504)	0.924 (1.762)	−0.242 (2.054)	1.598 (4.258)	0.958 (0.788)	0.758 (1.007)	−0.771 (1.764)
H6b	Log accumulated DTTs (LACDTT)	0.426 (0.344)	0.416 (0.474)	0.313 (0.572)	0.471 (0.805)	−1.966 (1.431)	−0.724 (1.628)	−4.874 (3.714)	0.470 (0.400)	0.430 (0.517)	1.366 (1.013)
H7	WTO/GATT membership (WTO)	1.201 (0.910)	2.042 (1.234)*	2.109 (1.448)	0.626 (2.067)	−1.313 (4.166)	1.049 (4.307)	—	0.893 (0.950)	0.451 (1.236)	0.782 (2.314)
H8	Cultural Proximity (CP)	1.909 (0.787)**	2.258 (1.268)*	4.219 (1.510)***	0.522 (1.812)	1.430 (1.318)	0.711 (1.631)	3.651 (2.863)	1.084 (1.465)	5.000 (1.942)**	−3.369 (3.591)
H9	Log geographic distance (LDIS)	1.221 (0.552)*	1.473 (0.899)	1.748 (1.038)*	−0.037 (1.281)	1.047 (1.578)	0.619 (2.099)	1.968 (2.966)	1.254 (0.920)	2.423 (1.117)*	−0.791 (2.422)
H10	Log political risk (LRISK)	−0.138 (1.716)	−0.163 (2.034)	2.283 (2.443)	0.078 (4.063)	−1.035 (5.939)	12.143 (8.295)	−8.685 (11.338)	0.735 (1.922)	0.450 (2.257)	4.868 (5.041)

H11 PPP	0.002 (0.002)	0.003 (0.002)	0.002 (0.002)	0.002 (0.013)	0.094 (0.027)***	0.039 (0.035)	0.175 (0.053)***	0.228 (0.002)	0.003 (0.002)	−0.009 (0.012)
H12 Log exchange rate (LERATE)	0.262 (0.104)**	0.453 (0.163)***	0.421 (0.190)**	0.147 (0.244)	0.604 (0.326)*	0.528 (0.443)	0.487 (0.612)	0.057 (0.125)	−0.056 (0.172)	0.214 (0.322)
H13 Log inflation (LINF)	−0.002 (0.001)	−0.002 (0.001)*	−0.002 (0.001)*	−0.005 (0.046)	0.071 (0.062)	0.166 (0.080)**	0.287 (0.292)	−0.181 (0.001)	−0.002 (0.001)	−0.023 (0.042)
H14 Log China's exports (LEXP)	1.689 (0.232)***	1.551 (0.295)***	1.380 (0.345)***	2.030 (0.540)***	1.758 (0.497)***	1.855 (0.611)***	0.671 (0.979)	1.652 (0.285)***	1.484 (0.338)***	1.965 (0.632)***
H15 Log China's imports (LIMP)	0.468 (0.158)***	0.506 (0.184)***	0.341 (0.227)	0.192 (0.344)	0.941 (0.442)**	0.924 (0.611)	1.481 (0.759)**	0.426 (0.183)**	0.333 (0.232)	0.421 (0.394)
H16 Log inward FDI (LINFDI)	0.802 (0.285)***	0.984 (0.355)***	0.441 (0.466)	0.342 (0.752)	1.903 (0.598)***	2.791 (0.825)***	−0.564 (1.503)	0.755 (0.383)**	0.136 (0.499)	0.935 (1.222)
Number of cases	715	715	440	275	286	176	110	429	264	165
Lagrange multiplier test		40.97***	16.59***	6.59**	n.s.	n.s.	5.76**	n.s.	n.s.	3.16*

Notes: Standard errors are in parentheses; n.s. = not significant. ***, ** and * indicate that the coefficient is significant at the 1 per cent, 5 per cent and 10 per cent levels respectively.

155

Table A7.4 Correlation matrix

	LFDI	LGDPPC	LOIL	LPATENT	BIT	LACBIT	DTT	LACDTT	WTO
LFDI	1.0000								
LGDPPC	0.0129	1.0000							
LOIL	0.2051	0.1357	1.0000						
LPATENT	0.0531	0.5580	0.0908	1.0000					
BIT	-0.0950	0.1426	-0.1025	0.0914	1.0000				
LACBIT	0.0420	0.2614	0.0950	0.2305	0.5727	1.0000			
DTT	0.0793	0.4648	-0.0085	0.4540	0.3325	0.4506	1.0000		
LACDTT	0.1296	0.4331	0.2265	0.4421	0.3749	0.6622	0.6639	1.0000	
WTO	-0.0792	-0.3255	0.0557	-0.0790	0.0502	-0.1057	-0.0746	-0.1619	1.0000
CP	0.3521	0.2073	0.1931	0.0627	-0.0583	-0.0759	0.1728	0.1396	-0.1626
LDIS	-0.1443	-0.0545	0.2630	-0.1794	-0.2172	-0.1057	-0.2849	-0.2542	0.0041
LRISK	-0.0044	0.7103	-0.0459	0.4574	0.2527	0.3757	0.4470	0.4736	-0.4551
PPP	-0.0607	-0.0812	-0.0464	-0.0345	0.0586	-0.0584	-0.1131	-0.1398	0.2234
LERATE	0.1016	-0.4710	-0.0716	-0.2618	-0.0594	-0.0608	-0.2534	-0.2744	0.0005
LINF	-0.0963	-0.1284	-0.0947	-0.0387	0.0005	-0.1281	-0.1123	-0.1829	0.2595
LEXP	0.4438	0.5221	0.1854	0.4087	0.0986	0.3765	0.3775	0.4803	-0.3026
LIMP	0.3809	0.5369	0.2197	0.4603	0.1694	0.3297	0.4213	0.4477	-0.2019
LINFDI	0.1805	0.2299	0.1619	-0.1321	0.0418	0.2737	0.0860	0.1180	-0.3490

Table A7.4 (continued)

	CP	LDIS	LRISK	PPP	LERATE	LINF	LEXP	LIMP	LINFDI
LFDI									
LGDPPC									
LOIL									
LPATENT									
BIT									
LACBIT									
DTT									
LACDTT									
WTO									
CP	1.0000								
LDIS	−0.2579	1.0000							
LRISK	0.1730	−0.0475	1.0000						
PPP	−0.0467	−0.0277	−0.0620	1.0000					
LERATE	−0.0478	−0.1936	−0.3546	−0.0628	1.0000				
LINF	−0.0713	0.0142	−0.1184	0.8652	−0.0901	1.0000			
LEXP	0.4096	−0.3872	0.3959	−0.1313	−0.1095	−0.1838	1.0000		
LIMP	0.4125	−0.3076	0.3995	−0.0183	−0.2047	−0.0417	0.8064	1.0000	
LINFDI	0.3698	0.1627	0.3090	−0.2360	−0.0481	−0.2890	0.2517	0.0950	1.0000

Note: The policy time dummy 1994 is excluded from the correlation matrix as it is a dummy.

157

8. Old wine in new bottles: a comparison of emerging-market TNCs today and developed-country TNCs thirty years ago

John H. Dunning, Changsu Kim and Donghyun Park

INTRODUCTION

Traditionally, the vast majority of transnational corporations (TNCs) that operate across borders have originated from developed countries such as the United States (US), Japan and members of the European Union (EU). Large and well-established TNCs such as Coca Cola, Toyota or Siemens are almost invariably from such countries. In the context of TNCs, we tend to associate the role of emerging markets[1] primarily as the destination of TNCs from developed countries, for example, US software companies setting up research facilities in India, Japanese manufacturers establishing production facilities in China, or British banks acquiring financial institutions in Brazil. Until quite recently, this widespread perception of developed countries as homes of TNCs, and emerging markets as hosts of TNCs, had been firmly rooted in empirical reality (Dunning 1993). While there were TNCs from emerging markets in the past, as will be described elsewhere in this chapter, they were nowhere near as active or visible as they are today.

In line with their growing relative significance in the global economy, many emerging markets are now becoming important outward foreign direct investors (UNCTAD 2006). At a broader level, the growth of TNCs from emerging markets reflects their rapid economic development and growth (Dunning and Narula 1996). The four newly industrialized economies of Hong Kong (China), the Republic of Korea, Singapore and Taiwan Province of China now have per capita income levels approaching those of developed countries. In other words, some emerging markets have become rich enough to export capital to the rest of the world. However, the growth of TNCs from emerging markets is by no means limited to the most successful or the most industrialized developing countries. Asian countries other than the newly industrialized economies, including China and India, and major Latin American economies such as Brazil and Mexico, as well as South Africa, have all spawned their own TNCs. It is possible to interpret the growth of such cross-border activity as evidence of the growing ability and willingness of emerging-market firms to make investments outside of their home countries (Bartlett and Ghoshal 2000). Indeed some of these firms, such as the Republic of Korea's Samsung and Hyundai, India's Tata and Malaysia's Sime Darby, have become truly global players with operations all over the world (UNCTAD 2006).

Given that most TNCs have come from developed countries in the past but that an increasing number of emerging market firms are investing outside their national boundaries, it is both interesting and worthwhile to examine the differences between the two groups of firms. Indeed, the central objective of this chapter is to compare and contrast the contemporary emerging-market TNCs with the traditional developed-country TNCs. We shall set out some similarities and differences in the industrial and geographical patterns of outward FDI from the two groups of countries and shall suggest that these similarities and differences may be due both to factors that are exogenous to both groups – especially the current wave of economic globalization – and to those endogenous to them, such as government policies toward outward FDI. We hope that our comparative study will help provide the reader with a better understanding of outward FDI and TNCs from emerging markets, which is an issue of growing global significance.

8.1 QUANTITATIVE SIGNIFICANCE OF EMERGING-MARKET FDI AND TNCs

In 1980, the average GDP per capita of emerging markets that were new players in the global economy amounted to about $1400, or just 14 per cent of the level of developed countries. This figure had risen only marginally to 15 per cent by 2004 (World Bank 2006). However, some emerging markets, most notably in East Asia, have experienced spectacular sustained economic growth that has transformed them from being typical poor Third World countries into dynamic industrialized economies on the brink of first world prosperity. The newly industrialized economies of Hong Kong (China), the Republic of Korea, Singapore and Taiwan Province of China have been the front-runners of this East Asian miracle, followed by Indonesia, Malaysia and Thailand. In fact, Hong Kong (China) and Singapore had higher GDP per capita than Italy or Australia in 2004, while the Republic of Korea and Taiwan Province of China had a GDP per capita equal to that of Israel and Spain. All four newly industrialized economies are now classified by international organizations as high-income economies. More recently, China, India and Viet Nam have begun to experience rapid economic growth on a sustained basis. Yet despite the impressive economic performance of many East Asian economies, the overall performance of emerging markets since 1980 has been mixed.[2]

The most successful emerging markets have benefited enormously from globalization (Mathews 2006). Integration into the global economy has not been confined to those countries but has extended to virtually all emerging markets (Hoskisson *et al.* 2000). The overall performance of the emerging economies in terms of exports and investments has been impressive indeed. In 1980, the major emerging markets of Asia and Latin America accounted for 10 per cent of the world's exports. Their share rose to 15 per cent by 1990, to 21 per cent by 1995 and to 24 per cent by 2003. China has now become the fourth largest exporter in the world, after Germany, the US and Japan.[3] Hong Kong (China) and the Republic of Korea are among the top 12 largest world exporters as well. However, as Table 8.1 somewhat surprisingly shows, the share of emerging markets in the global stock of inward and outward FDI has not changed much since 1980. A likely explanation for this is the massive volume of cross-border mergers and acquisitions (M&As) within the Triad – the US, Japan and the EU – in the 1990s. One important indicator that has clearly changed is the ratio between the outward and inward FDI stock of emerging markets.

Table 8.1   Inward and outward FDI stock in developed and developing countries, 1980–2004

Region	1980		1990		1995		2004	
	US$b	**%[1]**	**US$b**	**%**	**US$b**	**%**	**US$b**	**%**
Developed countries								
Inward FDI	391	56	1404	79	2036	69	6470	74
Outward FDI	499	89	1638	92	2583	89	8610	89
Outward/Inward	1.28	1.59	1.17	1.16	1.27	1.29	1.33	1.20
Developing countries								
Inward FDI	302	44	364	21	917	31	2226	26
Outward FDI	60	11	147	8	309	11	1036	11
Outward/Inward	0.20	0.25	0.40	0.38	0.34	0.35	0.47	0.42

Note: 1. Of developed plus developing countries.

Source: the authors' calculations, based on data in UNCTAD (2004, 2005).

Developed countries

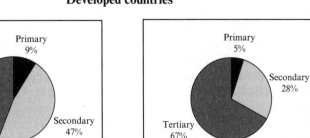

Developing countries

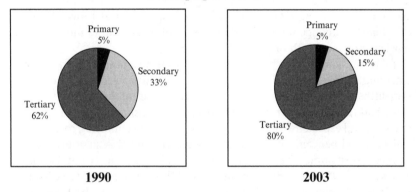

| 1990 | 2003 |

Source: UNCTAD (2005).

Figure 8.1 Sectoral distribution of the outward FDI stock of traditional and new FDI players, 1990–2003 (%)

As we can see in Figure 8.1 in 2003, around 80 per cent of the stock of the new players' outward FDI was in services such as trade, finance and business activities, compared to 62 per cent in 1990. The corresponding shares for developed-country TNCs were 44 per cent in 1990 and 67 per cent in 2003. As is the case of their developed-country counterparts, the share of primary and secondary sectors in developing-country TNCs' outward FDI is declining. The increase in the share of services in outward FDI of emerging markets mirrors the increase in the share of services in their gross domestic products (GDP). Furthermore, service-oriented economies such as Hong Kong (China) and Singapore invest abroad primarily in services – especially offshore centers and financial services – and thus help to raise the share of services in outward FDI of emerging markets as a whole.

Let us now look at the share of inward FDI accounted for by different emerging markets. In 2002–4, Latin America and Asia accounted for almost all of emerging markets' inward FDI. Given the growing interest of foreign TNCs in Asia in general and China in particular, one might have expected Asia's share of emerging markets' inward FDI to rise at the expense of Latin America; this, however, has not been the case. In 1980, Latin America and Asia accounted respectively for 17 per cent and 83 per cent of emerging markets' inward FDI. The corresponding ratios for 2004 were 28 per cent and 64 per cent. Taking a closer look at Asian economies' inward FDI, by 2004, Hong Kong (China) had accumulated the fourth largest stock of inward FDI, after the US, the United Kingdom (UK) and France. China was the third largest recipient of FDI inflows in 2003 to 2005, after the US and the UK. During this period, the Chinese-speaking economies of China, Hong Kong (China), Singapore and Taiwan Province of China jointly accounted for 45 per cent of FDI inflows into emerging markets and a seventh of global FDI inflows.

Table 8.2. shows the share of outward FDI accounted for by different emerging markets. In 1980, Latin American countries accounted for nearly four-fifths of the total outward FDI by emerging markets. By 2004, their share had fallen to 28 per cent. The corresponding share of Asian emerging markets, and especially that of the Chinese-speaking countries, rose dramatically from 11 per cent to 69 per cent. The growth rate of Asia's outward FDI has been most impressive. Table 8.2 shows that Hong Kong (China) leads the way with a $405 billion stock of outward FDI in 2004, a sum exceeded only by France, Germany, the UK and the US. Brazil, China, the Republic of Korea, Singapore and Taiwan Province of China are the other main sources of outward FDI from emerging markets. Along with Hong Kong (China), they accounted for 70 per cent of the stock of outward FDI from emerging markets in 2004 and 7 per cent of the global stock of outward FDI. The corresponding figures for 1990 were 66 per cent and 5 per cent.[4]

Central and Eastern European countries are the other new actors on the world economic stage. However, as recently as 1980, there were virtually no FDI inflows into those economies. The Czech Republic, Hungary and Poland started to open their borders to foreign TNCs around 1990. By 1995, the Central and Eastern European countries accounted for 1 per cent of global inward FDI stock. They continued to experience rapid growth of inward FDI, in part due to extensive privatization of state-owned assets; by 2004, their share had risen to 3 per cent. Today, the Czech Republic, Hungary, Poland and Russia each exceed Argentina, India, the Republic of Korea and Taiwan Province of China as FDI destinations. However, as might

Table 8.2 Origin of outward FDI stock of developing economies (US$m)

Region	1980	%	1995	%	2004	%
Asia	6 440	10.7	189 064	61.2	717 997	69.3
China	nsa	–	15 802	5.1	38 825	3.7
Hong Kong (China)	148	0.2	78 833	25.5	405 589	39.2
India	4	neg	264	0.1	6 592	0.6
Republic of Korea	127	0.2	10 231	3.3	39 319	3.8
Malaysia	197	0.3	11 042	3.6	13 796	1.3
Singapore	3 718	0.2	35 050	11.4	100 910	9.7
Taiwan Province of China	97	0.2	25 144	8.1	91 237	8.8
Thailand	13	neg	2 274	0.7	3 393	0.3
Latin America	46 915	77.9	86 263	28.0	271 690	26.2
Argentina	5 997	10.0	10 696	3.5	21 819	2.1
Brazil	38 545	64.0	44 474	14.4	64.363	6.2
Chile	42	0.1	2 425	0.8	14 447	1.4
Columbia	137	0.2	1 027	0.3	4 284	0.4
Mexico	31	0.1	2 572	0.8	15 885	1.5
Other	6 884	11.4	33 297	10.8	45 989	4.5
Of which						
South Africa	5 722	9.4	23 305	7.6	28 790	2.8
Total	60 239	100.0	308 624	100.0	1 035 676	100.0

Note: . . . nsa = not separately available; neg = negligible.

Source: Dunning, Van Hoesel and Narula (1998); UNCTAD (2004, 2005).

be expected, their outward FDI is lagging behind. Even in 2004, the combined share of Central and Eastern European countries was only 1 per cent of the global stock of outward FDI (UNCTAD 2005). If we exclude FDI outflows from Russia, which have mainly taken the form of flight capital, investment in oil and mineral exploration and strategic asset-augmenting investment in neighboring ex-socialist countries,[5] their combined share was only 0.2 per cent. Nevertheless, the Czech Republic, Hungary, Poland and Slovenia are now beginning to invest in neighboring countries.

8.2 AN EXPLANATORY FRAMEWORK OF THE NEW PLAYERS' FDI

The most generally accepted scholarly explanation for the emergence of new players on the global investment scene is the investment development path, a concept that was first put forward by one of the authors of this chapter in 1979 (Dunning 1981). This suggests that as countries' per capita income rises, they initially draw in increasing amounts of FDI, and subsequently become outward investors. Eventually, as demonstrated in the case of most industrialized countries, outward FDI either exceeds inward FDI, or the two types of FDI fluctuate around a rough balance. This trajectory of the investment development path essentially reflects the changing competitive advantages of firms from particular countries vis-à-vis their foreign competitors, and the changing attractiveness of countries with respect to costs, market opportunities and natural or created resource endowments. The principle of comparative dynamic advantage suggests a continuing restructuring of economic activity as countries move upwards along their investment development path. Both inward and outward investment have a role to play in easing this process. Figure 8.2 depicts a freehand drawing of

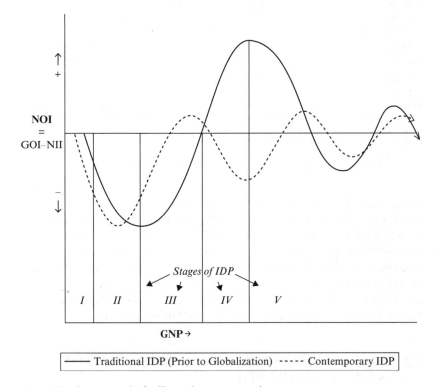

Note: Not drawn to scale; for illustrative purposes only.

Figure 8.2   The investment development path

the relationship between per capita GNP and net outward FDI, which is the difference between gross outward investment and gross inward investment. This figure shows two different investment development paths – a traditional path and a more contemporary path that reflects the influence of globalization.

In Figure 8.3, we plot the ratio of actual outward FDI to inward FDI (O/I) on the vertical axis and per capita GNP on the horizontal axis for selected developed countries and emerging markets for the year 2004. As might be expected, this figure shows virtually all the new players as having an outward to inward FDI ratio of less than one, with the notable exception of Taiwan Province of China. Perhaps more significantly, this figure also shows that there is a positive relationship between per capita GNP and the outward-to-inward FDI ratio. So the general proposition of the investment development path remains valid, even though other research has shown that the outward-to-inward FDI ratio also depends on other

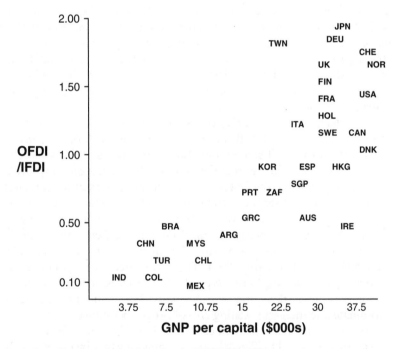

Source: the authors' calculation from data in UNCTAD (2005).

Figure 8.3 The relationship between stock of outward and inward FDI (2004) and GNP per capita of selected developing and developed economies (2003)

country-specific factors, such as the quality of a country's institutions, its economic structure, its openness to international trade and capital flows, and its government policy toward FDI.[6]

The home economies of emerging-market TNCs differ widely in terms of size, income level, economic structure, natural resources, technological capabilities, trade openness, government policies and other characteristics (Hoskisson *et al.* 2000). For example, the economies range from small ones such as Hong Kong (China) and Singapore to very large ones such as China, India, Brazil and Russia. Some home economies such as the Republic of Korea, China and India have modest endowments of natural resources, whereas others such as Brazil, Russia and Malaysia have abundant endowments. East Asian economies are relatively more dependent on manufacturing and exports than other emerging markets. It is therefore not surprising that each emerging market has its own particular FDI objectives, which are shown in Table 8.3. For example, Singapore's FDI is associated with market access and low labor costs, the Republic of Korea's FDI with escaping high labor costs and militant labor unions at home, China's FDI with the search for markets and natural resources, India's FDI with new market access and escape from home-country government restrictions, Brazil's FDI with substantial investment in the financial and business sectors, Mexico's FDI with access to markets and knowledge, and Russia's FDI with the energy and mining industries and privatization programs in transition economies.

While each emerging-market economy and firm has its own particular motives for outward FDI, there are also a number of broader considerations that motivate all emerging-market economies and firms to venture abroad. Broadly speaking, there are two groups of reasons why any firm would engage in FDI: the first is to exploit its existing assets or competitive capabilities, and the second is to augment them. Whereas asset-exploiting FDI is associated with an investing firm's making use of its existing ownership advantages, asset-augmenting FDI is associated with an investing firm acquiring important ownership (O) advantages that it currently lacks (Kuemmerle 1999; Wesson 1993). There are three more specific motives underlying the asset-exploiting type of FDI: to access natural resources, to exploit existing markets or seek out new markets, and more effectively to coordinate and integrate existing cross-border operations.

An interesting issue in connection with FDI motives is its geographical distribution. Do TNCs from emerging markets invest primarily in other emerging markets or in developed countries? Do they largely stay close to home or venture farther a field to distant countries? Table 8.4 and Figure 8.4 summarize the most salient features of the geography of the new wave of FDI.

Table 8.3 Selected country-specific motives of emerging-market TNCs for outward FDI

Country	Characteristics
Brazil	Largely regional, e.g. Latin America; but recent expansion into Canada; substantial petroleum and financial investments, some of the latter to tax haven countries.
China	Largely market- and natural-resource seeking, but recently knowledge-related activities and in brands. Considerable state support – directly or indirectly.
Hong Kong (China)	Mainly in Mainland China, but some in other poorer Asian and African countries, motivated both by cost reduction and market seeking in both manufacturing and service sectors.
India	Initially to penetrate new markets and escape government restrictions, but recently more on accessing and acquiring technology/brand names.
Republic of Korea	Escaping high-cost and difficult labor markets at home, as well as saturated product market. Increasing asset-seeking FDI in Europe and US.
Malaysia	Importance of offshore banking, transport and a range of diversified activities. Some asset-augmenting FDI in Europe and the US.
Mexico	Largely within North and South America. Market access and knowledge seeking in an attempt to become major global players, e.g., Cemex.
Russia	Largely energy and mining investments. Avoidance of domestic regulatory constraints.
Singapore	Market access dominates, but low-cost labor seeking also a factor. For some more technology-intensive activities, following the client is important. Exploiting its own advantages as a regional service center.
South Africa	Both mining and market-seeking FDI. Becoming an important center for regional headquarters of TNCs in sub-Saharan Africa.
Thailand	Initially opportunistic and ill-planned, and now increasingly regional market access seeking.

Source: the authors' evaluation from various country studies in 2005–2006. See also UNCTAD (2006).

Table 8.4   The geography of outward FDI of the new players

1. Asian TNCs are more globalized than those of Latin America or those of Central and Eastern Europe.

2. First wave of outward FDI (1970s) was mainly to developing countries; second wave (1980s) more to developed countries; third wave (1990s) back to own regions; fourth wave (2002 onward), increasingly (via M&As), to developed countries.

3. Up to 2001, mostly greenfield FDI; now M&As are playing a more important role.

4. In 2004, only five developing economies (China, Hong Kong, the Republic of Korea, Malaysia and Singapore) TNCs are listed in the top 100 non-financial TNCs identified by UNCTAD. However, at least 80 such TNCs, of which 61 were from Asia, had foreign assets of $1 billion or more in 2004. Ten of the top 100 developing country TNCs recorded 50 or more foreign affiliates (UNCTAD 2006).

Source: the authors' views. See also UNCTAD (2006).

While TNCs from Asia tend to be more geographically diversified and more active outside their home regions, those from Latin America and Central and Eastern Europe tend to be more concentrated in their home markets or adjacent markets – notably, North America for Latin American TNCs, Asia for Asian TNCs and Western Europe for Central and Eastern European TNCs. The first wave of outward FDI from both Asia and Latin America in the 1970s was directed to other parts of the same region. The second wave in the 1980s was attracted more to developed countries. During the third wave in the 1990s, an increasing share of new FDI returned to the home region, due mainly to the economic vigor of both regions, especially that of China and the rest of East Asia. However, there are signs of a fourth wave now emerging with a focus on seeking out new technologies, brand names and organizational competences (Moon and Roehl 2001) – namely asset-augmenting FDI – and this is directed primarily towards the developed economies. In 2004 and in the first half of 2005, some 85 per cent of the $18 billion of cross-border M&As valued at over $300 million undertaken by TNCs from emerging markets involved targets in developed economies, and all were in manufacturing or service sectors.[7]

Table 8.5 summarizes the suggested relationship between the investment development path and types of FDI and the ownership, locational and internalization (OLI) advantages of investing firms. This depicts the framework as we see it as of 2006 – and it paves the way for the analysis of the following section.

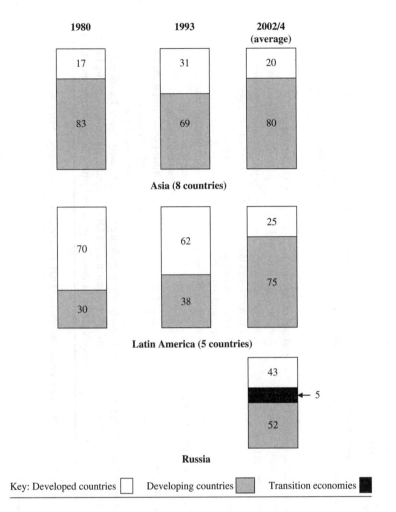

Source: UNCTAD (2005, 2006); the authors' calculations are from country data.

Figure 8.4 Regional destinations of new players' outward FDI stock, 1980–2002/4 (%)

8.3 A COMPARISON OF TODAY'S EMERGING-MARKET TNCs AND YESTERDAY'S DEVELOPED-COUNTRY TNCs

We now turn to the main contribution of this chapter, which is to compare the attributes of emerging-market TNCs today with those of

Table 8.5   The investment development path

Investment Development Path	FDI position	FDI types	Ownership, location, internalization advantages
Stage I (GNP pc: < $2000) **Stage II** (GNP pc: $2000–$3500)	• Modest IDI & limited ODI • ODI beginning in lower technology sectors	• Asset exploiting – natural resource seeking – market seeking – efficiency seeking	• **Ownership:** initially, mainly country specific; later becoming more firm specific
Stage III (GNP pc: $3500–$8000) **Stage IV** (GNP pc: > $8000)	• Intra-industry FDI increases • FDI in higher technology sectors & ODI rising faster than IDI	• Asset augmenting – created asset & competence seeking	• **Location:** access & use of local resources, capabilities, institutions & markets • **Internalization:** utilization of ownership & location through internalization
Stage V	• Balanced NOI		
Comment	• In early 2000s, ODI appears to be occurring in stage II	• In early 2000s, evidence of asset-augmenting FDI occurring in stage II	• In early 2000s, locational advantages are tending to be more of an institutional kind

Notes: pc = per capita; GNP = gross national product; IDI = inward direct investment; ODI = outward direct investment; NOI = net outward investment.

Source: adapted from Dunning, Kim and Lin (2001).

Table 8.6   Features of outward FDI for developed and developing countries, 1960–2006

Country group	1960–1980 (Pre-globalization period)	1980–2006 (Post-globalization period)
Developed countries	• Growth of market/efficiency-seeking FDI of intra-Triad kind • Rise of Japanese FDI • Mainly greenfield FDI but some Anglo-US M&As • More joint ventures and contractual agreements • Ownership advantages, both country- and firm-specific • Mainly privately-owned TNCs	• Large expansion of all kinds of FDI, both horizontal and vertical • Opening up of new FDI destinations, especially in Asia • Intra-Triad M&A boom: 1990–2000 and 2004–2006, particularly of asset-augmenting FDI • Increasing firm-specific ownership advantages arising from global/regional activities • Almost exclusively privately-owned TNCs
Developing countries	• Limited amount of market/resource seeking by Latin American/Indian TNCs, mainly in adjacent regions • Mainly country-specific ownership advantages • Some state-owned TNCs	• Growth of Asian FDI and the beginning of emerging market • Initially, market/resource-seeking kind • Lately, since 2000, some asset-augmenting FDI by Asian, especially Chinese and Indian firms • Ownership advantages, primarily country-specific, except in case of large and more globalized TNCs • Some state-owned TNCs, e.g. in natural resource sectors

developed-country TNCs 30 years ago. This is summarized in Table 8.6. In this connection, the current wave of globalization, which started around 1980, provides a natural dividing line between the present and the past. 'Economic globalization' refers to the progressive removal of barriers to cross-border flows of goods, services, capital and labor, or, equivalently, the progressive integration of national economies into a single global economy.

Of course, globalization is an evolutionary process and, in the broader sense, has been moving forward ever since the end of the Second World War (Wolf 2004). However, there has been an unmistakable acceleration in the momentum of globalization processes since around 1980. This has reflected the introduction and/or convergence of a number of different phenomena. For one, China's historic decision to move away from a centrally planned economic system to a more market-oriented system in the late 1970s heralded the reincorporation of a substantial part of the world population into the global economic arena. The impressive performance of another Asian giant, India, especially since the economic reforms of the early 1990s, has further reinforced this trend. The great majority of developing countries turned away from protectionism and toward trade liberalization when it became clear that the import substitution strategy of previous years had been ineffective in delivering economic growth. Globalization received a further boost from the demise of central planning in the USSR and Central and Eastern Europe. The upshot of the current wave of globalization is the phenomenal growth of cross-border flows of goods and services, capital and labor. National economies today interact with each other to a much greater degree than in 1980.

First, we will briefly look at the history of FDI for two time periods (pre- and post-globalization), of two groups (developing and developed economies). In the pre-globalization period, the great majority of FDI from developed economies was either market seeking or efficiency seeking; it was particularly of an intra-Triad kind. During that period, there was only a very limited amount of FDI from developing economies. The post-globalization era was most noticeable for the growth of FDI from developing countries and the emergence of emerging-market TNCs. Initially, the majority of developing-country FDI was of the market- and resource-seeking kind. However, since 2000, there has been a noticeable growth of asset-augmenting FDI, especially by Asian firms.

We believe that a comparison of post-globalization emerging-market TNCs and pre-globalization developed-country TNCs is a useful exercise because it helps us identify the exogenous and endogenous differences between the two groups of firms. By far the most important exogenous difference between these two types of TNC is that of globalization itself. The current wave of globalization has integrated global markets to a much greater extent than before. The combination of liberalizing government policies and fast-paced technological progress in transportation and communications has sharply diluted the significance of national boundaries in the global economy.

Let us focus, first, on the massive flows of capital across borders taking place during the current wave of globalization. Such flows comprise financial assets such as bonds, equities and bank loans as well as real assets such as production facilities, real estate and infrastructure. Relative to trade liberalization that began in the immediate postwar years within the multi- lateral framework of GATT, the liberalization of international capital flows is a much more recent phenomenon. In fact, even among the major developed countries, the movement of portfolio investment across borders did not become fully liberalized until the late 1970s. Prior to the current wave of globalization, government policy in both developed countries and emerging markets had restricted the international movement of capital flows, although the degree of restriction was higher in the latter. Such gov- ernment restrictions applied to inflows of both financial assets and FDI.

Historically, economic nationalism and, more particularly, the notion that unique and valuable productive assets should not be in the hands of foreigners, has been the underlying rationale for many government restric- tions on FDI inflows. However, during the current wave of globalization, there was a sea change in the attitudes of governments from both developed countries and emerging markets toward FDI. The change is all the more pronounced in emerging markets due to their past hostility toward FDI. Virtually all countries now compete fiercely with each other in order to attract foreign firms to their midst (UNCTAD 2005). The perceived benefits of FDI, in the form of employment creation, access to new tech- nologies, management capabilities, institutions and markets, and ultimately economic growth, are now widely perceived to outweigh any costs associ- ated with the abrogation of national sovereignty or cultural identity. The backlash in emerging markets against foreign capital in the aftermath of the Asian crisis was limited to short-term inflows. In fact, the crisis high- lighted the superiority of long-term inflows such as FDI, which are per- ceived to be less volatile and hence less destabilizing to economic growth. A further impetus for the pro-FDI policy shift in emerging markets was the success of pioneering economies such as Singapore and Hong Kong (China), which had embraced FDI before it became fashionable to do so.[8]

Having examined the exogenous factors, we now turn to consider the endogenous factors, which include home government policies toward FDI, intra-regional FDI, endowments of natural and created assets, institutions, geography and country size, GDP and per capita GDP, and the ownership, location and internalization (OLI) advantage components of firms. We shall focus on two observations about the endogenous differences between emerging-market TNCs and developed-country TNCs. First, home gov- ernments from emerging markets tend to exert more influence on the investment decisions of their firms than do their developed-country coun- terparts. Although the influence of such governments over their own TNCs is especially evident in the case of state-owned TNCs, private sector emerging-market TNCs are also more constrained by national economic policies and the content and quality of domestic institutions than are those from developed countries. To a much greater extent than in developed countries, the governments of emerging markets view outward FDI – whether or not it is undertaken by state-owned companies or the private sector – as an important vehicle for advancing strategic national objectives and upgrading the competitiveness of their economies. Historically, many developing countries have moved from active support for an import-substituting industrialization policy toward a greater involvement in establishing export-generating industries. In fact, an active, export-oriented outward-looking policy during the past decades has helped enhance the global reach of emerging-market TNCs (UNCTAD 2006).

Second, it is possible to view any differences in the motivation for FDI from emerging-market firms and developed-country firms in terms of their comparative ownership, location and internalization (OLI) advantages. Sustainable ownership-specific (O) advantages primarily consist of the possession of intangible assets such as globally well-known brands, and those arising from the common governance of cross-border value-added operations. Internalization-specific (I) advantages arise from a firm's managerial, organizational and institutional capabilities to exploit efficiently its ownership-specific assets. Location-specific (L) advantages refer to the benefits of locating in a particular foreign country that are conducive to a firm creating or utilizing ownership advantages.

Prior to 1980, the overwhelming majority of outward FDI came from developed countries, and outward FDI from emerging markets was confined to just a handful of countries. It was only after the start of globalization that firms from emerging markets became a visible and integral part of the global TNC landscape. The traditional developed-country TNCs, in general, expand abroad in order to exploit ownership-specific advantages which they have developed in their large internal home markets (Buckley and Casson 1976; Rugman 1981; Vernon 1966). At the same time, the relative lack of firm-specific ownership advantages among emerging-market firms suggests the relative importance of country-specific ownership advantages in determining the scope and pattern of their FDI. This is not to deny that emerging-market firms may have their own unique competitive advantages (Lall 1983; Tolentino 1993; Wells 1983). For example, they may be more knowledgeable about the resources, capabilities and consumer needs in other emerging markets due to their own domestic experiences. They may also be in a better position to offer the kinds of technologies and management skills that the smaller and least-developed countries need. However, in general, these firm-specific advantages are much less determinative of outward FDI by emerging economies today than they were for developed countries half a century or more ago. What they have, as one of the main drivers of home-based TNC activity by countries like China illustrates, is a number of country-specific advantages, such as a plentiful supply of liquid assets (UNCTAD 2006).

We shall make one final observation in connection with the interplay between exogenous and endogenous factors. Globalization has enabled firms from emerging countries to venture abroad at a much earlier stage of corporate evolution than their developed-country predecessors (Mathews 2006). In other words, in the current wave of globalization, emerging-market firms are investing overseas well before they have become large and well-established players in their own industries. The liberalization and deregulation of FDI inflows has reduced the cost of outward FDI relative to that of domestic investment. The lowering of corporate income tax rates and other fiscal incentives represents further reductions in the cost of investing abroad. Therefore, it is hardly surprising that firms in the post-globalization period face stronger institutional and other inducements to invest abroad than firms in the pre-globalization period.

At the same time, the growing integration of national markets into a single regional or global market signifies intense competitive pressures in both domestic and foreign markets. Inefficient firms that cannot compete in the global marketplace can no longer shelter behind protectionist barriers (Bartlett and Ghoshal 2000); indeed their very existence may be threatened by the onslaught of cross-border competition. Under these circumstances, a firm with limited assets faces a much stronger inducement to access the assets strategically – particularly created assets such as brands, distribution networks and R&D facilities – in foreign countries in order to protect or enhance its global competitiveness. In other words, the intense competitive pressures unleashed by the current wave of globalization are inducing firms to engage in strategic asset-augmenting FDI. Examples include several M&As, including Lenovo's purchase of IBM's PC business and Tata's acquisition of the steel giant Corus. Again, differing circumstances encourage post-globalization emerging-market firms to undertake strategic asset-augmenting at a much earlier stage of their corporate development than pre-globalization developed-country firms (Sim and Pandian 2003; Zeng and Williamson 2003).

CONCLUSION

The current wave of economic globalization has been characterized by an explosive growth in cross-border flows of goods, services, capital and labor. Although globalization is an ongoing evolutionary process that started at the end of the Second World War, the period since around 1980 has witnessed the integration of large parts of the world, in particular China and India, into the global economy. Emerging markets have traditionally been destinations of FDI rather than sources of it. In the post-1980 period, however, TNCs from these countries have become an increasingly significant part of the global FDI landscape.

Globalization is partly a result of the growing integration of emerging markets into the world economy. At the same time, the emergence of TNCs from emerging markets is partly a result of globalization. To some extent, today's FDI from emerging markets resembles yesterday's FDI from developed countries. This is particularly the case for most natural resource- and market-seeking FDI. However, as summarized in Table 8.7 there are motivational and behavioral differences between the emerging-market TNCs today and the developed-country TNCs of yesterday. Perhaps the most noticeable of these is the much earlier outward direct investment thrust by developing country firms from such countries as China and India than would have been predicted by the investment development path. Other

Table 8.7   Comparing developed country TNCs (1960s) with emerging market TNCs (2000s)

Criterion	Developed country TNCs 1960s	Emerging market TNCs 2000s
1. Motivation	FDI to exploit ownership advantages	Growing significance of asset augmentation
2. Resources	Firm-specific ownership advantages	Country ownership-specific advantages
3. Managerial approach	Ethnocentric/polycentric	Geocentric/regiocentric
4. Theoretical approach	Neo-classical perspective	Evolutionary/institutional perspective
5. Form of entry	Mainly greenfield	Increasingly strategic alliances and networking
6. Type of FDI	First, resources/market seeking, then, asset augmenting/rationalizing	Simultaneously, all kinds
7. Time frame	Gradual internationalization	Accelerated internationalization
8. Destination	Intra-triad	Largely 'regional'
9. Role of home government	Moderate	Orchestrating a catch-up strategy

differences include the form of entry, its management approach and the timeframe. This, in turn, reflects the perceived need of these countries and their firms to augment their ownership-specific advantages; in so doing, this helps them to become global players. Such a driving force was generally absent from first-world TNCs in the 1960s and 1970s.

Table 8.7 also identifies other differences between contemporary emerging-market TNCs and their developed-country counterparts 40 years ago. These include (1) the form of foreign entry – emerging-market TNCs tend to opt for more collaborative and network-related modes than those earlier preferred by developed country TNCs; (2) the managerial approach – from the start of their foreign involvement, the organizational strategy of emerging-market TNCs has been mainly regional or geocentric; (3) the role of home government – most emerging-market TNCs have active, and often financial, backing from their governments, unlike that provided by developed-country governments in the 1960s; (4) the destinations of FDI, which, until quite recently, had been primarily intra-regional; and (5) the theoretical approach – in the case of emerging market TNCs this has veered toward evolutionary and institutional models, away from (extensions of) neoclassical models originally used to explain developed country FDI.

At the same time, as already noted in this chapter, we would accept that global events, technological events and learning experiences over the past 40 years have compelled established and new TNCs from industrialized countries to review their global strategies, some of which (for example, their mode of entry, organizational structures and the geography of their operations) are becoming quite similar to those adopted by emerging-market TNCs.

But perhaps most important of all, unlike yesterday's developed-country TNCs, today's emerging-market TNCs rarely have the firm-specific ownership advantages (notably organizational and management skills) to ensure success in their outward FDI. What they do appear to have is a variety of home-country-specific advantages that they are able to internalize and use outside their national boundaries. The most obvious example is access by Chinese firms to ample financial assets. Only time will tell whether the current truncation of the investment development path will pay off for emerging-market TNCs. Much of their future will depend on how successful they are in bridging firm- and country-specific institutional distance, particularly with respect to issues such as environmental and corporate social responsibility (Dunning 2006).[9] However, given that many of these challenges can be met over the next decade or more, we would foresee that the industrial and geographical patterns of emerging-market TNCs will come to resemble those of their developed-country predecessors.

NOTES

1. The *World Investment Report* (United Conference on Trade and Development 2004–2006) defines 'developing and transition economies' as comprising all developing countries plus countries in South-East Europe and the Commonwealth of Independent States (CIS). Occasionally, the term 'South' or 'Third World' is also used to denote these economies. In this chapter, the term 'emerging markets' is more narrowly defined and refers to the major sources of FDI from the 'South', including Argentina, Brazil, Chile, China, Columbia, Hong Kong (China), India, the Republic of Korea, Malaysia, Mexico, Nigeria, Russia, Singapore, South Africa, Turkey, Taiwan Province of China and Venezuela, which accounted for 90 per cent of FDI from emerging markets in 2004.
2. FDI by TNCs from developing countries has changed in both significance and pattern over the past decades. The early increase of FDI from developing countries in the 1970s and 1980s was from all parts of the developing world, including Africa, Asia and Latin America. From the mid-1980s onward, however, Asia began to take the lead (Dunning, Van Hoesel and Narula 1998).
3. In 2003, the value of exports was $748 billion, $724 billion $472 billion and $438 billion for Germany, the US, Japan and China respectively (World Bank 2006).
4. These same six economies accounted for 79 per cent of FDI outflows from developing countries between 2002 and 2004, and 6 per cent of global FDI outflows.
5. Five of the top ten TNCs from Central and Eastern Europe were Russian, including a $7.2 billion stake in petroleum and natural gas by JSC (UNCTAD 2005).
6. From a government perspective, outward and inward FDI can be used as a wider policy to upgrade national competitiveness. Certain countries might be in a favorable position to exploit or gain new assets via outward FDI, while others might best advance their competitive or comparative advantage by encouraging inward FDI from a different group of countries. The application of the investment development path to understanding the growth of outward FDI of developing countries is set out in UNCTAD (2006).
7. They included a $7.8 billion purchase of the Canadian company John Labatt by the Brazilian company Ambex, a $1.7 billion acquisition of IBM's PC business by the Chinese company Lenovo and a $4.2 billion investment in the Canadian oil group Petro-kazakhstan by the Chinese energy group CNPO (UNCTAD 2006).
8. There are signs, however, of a new backlash against FDI, which *inter alia* is associated with a move by some countries toward protectionism and toward more left-wing governments (Sauvant 2006).
9. UNCTAD (2006) also explores these issues and suggests that the (current) differences between today's emerging-market TNCs and yesterday's developed-country TNCs may have more to do with the former's ideological, cultural and social distinctiveness rather than economic or technical characteristics.

REFERENCES

Bartlett, C.A. and S. Ghoshal (2000). 'Going global: lessons from late movers', *Harvard Business Review*, 78, pp. 132–142.
Buckley, P.J. and M.C. Casson (1976). *The Future of the Multinational Enterprise* (London: Macmillan).
Dunning, J.H. (1981). 'Explaining the international direct investment position of countries: towards a dynamic or developmental approach', *Weltwirtschaftliches Archiv*, 117, pp. 30–64.

Dunning, J.H. (1993). *Multinational Enterprises and the Global Economy* (Wokingham, England: Addison Wesley).

Dunning, J.H. (2006). 'Space, location and distance in international business activities'. Paper presented at the *Annual Meeting of the European Academy of International Business*, 7–9 December, Fribourg, Switzerland.

Dunning, J.H., C. Kim and J.-D. Lin (2001). 'Incorporating trade into the investment development path: a case study of the Republic of Korea and Taiwan', *Oxford Development Studies*, 29, pp. 145–154.

Dunning, J.H. and R. Narula (1996). *Foreign Direct Investment and Governments* (London and New York: Routledge).

Dunning, J.H., R. Van Hoesel and R. Narula (1998). 'Third World multinationals revisited: new developments and theoretical implications', in John H. Dunning, ed., *Globalization, Trade and Foreign Direct Investment* (Oxford: Pergamon Press), pp. 255–286.

Hoskisson, R.E., L. Eden, C.M. Lau and M. Wright (2000). 'Strategy in emerging economies', *Academy of Management Journal*, 43, pp. 249–267.

Kuemmerle, W. (1999). 'The drivers of foreign direct investment into research and development: an empirical investigation', *Journal of International Business Studies*, 30, pp. 1–24.

Lall, S. (1983). *The New Multinationals: The Spread of Third World Enterprises* (Chichester: John Wiley).

Mathews, J.A. (2006). 'Dragon multinationals: new players in 21st century globalization', *Asia Pacific Journal of Management*, 23, pp. 5–27.

Moon, H.-C. and T.W. Roehl (2001). 'Unconventional foreign direct investment and the imbalance theory', *International Business Review*, 10, pp. 197–215.

Rugman, A.M. (1981). *Inside the Multinationals: The Economics of Internal Markets* (New York: Columbia University Press).

Sauvant, Karl P. (2006). 'A backlash against foreign direct investment', in Laza Kekic and Karl P. Sauvant, eds, *World Investment Prospects to 2010: Boom or Backlash?* (London: Economist Intelligence Unit), pp. 71–77.

Sim, A.B. and J.R. Pandian (2003). 'Emerging Asian MNEs and their internationalization strategies: case study evidence on Taiwanese and Singaporean firms', *Asia Pacific Journal of Management*, 20, pp. 27–50.

Tolentino, P.E. (1993). *Technological Innovation and Third World Multinationals* (London: Routledge).

United Nations Conference on Trade and Development (UNCTAD) (2004). *World Investment Report 2004: The Shift Towards Services* (New York and Geneva: UNCTAD).

United Nations Conference on Trade and Development (UNCTAD) (2005). *World Investment Report 2005: Transnational Corporations and the Internationalization of R&D* (New York and Geneva: UNCTAD).

United Nations Conference on Trade and Development (UNCTAD) (2006). *World Investment Report 2006: FDI from Developing and Transition Economies: Implications for Development* (New York and Geneva: UNCTAD).

Vernon, R. (1966). 'International investment and international trade in the product cycle', *Quarterly Journal of Economics*, 80, pp. 190–207.

Wells, L.T. (1983). *Third World Multinationals: the Rise of Foreign Investment from Developing Countries* (Cambridge MA: MIT Press).

Wesson, T.J. (1993). *An Alternative Motivation for Foreign Direct Investment*, Ph.D. dissertation, Harvard University.

Wolf, M. (2004). *Why Globalization Works* (New Haven and London: Yale University Press).

World Bank (2006). *World Development Report 2006: Equity and Development* (New York: Oxford University Press).

Zeng, M. and P.J. Williamson (2003). 'The hidden dragons', *Harvard Business Review*, 81, pp. 92–99.

PART III

What's in it for host countries?

9. Who's afraid of emerging-market TNCs? Or: are developing countries missing something in the globalization debate?

Andrea Goldstein

INTRODUCTION

This chapter discusses the consequences of South-to-North FDI flows for OECD governments and firms. Emerging-market transnational corporations (TNCs) from non-OECD countries wish – and indeed need – to establish a direct presence in OECD countries to develop new resources and capabilities.[1] Their rise introduces a wide range of new issues in the policy debate in OECD countries. These include the importance of nationality in determining corporate behavior, the adaptability of non-OECD investors to the policy environment and the informal norms that characterize business in OECD countries, and the consequences for national security.

The current wave of globalization is characterized by the unprecedented international scope of distribution systems and markets for goods and services, capital, labor and technology (Feenstra and Hamilton 2006). Yet the rising interdependence of national economies poses challenges to national sovereignty and, somehow paradoxically, opens the door to protectionism, possibly more in the investment than on the trade front. In Europe, in the first five months of 2006, the governments of France, Italy, Poland, and Spain sought to check takeover bids by German (E.On), Italian (ENEL, Unicredit) and Spanish (Abertis) companies, while Korean politicians described foreign investors as 'vultures'. Still, if recent developments provide any guidance, TNCs from non-OECD countries are particularly exposed to the risk of the 'selective globalization syndrome' (Gross 2006), which makes globalization opportunities available *à la carte* (that is, according to demand) or *prix fixe* (that is, with constraints) depending on who orders the menu.[2]

Public opinion is sensitive to an investor's nationality. In the Czech Republic, 52 per cent of respondents emphasized the importance of country of origin (Gabal, Analysis and Consulting 2001); 70 per cent of Americans (and 58 per cent of Republicans) opposed the DP World takeover of P&O (*CBS News Poll* 2006);[3] in France, 65 per cent believed it was the Government's role to stop foreign bids (TNS-Sofres 2006). In a way, this is not surprising. Much like naive predictions about the demise of the sovereign state have been long proven unsubstantiated, so have been expectations of a convergence of business systems toward a seamless and landless model. Even while their assets and liabilities become increasingly global, corporations continue to be shaped decisively by the policies and values of their home countries (Doremus *et al*. 1999). If people, for what-ever reason, have a negative appreciation of a country, they do not like their corporations either.[4] At the same time, when they operate beyond their national borders, TNCs internalize many characteristics of the host envi-ronment and, to some extent, they do so to a larger degree than they influence such environments. At the end of the day, many corporate behav-iors happen in reaction to government rules – and if the former are malicious, it is probably because the latter are faulty in design or imple-mentation.

This chapter is organized as follows. The next section summarizes the arguments made in some high-visibility business deals (attempted and real-ized) that saw emerging TNCs as suitors. Section 9.2 goes back in time and analyzes the reaction of European and North American elites and public opinion regarding the emergence of Japanese TNCs in the 1980s, to gauge the extent to which parallels can be drawn with the most recent episodes. Section 9.3 moves to the policy implications and the final section concludes.

9.1   WHAT DO BUSINESSES, GOVERNMENTS AND PEOPLE FEAR?

Since 2003, the amount of inward FDI from non-traditional source coun-tries into the OECD has grown dramatically. Non-traditional source coun-tries are those that are still not in the OECD, plus those that have joined the OECD since 1994 (Mexico, the Republic of Korea, the Czech Republic, Hungary, Poland and Slovakia, in chronological order). Over this short period, a number of big acquisitions have generated considerable contro-versy, to the point that some deals have had to be repackaged or shelved. Those of particular interest for this chapter are summarized in Table 9.1.[5] What arguments have been advanced to oppose such deals? In each case, emerging-market TNCs have been accused of following different rules in a number of policy domains. A note of caution on this approach is warranted. Making comparisons is useful to uncover perhaps hidden motives and

Table 9.1 Selected cross-border mergers and acquisitions by emerging TNCs, 2003–2006

Bidder (nation)	Target (nation)	Year	Description
Mahindra and Mahindra (India)	Valtra (Finland)	2003	In June, M&M proposed to create the world's largest manufacturer of tractors. In August, the Minister of Trade and Industry was reported as saying that the State's Finnish Industrial Investment Ltd was ready to join the bid to preserve Finnish ownership, before US AGCO bought Valtra at almost double the €350m that M&M had offered.
Lenovo (China)	IBM PC (US)	2004	Lenovo paid $1.25 billion ($650 million in cash) and assumed $500 million in debt obligations; IBM took an 18.9% stake in Lenovo.
CNOOC (China)	Unocal (US)	2005	In June, CNOOC made a $19.6 billion all-cash hostile bid. In July, it asked CFIUS to review its offer. In August, it withdrew.
Haier (China)	Hoover (US)	2005	In June, it teamed up with Bain Capital and the Blackstone Group to make a $1.28 billion offer, which was withdrawn in July.
Old Mutual (South Africa)	Skandia (Sweden)	2005–06	Launched a $6.04 billion takeover bid in September, which ABN Amro found to be fair from a financial point of view; 8 of Skandia's 11 directors (but not the chairperson) rejected the offer; in January, after extending its offer period three times, OM declared its offer unconditional.
DP World (UAE)	P&O (UK, US assets)	2006	After CFIUS approved the deal in February (following a standard 30-day review), DPW agreed to an additional 45-day security review. In March, following a 62-to-2 Congress vote forbidding the acquisition, DPW agreed to spin off the U.S. assets.
Mittal (Netherlands)	Arcelor (France, Luxembourg, Spain, Belgium)	2006	Unexpected €18.6 billion offer in January, raised to €25.8 billion in May. Mittal's choice of Severstal as a white knight met shareholders' resistance. Arcelor agreed in June to a merger valued at €26.8 billion. Arcelor shareholders would have 50.6% of the new company, named Arcelor-Mittal and headquartered in Luxembourg. Joseph Kinsch, chairperson of Arcelor, would be chairperson of the combined company, and when he retired, which was expected shortly, he would be succeeded by Lakshmi Mittal.

Source: the author, from various sources.

possibly contribute to grounded theory building. However, the cases that are analyzed here are relatively few and are different in nature; emerging markets are not a homogenous group and the potential threats they pose to host countries vary significantly; and different host countries are concerned about different dimensions. It is also important to underline that, while emerging-market investors have been treated rudely in some cases, they have been welcomed in other instances. Interestingly enough, it is hard to detect any regularity. For example, in Italy, the purchase of the second-largest telecom provider and of the second-largest steel maker by Egyptian and Russian TNCs respectively, hardly raised any eyebrow, while European takeover bids in other sectors met with fierce resistance (Goldstein 2006).

In the area of finance, business in emerging economies is accused of having access to cheap credit. Chevron claimed that CNOOC's offer was funded partly by subordinated loans from the state-owned parent firm which gave it an advantage equivalent to about $10 per Unocal share over the US oil major's bid. A close inspection of the terms of the deal by the *Financial Times*, however, revealed that the parent company was not being directly funded by the government, that the three Chinese lenders that lent to the parent firm were following commercial behavior and that a clause in the contract allowed the parent firm to demand repayment of the funds from five years after the completion of the deal.[6] Moreover, there are fears that emerging-market TNCs do not master fully the intricacies of Western financial markets. For instance, one of the rumored reasons why Minmetals lost out to Noranda, a Canadian company, was that, on the bid deadline date, the Chinese company's chief executive could not be reached because he was accompanying leading politicians on an official visit to South America.[7]

Questionable corporate governance and scant regard for minority investors are among further accusations. CNOOC's four non-executive directors (out of eight members) went as far as hiring independent advisers to review management's preliminary plans for a possible Unocal bid. Mittal has been accused of being 'a sort of UFO in the world of steel . . . one cannot but be intrigued by the conditions under which many [of its acquisitions in the mid-1990s] were made and the problems they have raised' (Roche 2006). While it is true that 'family corporations are less shackled, because their feet are not held to the fire by independent directors and investors',[8] the literature is far from conclusive on the welfare consequences of family ownership.[9] It is also argued that prestige and empire building are the drivers of foreign acquisitions – that CNOOC, for instance, was chasing the wrong target (the bulk of Unocal's Asian production is dedicated to supplying local power stations and is not available for exports to China) and offering too much.[10]

In terms of strategy, the charge levied at emerging-market TNCs is that they do not have the traditional ownership advantage – a brand, a portfolio of patents, a unique product – that define established TNCs. According to Arcelor CEO Guy Dollé, who compared Mittal to eau de cologne and his company to expensive perfume, the industrial logic behind the proposed deal was 'extremely slim' since several of Mittal's US sites had 'come out of Chapter 7 and 11'[11] and were in poor shape compared with other steel plants.[12] While the two companies have, in fact, very different cultures – Mittal is focused on making commercial-grade products while Arcelor is a very technical company geared more to producing a higher-value type of steel – in this industry, the most successful players are those that have constructed mills on the cheap and worked their way up.[13] The Swedish managers of Skandia, Scandinavia's largest insurer, contrasted its strategy as a niche player in the unit-linked savings market with Old Mutual's business plan as a financial conglomerate.[14] The Swedish state pension funds also argued against Old Mutual's offer, saying that it entailed unacceptable currency and political risks, even if foreign shareholders deemed the offer for the loss-making operation fair.[15]

Corporate social responsibility has been another hot issue. European politicians opposing the Arcelor takeover cited concerns about industrial relations, even when trade unions themselves defended the record of the 'Indian' company and in fact argued that Arcelor was less sensitive to their concerns.[16] The Attorney-Generals of California, Texas, Montana and New Mexico also wrote to Unocal in June 2005, fearing for the environment, the health of their citizens and the solvency of their state treasuries if a deal with CNOOC went through.

As Congressional *angst* about the US trade deficit mounted, another area of contention has surrounded the terms of investment and market access, especially to China. A report by Senator Charles Schumer, a New York Democrat who has proposed 27.5 per cent tariffs on all Chinese imports if China refuses to revalue the renminbi, argues that Beijing limits foreign business activity by limiting partnerships and joint ventures, requiring technology transfers, and by targeting industries such as steel, aviation and high-technology.[17] Senator Byron Dorgan, a North Dakota Democrat, has argued that since Beijing would not allow a US company to buy a Chinese oil company, 'why on earth should they be able to buy an American oil company?'[18] Although Gazprom was only rumored to be interested in bidding for Centrica in the United Kingdom, the lack of reciprocity in access to the Russian gas distribution network was the reason allegedly advanced by the British government to scare it off.

National security is another area of concern. In December 2004, the landmark IBM unit purchase sparked fears that Lenovo could be acting as a screen for the Chinese government and army to transfer 'advanced' and sensitive technology.[19] Following complaints from a trio of senior Republicans, the deal was reviewed by the Committee on Foreign Investments in the United States (CFIUS), a body created in 1975 to gauge any impact on national security.[20] The IBM inquiry was a full investigation, which occurs in far fewer than 1 per cent of cross-border deals. The Committee's proceedings are secret, and IBM would not say what steps it took to address the concerns of the group. Information leaked to the press, however, indicates that IBM apparently made more in the way of commitments and assurances than concessions which might restrain its sales or product development.[21] The steps included agreeing to separate Lenovo's US employees, mainly in the Research Triangle Park in North Carolina, from IBM workers there who work on other products, like larger server computers and software.[22] The national security argument was raised again at the time of the Unocal deal – that, in a tight energy market, foreign control of a company hooked up to US strategic oil reserves and owning the country's only rare-earth mine was risky.[23] And when the State Department announced a $13 million purchase of 16 000 Lenovo computers in 2006, Frank Wolf, a Virginia Republican who chairs the House Appropriations Subcommittee on Commerce, Justice, State and the Judiciary, objected to their use in a classified network connecting embassies and consulates. The State Department eventually agreed to use Lenovo computers only in unclassified settings.

Government ownership and control of some emerging TNCs is an additional concern. Following a recommendation by the US–China Economic and Security Review Commission, the House passed a resolution warning that the CNOOC bid could impair national security and favored an amendment aimed at barring the Administration from approving the deal. The Chinese Foreign Ministry chastised Congress and called on it to 'correct its mistaken ways of politicizing economic and trade issues'.[24] In a similar vein, the energy bill was amended, threatening to increase the time it would take for CNOOC to complete the regulatory process to buy Unocal from a maximum of 90 days to at least 141 days. When announcing its decision to abandon the deal, CNOOC issued a tersely worded written statement and called the political opposition in the United States 'regrettable and unjustified'. In fact, while not openly opposing CNOOC's bid, Beijing was believed to be ill-at-ease with the possibility that the takeover tussle could overshadow President Hu Jintao's September 2005 visit to Washington. As *The New York Times* put it in a leader on the P&O deal, 'it is not irrational for the United States to resist putting port operators, perhaps the most vulnerable part of the security infrastructure, under [the] control [of an ally whose] record in the war on terror is mixed'.[25] After emphasizing terrorism fears in the public mind, it was of course a paradox that the Bush administration could be accused of being soft on security matters. In the Arcelor case, Dollé underplayed the degree of government influence on the Russian economy – even if Alexei Mordashov, the owner of Severstal, had previously discussed the deal with the Kremlin – while arguing that the Mittal offer carried a higher political risk – even if the Indians only sought political support in Delhi after presenting the unsolicited offer.[26]

Last but not least, racial stereotyping lurks behind some of the opponents' arguments. Arcelor executives dismissed Mittal as a 'company full of Indians' trying to buy their firm with Monopoly money (*monnaie de singe*), while defining Mordashov as a 'true European'.[27] More generally, prejudice can be deduced through comparative analysis: extreme double standards, for example, are usually a sign that something strange is going on, even if comments or concerns look reasonable in isolation.[28] In fact, the origins of Mordashov's fortunes are at least as suspicious as those of Mittal, a point that many opponents of his bid (and supporters of Severstal's) have somewhat missed.[29]

9.2 DÉJÀ VU? THE RESPONSE TO JAPANESE INVESTMENTS IN THE 1980s

In the 1980s, Japan rapidly emerged as one of the world's leading sources of FDI. Outflows rose from less than $5 billion in 1980 to a $68 billion peak in 1989, after the Plaza Accord allowed for an appreciation of the Japanese yen (Farrell 2000). Japanese TNCs' FDI outflows to the United States rose from $3.4 billion in 1985 to an average of $17.6 billion in 1988–89. Many of the arguments made recently against emerging TNCs echo those that were heard in the United States and Europe in the 1980s.

In an elegant summary of the views of the US critics, Yamamura (1989) referred to unfair trade and other practices that allowed Japanese firms to displace competitors, destroy jobs and accumulate in turn the resources needed to invest overseas; strong reservations regarding the culture-bound and anti-union Japanese managerial style; 'serious concern for the likelihood of diminished US ability to innovate and adopt innovations as US firms lose domestic market share to Japanese exports and the Japanese firms in their midst'; and to the risk that 'the political influence of Japanese interests [may have] undue effect on US defense capabilities and foreign policy'.[30]

The policy reaction at the time was swift: in 1988, Felix Rohatyn, the influential New York banker, proposed setting up a special vetting process for foreign investment to avoid threats to national security. Later in the year, Congress passed the Exon-Florio Amendment to the Defense Production

Act of 1950, empowering the President to block foreign acquisitions that threaten national security. President Reagan designated the Committee on Foreign Investments in the United States to review such transactions.

Although the arguments are similar, there are at least five aspects under which the economic situation in the 1980s that led to the decision of many Japanese firms to establish themselves in Europe and North America was different from the one currently prevailing. To say nothing about the political situation; this will be reviewed in the following section.

First, controlling for market size and relative labor costs, Japanese investment was significantly influenced by trade protection measures, and in particular, by the level of anti-dumping actions (Barrell and Pain 1999). In a context of an expected dollar depreciation and expected tougher labor standards, Japanese automobile companies responded to the introduction of 'gray-area' measures like Voluntary Export Restraints (VERs) by hastening the process of direct investment (Co 1997). Similarly, in the United Kingdom, trade policy and anti-dumping actions influenced the level and distribution of Japanese investment across sectors (Girma *et al.* 1999). It was not only avoiding protectionist measures in place by establishing production facilities that counted. As the probability of protection rose, Japanese firms engaged in more FDI as an insurance policy – an especially important strategy in those sectors in which a firm may lose substantial market share if it does not have a plant in the host country when protectionism is put in place (Blonigen and Feenstra 1997). In short, the threat of protection had a substantial impact on non-acquisition Japanese FDI in the United States in the 1980s. In addition, threat-responding FDI by Japanese firms had political intentions of defusing the threat of protection as suggested by *quid pro quo* theory.

Most current US actions toward China are fully consistent with current WTO rules, including the special terms of China's 2001 WTO accession (Bown and McCulloch 2005).[31] In this sense, the situation has changed. Still, it is very interesting to see South Carolina emerging as the biggest host state for Chinese investment in the United States in terms of jobs created. In the 1980s, Japanese firms

> intentionally located some of their factories within the states and districts of senators and representatives considered protectionist toward their particular industry. Having sizable numbers of constituents drawing paychecks from Japanese firms can have a moderating influence on politicians who might otherwise be inclined to support protectionism (Lincoln 2003, p. 115).

It helped that these were also 'Right to Work' states, where it is easier to operate without unions. Senator Graham from South Carolina is possibly the most prominent of this breed of Capitol Hill politicians, and it is probable, although difficult to prove, that the Chinese government encouraged or coordinated such location decisions.

Second, Japan at the time (and to some extent still today) had a very *sui generis* model of industrial organization. Inter-corporate linkages that define *keiretsu* groups of firms played a significant role, especially in core electronics and automobile industries, as supplier–buyer relationships were transferred to the foreign countries where FDI took place (Kimura and Pugel 1995). In fact, one possible reason why Japanese-owned establishments in the United States held large inventories – a counterintuitive circumstance given their supposed competence in supply chain management – is their particularly heavy reliance on purchased materials, much of which are imported from Japan (Howenstine and Shannon 1996). The worry at the time was that 'a concentrated Japanese oligopoly [in semiconductors] poses a threat to downstream producers throughout the world [and] poses a threat to American military capabilities that rely on high-technology electronics' (Tyson 1992, p. 146). China does not have industrial conglomerates and the degree of supply concentration is generally low.[32]

Third, as early as 1992, Japanese TNCs employed 737 000 people in the United States versus 410 000 people employed by US TNCs in Japan. In contrast, TNCs from Brazil, Russia, India and China (the so-called BRIC countries) had a combined US employment of 10 200 in 2003, which is only marginally higher than 1 per cent of the employment in US TNCs in the BRICs (982 000).[33] In other words, FDI has played a major role in China's recent catch-up that it obviously did not for Japan. This imbalance may mean different things. On the one hand, it can mean that the possibility for mutually penetrating TNCs to act as an alternative to fierce head-on competition is far less relevant today; on the other hand, it can mean that US (and, more generally, Western) TNCs have a lot at stake if emerging TNCs receive a brusque welcome in their overseas forays. One would expect the asymmetry between limited BRIC investment in the West and the explosion of Western FDI in emerging markets to caution against perceptions of the BRICs as unfair partners. And yet, few of the pro-China business lobbyists, who in many cases acted to fend off congressional actions against China trade, proved willing to back CNOOC. Understanding why this occurred is a theme for future research.

Fourth, Japanese firms have not been passive actors in the process of business convergence. If they now walk the talk of shareholders' value and corporate governance, they have influenced Western business practices in innumerable ways, from just-in-time to *keizen*.[34] It remains to be seen whether emerging-market TNCs can also contribute to this two-way dialectic.

Finally, nowadays nobody disputes that Chinese and Arab central banks are as important as buyers of US government bonds as the US is as a market for Chinese goods and Arab oil. In contrast, in the 1980s, critics saw the fact that current and future US generations may pay debt service to Japanese households and financial institutions as a central preoccupation.

9.3   POLICY IMPLICATIONS, WITH A FOCUS ON THE CURRENT US DEBATE

It is in the US that the threat of having emerging-market TNC as the barbarians at the gate has generated the most heated debate on policy remedies, with a focus on modifying the rules governing the Committee on Foreign Investments in the United States. According to Tyson (2005), 'this review process has been mainly applied to foreign acquisitions of American companies producing military goods or components. Recently, such reviews have been extended to foreign acquisitions involving dual-use technologies in the telecommunications, Internet, and computer industries.'[35]

Different proposals were presented in the summer of 2006. One set of bills would give Congress a greater role in overseeing individual investments by unprecedented, intrusive reporting requirements of all filings with CFIUS, including reports that identify disagreements by agencies. Another legislative initiative would transfer congressional jurisdiction over CFIUS from the Banking Committee, which has traditionally balanced security concerns with recognition of the importance of foreign investment, to the Homeland Security Committee, tilting the balance away from investment. A troubling proposal would require a mandatory 45-day investigation – now reserved for only the most controversial deals with genuine national security concerns – for all foreign investments (or, under current law, foreign acquisitions) in 'critical infrastructure', even by purely private firms. This would include a dozen industries, from agriculture to telecoms and banking, which account for about 25 per cent of the US economy (Graham and Marchick 2006).[36] Proposed emergency legislation by Senators Hillary Clinton and Robert Menendez would prevent foreign governments from controlling US-container port assets and bar companies such as APL, a Californian line owned by Singapore's state-owned NOL.[37]

The suggested legislation to overhaul completely the national security vetting system, however, risks adding to the problem instead of offering a solution.[38] By legislating what was an administrative procedure, the reform could multiply excessive and wasteful scrutiny of routine transactions, politicize foreign investment decisions, encourage agencies to go on record in opposition to foreign investment deals, and potentially lead to leaks of proprietary information. But confidentiality is central to acquisitions. Thus, to meet overall objectives, it is essential to pair policies that support well-functioning, open capital markets with specific carve-outs for transactions that pose a strategic threat (Holtz-Eakin 2006). A policy mechanism to accomplish this aim should specify clearly which transactions may generate legitimate national security concerns, identify transparently how the strategic impact of the transaction would be evaluated, ensure a leak-proof degree of confidentiality to the process, and provide for flexible arrangements that permit means to augment security or otherwise satisfy these criteria as part of the transaction itself.

Reciprocity is also a two-edged sword. In a mutually connected and increasingly complex world, where it is impossible to write contracts that incorporate all possible contingencies, trust is crucial and must be built over time. In the logistics business, for instance, 'the US is relying on the goodwill of Dubai Ports and other port operators to do overseas security checks for them and the furor over DP World obviously doesn't help secure such co-operation'.[39] Already, Dubai participates in the container security initiative, through which US customs officers are allowed to check US-bound containers for suspicious material. And the same Chevron executive who in June 2005 accused CNOOC of 'clearly not being a commercial company', had previously called his company's collaboration with the Chinese 'extremely successful'.[40] It is a further irony of the saga that the failure to offer any commitment in the WTO services negotiations involving maritime services that involve port activities has put the US, usually at the forefront of efforts to open up foreign markets, on the receiving end of a plurilateral request.

Moreover, rather mundane considerations lurk behind some of the more lurid accusations levied at emerging-market TNCs. Of the 41 House of Representatives members of both parties who wrote to President Bush expressing their concern that any run on Unocal by CNOOC represented a threat to national security, 22 had received contributions from Chevron in the past three electoral cycles.[41] Many political winds – including the freedom with which Republicans have criticized the President when his approval numbers were very low and the chance for Democrats to look tough on homeland security – have fanned the jingoistic indignation in the DP World case, which has spawned eight congressional hearings and some twenty bills. Opponents of the deal included the provision to block it as an amendment to a 'must pass' emergency spending bill for the Iraq war and Hurricane Katrina, thus complicating the situation for the administration.[42]

In a similar vein, it is at least disingenuous to forget that proposed legislation on foreign ownership could inhibit consolidation of the inefficient containers industry. This remains undersized and mostly family-owned and enjoys generally good business conditions.[43] In many cases, the responsibility for security is not with the private sector. In the case of ports, the evaluation and inspection of shipments is the federal government's responsibility, through the US Coast Guard and Customs, and not the port owners' or the terminal operators'. Ports authorities subject all dock workers, including those employed by terminal operators such as DP World, to stringent background checks. In fact, most managers in the US maritime industry did not think the P&O takeover endangered national security and thought instead that political critics had failed to understand the issue.[44] Similarly, rigging the market for corporate control is hardly the most appropriate measure to improve energy security.

9.4   MAY OWNERSHIP MATTER AFTER ALL?

Economists have often looked with disdain at some of the pundits' views reported in the previous section. The truth of the matter is that then and now 'much of the debate [on corporate ownership] is ideological, complicated by nationalism, conflicts of regional interest, and, in a few instances, racism' (Yamamura 1989, p. 24).[45] Ideology, of course, is visible on both sides of the fence; for instance, the optimality of free trade and capital flows remains an issue where science counts as much as faith, especially when theory is translated into policy decisions (McCulloch 1993). Leaving aside those cross-border transactions that show risk of affecting security directly or indirectly because of breaches of export control laws and regulations (see Chapter 14 of this book), the link between corporate nationality and competitiveness is, on three dimensions at least, strong enough to warrant policy consideration.

First, because of the spatially bound nature of spillovers and linkages, geography and proximity still play an important role in the generation of new products and processes (Breschi *et al.* 2005). Moreover, despite the growing importance of R&D activities of foreign affiliates in most host economies (Narula and Zanfei 2004), foreign affiliates still play an ancillary role in innovation (Singh and Khanna 2003).[46] In this context, laggard firms might invest abroad to capture local advantages through geographical proximity of plant location, rather than to exploit existing ones (Fosfuri and Motta 1999). When these factors are combined, they point to the fact that having companies with strong local roots is important for a nation's long-term competitiveness. In fact, the Pechiney precedent is important to understand the French unease with the Mittal offer. A few years ago, the French aluminum company was a French *fleuron technologique* and a global leader in electrolysis technology. Following the takeover by Alcan in 2003, Pechiney's excellence centers in France were shut down (Cohen 2006).

Similarly, corporations are social actors and play a role in identifying national priorities and drawing appropriate policies. In modern capitalist societies, business must pay attention to long-term societal concerns – in areas ranging from diversity to equal opportunity, the environment, and workforce policies (Palmisano 2006) – and in turn, business exercises increasing influence on social and political dynamics and may even acquire decision-making authority (Rohatyn 2005). Based on a number of empiri- cal studies, Khanna (2006) argued that 'companies rooted in a particular country are more likely than footloose multinationals to make a nation's problems their own'. A strong identification with a particular country increases the economic interest that a company finds in investing in public goods for the country – from education to infrastructure and better govern- ance standards. To the extent that China and, to a lesser extent, Russia and various Arab countries are far from being consolidated democracies, it is natural to see stakeholders worried about takeover bids by companies from these countries.

A third reason why the emergence of this new breed of TNCs deserves to be treated carefully has to do with their behavior in third markets. To the extent that investment by Chinese and other emerging-market investors is not subject to political and governance conditionality, as is increasingly the case with Western TNCs, FDI and the strengthening of autocratic regimes in rogue states may proceed in parallel, especially in countries that produce oil and other raw materials.[47] The risk of falling into the protectionist trap is that emerging-market TNCs may prefer to search for alternative acquisi- tion strategies in the future – in the case of CNOOC, which is listed, to strengthen cooperation with its state-owned parent firm, China National Offshore Oil Corporation, and to redirect its efforts toward countries with a patchy history in terms of human rights and corruption.

The accusation that emerging-market TNCs are acting as instruments of the foreign policy ambitions of their home governments is sometimes naive, or may simply conceal deep-rooted protectionist reflexes. The interpene- tration of business and political dynamics is obviously germane to the study of TNCs from their very origin. As summarized by Jones (2005, p. 218), 'from the [nineteenth] century, governments were aware that national diplomatic influence and national economic influence were related'. Still, many emerging-market TNCs maintain closer ties with their governments than their OECD peers, often because they remain state- owned or state-controlled, in particular in oil and other natural resources. It would be unfortunate if government support and weak checks and balances from other stakeholders led emerging-market TNCs to adopt sub-par behavioral and operational standards in low-income developing countries.

The onus is also on emerging-market TNCs' shoulders to prove, through open information and legal lobbying, that the perception that they are instruments of a foreign country's policy is flawed. Although these firms are now ready to spend a lot of money to enlist lobbyists, policy and media advisers, naiveté also plays a role. CNOOC misread the political environment in Washington as its path would have been smoother if it had joined with a US oil company as a partner in its bid, an option that was considered briefly but rejected. It then further undermined its bid by asking Unocal to join forces in lobbying Congress and to pick up the break-up fee due to Chevron.[48] The commanding heights of business in key emerging markets are very conscious of this quandary and of the risk of mismanaging the process. Ranbaxy Laboratories' CEO wrote that 'India has to recognize that the onus is on us to demonstrate our good intent' (Singh 2006, p. 15).[49]

CONCLUSIONS

From the previous discussions, it is clear that most arguments deployed in Western countries to block foreign acquisitions, especially by emerging-market TNCs, are specious, and more often than not, they amount to a not-so-veiled protectionism. For example, the CNOOC and DP storms were both ignited by third-party US firms that stood to lose from the deals.[50] In principle, applying globally the tools that have sustained the integration of the BRICs and other emerging economies into the world economy can contribute to world prosperity. Outward FDI is a further form of engagement with the global economy and as such brings new forces to bear in the direction of better political and corporate governance. As emerging-market TNCs become increasingly active as competitors in developed markets, they will have to conform to higher standards of corporate governance, accountability, transparency and social responsibility. To a large extent, this is what has happened with Japanese TNCs over the past three decades.[51] In fact, the BRICs and others may eventually also 'gain a new stake in placing limits on host-country investment policies' as had happened with Europe, Canada and Japan vis-à-vis the US (McCulloch 1991, p. 181).

Regardless of the country, investments should be made on a level playing field. Nonetheless, the path toward win-win globalization is paved with good, but ultimately unfulfilled, intentions. As it is unlikely that extreme protectionism will win the day, the risk is rather the emergence of a creeping variety. In an unbalanced playing field, acquisitions by trusted and well-established companies are cleared rapidly whereas any purchase by an emerging-market TNC can take much longer. According to the *Financial Times*, 'the regulatory process extended by Congress, in effect, cut the extra payment offered by CNOOC from US$3 a share to 1.38: not enough to compensate for the risk that it would end in refusal'.[52]

Still, arguing that blocking the doors of the global economy to Chinese and other up-and-coming investors is unfair – after opening the doors of their markets and praising the mostly positive consequences – is not enough. The global economy is experiencing a phase of profound changes that generate fears. This does not obviously have to translate into protectionism, but it helps to understand why 'nearly every country wants FDI, but only on its own terms' (Wilkins 1990, p. 627). In the US, and to a lesser extent in Europe and elsewhere in the West, the big question concerns China and Russia: are they an opportunity for ever-growing commercial and strategic alliances, or a threat likely to follow ever-more muscular practices?

Even without formal changes, the Lenovo, CNOOC and DP World controversies 'will lead to greater scrutiny of foreign investment, with more split decisions between agencies, and thus more decisions landing on the president's desk, subjecting him to case-by-case lobbying' (Eizenstat and Maibach 2006, p. A14). Efforts to gain a better understanding of the underlying trends, the emerging issues and the necessary adaptations to the policy environment must encompass all stakeholders. It would be ideal to introduce mechanisms of policy dialogue 'to begin talking about these things ahead of time so that we don't have a crisis if two days from now it turns out that some Chinese company wants to buy John Deere or something' (Rohatyn 2005, p. 8).

This chapter is a first and modest attempt to build a more robust theory of the political economy of South-to-North FDI. Insofar as there are few cases to study, it is rather difficult to define rigorously two contrasting groups – for instance, to compare current US–China (or US–India) investments with US–Japan deals in the 1980s (of which there were many more, although the literature has mostly focused on the controversial ones). Finally, in the future, more work will have to be done to learn from acquisitions that were not problematic.

ACKNOWLEDGEMENTS

The author thanks Giovanni Balcet, Christian Bellak, Hans Christiansen, Monty Graham, Rachel McCulloch, Cino Molajoni, Karl P. Sauvant and five anonymous referees, as well as Tarun Khanna and other participants at the National Conference on *Emerging Indian MNCs* (Delhi, 6 October 2006), for comments and suggestions on earlier drafts, and Meria Puhakka and Anna Salonen for help with Finnish sources. The opinions expressed and arguments employed are the author's sole responsibility and do not necessarily reflect those of the OECD or their members.

NOTES

1. While emerging TNCs are, almost by definition, a new phenomenon, there were about 100 pre-World War II Chinese TNCs. Mira Wilkins, personal communication, 16 June 2006.
2. Large emerging markets themselves are not immune to economic nationalism. Chinese officials have called for actions to limit malicious moves to take over local companies as a way of establishing monopolies in the local market and, in August 2006, the State Council ordered an unusual inquiry into the proposed takeover of state-owned Luoyang Bearings by Germany's Schaeffler, to make sure the bid represented fair value and did not damage national security. Russian authorities intend to limit foreign ownership in no fewer than 39 'strategic' sectors. The Indian government has asked the Foreign Investment Promotion Board and state-owned firms to screen out foreign investments seen as potential threats.
3. It is small consolation that a 1988 poll found 78 per cent of Americans to be in favor of restrictions on FDI (Wong 1989).
4. Bilateral opinions have been found to have a statistically robust and relatively large effect on imports, even when standard and new covariates capturing proximity between countries are controlled for (Disdier and Mayer 2006).
5. Although Mittal Steel has double headquarters in Amsterdam and London, shares listed on the New York and Amsterdam stock exchanges, and no assets in India, Lakshmi Mittal ('the Carnegie from Calcutta') is a non-resident Indian, and many perceive the company to be an Indian TNC. Gazprom, the Russian state-controlled gas monopoly, has also been at the center of speculation about a possible takeover of Centrica, the United Kingdom's biggest energy supplier.
6. 'Antagonists argue over Chinese group's financing', *Financial Times*, 6 July 2005.
7. 'CNOOC retreat makes a martyr of chairman', *Financial Times*, 3 August 2005.
8. Tarun Khanna cited in 'Mittal plays family card in his bid', *International Herald Tribune*, 8 March 2006.
9. Although most models in financial economics predict that minority shareholders are adversely affected by family ownership (for example, Burkart *et al.* 2003), according to Anderson *et al.* (2003) family firms perform better than non-family firms. Additional analysis reveals that the relation between family holdings and firm performance is non-linear and that when family members serve as CEOs, performance is better than with outside CEOs.
10. CNOOC offered about $10.55 per barrel of oil equivalent compared to $1.98 it paid for its stake in Australia's Northwest shelf gas project and $0.98 for raising its stake in Indonesia's Tangguh LNG project ('Unocal's cost puts spotlight on CNOOC', *Financial Times*, 4 April 2005).
11. Under the bankruptcy laws of the United States, Chapters 7 and 11 govern the process of reorganization of a debtor in bankruptcy, respectively.
12. 'Arcelor claims Mittal needs upgrade in U.S.', *Financial Times*, 23 February 2006.
13. In the first nine months of 2005, Mittal had slightly higher margins ('Steeled for marathon takeover battle', *Financial Times*, 31 January 2006).

14. 'Skandia takes flight to Old Mutual', *Financial Times*, 20 October 2005.
15. In particular, Old Mutual holds investments on the Zimbabwe Stock exchange, including a 19 per cent stake in Zimbabwe Newspapers, worth about 16 per cent of the bourse's total market capitalization. While this represents a modest slice of the London-listed group's global portfolio, it has drawn scrutiny in Sweden, a country that prides itself on ethical dealings.
16. 'Integrity surfaces as key concern in Arcelor battle', *Financial Times*, 1 February 2006, and 'Présent dans l'Ain depuis 1999, Mittal est plutôt un bon employeur', *Le Monde*, 3 February 2006.
17. 'US senator steps up attack on China over markets access', *Financial Times*, 19 April 2005.
18. 'Who's afraid of China Inc.?' *The New York Times*, 24 July 2005.
19. 'Lenovo chief dismisses US security fears', *Financial Times*, 3 February 2005.
20. CFIUS is chaired by the Secretary of the Treasury and includes eleven other members: the Secretaries of State, Defense, Commerce and Homeland Security, the Attorney General, the Director of the Office of Management and Budget, the US Trade Representative, the Chairperson of the Council of Economic Advisors, the Director of the Office of Science and Technology Policy, the Assistant to the President for National Security Affairs and the Assistant to the President for Economic Policy.
21. 'Sale of I.B.M. unit to China passes US security muster', *The New York Times*, 10 March 2005.
22. IBM also agreed to ensure that the chips and other parts in desktop PCs and notebooks were stamped with the name of their manufacturer and country of origin. Such labeling is fairly common among PC makers.
23. 'Unocal deal: a lot more than money is at issue', *The New York Times*, 24 June 2005.
24. 'CNOOC faces wall of opposition from US', *Financial Times*, 8 July 2005.
25. 'The President and the ports', *The New York Times*, 22 February 2006.
26. 'Il ne faut pas laisser une minorité d'actionnaires dicter l'avenir d'Arcelor', *La Tribune*, 6 June 2006; 'Le président du métallurgiste de Tcherepovets aurait demandé l'accord du Kremlin pour cette opération', *Le Monde*, 27 May 2006 and 'India ask Chirac to be fair to Mittal', *Financial Times*, 21 February 2006 respectively. On the position taken by the French authorities, see 'L'Elysée défend avec vigueur la fusion d'Arcelor avec Severstal', *Le Monde*, 30 May 2006.
27. 'Russian roulette', *The Wall Street Journal*, 30 May 2006.
28. Gideon Rose, personal communication, 19 June 2006.
29. Of course, this should not obscure the fact that many French media have raised this issue. See 'Tout sauf Mittal?' *Le Monde*, 28–29 May 2006 and 'Bataille de milliardaires', *La Tribune*, 6 June 2006.
30. The reaction was more muted in Europe – French Prime Minister Edith Cresson's infamous remarks about 'Japanese ants' notwithstanding. See Mason (1995).
31. As Rachel McCulloch reminded me, 'the trade barriers on Chinese textiles and apparel the US has put into place via OTEXA include some very much like VERs'. The difference is that most Japanese companies that engaged in VER-jumping FDI were in capital-intensive sectors.
32. According to Deutsche Bank data, the market share of the top three companies in three sectors (notebook PCs, desktop PCs, color TVs) is around 50 per cent ('Being tough at the top', *Financial Times*, 28 February 2006).
33. All data come from a series of articles produced by the Bureau of Economic Analysis.
34. *Keizen* (Japanese for 'change for the better') refers to a business strategy aimed at improving workplace quality and eliminating waste. It's often associated with the Toyota Production System.
35. So far, over 1600 deals have been subject to investigations, of which only 25 were extended (intervention by Robert M. Kimmitt, US Deputy Secretary of the Treasury, at the World Economic Forum Annual Meeting, 28 January 2006). Only one deal was blocked on national security grounds: the 1990 sale of an airplane-parts maker based in Seattle – Mamco Manufacturing – to the China National Aero-Technology Import and

Export Corporation. A rare negative review in 2003 caused Hutchinson Whampoa, which is based in Hong Kong (China), to withdraw a bid for Global Crossings, the telecommunications company that was later bought by Singapore Technologies Telemedia.

36. The definition of 'critical infrastructure' embodied in homeland security objectives could potentially include all transactions in the food supply chain. Similarly, definitions that include 'economic security' are too broad and likely to generate uncertainty regarding investments. It is useful to retain a targeted and clear definition of those transactions covered by CFIUS, and to focus on operational control of new technologies or sensitive locations (Eizenstat and Maibach 2006; Holtz-Eakin 2006).

37. Already, the Jones Act, a law enacted in 1920 that was intended to protect national security, requires that all ships moving people and cargo between domestic ports be US-owned, US-built and sailed by US crews.

38. H.R.5337, *Reform of National Security Reviews of Foreign Direct Investments Act* (Introduced in House on 10 May 2006).

39. John Meredith, group managing director of Hutchinson Port Holdings, in 'US warned about hardline ports stance', *Financial Times*, 18 April 2006.

40. 'Why China scares big oil', *Fortune*, 8 August 2005.

41. Rep. Richard Pombo (R-CA), a sixth-term member of Congress representing the 11th district of California, who sponsored a resolution criticizing the CNOOC bid, has received $13,000 from Chevron since 2003.

42. The White House also made its 'mea culpa in that we did not do a good job of informing Congress in advance about this proposed acquisition'. In fact, a 1993 amendment to the law stipulates that an extended investigation is mandatory when the acquiring company is controlled by or acting on behalf of a foreign government. Intervention of Allan Hubbard Director, National Economic Council in the C. Peter McColough Series on International Economics, Council on Foreign Relations, 18 April 2006.

43. 'Danger for US ports in backlash to Dubai deal', *Financial Times*, 22 February 2006.

44. 'Most maritime managers see little risk in P&O takeover', *Financial Times*, 6 March 2006. Close to 75–80 per cent of terminal capacity at US ports already involves some foreign ownership and nearly 100 per cent of shipping capacity serving the country is foreign.

45. The term 'sake-sipper beholden to Japan' indicated 'individuals who thought Japanese were not all that terrible' (Wilkins 1990, p. 626).

46. To the extent that Japanese TNCs are embedded in more tightly integrated organizational and business systems, their transnational learning may be more limited (see Lam 2003 in the case of Japanese R&D laboratories in the United Kingdom).

47. According to the 2005 Report to Congress of the United States–China Economic and Security Review Commission, 'China's practice contrasts with the practice of most other nations to buy energy supplies on the open market'. (USCC 2005, p. 29) To be fair, US TNCs recorded higher rates of return in the periphery under authoritarian regimes, although flows have not been significantly related to regime type and the overall performance has been better in developed democracies (Oneal 1994).

48. 'CNOOC at odds with Congress over worth of Unocal deal', *Financial Times*, 27 July 2005.

49. Marchick and Graham (2006, p. 13) similarly advised Chinese companies that wish to enter the US market 'to become more sophisticated in addressing the potential political opposition that may arise'.

50. I thank Monty Graham for drawing my attention to this point.

51. The 1995 US–Japan Investment Agreement focused on both structural change and government facilitation designed to attract FDI to Japan. There are continuing consultations on measures needed to remove existing barriers in order to improve the FDI climate in Japan.

52. 'CNOOC deal sunk in a perfect storm', 3 August 2005.

REFERENCES

Anderson, Ronald C. and David M. Reeb (2003). 'Founding-family ownership and firm performance: evidence from the S&P 500', *Journal of Finance*, 58(3), pp. 1301–1327.

Barrell, Ray and Nigel Pain (1999). 'Trade restraints and Japanese direct investment flows', *European Economic Review*, 43(1), pp. 29–45.

Blonigen, Bruce A. and Robert C. Feenstra (1997). 'Protectionist threats and foreign direct investment', in R. Feenstra, ed., *The Effects of US Trade Protection and Promotion Policies* (Chicago, IL: University of Chicago Press), pp. 69–76.

Bown, Chad P. and Rachel McCulloch (2005). 'US trade policy toward China: discrimination and its implications'. Paper presented at the *PAFTAD 30 conference*, East-West Center, Honolulu, 19–21 February, mimeo.

Breschi, Stefano, Francesco Lissoni and Fabio Montobbio (2005). 'The geography of knowledge spillovers: conceptual issues and measurement problems', in Breschi and Franco Malerba, eds, *Clusters, Networks and Innovation* (Oxford: Oxford University Press), pp. 343–371.

Burkart, Mike, Fausto Panunzi and Andrei Shleifer (2003). 'Family firms', *Journal of Finance*, 58(5), pp. 2167–2202.

CBS News Poll (2006). 'President Bush, the ports, and Iraq', available at www.cbsnews.com/htdocs/pdf/poll_bush_022706.pdf (last visited 23 March 2007).

Co, Catherine Y. (1997). 'Japanese FDI into the US automobile industry: an empirical investigation', *Japan and the World Economy*, 9(1), pp. 93–108.

Cohen, Elie (2006). 'Malaise dans la mondialisation ou "patriotisme économique"', *La Revue Parlementaire*, 887.

Disdier, Anne-Celia and Thierry Mayer (2006). *Je t'Aime, Moi Non Plus: Bilateral Opinions and International Trade*, CEPII Working Papers, No. 2006–01 (Paris: Centre d'Etuder Prospectives et d' Informations Internationales), mimeo.

Doremus, Paul, William W. Keller, Louis W. Pauly and Simon Reich (1999). *The Myth of the Global Corporation* (Princeton, NJ: Princeton University Press).

Eizenstat, Stuart E. and Michael C. Maibach (2006). 'Protect our heritage', *Wall Street Journal*, 30 March.

Farrell, Roger (2000). *Japanese Foreign Direct Investment in the World Economy 1951–1997*, Pacific Economic Papers, No. 299 (Canberra: Australian National University), mimeo.

Feenstra, Robert and Gary Hamilton (2006). *Emergent Economies, Divergent Paths* (Cambridge: Cambridge University Press).

Fosfuri, Andrea and Massimo Motta (1999). 'Multinationals without advantages', *Scandinavian Journal of Economics*, 101(4), pp. 617–630.

Gabal Analysis and Consulting (2001). *Attitudes towards Foreign Investors and Employers*. Project commissioned by CzechInvest (Prague: Gabal).

Girma, Sourafel, David Greenaway and Katharine Wakelin (1999). *Anti-dumping, Trade Barriers and Japanese Direct Investment in the UK*, Centre for Research on Globalisation and Labour Markets Research Paper No. 99/4 (Nottingham: University of Nottingham, The Centre), mimeo.

Goldstein, Andrea (2006). 'Verso una nuova geografia degli investimenti internazionali?', *L'Italia nell'economia internazionale. Rapporto ICE 2005–2006* (Rome: ICE–ISTAT).

Graham, Edward and David Marchick (2006). *US National Security and Foreign Direct Investment* (Washington, DC: Peter G. Peterson Institute for International Economics), mimeo.

Gross, Daniel (2006). 'Globalization offered two ways: à la carte and prix fixe', *The New York Times*, 12 March.

Holtz-Eakin, Douglas (2006). *Testimony before the Subcommittee on Domestic and International Monetary Policy, Trade, and Technology of the Committee on Financial Services U.S. House of Representatives*, 17 May (Washington, DC: USGPO), mimeo.

Howenstine, Ned G. and Dale P. Shannon (1996). 'Differences in foreign-owned US manufacturing establishments by country of owner', *Survey of Current Business*, 76(3), pp. 43–60.

Jones, Geoffrey (2005). *Multinationals and Global Capitalism from the Nineteenth to the Twenty-first Century* (Oxford: Oxford University Press).

Khanna, Tarun (2006). 'At home, it's not just profits that matter', *International Herald Tribune*, 21 February.

Kimura, Yui and Thomas A. Pugel (1995). 'Keiretsu and Japanese direct investment in US manufacturing', *Japan and the World Economy*, 7(4), pp. 481–503.

Lam, Alice (2003). 'Organisational learning in multinationals: R&D networks of Japanese and U.S. MNEs in the U.K.', *Journal of Management Studies*, 40(3), pp. 673–703.

Lincoln, Edward J. (2003). 'Japan: using power narrowly', *The Washington Quarterly*, 27(1), pp. 111–127.

Marchick, David M. and Edward M. Graham (2006). 'How China can break down America's wall', *Far Eastern Economic Review*, 169(6), pp. 10–14.

Mason, Mark (1995). 'Historical perspectives on Japanese direct investment in Europe', in Mark Mason and Dennis Encarnation, eds, *Does Ownership Matter? Japanese Multinationals in Europe* (Oxford: Oxford University Press), pp. 3–38.

McCulloch, Rachel (1991). 'Why foreign corporations are buying into U.S. business', *Annals of the American Academy of Political Science*, 516(1), pp. 169–182.

McCulloch, Rachel (1993). 'The optimality of free trade: science or religion?', *American Economic Review*, 83(2), pp. 367–371.

Narula, Rajneesh and Antonello Zanfei (2004). 'Globalisation of innovation: the role of multinational enterprises', in J. Fagerberg, D. Mowery and R. Nelson, eds, *Handbook of Innovation* (Oxford: Oxford University Press), pp. 318–345.

Oneal John R. (1994). 'The affinity of foreign investors for authoritarian regimes', *Political Research Quarterly*, 47(3), pp. 565–588.

Palmisano, Samuel J. (2006). 'The globally integrated enterprise', *Foreign Affairs*, 85(3), pp. 127–136.

Roche, François (2006). 'Mittal-Arcelor: le choc de deux modèles', *La Tribune*, 28 April.

Rohatyn, Felix (2005). *Where Now for the U.S. Economy? Domestic Public Investment, Foreign Direct Investment, and America's Position in the World*, speech at the Center for American Progress, 22 September, available at www.americanprogress.org/kf/transcript0922.pdf, last visited 25 October 2007.

Singh, Jasjit and Tarun Khanna (2003). *What Drives Innovation by Multinationals? Evidence Using Patent Data*, Strategy Unit Working Papers, No. 03-058 (Cambridge, MA: Harvard University), mimeo.

Singh, Malvinder Mohan (2006). 'The onus is on India to show its gentle intent', *Financial Times*, 2 June.

TNS Sofres (2006). *'Les Français et la Fusion Suez / Gaz de France', Résultats d'une Étude Réalisée pour Le Figaro*, 3 March, available at www.tns-sofres.com/etudes/pol/060306_suez_r.htm, last visited 25 October 2007.

Tyson, Laura D'Andrea (1992). *Who's Bashing Whom? Trade Conflict in High-Technology Industries* (Washington, DC: Institute for International Economics).

Tyson, Laura D'Andrea (2005). 'What CNOOC leaves behind', *Business Week*, 15 August.

USCC (2005). *2005 Report to Congress of the U.S. – China Economic and Security Review Commission* (Washington, DC: USGPO).

Wilkins, Mira (1990). 'Japanese multinationals in the United States: continuity and change, 1879–1990', *Business History Review*, 64, pp. 585–629.

Wong, Kar-Yiu (1989). 'The Japanese challenge: Japanese direct investment in the United States', in Kozo Yamamura, ed., *Japanese Investment in the United States: Should We Be Concerned?* (Seattle: Society for Japanese Studies), pp. 63–96.

Yamamura, Kozo (1989). 'The significance of Japanese investment in the United States: how should we react?' in Kozo Yamamura, ed., *Japanese Investment in the United States: Should We Be Concerned?* (Seattle: Society for Japanese Studies), pp. 5–40.

10. Corporate governance of emerging-market TNCs: why does it matter?

Rainer Geiger

INTRODUCTION

This chapter is about the link between corporate governance and investment policy. Attempted takeovers of domestic enterprises by foreign transnational corporations (TNCs) have raised concerns and fuelled debate by legislators and the general public. Corporate governance has figured prominently among the issues raised: What are the ownership and control structures of the bidder? Is there adequate disclosure of the TNCs' decision-making process in the country of origin? If a foreign TNC is government-owned, is it used as a tool of government strategy? Do the TNCs involved have a track record of responsible business conduct?

Are such concerns legitimate? To a large degree, the answer depends on the extent of differences between the TNCs of industrialized countries and those of emerging markets. Insofar as there are important differences, authorities need to consider the appropriate policy responses.

There is not enough empirical evidence to demonstrate that corporate governance patterns in emerging markets are fundamentally different from those in OECD economies. It appears, however, that ownership is often more concentrated in comparison with several of the developed economies, that state ownership is sometimes stronger and that transparency and corporate accountability are not always particularly well-developed. The key message of this chapter is that, even where the nationality of the bidding company is not deemed important by host country authorities, the bidder's corporate governance does matter and is likely to have an impact on the outcome of investment policy decisions.

In order to make this case, this chapter briefly describes the yardsticks of corporate governance in industrial and emerging markets and discusses the importance of good corporate practices for inward and outward investment. It reviews the ownership structures and board practices of firms in emerging markets and suggests possible policy responses to potential problems.

10.1   YARDSTICKS FOR GOOD CORPORATE GOVERNANCE

Corporate governance is about the way companies are managed and controlled. Good governance implies transparency of company structures and operations; equitable treatment of all shareholders, including minority shareholders; good relations between the company and stakeholders (for example, all groups providing resources to the company and sharing risks and benefits); reliability, accessibility and timely disclosure of financial and non-financial information about a company; as well as competent and accountable corporate boards.

In a globalized economy, it is essential that good corporate governance practices be widely shared among home and host countries for capital to flow freely across national borders and for liberalized markets to function properly. As shown by past experience, financial crisis situations often have their origin in poor corporate governance (Geiger 2003). Globalized markets need global standards to deal with systemic risks, and corporate governance standards are part of the level playing field.

The *OECD Principles for Corporate Governance* of 1998 were elaborated in the aftermath of the Asian financial crisis. They were revised and strengthened in 2004 to take into account corporate governance developments in developed and emerging markets as well as problems highlighted by major corporate scandals (Enron and others) (OECD 2004b). These scandals undermined the confidence of investors, threatened the functioning of financial markets and destroyed shareholder value.

The OECD Principles are non-prescriptive but globally recognized as good practice standards that can and should be implemented in all countries. They cover shareholders rights, equitable treatment of minority shareholders, stakeholder relations, disclosure of financial and non-financial information, and board responsibilities. The Principles are being disseminated and promoted worldwide through regional roundtables and recommendations (for example, the so-called White Papers) organized in partnership between the OECD and the IFC/World Bank Global Corporate Governance Forum.[1]

To be effective, the OECD Principles need to be translated into action, adjusted as necessary to specific national and regional circumstances and legal traditions. Market discipline can be a powerful driving force for good corporate governance, in particular for listed companies, as good practice is rewarded by better access to capital while bad practice may lead to loss of reputation and exposure to risk, of both a commercial and a legal nature. Market intermediaries like banks and brokers, as well as corporate gatekeepers such as financial analysts, lawyers, accountants and consultants can play an important role. And finally, regulation and market supervision are necessary for enforcement and punishment of violations.

For the reasons stated above, corporate governance can provide a strong ingredient to countries' investment environment. It is part of the Policy Framework for Investment adopted in 2006 at the OECD by a task force composed of OECD countries, transition economies and developing countries (OECD 2006a). The Policy Framework for Investment is a comprehensive and non-prescriptive tool aimed at improving the environment for both domestic and foreign investment. As stated in Chapter 6 of the framework,

> The degree to which corporations observe basic principles of sound corporate governance is a determinant of investment decisions, influencing the confidence of investors, the cost of capital, the overall functioning of financial markets and ultimately the development of more sustainable sources of financing.

Corporate governance has also been incorporated into regional investment frameworks such as the Investment Compact for South East Europe and the Investment Programme for Middle East and North Africa operated by the OECD (OECD 2006b, Chapter 3).

There are several aspects of corporate governance that matter for takeovers and acquisitions. First, there is a legitimate desire by a target company and its stakeholders as well as by a host country to know about the structure of ownership and control of the bidding company. If a takeover bid occurs in an industry considered of strategic importance, and if a foreign company is involved, the concern to 'know your investor' is obvious.

Share ownership and effective control are not always commensurate. Corporate structures characterized by multiple voting rights, preferential shares and ceilings for the exercise of voting rights are still frequent in a number of developed and developing economies. Company groups can be based on contractual arrangements totally dissociated from share participation. Pyramidal schemes, cascading ownerships and certain other holding constructions are among the strongest expressions of dissociation of ownership from corporate control (Kirkpatrick 2004). These conditions present opportunities and incentives for the inequitable treatment of minority shareholders. The OECD Principles call for comprehensive, timely and easy-to-access disclosure about capital structures and arrangements that enable certain shareholders to obtain a degree of control disproportionate to their equity ownership.

Problems of transparency can arise when the ultimate beneficial owner at the top of a holding or a pyramid is controlled by a family or a state-owned enterprise, since these persons, groups or entities are not always subject to the same type of disclosure requirements as listed companies. In addition, certain legal devices are sometimes employed to make ownership structures completely opaque by separating legal owners (for example, a trust) from the real beneficiary, which remains undisclosed (OECD 2001; OECD 2002b; Financial Action Task Force 2006). Another source of concern may be the stakeholder relations of the acquiring company. If a company has a track record of bad labour practices, poor environment performance or illegal or unethical behavior (for example, systematic use of bribery), it may not be welcome as an investor in a host country.

10.2 OWNERSHIP AND CONTROL STRUCTURES IN EMERGING MARKETS

The issues discussed below raise relevant questions and concerns about any potential acquirer, whether it is a TNC from the OECD or from an emerging market.

As suggested by economic research, opaque group structures can have a negative effect on economic performance (OECD 2006c).[2] They certainly can affect the interests of minority shareholders in a group's companies as the interests of these companies may be systematically subordinated to the overall group strategy. At a minimum, shareholders and stakeholders should know about the real control structure and the decision-making process within a group, as well as about the existence or absence of safeguards for corporate accountability.

Host countries may have additional legitimate concerns about ownership and control if a takeover by a foreign company is to occur in a sector of 'strategic' importance to their economies – most basically defense-related production, but in some cases also essential infrastructure and/or high technology. The knowledge of the beneficial owner can have a national security dimension when there is reason to believe that an investor may be controlled by criminal or terrorist networks, is involved in money laundering or is likely to use its control of the acquired enterprise in ways otherwise contrary to the national interest.

A number of risks are associated with concentrated and non-transparent ownership, for example, controlling shareholders may engage in abusive insider deals and related-party transactions (Lemmon and Lins 2003). They may indulge in asset stripping to the detriment of a dependent subsidiary. Minority shareholders may see their positions diluted and ultimately devalued. Entrenchment of management at the top of the group as well as in controlled subsidiaries is another area for concern if a company is not subject to any financial market discipline. Specific risks may be associated with state ownership where governments use enterprises they control as instruments of their own policy. Such practices are often prohibited by law, but there can be difficulties in enforcing laws and in providing swift and effective remedies to minority shareholders harmed by such misconduct.

As mentioned above, there is no empirical evidence to suggest that investment from emerging markets warrants any type of scrutiny that is not applied to either domestic investment or investment from OECD economies. However, there are a few indicators that do militate toward vigilance. In a number of emerging markets, the degree of concentration of ownership and control is particularly high and disclosure practices are not as well-developed.

For instance, in the Russian Federation, there are large government shareholdings in the energy and financial sectors, as well as concentrated private ownership in heavy industries. China is characterized by government control of key companies (including TNCs), and outward investment strategies benefit from strong government support (OECD 2003a).[3] Moreover, state-owned companies in countries like India and China cause concerns due to perceived efficiency gaps in management and a lack of accountability. Many other Asian countries also have a highly concentrated control of the corporate sector, with important residual government ownership. In Middle-East and North African countries, there are relatively few companies listed on stock exchanges and subject to the associated financial market discipline. Family controlled groups still predominate and government shareholdings remain important in key industries.

State-owned enterprises and family groups are often not subjected to financial market discipline, and certain regions like the Middle-East and the Gulf suffer from the limited capacity of stock markets with an inadequate supply of traded shares.

As far as the regulatory environment is concerned, the situation varies from country to country, but there is a clear trend toward improvement, in line with international standards. However, in some countries like Russia and China, there are persisting regulatory gaps, in particular with respect to corporate accountability, disclosure and related party transactions. In some jurisdictions where reasonably comprehensive financial market regulations exist, as in the Russian Federation, rules are not adequately enforced since regulatory agencies do not have the power or capacity to impose sanctions that have deterrent effects.

10.3   BOARD PRACTICES IN EMERGING MARKETS

Company boards are the cornerstones of corporate governance. They are crucial to providing strategic guidance for a company and to control management. This requires competence and responsibility. In the terms of the OECD Principles for Corporate Governance, 'boards should be able to exercise objective independent judgment on corporate affairs' (OECD 2004b; Principle VI E).

In company groups with concentrated ownership, uncertainty may arise with respect to the definition of directors' duty of loyalty. Does it imply loyalty to the individual company, in accordance with national company law or to the group as a whole? How is the process of nomination of directors organized? Is there sufficient scope for independent directors? Does this imply independence in relation to controlling shareholders? What about the independence and accountability of boards of state-owned enterprises?

There has been no systematic research on board practices in emerging markets. But according to the studies that do exist, the situation seems to be bleaker than in many OECD countries (Maassen and Van de Coevering 2005). Boards are not always empowered as effective instruments to control management. The board's composition does not necessarily reflect competence, and independent directors may be difficult to find. There is also an absence of consistent court practice to enforce the personal liability of directors for acts of negligence and breach of their duties of loyalty and care. However, shortcomings of board practices are now being addressed, and reforms are being put in place, following the recommendations of the OECD Principles. National and regional corporate governance associations and institutes of directors are developing recommendations for good practice and providing necessary training.[4]

10.4 POLICY CHALLENGES

Foreign investment is continuing to expand; corporate mergers and acquisitions reached new records in 2006. The benefits of attracting investment are still widely shared among nations. The network of bilateral investment agreements is also expanding. OECD and developing countries have jointly elaborated a policy framework which, to the extent that it is applied, provides a strong underpinning for an open investment climate. Regional investment frameworks have been adopted and are being used as a starting basis for policy reform (for example, in South East Europe, APEC, the Middle East and North Africa) (OECD 2006b). At the same time, interest in corporate governance and responsible business conduct is rising, and emphasis is given to the structural policies that allow countries to share the benefits of investment for their own development.

But international investment is no longer a one-way street (as other chapters in this volume document). Emerging markets are becoming major players in foreign mergers and acquisitions; this fact alone calls for a careful examination of international investment rules to ensure that these are based on common values and principles with which all actors are fully associated. This debate will have to include the following major elements: the maintenance of an open investment environment and the transparent use of any remaining investment controls as well as the systematic development of policies that promote responsible business conduct. Corporate governance will have to feature prominently in this debate.

There have been a number of spectacular instances in which takeovers and acquisitions by foreign TNCs have been blocked or discouraged, and some of these instances involved TNCs from emerging markets.[5] With respect to the latter, concerns have been expressed regarding the absence of a level playing field: it was argued, for example, that these companies are not subject in their home countries to the same demanding legislation and standards as Western companies (for example, labour, environment, corporate governance), that they benefit from state support for their foreign expansion strategies and that the investment environment in their home countries is far more restrictive than in the target countries (Deutsche Bank Research 2006). The question policy makers need to ask themselves is whether they represent a number of isolated incidents or a general backlash against an open investment environment. In other words, is there a real threat of investment protectionism?

10.5   POLICY INSTRUMENTS AND GOOD PRACTICES

The first consideration is the transparent and predictable use of the remaining investment controls. Within the OECD area, general investment screening and review procedures have largely been abandoned. They have only been maintained in a few countries – in many cases for mergers and acquisitions that exceed a specific threshold. Sector restrictions continue to be in place in a number of countries, mostly to protect a few prioritized economic activities or to shield traditional cultural patterns.

But even in the countries professing a liberal investment climate, controls based on national security considerations have moved to the forefront for a number of reasons: a heightened concern about security and international terrorism, the dependence on energy supplies and, more generally, public concern about the benefits of FDI in strategic sectors.[6] Even where there is no formal review mechanism, foreign mergers and acquisitions may be discouraged through informal barriers or political statements (OECD 2007).

As demonstrated above, issues like corporate governance and responsible business conduct are relevant to this debate. Will it be possible to limit the national security exception to genuine concerns or will the door be opened to uncontrollable abuse? There could be a need to agree on criteria to define good practice in order to rationalize the decision-making process across all members of the international community in a new context of shared responsibility.

A fundamental principle that is increasingly shared is that issues of corporate ownership change should, to the greatest extent possible, be addressed by general regulation applicable to all types of companies rather than foreign investment controls. Apart from competition policy, such regulation includes securities regulation, financial supervision and taxation. Emerging markets should be invited to participate fully in the process of developing and applying international standards, and in the evaluation of results.

In the area of corporate governance:

- They should apply the OECD Principles and participate in implementation through national policy assessment and international peer review. This will have to include greater transparency of ownership and control structures, more efficient and accountable corporate boards, timely disclosure of reliable financial and non-financial information about their activities and responsible stakeholder relations.
- Corporate governance patterns of state-owned enterprises need to be systematically improved in accordance with the OECD *Guidelines on Corporate Governance of State-Owned Enterprises*. In many jurisdictions, this will mean wider implementation of good corporate governance standards relating to the transparency of ownership policies, accountable management and empowerment of boards as a competent body for corporate strategy and control. State-owned enterprises should be subject to the same rules as private enterprises in terms of market regulation and corporate behavior (OECD 2005).
- Procedures should be put in place to disclose systematically and verify beneficial ownership of corporations, both for individual corporate entities and holding company structures.

The foregoing are challenges that all countries need to address, but the benefits for emerging markets to do so are particularly strong because they have much to gain from greater participation in policy development and implementation efforts. These issues are being addressed in regional roundtables in Latin America, Asia, the Middle-East and North Africa,

South-East Europe and Eurasia, organized by the OECD and the IFC/ World Bank, as well in country policy dialogues for Russia and China.

It would also be desirable if emerging markets applied international instruments for responsible corporate conduct like the *OECD Guidelines for Multinational Enterprises* and fully cooperated in the international fight against corruption on the basis of applicable conventions and international action plans. As stated in Chapter 7 of the *Policy Framework for Investment*, 'Public policies promoting recognized concepts and principles for responsible business conduct, such as those recommended in the OECD Guidelines for multinational enterprises, help attract investments that contribute to sustainable development' (OECD 2006a, p. 19).

Brazil is a signatory to the *OECD Convention on Combating Bribery of Foreign Public Officials in International Business Transactions* and South Africa has been invited to sign that Convention; India and China have adhered to the Asian–Pacific Action Plan against corruption managed by the OECD and the Asian Development Bank. Discussions are being pursued with Russia on business integrity and responsible corporate conduct. Brazil, together with eight other non-OECD countries, has adopted the OECD investment instruments which include the Principle of National Treatment and the OECD *Guidelines for Multinational Enterprises*.

There is clear progress on all these issues, but systematic procedures for integrating emerging markets in the OECD policy debate need to be developed. This could include a mechanism for consultation on specific issues arising in the international investment process, linked to any of the policy areas above.[7]

CONCLUSIONS

In summary, while the bidder's nationality itself should generally not be cause for regulatory action toward mergers and acquisitions, the quality of corporate governance does play a role. Corporate governance should therefore be integrated in the ongoing policy debate on international investment. There are serious and legitimate concerns in this area that need to be addressed if a relapse into investment protectionism is to be avoided.

Emerging-market TNCs can act as drivers for economic development if they live up, in both home and host countries, to international standards of corporate governance and responsible business conduct. This would have a useful demonstration effect, facilitating acceptance of mergers and acquisitions and countering protectionist pressures in political circles and public opinion.

This also means that emerging markets that are home countries to outward investment may need to upgrade their regulatory environment to facilitate responsible business conduct. To quote the OECD:

> Such policies include: providing an enabling environment which clearly defines respective roles of government and business; promoting dialogue on norms for business conduct; supporting private initiatives for responsible business conduct; and participating in international co-operation in support of responsible business conduct (OECD 2006a, p. 19).

For their part, host countries in the OECD and other mature economies are well advised to put in place a comprehensive framework of policies and to undertake timely structural reform to enable them to reap the full benefits of investment from emerging markets.

The way forward for OECD countries and emerging markets as well as for other countries is to engage in a far-reaching dialogue on the application of international standards that combine the advantages of both investment and corporate governance.

ACKNOWLEDGEMENTS

The chapter reflects the personal views of the author. The author thanks Janet Holmes and Hans Christiansen, Corporate Affairs Division, OECD, for their comments.

NOTES

1. See, for example, OECD 2002a, 2003a, 2003b, and 2004a. More information about the regional roundtables can be found at www.oecd.org/document/9/0,3343,en_2649_34795_2048457_1_1_1_1,00.html, last visited 25 October, 2007.
2. See especially the commentary regarding OECD Principle III.A.2.
3. See also the proceedings of the Second Policy Dialogue on Corporate Governance in China, Beijing, 19 May 2005, which focused on corporate governance of state-owned enterprises. Documentations relating to the proceedings can be accessed at www.oecd.org/daf/corporate-affairs through the link for Information by country and then China.
4. National and regional director institutes have been set up in, among other countries and regions, India, Nigeria, the Philippines, Singapore, South Africa, Southern Africa, Thailand, Zambia and Zimbabwe.
5. Two of the most widely quoted cases were the controversies surrounding Dubai Ports World's acquisition of the Peninsular and Oriental Steam Navigation Company of the United Kingdom (including the latter company's US port operations) and the Chinese oil company CNOOC's unsuccessful bid for UNOCAL of the US.

6. These issues are discussed in the context of the OECD's ongoing project on 'Freedom of Investment, National Security and "Strategic" Industries'. Information and outputs from the exercise are available at www.oecd.org/investment.
7. These issues featured prominently on the agenda for the 2007 G8 Summit.

REFERENCES

Deutsche Bank Research (2006). *Chinesische Firmen auf dem Vormarsch* (Frankfurt: Deutsche Bank).

Financial Action Task Force (2006). *The Misuse of Corporate Vehicles, Including Trust and Company Service Providers*, available at www.fatf-gafi.com.

Geiger, Rainer (2003). *Managing the Global Economy: The Role of Governance*, Current Developments in Monetary and Financial Law, 2 (Washington, DC: International Monetary Fund).

Kirkpatrick, Grant (2004). 'Corporate governance and company groups: considerations from the OECD principles', Working Paper presented at *KDI Conference on Corporate Governance of Company Groups*, Seoul, mimeo.

Lemmon, Michael L. and Karl V. Lins (2003). 'Ownership structure, corporate governance and firm value: evidence from the East Asian financial crisis', *Journal of Finance*, 58, pp. 1445–1468.

Maassen, Gregory F. and Patrick van de Coevering (2005). *Reform Strategies for Boards of Directors in Emerging Markets: How the Private Sector can be Involved in the Development of and Implementation of Modern Business Standards* (Rotterdam: Rotterdam School of Management), mimeo.

OECD (2001). *Behind the Corporate Veil: Using Corporate Entities for Illicit Purposes* (Paris: OECD).

OECD (2002a). *White Paper on Corporate Governance in Russia* (Paris: OECD).

OECD (2002b). *Options for Obtaining Beneficial Ownership and Control Information: A Template* (Paris: OECD).

OECD (2003a). *White Paper on Corporate Governance in Asia* (Paris: OECD).

OECD (2003b). *White Paper on Corporate Governance in Latin America* (Paris: OECD).

OECD (2004a). *Experiences from the Regional Corporate Governance Roundtables* (Paris: OECD).

OECD (2004b). *OECD Principles of Corporate Governance* (Paris: OECD).

OECD (2005). *OECD Guidelines on Corporate Governance of State-Owned Enterprises* (Paris: OECD).

OECD (2006a). *Policy Framework for Investment* (Paris: OECD).

OECD (2006b). *Investment for Development, Annual Report 2006* (Paris: OECD).

OECD (2006c). *Methodology for Assessing Implementation of the OECD Principles of Corporate Governance* (Paris: OECD).

OECD (2007) 'Freedom of investment, national security and "strategic" industries: Interim report', in *International Investment Perspectives 2007* (Paris: OECD).

11. Are emerging-market TNCs sensitive to corporate responsibility issues?

Carrie Hall

INTRODUCTION

The past decade has seen a rapid increase in the number, size and scope of transnational corporations (TNCs) based in emerging markets – growing from 3000 in 1990 to 13 000 within 10 years (UNCTAD 2006). Only a small number of these TNCs have become global competitors able to square off with traditional Western business leaders. Yet this limited occurrence, combined with the notion that multitudes of lesser-known emerging-market TNCs are expanding into foreign markets, has been enough to garner significant attention from almost every constituency – government, business, civil society, media and investors.

For the United Nations Global Compact, the world's largest voluntary corporate citizenship initiative, questions abound related to the business practices of emerging-market TNCs, practices that have been cultivated in areas renowned for deficient economic, political and social frameworks that often lead to low thresholds of ethical behavior and accountability for business. Currently, there is no clear indication of the prevalence of basic corporate citizenship tenets – human rights, labor rights, environmental protection, anti-corruption – within emerging-market TNCs.

On the one hand, the corporate responsibility actions of leading emerging-market TNCs can be as sophisticated as those taken by the most advanced Western companies, and there are signs that corporate citizenship is becoming a global phenomenon. The Global Compact (through its participants and local networks) can be found in approximately 100 countries, a majority of them in the developing world. From Chile to China and South Africa to Sri Lanka, corporate responsibility seminars and summits are teeming with local participants wanting to learn about the value of implementing universal principles into business practices. On the other hand, new examples of human rights violations, worker exploitation and corruption being carried out by emerging-market TNCs (as well as developed-country TNCs) are frequently revealed. It is no secret that companies devoid of responsible practices are winning contracts and making profits in developing countries despite their unsavory behavior.

If emerging-market TNCs can profit from unprincipled – or simply un-evolved – behavior in markets that do not demand higher standards, then why are so many voluntarily committing to implement the Global Compact's ten principles on human rights, labor, environment and anti-corruption?[1] And why are a number of these businesses rallying together to take collective action against corruption and for environmental protection? The growing interest in corporate citizenship exhibited by leading emerging-market TNCs around the world suggests that these companies are in fact deriving strategic value from responsible business practices, and in some cases even finding that principled behavior is essential to business survival and success.

Emerging-market TNCs have a particular stake in the corporate respon-sibility movement. Many of the 'emerging giants'[2] are engaged in the Global Compact, including Cemex, Infosys, Eskom, Haier, Embraco, Koç and several key Tata Group companies.[3] Beyond this small but growing group of world-class emerging-market TNCs, the Global Compact counts over half of its 3000 participating companies from developing countries, with participant representation along the spectrum of developing econ-omies from the weakest to the most advanced emerging markets. The ini-tiative has experienced particularly strong engagement in Brazil, China, Egypt, India, Mexico, South Africa and Turkey, as well as growing partici-pation in such countries as Pakistan, Singapore and Thailand in Asia; Ghana, Malawi, Nigeria and Zambia in Africa; and Argentina, Chile, Panama and Peru in Latin America.

Global Compact experience shows that the leading emerging-market TNCs provide some of the most effective and comprehensive examples of corporate responsibility. What is remarkable about such behavior by these companies is the underlying motivation for action, not necessarily the actual corporate citizenship practices. In fact, the approaches taken by world-class emerging-market TNCs to implement human rights, labor, environment and anti-corruption principles in day-to-day operations and business strat-egy are not wholly dissimilar to those taken by leading Western corporate citizens, for example, in regard to environmental, health and safety systems or the production of sophisticated reports with advanced social perform-ance indicators.

However, for emerging-market TNCs, often the earliest driving force for corporate citizenship is the highly challenging societal and economic framework found in the home country. This is a core distinction from Western TNCs, which typically are first able to cultivate their business operations under more stable socio-economic circumstances before expanding abroad. Arguably, corporate responsibility practices take on a heightened significance for emerging-market TNCs and, ultimately, can be a matter of survival.

11.1 SOCIO-ECONOMIC CHALLENGES NECESSITATE INNOVATIVE ACTION BY EMERGING-MARKET TNCs

Business simply cannot thrive if society fails. For emerging-market companies with ambitions for a strong domestic or international presence, socio-economic issues can become most pressing. In environments that lack adequate economic, political and social institutions for development, achieving success can demand innovative business approaches that serve both corporate and societal interests. Even more, society may need to become a key consideration in business mission and strategy. The experiences of many leading emerging-market TNCs demonstrate how responsible corporate practices can play a strategic role in managing a variety of risks endemic to developing countries, including a weak state, ineffective regulations, faulty tax structures, lack of skilled labor, social unrest and generally poor living and health conditions.

BOX 11.1 CEMEX: SOCIETAL FOCUS GENERATES VALUABLE NEW CUSTOMER BASE

CEMEX S.A., de C.V. (CEMEX) is one of the world's leading building-solutions companies. Since its founding in Mexico in 1906, the company has grown from a purely domestic position to a presence in over 50 countries around the world. CEMEX has comprehensive programs underway to address social, economic and environmental issues, not only in Mexico, but also in other countries where it operates.

Among the company's most innovative programs is 'Patrimonio Hoy', an initiative that provides low-income families with access to low-cost materials to build or upgrade a home. The program addresses the limited financing options that prevent families from residing in or improving a dwelling. The company has established

---

centers throughout Mexico that have so far aided 123 000 families. Through the 'Construmex' program, Mexicans living in the United States can transfer money home for their families' construction needs. For only a dollar each, clients can transfer orders directly through the network of more than 20 000 CEMEX distributors across Mexico, who then deliver the building materials to the clients' designated recipients. Another notable program is 'Piso Firme', which has helped over 200 000 disadvantaged families replace dirt floors with concrete. CEMEX is visibly leveraging its core strengths as a cement and building-solutions company to help reduce slum housing and the unsanitary, violent outcomes that result from this environment. In the process, the company is gaining thousands of loyal customers from a previously untapped sector of the population.

CEMEX carries its spirit of community investment and improvement to countries where it operates. In addition to winning awards for its environmental performance in Costa Rica, Panama and Venezuela, as well as awards for its safety performance in Colombia and Costa Rica, CEMEX is involved in a wide array of community development projects around the world. 'Patrimonio Hoy' is underway in Colombia, Costa Rica, Nicaragua and Venezuela. The company supports or leads education initiatives in countries including Costa Rica (scholarships), Egypt (education for girls) and the Philippines ('One Paper, One Pencil' program for children). Examples of other programs include centers for disabled people in Venezuela, mobile health diagnostic teams in Nicaragua, a labor risk program in the Dominican Republic and a cultural center in Colombia that will promote children's rights and cultural development in the community.

These programs bring alive the commitment of CEMEX's CEO Lorenzo Zambrano that 'wherever we operate around the world, our code of ethics, our company values, and our governance standards will guide our actions.'*

Source: UN Global Compact.

* Building for Future Generations: 2004 Sustainability Report, available at www.cemex.com/sr2004/eng/pdf/SR04english.pdf (last visited 5 December 2006).

India's Tata Steel and Turkey's Koç Group each operate on founding missions that identify the overall development of the home country and its people as being of paramount importance. Vehbi Koç, founder of Koç

Group, instituted the following code for the company: 'I live and prosper with my country . . . We shall do our utmost to strengthen our economy. As our economy prospers, so will democracy and our standing in the world.'[4]

BOX 11.2   TATA STEEL: PIONEERING APPROACH
            PUTS FOCUS ON EMPLOYEES AND
            COMMUNITY

From its founding in 1907, Tata Steel has operated on the belief that the success of the business was tied to the well-being of society. The company took early and decisive steps to act on this principle. In 1912, the founders of the London School of Economics were invited to India to prepare a Memorandum of Health for the company. In the same year, an eight-hour workday was instituted. Other milestones included: free medical aid in 1915; a Welfare Department in 1917; leave with pay, Workers Provident Fund and Workmen's Compensation in 1920; and maternity benefits for women in 1928. Labor welfare practices were established before these were made statutory across the world.

Nearly a century after its founding, Tata Steel is engaged in nearly every angle of socio-economic development in and around the areas where it has operations. A sample of the company's activities include: health care facilities that can treat thousands of people; educational support from pre-school to postgraduate levels involving the management of hundreds of schools; employment training; promoting entrepreneurship through supporting local suppliers and micro-finance programs; and development and maintenance of civic amenities including roads, water, emergency services and parks. The company undertakes many of these activities in rural areas near its operations to ensure that rural communities are not left out of the wealth generated in urban centers. Tata Steel's extensive activities related to HIV/AIDS awareness are notable – the company is a founding member of the Global Business Coalition on HIV/AIDS.

Today, Tata Steel spends 30 per cent of its profits after tax on community development based on the philosophy that 'no success in material terms is worthwhile unless it serves the interest of the nation and is achieved by fair and honest means'.* The company's extensive efforts not only help to improve the quality of life for many people in India, but also help to build sustainable communities capable of producing qualified and healthy workers for the company's operations.

Source: UN Global Compact.

* Tata Steel, 'Setting sustainability standards', available at www.tatasteel.com/corporatesustainability/default.asp (last visited 5 December 2006).

Community development efforts (both at home and in other emerging markets) can have strategic significance for emerging-market TNCs. The deep and broad commitment exhibited in areas such as education, health, job creation, disaster relief, arts, culture and sports serves as far more than 'philanthropy'. Tendencies to view such activities as peripheral – not 'true' corporate responsibility – should be reconsidered, as community investment can address aspects of the societal context that are lacking or insufficient – voids that can greatly impact a company's ability to operate, compete and thrive.

Consider that, for over 100 years, the Tata Group has embedded its mission for societal development throughout its business strategy. The group's companies are renowned for their unwavering, acute focus on 'society' wherever they operate, whether in India, Bangladesh or Africa. In so doing, the Tata Group has grown to be India's largest conglomerate, with annual revenues of US$21 billion, and it is now a global player in many industries: 'the world's second largest tea business (Tata Tea); Asia's largest software firm (Tata Consultancy Services); a steel giant (Tata Steel); a worldwide hotel chain (Indian Hotels); and a sprawling vehicle-manufacturing arm (Tata Motors)' (Perry 2006).

Enlightened emerging-market TNCs recognize that 'businesses that . . . proactively understand and engage with social issues will benefit most. They will be better able to shape the social contract and to identify ways of creating value from the opportunities and risks arising from sociopolitical issues' (Bonini *et al.* 2006). Consider the decision of CEMEX, the global building company based in Mexico, to develop a micro-lending program for poor customers in the 1990s when the devaluation of the Mexican peso resulted in rises in unemployment and a weakening of the currency, a situation that caused both society and business to suffer. Now, approximately 123 000 families across Mexico live in decent homes and CEMEX has a new customer base, along with a large amount of accumulated goodwill (Box 11.1).

Socio-economic deficiencies found in emerging markets can have even more grave implications for the success of native companies, as they are increasingly confronted with tough international competition in home markets due to the globalization of trade and investment flows. In many cases, a widespread shift toward market liberalization is causing strong local companies to turn to the global marketplace for the financing, technology or talent needed to compete domestically, and in some cases internationally, with more advanced companies (Khanna and Palepu 2005). Arguably, this growing need for emerging-market companies to 'adopt an international vision' (UNCTAD 2006) relatively early in business strategy development – even just to thrive domestically – must extend to environmental, social and governance issues.

With a home base in a high risk or less enabling environment, an emerging-market TNC must take special efforts to ensure transparency in business dealings, maintain or improve the quality and health of its workforce, and manage social and environmental risks, whether to attract trade and investment, take part in a supply chain, build a brand or export products. Finding systematic methods for addressing 'institutional voids' has not just allowed leading emerging-market TNCs 'to compete effectively against [foreign] multinationals. Further, as a result of their distinguished track record, they have been able to develop a corporate brand name that signifies quality, trust and transparency' (Khanna and Palepu 2005, p. 4).

Actions taken by leading emerging-market TNCs to reach high global standards for human and labor rights, environmental protection and anti-corruption within their operations is an important aspect of applying 'international' thinking. A 2005 McKinsey study of global leaders from emerging markets found that 'all brought their key processes up to or above global benchmarks before globalizing' (Sinha 2005). Meeting international standards for the environment and health and safety systems or implementing widespread policies concerning bribery and extortion can help allay concerns of international investors, partners or customers related to the stability and integrity of an emerging-market TNC's operations.[5]

BOX 11.3   ESQUEL: REDEFINING EXPECTATIONS FOR TEXTILE SUPPLY CHAIN PARTNERS

Though not a household name, Esquel is a supplier to some of the Western world's best-known clothing companies including Marks and Spencer, Hugo Boss, Nike and Tommy Hilfiger. The nearly 30 year-old textile company is based in China and has expanded operations to Malaysia, Mauritius, Sri Lanka and Vietnam. Of the company's 45 000 employees, roughly 95 per cent work in factories, weaving, dyeing and sewing cotton shirts for its leading

Western clients. Esquel is determined to be seen as a reformer in the textile industry.

Esquel's corporate responsibility approach is wide-ranging – from fair wages and benefits, extensive employee training and codes of conduct tied to international labor standards, to comprehensive efforts to reduce the company's environmental footprint across its production process. Its factories are each audited up to 30 times per year on ethical compliance issues. When the company needed to close a factory in Mauritius in 2003, it set up a support program that helped a majority of employees find new jobs, and in the meantime suffered no disruption to production until closing. In Malaysia, the company saw production time decrease and quality (and worker morale) increase as a result of employee skills training. In China, HIV/AIDS education was provided to over 30 000 employees once it became clear that many were not properly aware of the disease. In addition to all factories being ISO 14000 and 9000 certified, Esquel's work in the area of environmental sustainability is thorough: tracking water and energy consumption in garment manufacturing for each process (for example, spinning, weaving), wastewater pollution; air emissions in the factories, exhaust of vehicles transporting goods, and packaging materials.

Esquel has won accolades from clients, media and industry for its enlightened approach to business, suggesting that the company is making progress toward its goal of dispelling broad generalizations of the conditions and standards found in Asian textile factories.

Source: UN Global Compact.

The sustainability reporting practices of leading emerging-market TNCs support this position. Thailand's Charoen Pokphand Group, one the country's key conglomerates, lists the dozens of awards its companies have won related to occupational health and safety and the environment, proclaiming that it seeks to meet world-class standards in these areas. Brazil's Embraco, a producer of compressors, reports on efforts throughout its plants in China, Slovakia, Italy and Brazil to maintain key certifications including ISO 14001, ISO 9001 and OHSAS18001, and uses thorough methods for quantitatively reporting on social, labor and environmental performance. In South Africa, leading companies (including SASOL, Eskom and Barloworld) all use Global Reporting Initiative indicators to report on social performance.

11.2 FROM LEADING EXAMPLES TO WIDESPREAD ACTION

Despite the heightened sensitivity of emerging-market TNCs to socio-economic issues, general awareness and active interest in corporate responsibility by the majority of these 13 000 companies is lacking. Examples of enlightened and innovative practices implemented by some of the leaders in this pack cannot and should not obscure the fact that there are still many shortcomings related to the behavior of emerging-market TNCs, both at home and abroad. However, good-practice examples showing why and how the best emerging-market TNCs seek to balance corporate and social interests do serve an important purpose.

The decision of a seemingly small number of emerging-market TNCs to implement corporate responsibility actively in business – despite the current ability to profit with less evolved behavior – is noteworthy and precedent-setting. Leading emerging-market companies are rapidly making history and setting benchmarks for others to meet. Not only are these companies dispelling traditional notions that business is only driven by the West, but world-class emerging-market TNCs are also showing that in order to break this mold they are addressing issues of human rights, labor standards, the environment, corruption and community development.

Leading emerging-market TNCs are proving that low thresholds for corporate behavior and insufficient socio-economic frameworks are no excuse for ignoring societal well being. Further, they are making the case for companies with a home base in such environments to take the earliest possible opportunity to address pressing socio-economic obstacles in order to succeed and compete in a globalized world.

Many societal actors have a role in taking this call to the thousands of emerging-market TNCs yet to engage in corporate citizenship. It is critical that media and civil society, among others, continue to bring to light the unethical behavior of such companies, as well as report on the good practices being carried out by leaders. In addition, more widespread research must be conducted to understand how the majority of TNCs based in emerging markets are behaving in relation to human and workplace rights, environmental protection and corruption. While the likely hypothesis is that the lion's share of progress remains to be made in these areas, it is critical to have a more comprehensive understanding of the situation so that it can be addressed effectively – for example, by region or industry.

Leading emerging-market TNCs have an important role to play. Not only through continuing to improve their business and societal practices, but also by acting as champions in the corporate responsibility movement and as mentors to emerging-market peers at home and abroad. Because many leading emerging-market TNCs have been forced to reconcile business objectives with social limitations from a nascent stage, these companies are in an excellent position to be multipliers of corporate citizenship in locations where they operate under similar challenging conditions.

Finally, the Global Compact is committed to providing a platform for dialogue and learning among all societal actors on corporate responsibility in emerging markets. Education, awareness raising and advocacy of the business case for responsible practices by emerging-market TNCs is one way that the Global Compact can help achieve serious changes in the business practices of these companies.

Leading emerging-market TNCs are defining expectations for responsible practices by companies based in developing economies. If these good-practice examples are not enough to convince less evolved peers to engage in principled behavior now, then the continued integration of economies and societies should serve as an important impetus. Today's globalized society is engaged in a race to better standards for corporate behavior, not worse ones. As more companies like Tata Steel, Cemex, Haier, Koç and SAB Miller emerge as global players, it will become evident that principled corporate behavior is essential to a winning business strategy for emerging-market TNCs.

BOX 11.4   PETROBRAS: HELPING COMMUNITIES FACE THE EFFECTS OF VIOLENCE AND CONFLICT

Petróleo Brasileiro S.A. (Petrobras), a global petroleum company involved in exploration, production, refining, trading and transportation, is the largest company in Brazil. The company's roots are in Brazil (where it actively seeks to contribute to the development of the country) but its operations span 21 countries, many of which have unstable social or political climates. Today, Petrobras is investing US$200 million per year in corporate social responsibility and environmental programs that span 1200 related projects. At home, Petrobras recognizes the importance of community investment and has extensive programs underway related to poverty reduction across Brazil ('Zero Hunger'), education, child labor, child sexual abuse and fundamental rights for people with special needs, among many other issues.

The company also has corporate responsibility programs ongoing in foreign countries where it operates; such efforts take on a special meaning in countries or communities emerging from or still suffering from conflict and violence. In Angola, Petrobras is involved in reconstruction projects through humanitarian programs related to schools, daycare centers, hospitals and rural communities, as well as supporting Angolan socio-cultural organizations, including the National Historic Archives and Agostinho Neto University. In addition, Petrobras supports management-training programs to develop skilled laborers for the country's oil industry. In Colombia, the company works to build the capacity of Junta leaders near its operations and to train community health agents. Examples of Petrobras's initiatives in Nigeria include donation of supplies to schools that educate 12 000 pupils, provision of food and blankets to orphanages in the Lagos region, and an HIV/AIDS prevention campaign in 40 secondary schools in coordination with a local civil society organization.

Source: UN Global Compact.

NOTES

1. Information on the United Nations Global Compact and the ten principles in the areas of human rights, labor, environment and anti-corruption can be found at www.unglobalcompact.org.
2. Several recent articles point to the emergence of global business players from emerging markets and assess business strategies undertaken by such companies to compete globally, including Boston Consulting Group (2006) and Khanna and Palepu (2006).
3. All companies referenced in this chapter (including through case examples) are UN Global Compact participants.
4. The Koç Group Vision and Values, available at www.koc.com.tr/en-US, (last visited 25 October 2007).
5. Karl P. Sauvant (2006, p. 75), notes that, 'Emerging market MNCs are sometimes (rightly or wrongly) seen as having an unfair advantage (explicit backing and support from their governments) or being more prone than their developed-country counterparts to undesirable behaviour)'.

REFERENCES

Bonini, S., Mendonca, L. and J. Oppenheim (2006). 'When social issues become strategic', *The McKinsey Quarterly*, 2, pp. 20–32.
Boston Consulting Group (2006). *The New Global Challengers* (Boston: Boston Consulting Group).
Khanna, T. and K. Palepu (2005). *Emerging Giants: Building World Class Companies in Developing Countries*, Harvard Business School Note No. 9-703-431 (Boston, MA: Harvard Business School), pp. 1–19.
Khanna, T. and K. Palepu (2006). 'Emerging giants: building world class companies in developing countries', *Harvard Business Review*, 84 October, pp. 60–69.

Perry, Alex (2006). 'How Ratan Tata turned the country's oldest conglomerate into a global force', *Time Asia Magazine*, 19 June.

Sauvant, Karl P. (2006). 'A backlash against foreign direct investment?' in Laza Kekic and Karl P. Sauvant, eds, *World Investment Prospects to 2010: Boom or Backlash?* (London, UK: The Economist Intelligence Unit Ltd), pp. 71–77.

Sinha, J. (2005). 'Global champions from emerging markets', *The McKinsey Quarterly*, Number 2, pp. 26–35.

UNCTAD (2006). *World Investment Report 2006: FDI from Developing and Transition Economies: Implications for Development* (New York and Geneva: UNCTAD).

PART IV

What's in it for home countries and the
international community?

12. Outward FDI and the economic performance of emerging markets

Steven Globerman and Daniel M. Shapiro

INTRODUCTION

A fairly substantial literature exists that evaluates the impacts of outward foreign direct investment (OFDI) on home countries.[1] The emphasis of the relevant studies has been on OFDI from developed countries, reflecting the historic propensity for OFDI to be undertaken by transnational corporations (TNCs) headquartered in those countries. However, OFDI from emerging markets has been growing in both absolute and relative importance in recent years. As a result, researchers and policy makers are paying increasing attention to OFDI by TNCs headquartered in emerging markets, particularly those from Brazil, China, India, and Russia (the so-called BRICs).[2] Nevertheless, there is relatively little published research on the home country impacts of OFDI for emerging economies.

Studies for developed home economies focus on a wide range of potential economic impacts of OFDI, including impacts on domestic employment, wages, expenditures on research and development and innovation, trade flows and tax revenues (Kokko 2006). While there is some conflicting evidence, the broad conclusion to be drawn from the relevant studies for developed countries is that OFDI is associated with net productivity benefits to the home country that are manifested in higher per capita real income levels.[3] The evidence suggests that the productivity benefits of OFDI are achieved primarily through efficiency gains tied to the specialization and scale advantages of firms competing in international markets, and the indirect importation of knowledge and technology through imports and internal spillovers. In this sense, OFDI benefits are ultimately linked to international economic integration, which, in turn, has resulted in rising per capita incomes in developed home economies. In short, OFDI in developed economies is part of a tightly coupled system of complementary relationships that includes inward FDI (IFDI) and trade flows, and the benefits to OFDI are best understood in the context of these complementary relationships.

While recent studies suggest that rising levels of OFDI characterize newly developed countries (Duran and Ubeda 2005), one should not assume that the home country impacts of OFDI for emerging markets mirror those observed for developed countries. Differences of various sorts between developed and emerging markets, as well as between developed- and emerging-market TNCs, may contribute to different motives for OFDI, as well as to different consequences of the OFDI that is undertaken. In fact, we present and discuss evidence in this chapter suggesting that the OFDI undertaken by emerging markets has been quite limited to date, and does not appear to be embodied in a strong nexus of international economic linkages encompassing trade and IFDI.

Dunning (1981) and Dunning *et al.* (2000) emphasized the strong complementarity among OFDI, IFDI and trade in the various versions of the Investment Development Path (IDP). Although the direction of causality is not unambiguous, the IDP studies consistently indicate that economic development is associated with high levels of trade and FDI. Hence, the weak linkages observed between OFDI, IFDI and trade for emerging markets suggests the difficulties that many of them face in achieving sustained productivity growth. While the precise reasons for the weak observed linkages between OFDI and other measures of globalization are uncertain, we argue in a later section that corporate governance attributes of emerging markets may be an important factor limiting the economic benefits that they realize from the OFDI undertaken by their TNCs.

While some observers argue that the globalization process broadly defined, as well as OFDI specifically, will inevitably lead to governance reform in emerging-market TNCs, others argue that increased OFDI, IFDI and international trade, both individually and collectively, have not been a robust source of governance reform. In particular, the latter argue that political actions within emerging markets are required to introduce competition and market transparency that will promote new forms of corporate governance, and such political changes are difficult to implement. In many cases, political actions have been the result of financial crises afflicting emerging economies, with pressure for changes being exerted by international agencies such as the IMF. Obviously, it would be preferable for the relevant changes to be implemented in a proactive manner. In this regard, our broad policy conclusion is not dissimilar to Moran's suggestion in Chapter 13 that an appropriate public policy stance towards OFDI is one that is 'predisposed toward eliminating market failures that might impede home country firms from engaging in FDI'.

In summary, our analysis leads us to conclude that corporate governance shortcomings, as well as relatively weak supporting public sector institutions, contribute to relatively weak linkages between OFDI and other manifestations of globalization among emerging markets, thereby limiting the productivity benefits realized from OFDI. At the same time, the limited amount of OFDI undertaken relative to domestic savings mitigates against concerns that OFDI will adversely affect domestic capital formation and macroeconomic stability in emerging markets. In this regard, it is appropriate to highlight the fact that OFDI, to date, has been highly concentrated among a small number of countries. Equally relevant, OFDI from emerging markets has also been highly concentrated among a relatively small number of TNCs (UNCTAD 2005, p. 17).[4] This concentration serves as a caution against generalizing our findings and conclusions to all emerging markets.

The chapter proceeds as follows. Section 12.1 outlines the potential economic consequences of OFDI, particularly as they reflect the linkages between OFDI, IFDI and trade and the economic benefits of those linkages, and summarizes the evidence for developed countries regarding the linkages and their economic benefits. Section 12.2 identifies possible reasons why the linkages and their benefits observed for developed economies described in section 12.1 may not be characteristic of the emerging market experience. Section 12.3 provides some empirical evidence on the extent to which the empirical relationships between OFDI, on the one hand, and IFDI, trade and domestic capital formation rates, on the other hand, differ between developed and emerging economies, as well as among emerging markets. Section 12.4 discusses some research that focuses on the relationship between international economic integration and the restructuring of emerging markets, particularly the degree of convergence between public and private sector governance practices in developed and developing countries. Finally, the chapter ends with a brief set of policy conclusions.

12.1 THE POTENTIAL ECONOMIC IMPACTS OF OFDI

While there are numerous potential economic impacts of OFDI, of greatest significance, particularly to developing countries, is whether OFDI, on balance, contributes to higher real per capita income levels over time. In this context, per capita income growth will be a function primarily of increases in the amount of capital per worker and improvements in total factor productivity. Hence, our consideration of the potential economic consequences of OFDI focuses particularly on how OFDI is related to productivity improvements and domestic capital formation in the home country.

As suggested in the Introduction, the potential productivity benefits of OFDI can best be appreciated in the context of how OFDI contributes to a nation's international economic integration.[5] A particularly important issue in this regard is whether and how OFDI is linked to international trade, as well as to IFDI, for individual countries. To the extent that OFDI is linked to increased international trade and IFDI, it can be expected to have important direct and indirect consequences for productivity through increased specialization of production and inflows to the home country of factor inputs, such as new technology and new management practices. In this regard, the potential linkage between OFDI and trade might well be the most important channel through which OFDI impacts the home economy. Certainly, it has received the most attention in the literature evaluating the consequences of OFDI for developed economies.

12.1.1   OFDI and Trade

The conceptual basis for understanding the location of international production and the role played by direct investment was originally established by Dunning's (1973) eclectic paradigm. This identifies the international distribution of production facilities as the outcome of the interaction between location-specific advantages, firm-specific ownership advantages and internalization advantages. Location-specific advantages are derived from traditional and non-traditional determinants of country-level comparative advantages. Firm-specific ownership advantages are primarily related to the ownership of proprietary assets – often tacit knowledge – which enables a firm to establish a competitive advantage in specific activities. Internalization advantages are linked to market imperfections that make it more efficient to carry out specific economic activities within a single organization, rather than across the boundaries of independently owned organizations.

While the eclectic paradigm has been substantially refined and extended since its introduction, its basic insights into the potential linkages between trade and OFDI remain salient. Specifically, if international transactions are most efficiently carried out by home country-based TNCs, OFDI will stimulate international trade by expanding an efficient channel through which trade takes place. Home country-based TNCs may be more efficient at carrying out specific international transactions because they possess firm-specific advantages in those activities. Furthermore, market imperfections may render arms-length international transactions less efficient than intra-firm exchanges as channels for international trade. In this broad context, OFDI encourages increased international trade in specific economic activities because it reflects an efficient firm-specific channel for carrying out such trade. It is important to note, however, that while there is a strong theoretical basis for expecting OFDI to promote international trade, the causal linkage between the two is difficult to identify empirically (Duran and Ubeda 2005).

Increased trade, in turn, can take the form of both increased exports and imports. Presumably, OFDI will encourage increased exports of goods for which the home country has a location advantage. At the same time, home-country TNCs can be efficient channels for the importation of goods (including factors of production) for which the home country suffers a location disadvantage. In this context, OFDI promotes inter-industry trade and a resulting specialization of production within the home country along traditional lines of comparative advantage. However, home-country TNCs can also be an efficient channel for coordinating the geographical specialization of value chain activities within industries, where economies of scale (including agglomeration economies) underlie the imperative for geographical specialization of specific value chain activities. Here, OFDI also promotes intra-industry trade between the home country and its trading partners.[6]

Evidence bearing upon the quantitative importance of the linkages between OFDI and inter- and intra-industry specialization among developed countries is somewhat equivocal. For example, Lipsey (2002) found that transnational operations have led to a shift by parent firms in the United States toward more capital-intensive and skill-intensive domestic production consistent with inter-industry specialization along comparative advantage lines; however, this type of sectoral reallocation does not appear to have taken place in Sweden and Japan. In another study, Lipsey (2000) concluded that, within most broad industry groups, US FDI tends to move to countries with comparative disadvantages in trade relative to the United States. In resource-intensive industries, however, it moves to countries with comparative advantages in trade relative to the United States. On balance, it seems fair to conclude that OFDI contributes to increased and more specialized international trade for the home country.

Increased real income levels associated with traditional gains from trade, as well as the efficiency improvements associated with economies of scale and specialization from intra-industry trade, may therefore be seen as important potential indirect benefits of OFDI to the home country. These benefits are magnified to the extent that new technology (to the home country) is embodied in imports such that imports contribute to international R&D spillovers from exporting to importing countries. Bernstein and Mohnen (1998) and Coe and Helpman (1995), among others, assessed the influence of trade volume-weighted foreign R&D capital stocks on domestic productivity levels among OECD countries and identified substantial international R&D spillovers linked to trade.[7]

It is not possible to review comprehensively the extensive literature evaluating the impact of increased production specialization associated with international trade on productivity change in developed countries. Suffice it to say, the consensus opinion of economists remains that international trade is ultimately linked to improved productivity and higher real per capita income levels. The relevant issue for this study is whether the linkage between OFDI and trade, both in terms of the strength of the linkage and its economic consequences, is likely to differ between developed and emerging economies. This issue is considered in detail in later sections of this chapter.

12.1.2 OFDI and Technological Change

As discussed in the preceding subsection, increased imports are a channel for R&D spillovers that increase productivity and real income levels in the importing country. Moreover, OFDI might also promote technological change in the home economy more directly through the transfer of knowledge about new production and management techniques from foreign affiliates to the parent company. Such reverse transfers of technology are potentially derived from 'knowledge-seeking' OFDI, particularly investments that are located in regions where clusters of expertise in specific technologies reside. However, as noted in several studies, the benefits of these reverse transfers depend quite critically on the absorptive capacity of the home firm (Tavares and Young 2005). More generally, realizing the benefits of foreign technology spillovers, whatever the specific channel through which the technology is potentially available, requires that the receiving country possesses the capabilities to adopt and effectively utilize the relevant technology.[8]

The evidence on the economic importance of international transfers of disembodied technology is more equivocal than the evidence on R&D spillovers associated with imports of capital goods. For example, Jaffe and Trajtenberg (1999) used patent citations as a measure of knowledge spillovers for France, Germany, Japan, the UK, and the US. They found that patent citations are geographically localized. More generally, Globerman, Shapiro and Vining (2005) found that geographical proximity of Canadian software companies to US-based clusters of innovation activity does not seem to improve the economic performance of the Canadian companies. It is certainly possible that there is limited scope for transfers of disembodied technology among developed countries given similar levels of economic development across those countries. In this regard, transfers of technology from developed to developing countries may be more readily identifiable, given a more substantial divergence in technology levels.

On the other hand, developing countries arguably have weaker absorptive capabilities than developed countries.

12.1.3 Domestic Capital Formation and FDI Inflows

Relatively little attention has been paid to the relationship between OFDI and domestic capital formation rates for developed home countries. This probably reflects two empirical observations highlighted by Lipsey (2000). The first is that inward and outward FDI stocks tend to coincide for developed countries, that is, nations that invest abroad are usually major recipients of FDI. Analyzing data for individual OECD countries from 1970–1995, Lipsey found that the relationship between inflows and outflows of foreign direct investment relative to total output is positive and significant in most of the sample countries. The second observation is that neither inflows nor outflows of direct investment are crucial to determining the level of capital formation in a given country. Lipsey showed that even gross FDI inflows have been small relative to gross fixed capital formation. In most countries, gross inflows of FDI averaged 5 per cent or less of gross fixed capital formation. Thus, it is unlikely that OFDI has a significant negative impact on domestic capital formation; for developed countries, any potential losses are offset by capital inflows.

Lipsey did not argue that OFDI and IFDI are causally linked. Rather, he believed that the 'co-evolution' of the two phenomena among developed countries primarily reflected economic conditions that influenced the turnover of assets among TNCs from developed countries. In the language of the eclectic paradigm, this means that differences in firm-specific advantages lead to mergers and acquisitions across developed home and host economies. As noted above, Dunning (1981, 1988) explicitly linked OFDI and IFDI flows to levels of economic development in the home country. In his investment development path (IDP) model, the magnitude and nature of OFDI varies discretely as the home country becomes wealthier. At the same time, inward IFDI is attracted to wealthier countries. It is important to emphasize, however, that the IDP of each individual country may be path dependent and fundamentally idiosyncratic.

The link between OFDI and IFDI is less widely studied, and perhaps less widely understood than the link between OFDI and trade. Indeed, Tavares and Young (2005) argued that policy makers have not generally understood the implications of the connection for competitiveness and development. In terms of the eclectic paradigm, OFDI and IFDI are linked because the firm-specific advantages required to be internationally competitive are more likely to be acquired when the home economy has location advantages that attract IFDI, which in turn provides spillover benefits to home-country firms, some of whom become TNCs.[9] Thus there is a dynamic interaction between OFDI and IFDI, resulting in high levels of both for developed countries.

We are not concerned with whether observed linkages between OFDI and IFDI are causally related or merely reflect the influence of broad economic determinants common to both. Our main concern is whether the linkage observed for developed countries can also be identified for developing countries. To the extent that it exists, concerns about OFDI suppressing domestic capital formation rates in developing countries are mitigated. Specifically, FDI inflows would help mitigate the impact of FDI outflows for emerging markets. In addition, strong links between OFDI and IFDI suggest the presence of both firm-specific and location advantages in the home country.

12.1.4   Summary

OFDI is a component of globalization. Hence, the economic consequences for the home country, particularly with regard to improvements in productivity and increases in real per capita income levels, will reflect the strength of the linkages between OFDI and manifestations of globalization including increased international trade, as well as direct and indirect international transfers of technology, information and governance practices. Theory, as well as evidence for developed countries, tends to support a view that OFDI has net economic benefits for the home country. In particular, OFDI promotes increased specialization of production with resulting economies of scale and specialization, as well as the transfer of technology into the home market through imports of capital goods, IFDI spillovers and inter-affiliate transfers of knowledge by home-country TNCs. It is through these linkage channels to other manifestations of globalization that OFDI arguably contributes to higher real incomes in the home country.

Differences in economic and political conditions between developed and emerging markets caution against assuming that the consequences of OFDI for emerging economies mirror those for developed economies. In the next section of this chapter, we identify characteristics of emerging markets that may contribute to those markets experiencing different economic consequences from OFDI than those experienced by host developed economies.

12.2   EMERGING MARKETS AND OFDI

There are numerous differences between developed and emerging markets that could potentially contribute to differences in the home country impacts of OFDI. In this section of the chapter, we focus on attributes of emerging markets that have been prominently discussed in the literature and explore the implications of those attributes for the home country impacts of OFDI. Since there are significant differences across emerging markets in the relevant attributes, the discussion in this section also highlights potential reasons for differences across emerging markets in OFDI impacts.

12.2.1 Business Groups, Ownership and Governance

Recent evidence indicates that the economies of most emerging and transition economies are dominated by large, diversified business groups (Khanna and Yafeh 2005a; Morck, Wolfenzon and Yeung 2005). Many, though not all of these groups are family-controlled corporations characterized by pyramid ownership structures. Others, such as those in China, have important links to the state. As their importance becomes increasingly well documented, scholars have begun to study their characteristics and their performance (Khanna and Rivkin 2001; Khanna and Yafeh 2005, 2005a). On balance, the existing literature offers equivocal evidence bearing upon the hypothesis that business group affiliation provides performance benefits in emerging and transition markets. Thus, it remains unclear whether such business groups are 'paragons or parasites' (Khanna and Yafeh 2005a).[10]

In developed economies, with well-functioning external markets, the access of firms to critical resources, particularly capital, labor and complementary assets, is achieved primarily through market-based transactions. These markets are supported by a governance infrastructure that protects property rights, including an independent judiciary, an efficient and relatively corruption-free government, and a transparent regulatory framework (Globerman and Shapiro 2002). Under these circumstances, external markets are probably more efficient than internal markets for many transactions, and especially those related to capital markets. The reliance on external markets also promotes specialization within industries and firms, and internationally competitive firms are relatively specialized (Meyer 2004).

On the other hand, in economies in which external markets are not efficient, property rights protection is weak, contract enforcement is difficult and corruption is widespread, large diversified business groups emerge to fill the voids created by market failures and missing institutions (Khanna and Palepu 1997). Khanna and Rivkin (2001) argued that the internal markets created by such business groups are relatively efficient in the face of the widespread market failures prevalent in emerging-market economies. These internal markets tend to favor the emergence of diversified companies, which are often highly successful in their home markets (Khanna and Palepu 1997; Nachum 2004). However, a lack of specialization may limit the capacity of business groups to compete effectively in international markets, unless they are able to refocus their activities effectively.[11]

There are other potentially adverse consequences of group ownership for economic efficiency, some of which are related specifically to concentrated family ownership. These include inefficient capital investment, obstructed entry of new firms, stunted development of domestic capital markets and political rent seeking on the part of the controlling family owners, whereby the latter invest in political connections to stifle competition and to obtain privileged access to domestic resources (Morck, Wolfenzon and Yeung 2005).

Another prevalent characteristic of family-owned business is the limited use of professional managers in favor of using family members or trusted associates as key decision makers in the business. For example, Claessens, Djankov and Lang (2000) reported that, in East Asian countries, top managers are family members in about 60 per cent of firms that have a dominant or controlling shareholder. They also found that the top 15 family-controlled pyramids in East Asian economies hold corporate assets worth a large fraction of GDP – 84 per cent of GDP in Hong Kong (China), 76.2 per cent in Malaysia, 48.3 per cent in Singapore, 46.7 per cent in the Philippines and 39.3 per cent in Thailand. The minimal use of outside expert managers may contribute to underperformance from an asset utilization viewpoint. Furthermore, the lack of effective external monitoring in pyramid firms whose governance is dominated by a powerful family may deprive even scrupulous managers of effective investor feedback regarding investment decisions (Morck, Wolfenzon and Yeung 2005, p. 686).

Reliance upon family members and close associates to fill key management positions is paralleled by an emphasis on personal networks rather than contracts as the governance mechanism for transactions. To the extent that the competitive success of family-owned conglomerates derives largely from network connections in the home country, they may be disinclined to invest abroad where different firm-specific advantages are prerequisites for competitive success (Erdener and Shapiro 2005). If true, emerging economies characterized by family-owned conglomerates may have much less OFDI than would otherwise be the case. In a related manner, reliance upon personal networks may predispose family-owned businesses in emerging economies to invest in foreign countries where personal relationships with business and government leaders are strong. This phenomenon implies that OFDI by family-owned businesses in emerging economies may not primarily be driven by efficiency considerations, which in turn might attenuate the benefits of OFDI.

A focus on foreign investing in order to exploit economic rents associated with network connections potentially comes at the expense of investing in order to acquire knowledge and other resources that can improve the productivity of TNCs headquartered in emerging economies. In this regard, Li, Park and Li (2004) asserted that there is a much lower level of innovation and entrepreneurship for firms characterized by relation-based governance. This is because innovation makes the 'sunken' investments in relationships less valuable. Furthermore, the anti-competitive environment promoted by relation-based governance means that firms have more to lose from intensified competition associated with innovation.

In some emerging economies, most notably China, public ownership is a key feature of corporate governance.[12] In principle, state ownership leads to a move away from efficiency considerations as motivators of investment decisions in favor of other objectives. It is unclear, *a priori*, if state ownership, on balance, promotes or discourages OFDI, other things constant; however, there is reason to believe that the OFDI that is undertaken will not be as economically beneficial to the home country as OFDI originating in publicly owned companies managed by professionals.[13] Indeed, Blumenthal and Swagel (2006) have criticized purchases of overseas energy assets by Chinese companies. They claim that Chinese oil companies have vastly overpaid for the oil assets they have purchased, partly because the Chinese Communist Party sees energy instability as a threat to its rule. In a similar vein, Pitts (2006) cited assertions made by management consultants that Chinese companies suffer from a lack of merger and acquisition capabilities, thereby leading to ill-advised acquisitions. More generally, Hoskisson *et al.* (2005) suggested that government-controlled business groups are the least likely to refocus in a way that promotes competitiveness.

Reflecting these problems, many observers argue that today's developing countries face a challenge unknown to many OECD countries, namely, how to move from heavily relationship-based to rules-based systems of corporate and public governance.[14] Reforms of this type should provide greater incentives for large firms to narrow their business scope and reduce efforts to exert political influence, as well as for new firms to enter (Hoskisson *et al.* 2005; Peng *et al.* 2005).[15] In this regard, Wai-chung Yeung (2005) argued that globalization itself will inevitably contribute to fundamental changes in public and private sector governance, especially in Asian emerging economies. Among other things, developed country affiliates of TNCs headquartered in emerging economies will employ managers trained and experienced in Western management practices, some of whom, in turn, will wind up managing at TNC headquarters. Their presence in senior management positions in emerging-market TNCs should contribute to an evolution away from family control in favor of professional managers. Furthermore, to the extent that emerging-market TNCs raise capital in global capital markets, they will be obliged to adopt accounting practices, as well as corporate governance practices, that are arguably more transparent and 'public investor-friendly' than those required to raise capital in the home countries.[16]

In summary, the nature of business groups and the corporate governance features of emerging-market TNCs may or may not discourage the total volume of OFDI undertaken by those companies. A stronger argument can be made that those features will result in the OFDI that is undertaken conveying smaller home country efficiency benefits than would be the case if the strategies and corporate governance of the companies more closely resembled those in developed countries. Some observers argue that OFDI itself will inevitably contribute to governance changes in emerging economies that will, in turn, enhance the efficiency benefits of globalization generally and OFDI specifically. To the extent that corporate and public sector governance in emerging countries improves as a function of OFDI, those improvements themselves will represent an indirect long-run benefit of OFDI to emerging economies.

12.2.2 Domestic Capital Formation

As noted earlier in this chapter, among the OECD countries, there has been little concern expressed about the potential for OFDI to discourage net domestic capital formation. One reason is that OFDI tends to be balanced by IFDI. A second is that domestic capital markets in most OECD countries tend to be relatively efficient and liquid, as well as integrated into global capital markets. As a consequence, reductions in the availability of domestic savings through OFDI should have relatively small impacts on costs of capital in the home economy.

This sanguine view of the potential linkage between OFDI and net domestic capital formation might be inappropriate in the context of emerging markets.[17] For one thing, many emerging markets may be unattractive host country locations for IFDI, given features such as public sector corruption and government restrictions on foreign ownership in a range of industrial sectors (Globerman and Shapiro 2002). For another, domestic capital markets, to the extent that they exist, are relatively inefficient and illiquid, thereby limiting the ability of domestic businesses to finance capital expenditures through local borrowing or equity issuance, at least to any significant degree. Rather, as noted earlier, domestic capital investment patterns will largely reflect the decisions made by family- and state-owned businesses regarding their deployment of retained earnings. This reflects the fact that capital markets in many emerging markets are internalized within large domestic conglomerates. In this context, increased capital investment by smaller, domestic firms might not offset reduced domestic investments by TNCs to the same extent as might be expected in the case of developed economies.[18]

A reduction in rates of domestic capital formation associated with OFDI is a different concern from temporary outflows of capital associated with foreign exchange crises. To be sure, exchange rate volatility tied to large and sudden inflows and outflows of capital can contribute to higher interest rates in emerging economies; however, this phenomenon has been tied primarily to flows of short-term financial capital rather than to flows of foreign direct investment. On balance, studies show that direct investment capital flows are generally not significant contributors to capital flight during currency crises experienced by developing countries (Sula 2006; Sula and Willett 2005); however, reduced long-term domestic capital formation rates associated with OFDI are potentially a more relevant concern in the case of developing markets than in the case of developed economies. For example, there is some evidence that some Russian companies have diversified internationally because of the business environment in Russia (Vahtra and Liuhto 2004). This concern is evaluated in sections 12.3 and 12.4.

12.2.3 Scarcity of Management and Technical Expertise

In the literature concerned with developed countries, an important potential benefit of OFDI is the reverse flow of managerial and technological expertise that results from the overseas operations of home-country affiliates, particularly when the affiliates are located in 'centers of excellence'. The ability to exploit spillover efficiency benefits from OFDI is, in turn, a function of the managerial and technical capabilities of developing country TNCs, or more broadly, their absorptive capacity (Tavares and Young 2005). Specifically, if the relevant capabilities are below some minimum threshold, the capacity of those TNCs to identify and exploit managerial and technological spillover opportunities from doing business abroad might be attenuated.

In this regard, there is some evidence that spillover efficiency benefits from inward FDI in developing markets are only realized if host countries have minimum critical levels of human capital to take advantage of spillover opportunities (Kokko 2006). Thus, the benefits of inward FDI are related to the absorptive capacity of domestic firms, which is, in turn, related to their international competitiveness (Tavares and Young 2005). This may be a particularly severe problem for small and medium-sized enterprises in the home emerging market that lack the technical and managerial expertise to link into global value chains (UNCTAD 2005a). As a consequence, the potential spillover efficiency benefits to other home-country firms from OFDI by emerging-market TNCs may be quite modest. This concern is supported by evidence that spillover efficiency benefits from IFDI are more difficult to identify for developing host country economies than for developed host country economies (Kokko 1992).

Another consideration related to spillover efficiency benefits from OFDI is that a substantial percentage of OFDI from developing markets goes to other developing countries.[19] This so-called South–South OFDI may not generate reverse efficiency spillovers to developing home countries because the OFDI is not located in clusters of specific technological expertise, and because most South–South OFDI is arguably not of the knowledge-seeking type. Rather, it is meant to facilitate sales in foreign markets or to secure access to natural resources. On the other hand, the World Bank (2006, p. 117) has argued that narrower technological gaps between home and host firms may facilitate absorption, but also notes that this benefit may be limited because most South–South FDI is concentrated in extractive industries and infrastructure, where spillovers are limited. Along similar lines, Kumar (1982) has argued that emerging-market TNCs have a greater propensity to establish linkages with local firms than do their counterparts from developed countries. This implies a deeper integration of emerging-market TNCs into host economies, and this deeper integration could be particularly beneficial in terms of reverse knowledge and technology flows back to the home country.

12.2.4   Summary

In summary, differences between developed and developing countries in specific attributes raise the possibility that the productivity benefits to emerging home markets from OFDI may not mirror those observed for OFDI from developed economies. Specifically, the strength of the linkages between OFDI and other manifestations of globalization, especially international trade and the international diffusion of technology and management expertise, is likely to be weaker in the case of developing countries, and the productivity benefits from any increased trade, IFDI and acquisition of technology and know-how that is linked to OFDI are likely to be smaller.

Of particular relevance, differences in private and public sector governance between developed and developing countries make it likely that

OFDI from emerging markets will be less consistent with the goal of improving efficiency in producing and distributing output than is the case for developed countries. Hence, efficiency benefits to the home country from increased specialization through international trade, spillover efficiency benefits from IFDI, and the importation of technological and managerial expertise from home-country TNC foreign affiliates may be limited in the case of OFDI from emerging economies. A key issue in this regard is whether state-owned enterprises and family-owned conglomerates are able and willing to adapt their governance practices in order to operate efficiently in internationally competitive markets. As noted above, it has been suggested that OFDI will inevitably lead to changes in private and public sector governance in emerging countries that, in turn, will both strengthen the linkages between OFDI and other aspects of globalization, as well as enhance the efficiency benefits that are realized by emerging economies from increased international economic integration. Given the potential importance of the relationship between OFDI and public and private sector governance, we offer a fairly detailed review of the literature in section 12.4.

In the next section of this chapter, we discuss some evidence bearing upon the strength of the empirical linkages between OFDI from emerging economies and other manifestations of globalization. We also provide some evidence regarding the linkage between OFDI and domestic capital formation rates in emerging economies.

12.3   EMPIRICAL LINKAGES BETWEEN OFDI, IFDI, TRADE AND CAPITAL FORMATION

We argued above that central to the assessment of the potential home country benefits of OFDI is the degree to which these flows are integrated with, and complementary to, trade and IFDI, as well as the impact of OFDI on domestic capital formation. In this section, we provide some evidence on the nature and magnitude of these relationships.

12.3.1   Descriptive Statistics

Table 12.1 provides descriptive statistics for the relevant variables for different sub-samples of countries. In particular, we focus on differences between developed economies and emerging and transition economies. As noted above, it is by no means clear how to classify economies in this simple way and, as a result, we employ several different samples.[20] We use two samples of developed economies. The first, Developed I, includes the

Table 12.1 Descriptive statistics for selected globalization variables

Variable		Developed I		Developed II		Transition + Developing + BRIC	
		1995–2004	2000–2004	1995–2004	2000–2004	1995–2004	2000–2004
OFDI/GDP	Mean	4.6	6.1	4.7	6.0	0.4	0.5
	SD	4.4	7.6	4.6	7.3	1.8	1.5
IFDI/GDP	Mean	4.4	6.0	4.7	6.2	3.6	3.8
	SD	4.4	7.7	4.7	7.5	3.3	4.4
Exports/GDP	Mean	36.9	38.5	40.3	42.5	40.6	42.0
	SD	18.9	19.9	27.9	30.3	21.3	21.7
Imports/GDP	Mean	34.0	36.3	39.3	41.1	44.4	44.1
	SD	15.8	16.6	26.4	28.1	19.8	20.0
Trade/GDP	Mean	71.7	74.7	80.4	84.4	85.5	86.7
	SD	34.4	36.1	54.3	58.5	37.1	37.7
GFCF/GDP	Mean	20.9	20.9	21.9	21.4	21.0	20.1
	SD	2.6	2.8	3.9	3.4	6.6	7.3

Table 12.1   (continued)

Variable		Transition + Developing		Developing		Transition Economies		BRIC	
		1995–2004	2000–2004	1995–2004	2000–2004	1995–2004	2000–2004	1995–2004	2000–2004
OFDI/GDP	Mean	0.5	0.5	0.5	0.5	0.3	0.4	0.4	0.5
	SD	1.8	1.5	2.1	1.7	0.5	0.8	0.4	0.6
IFDI/GDP	Mean	3.6	3.8	3.4	3.4	4.5	5.0	2.4	2.4
	SD	3.3	4.5	3.7	4.9	2.0	2.7	1.8	1.7
Exports/GDP	Mean	41.5	43.0	39.4	40.6	47.6	49.5	19.1	21.3
	SD	21.185	21.6	22.2	22.7	16.9	17.0	9.8	9.7
Imports/GDP	Mean	45.6	45.2	42.0	41.1	55.5	56.5	16.9	17.9
	SD	19.4	19.7	19.7	19.6	14.5	15.1	5.7	5.6
Trade/GDP	Mean	87.7	88.8	82.2	82.6	103.1	106.0	36.0	39.2
	SD	36.2	37.0	36.7	37.2	30.6	31.2	15.4	14.8
GFCF/GDP	Mean	20.9	20.0	20.8	19.5	21.3	21.2	23.2	22.9
	SD	6.6	7.2	7.2	7.9	4.5	4.7	8.3	9.8

Notes: Developed I countries are defined as the original OECD members (excluding Luxembourg); Developed II countries are Developed I plus Israel, Hong Kong (China), Singapore, Taiwan Province of China and the Republic of Korea. Developing Countries are as defined by UNCTAD, and exclude the least developed countries, as well as transition countries, BRIC countries (Brazil, Russia, India, China), and countries judged to be tax havens. Transition countries are as defined by the IMF. See Appendix A12 for a complete list. Trade equals the sum of exports and imports.

Sources: *Handbook of Statistics*, UNCTAD Statistical Databases On-line, www.unctad.org/Templates/Page.asp?intItemID=1890&lang=1 (last visited 21 January 2007); *Foreign Direct Investment*, UNCTAD Statistical Databases On-line, www.unctad.org/Template/ Page.asp?intItemID=19238&lang=1 (last visited 21 January 2007); *GDP and its Breakdown at Current Prices in US Dollars*, United Nations Statistics Division – National Accounts, http://unstats.un.org/unsd/snaama/dnllist.asp (last visited 21 January 2007).

original OECD members, excluding Luxemburg. To these we add five economies (Hong Kong (China), Israel, Singapore, Republic of Korea, Taiwan Province of China) that have grown rapidly over the past decade and whose levels of GDP per capita are now similar to some of the original OECD members. In addition, they have been integrated into the global economy (as measured by IFDI, OFDI and trade). This sample is referred to as Developed II. We then constructed various samples of emerging and transition economies. First of all, countries classified by UNCTAD as the least developed were not included in any sample. These countries simply do not generate enough OFDI (0.03 per cent of global outflows) to make any discussion of OFDI benefits meaningful. The emerging and transition sample therefore comprises countries that are neither defined as developed, nor defined as least developed. From this sample, we create several sub-samples by considering separately transition economies (as defined by the IMF) and BRIC countries. We examine ten years of data, covering the period 1995–2004, and we also examine the most recent five-year period, 2000–2004.

The data in Table 12.1 suggest that developed economies, however defined, are characterized by high (and rising) levels of IFDI, OFDI, exports, imports and trade (the sum of exports and imports), relative to GDP.[21] These results are consistent with Dunning's IDP (Dunning 1981) in that the richest economies in the highest stages of the IDP are most fully integrated into the global economy. Importantly, IFDI and OFDI flows are roughly in balance, so that capital inflows do offset capital outflows. These results hold even when Hong Kong (China), Israel, the Republic of Korea, Singapore, and Taiwan Province of China are included in the developed country sample, thus suggesting that these economies have reached the higher stages of the IDP.

The results are quite different when the emerging and transition economies are considered. In general, when all such economies are considered, the most important differences between them and the developed sample are found in the IFDI and OFDI variables. The ratio of IFDI to GDP is lower for the emerging and transition economies, and the ratio of OFDI to GDP is considerably lower. Thus, for these economies, capital inflows far exceed capital outflows, which is again consistent with their status as economies in the earlier stages of the IDP. Further, these variables are not increasing as fast as in the case of the developed economies. Interestingly, the import, export and trade ratios are not markedly dissimilar between the samples.

There are also important differences within the sample of emerging and transition economies, most notably for the transition and BRIC countries. Transition economies have higher rates of FDI inflows than do other economies, but their outflows are not higher. However, the OFDI rates for transition economies have been increasing more quickly. BRIC countries have lower rates of inflow, and their outflows are similar to the average for the entire developing sample. Of course, the BRIC sample comprises only four countries, but it is still striking that the FDI rates are so low, given the presence of China in the group. However, like the transition countries, the BRICs have seen their OFDI ratio increase more rapidly than other developing countries. Indeed, without the transition and BRIC countries, the OFDI ratio for the developing sample actually declined in the most recent five-year period.

The trade variables also show considerable variation. The developing sample that excludes transition and BRIC countries has about the same trade intensity as the Developed II sample (which includes highly trade-intensive small countries). However, the transition economies are considerably more trade-intensive than any other sample, while the BRIC countries are considerably less trade-intensive. Once again, the obvious conclusion is that emerging and transition economies are heterogeneous, and it is therefore likely that the impacts of OFDI will also differ by country.

There is one variable that exhibits relatively less variation across the samples, and that is the ratio of gross fixed capital formation to GDP. Thus, the notable differences across the samples arise from differences in the degree to which the countries participate in the global economy.

12.3.2 Correlation Results

Table 12.2 presents the correlation coefficients between OFDI and the other variables reported in Table 12.1. It is important at the outset to clarify both our reasons for undertaking this exercise, and its limitations. Our reading of the literature on the benefits of OFDI to the home country suggests that these benefits are related to the ability of home-country firms to compete effectively in international markets, which in turn allows them to expand in the home market (scale benefits and specialization benefits). In addition, home-country firms may obtain spillover benefits from their foreign operations, and these benefits depend both on where they locate and on their ability to absorb new knowledge and technology. All of these benefits are therefore linked to the degree to which OFDI links emerging economies into international markets.

As noted above, there is a considerable literature that focuses on the relationship between OFDI and trade as a measure of the degree to which OFDI creates home country benefits. While there has been less emphasis on the relationship between OFDI and IFDI in that literature, this particular

Table 12.2   Correlation coefficients between OFDI/GDP and selected globalization variables

Variable	Developed I		Developed II		Transition + Developing + BRIC	
OFDI/GDP and:	1995–2004	2000–2004	1995–2004	2000–2004	1995–2004	2000–2004
IFDI/GDP	0.8*	0.9*	0.9*	0.9*	0.2*	0.1
Trade/GDP	0.6	0.5*	0.7*	0.7*	0.2*	0.2*
Export/GDP	0.6*	0.5*	0.7*	0.6*	0.2*	0.2*
Imports/GDP	0.5	0.5*	0.7*	0.7*	0.2*	0.2
GFCF/GDP	−0.3	−0.2	0.1	−0.0	0.000	0.0

Table 12.2 (continued)

Variable	Transition + Developing		Developing		Transition Economies		BRIC	
OFDI/GDP and:	1995–2004	2000–2004	1995–2004	2000–2004	1995–2004	2000–2004	1995–2004	2000–2004
IFDI/GDP	0.2*	0.1	0.2	0.1	0.5*	0.5*	−0.3	−0.5
Trade/GDP	0.2*	0.2*	0.3*	0.2*	0.4*	0.3	0.8	0.7
Export/GDP	0.2*	0.2*	0.2*	0.2	0.4*	0.3	0.9	0.8
Imports/GDP	0.2*	0.2*	0.2	0.2	0.4	0.2	0.7	0.4
GFCF/GDP	0.0	0.0	0.0	0.1	−0.1	−0.1	−0.4	−0.5

Notes: The categories are as defined in Table 12.1. * indicates statistically significant at 95%.

Sources: *Handbook of Statistics*, UNCTAD Statistical Databases On-line, www.unctad.org/Templates/Page.asp?intItemID=1890&lang=1 (last visited 21 January 2007); *Foreign Direct Investment*, UNCTAD Statistical Databases On-line, www.unctad.org/Templates/ Page.asp?intItemID=19238&lang=1 (last visited 21 January 2007); *GDP and its Breakdown at Current Prices in US Dollars*, United Nations Statistics Division – National Accounts, http://unstats.un.org/unsd/snaama/dnllist.asp (last visited 21 January 2007).

relationship has been central to the IDP literature, beginning with Dunning (1981). In Dunning's terms, the relationship between OFDI and IFDI indicates the degree to which a country has developed the market and institutional capabilities to attract sophisticated forms of IFDI (L-advantages) *and* the degree to which these advantages spill over to domestic firms that then invest abroad (O-advantages). In subsequent work, Dunning *et al.* (2001) have extended the framework to encompass trade.

Thus, from both the perspective of the literature on the home country benefits of OFDI, and from the literature on the IDP, one expects that OFDI, IFDI and trade variables will be positively correlated. It is important to recognize that a positive correlation does not imply causality. In the IDP literature, which relies on a stage of growth framework, it is not always clear whether high levels of GDP per capita cause increases in these measures of globalization or whether the latter simply increase over time, as does GDP (Liu *et al.* 2005). Our purpose here is not to enter that debate; rather it is to use the correlations to explore the potential differences between developing and developed economies in the strength of the empirical linkages between OFDI, trade and IFDI. We argue generally that OFDI benefits are higher when it is embedded in a system of complementary relationship with other measures of international activity. Thus, to the extent that the correlations among these variables are lower for developing economies, the linkages between OFDI and other manifestations of globalization might also be presumed weaker for emerging economies.

The results in Table 12.2 for the variables representing international activity (IFDI, trade, exports and imports) broadly confirm that, for the developed economies, these variables are all positively correlated with OFDI. Trade, OFDI and IFDI are relatively strong complements, that is, they have positive correlations. While the complementarity is also found in the various samples of emerging and transition economies, it is much weaker in almost all cases, and the coefficients are often not statistically significant. For the developing country sample that excludes transition and BRIC countries, the results not only suggest that complementarity is weak, but also that it might be decreasing. Transition and BRIC economies apparently are closer to the degree of complementarity associated with the more developed economies. For the BRIC countries, the small number of observations makes it difficult to draw substantive inferences. For example, the negative correlation (which is not statistically significant) between IFDI and OFDI is caused by India, with below average IFDI and higher than average OFDI.

On balance, we conclude that the strong complementarities among measures of international activity that characterize developed economies are not generally characteristic of emerging economies. There is some evidence that transition and BRIC economies are possibly more integrated inter-nationally than other developing countries. These results are supportive of the premise that governance infrastructure is a prerequisite for 'deep' inter-national economic integration that, in turn, contributes economic benefits to home economies that are directly and indirectly tied to OFDI.

Table 12.2 also provides correlation coefficients between gross fixed capital formation and OFDI. Here we are attempting to determine whether OFDI is a substitute for domestic investment. To some degree, this issue has already been addressed by the correlation of IFDI and OFDI. The implication of a strong positive correlation between them is that FDI inflows typically offset any negative effects of capital outflows. Gross fixed capital formation includes FDI inflows so long as they create new physical capital. Thus, FDI accomplished via acquisition would not be included in gross fixed capital formation. It is therefore interesting that although we observe both positive and negative coefficients, none are statistically significant in any sample. For the purposes of this chapter, what is import-ant is that there is no evidence that OFDI and gross fixed capital formation are substitutes for any of the developing economy samples (including BRIC countries for which the coefficients are not statistically significant). These results support an inference drawn earlier that OFDI is unlikely to be a significant constraint on domestic capital investment.

Strong complementarity, particularly when related to knowledge-based activities, can lead to increasing returns (Easterly 2001). For example, to the extent that IFDI is knowledge intensive, and to the extent that it creates spillover efficiency benefits for the host economy, IFDI will lead to increased OFDI and increased international trade. The complementarity between OFDI and IFDI will, in turn, attract more IFDI and so on. Such a process can lead to increased disparities between countries whose initial investments are relatively high, and those whose initial investments are relatively low. Countries with low levels of OFDI may thus persist with low levels of OFDI. In terms of the IDP, they may not be able to advance to the stages characterized by relatively high levels of both OFDI and IFDI.

12.3.3   Regression Results

In order to investigate further the path dependency of the OFDI process, we undertook a simple exercise whereby current (2000–2004) OFDI flows are regressed on past (1995–1999) OFDI flows. OFDI is defined both in natural logarithms and as a percentage of GDP. The results are found in Table 12.3. It is useful to begin with the first set of regressions, since this is a simple first-order autoregression that has been widely used in a variety

Table 12.3   The persistence of OFDI: regression results

Country Group	lnOFDI(2000–2004)=b lnOFDI(1995–1999) + a	R^2
Developed I	lnOFDI(2000–2004) = 1.0950[a/] lnOFDI(1995–1999) – 3.5587	0.7
Developed II	lnOFDI(2000–2004) = 1.1716[a/] lnOFDI(1995–1999) – 4.1886	0.7
Transition Economies	lnOFDI(2000–2004) = 0.9145[b/] lnOFDI(1995–1999) + 0.7577	0.9
Developing	lnOFDI(2000–2004) = 0.9269[b/] lnOFDI(1995–1999) + 0.0751	0.4
Transition + Developing	lnOFDI(2000–2004) = 0.9144[b/] lnOFDI(1995–1999) + 0.2849	0.8
Transition + Developing + BRIC	lnOFDI(2000–2004) = 0.9192[b/] lnOFDI(1995–1999) + 0.2201	0.8

Country Group	OFDI/GDP(2000–2004)=b OFDI/GDP(1995–1999) + a	R^2
Developed I	OFDI/GDP(2000–2004) = 2.1078 OFDI/GDP(1995–1999) – 1.4036	0.8
Developed II	OFDI/GDP(2000–2004) = 1.6414 OFDI/GDP(1995–1999) – 0.2913	0.8
Transition Economies	OFDI/GDP(2000–2004) = 1.2753 OFDI/GDP(1995–1999) + 0.1256	0.5
Developing	OFDI/GDP(2000–2004) = 0.6408 OFDI/GDP(1995–1999) + 0.162	0.3
Transition + Developing	OFDI/GDP(2000–2004) = 0.7029 OFDI/GDP(1995–1999) + 0.1751	0.4
Transition + Developing + BRIC	OFDI/GDP(2000–2004) = 0.7097 OFDI/GDP(1995–1999) + 0.1784	0.4

Notes:
All estimated coefficients on the lagged terms are statistically significant at 95% confidence levels.
a/ indicates that the coefficient is not statistically different from unity.
b/ indicates that the coefficient is statistically different from unity.

of contexts. The important result is that for both samples of developed countries, the coefficient on the lagged OFDI term is statistically different from zero, but not from unity. In other words, for the cross-sections of developed countries, OFDI flows follow a random walk, which also implies that any disturbance to the system will result in permanent effects. For example, exogenous changes that facilitate global flows of capital will raise OFDI (and IFDI) permanently.

In contrast, when the relevant coefficient is less than unity, as is the case for all samples of developing economies, the underlying process is mean reverting. In other words, an exogenous shock to the system will not result in permanent changes, but will rather cause the relevant variables to return to their means in the long run. The same exogenous change that will raise permanently the OFDI of developed countries will, for developing countries, result in only a temporary increase. Thus, developing countries may lack the capabilities to generate the levels of OFDI (and IFDI) that are associated with the developed economies.

Of course, it must be acknowledged that estimates based on cross-sectional data over relatively short periods may not be representative of all countries and all time periods. Thus, one should not conclude from the results that no developing economy will ever become the next Hong Kong, Republic of Korea, or Taiwan Province of China. However, it does suggest that, on average, this is unlikely for most emerging economies should current circumstances persist.

Roughly the same conclusions emerge from the second set of regressions, which use the ratio of OFDI to GDP. In these equations, it is the size of the coefficient on the lagged term that matters. The relevant coefficients for the developed countries are higher than those for the developing country samples, suggesting that there is greater persistence in OFDI among developed countries. Developed countries with high initial ratios of OFDI to GDP tend to have high ratios in the future. On the other hand, for developing countries, there is considerably less persistence. Developing countries with initially high ratios of OFDI to GDP are less likely to see them persist in the future. In these equations, however, it is interesting to note that the sample of transition economies exhibits more persistence than does the sample of developing countries.

12.3.4 Summary

In summary, our empirical results confirm that, in general, emerging and transition economies receive less IFDI and generate less OFDI. Consistent with the IDP, these countries have not yet reached the highest stages of the investment cycle. Our correlation analysis indicates that, for developed countries, measures of international activity are strong complements, thereby suggesting a potential for a self-reinforcing, virtuous cycle whereby trade, IFDI and OFDI all increase over time. The same strong complementarity is not found for emerging and transition markets, suggesting that the same virtuous cycle may be absent. In addition, our regression analysis suggests that, for these countries, OFDI follows a mean-reverting process such that exogenously determined increases in OFDI are not permanent. The implication is that the efficiency benefits of OFDI that derive from the linkages between OFDI, on the one hand, and trade, IFDI and disembodied technology inflows on the other hand, are likely to be modest for emerging economies compared to developed economies.

None of this should be taken to imply that development through globalization is therefore impossible for emerging countries. In our view, discussed more fully below, it simply implies that policies directed specifically at OFDI are likely not to be very important. Policies that limit OFDI limit the growth and competitive potential of domestic firms. Polices that encourage OFDI are, on average, not likely to succeed, unless accompanied by changes in the underlying governance of private and public sector activities. We therefore turn in the next section to a consideration of the determinants of governance change in emerging economies.

12.4   IMPACTS OF GLOBALIZATION ON EMERGING MARKETS

The statistical results discussed in the preceding section underscore the fact that OFDI is part of an overall process of international economic integration that includes increased trade and IFDI. For developed countries, there is a strong complementarity among variables that measure the degree of international activity; however, emerging markets are less integrated into the global economy, and this is particularly true for OFDI. Our previous discussion suggests that emerging markets face barriers to the creation of internationally competitive firms, and thus to the realization of benefits from OFDI. In particular, the literature emphasizes the role of governance and absorptive capacity as potential barriers. Therefore, we first focus in this section on the potential for governance reform in emerging markets, and on the evidence regarding the diffusion of management practices. Our discussion suggests that slowness in implementing reforms in corporate and public sector governance delays the benefits of OFDI.

Given that efficiency benefits associated with OFDI might not be achieved in the short run, the question arises whether there are any costs to OFDI that might be incurred. Most of the discussion in this regard has focused on the impact of OFDI on exchange rate stability and its impact on domestic capital formation. Both of these are discussed in this section.

12.4.1 Globalization and Governance

Earlier, we discussed widespread concerns that have been expressed about private and public sector governance in emerging markets, and the potentially adverse consequences that diversified business groups, particularly those that are family-owned, pyramid-structured conglomerates, as well as state-owned businesses, can have in terms of truncating the benefits of international economic integration. We also noted the claims of a number of observers that globalization will lead to improvements in governance. To the extent that such improvements occur, they could constitute one of the major benefits of globalization, particularly for emerging markets.

At the broadest level, there is now some evidence that indices of globalization are highly correlated with measures of good governance at the country level. For example, the Federal Reserve Bank of Dallas (2005) reports that countries that are more integrated into the global economy also have superior measured levels of public sector governance, where the latter is identified by a series of widely available indices including strength of property rights, accountability of public officials and rule of law. As with other correlations, caution must be exercised against inferring that globalization causes good governance, or, for that matter, the reverse causality; however, the evidence does suggest that globalization and superior public governance are complements.

The evidence reported by the Federal Reserve Bank of Dallas measures public governance at the country level. There have also been some studies examining the relationship between globalization and governance at the firm level. In one study, Khanna and Palepu (2004) evaluated whether globalization has promoted convergence toward world standards in corporate governance among Indian software companies. They focused particular attention on Infosys, one of India's leading software companies. The authors claimed that Infosys has a reputation for sound corporate governance and for being committed to shareholder value creation in a country in which corporate governance has, historically, not been a first-order concern. Interviews and field research led them to conclude that Infosys's incentive to adopt world corporate governance standards was primarily inspired by the need to attract skilled workers who are in demand in a global labor market rather than by the need to attract financial capital.

A more direct test of whether OFDI specifically encourages governance reform is provided in a study by Bris and Cabolis (2004). They examined more than 15000 cross-border acquisitions in the period 1990–2001 encompassing 49 countries. Specifically, they constructed industry-wide corporate governance indices reflecting investor protection. Their measure of whether investor protection improves as a result of an acquisition was whether Tobin's Q, a valuation measure of an asset, increases. They found that, when firms are acquired by firms from countries with better shareholder protection and accounting standards, the Tobin's Q increases for the industry in which the weak governance firm participates. Interestingly, they found some weak evidence that, when a firm from a country with poor corporate governance acquires a firm from a country with better corporate governance, the Tobin's Q of the acquiring industry increases.

In another relevant study, Peng, Au and Wang (2001) evaluated whether or not there is any difference in the reliance upon interlocking directorates when comparing multinational enterprises based in Thailand to non-TNCs in that country. These authors argued that the heavy reliance upon interlocking directorships in emerging markets may derive from the need to acquire necessary financial and technical resources, particularly from developed countries. Hence, they argued that FDI should lead to closer direct management links between TNCs in emerging and developed markets. They found that Thai TNCs do have more interlocking directorships than purely domestic companies, although the differences are modest. Moreover, the composition of the directorships with respect to nationality and ethnic origins were similar across the two sets of companies.

Palepu, Khanna and Kogan (2002) combined a variety of datasets covering corporate governance practices in 24 developing countries in Asia, Latin America and Eastern Europe, as well as data on laws protecting shareholders and creditors. Their focus was whether there is a correlation between similarities in governance practices across countries and globalization. They found strong evidence that *de jure* similarity in governance is correlated with several of their proxies for globalization. Further, the *de jure* results are not driven by similarity with US corporate governance. Rather, pairs of economically linked countries display similarity to each other's systems, especially if both countries are economically developed ones; however, they found little evidence of *de facto* similarity. Their interpretation was that, even though countries might mimic the tenets of each other's systems, their implementation is subject to significant lags.[22]

Filatotchev *et al.* (2003) studied the impediments to corporate restructuring of privatized firms in transition markets. In particular, they focused on the factors that entrench poor management and boards. They concluded that foreign involvement is likely to facilitate the development of organizational capabilities which might, in turn, encourage the improved international competitiveness of the firms involved.

The limited firm-level evidence therefore suggests that governance practices in emerging markets have not necessarily converged substantially toward practices in developed countries as a consequence of globalization. This result might reflect, in part, the fact observed in an earlier section that integration into the international economy has been relatively limited in the case of many developing countries. It might also reflect the fact that Western governance practices remain inappropriate for domestic market conditions in many emerging markets. In particular, attenuated domestic capital markets, high transactions costs in arms-length product and labor markets, limited resource mobility and other market imperfections contribute to the viability of family-owned conglomerates and, state-owned enterprises (Qian 2001).

To be sure, governance changes have taken place in many emerging markets. Experience suggests that the contribution of globalization *per se* to the reform process is modest. Rather, government initiatives, in conjunction with pressure exerted by international organizations such as the IMF, have played a prominent role in the promotion of economic reforms. Corporate reform in the Republic of Korea in the wake of the Asian crisis is a case in point (Woo-Cumings 2001). The importance of internal forces in promoting changes in governance practices is also suggested by the experiences of OECD countries. As Oman and Blume (2005) noted, in many of today's OECD countries, the transformation from relationship to predominantly rules-based systems of economic and political governance took place largely before the rise and global spread of the large manufacturing company.

In short, changes in corporate governance may well primarily follow, rather than lead, the emergence of more efficient domestic market institutions. Furthermore, changes in domestic market institutions require political changes that are difficult to implement, particularly in countries characterized by weak public sector governance. In the latter regard, the forces of globalization may be limited in the extent to which they can encourage political change in emerging economies. To be sure, a substantial literature has emerged over time documenting the negative impact that poor public sector governance has on inward FDI, particularly in the case of emerging economies.[23] One might therefore expect that competition among emerging economies for IFDI would lead to substantial improvements in public sector governance in those economies. An explanation of the reason why governance changes have been relatively modest in the light of competition for IFDI is that financial assistance provided by developed governments and non-governmental organizations (NGOs) to emerging markets has apparently not been linked to reduced government corruption. Moreover, there is some indication that private foreign investors became less concerned about government corruption in host countries after around 1995, perhaps because they have learned how to work around the risks imposed by host government legal and regulatory regimes (Groslambert and Bouchet 2006).

Findings that public sector governance practices in emerging markets have not necessarily converged substantially toward governance practices in developed countries are not entirely surprising, since governance practices continue to differ across developed countries at comparable standards of economic development and degrees of international economic integration (Doremus *et al.* 1997; van Tulder and Kolk 2001). The inference drawn from these findings is that national differences can sustain meaningful differences in governance practices, notwithstanding ongoing international economic integration through trade, investment and other phenomena.

Thus, the evidence highlights the difficulties in reforming corporate and public sector governance practices in emerging markets. In particular, the globalization process, by itself, should not be expected to transform substantially political institutions and government performance, which in turn, seems to be an important precondition for substantial changes in corporate governance. Nevertheless, international trade agreements, as well as pressure exerted by international organizations such as the IMF, can help encourage internal forces for change.

12.4.2 Managers and Corporate Strategies

Our previous discussion also pointed to a shortage of skilled managers as attenuating the capabilities of emerging markets to benefit from globalization. One consideration is that shortages of skilled managers limit the capacity of emerging economies to absorb new technology that is transferred from abroad, either through inward FDI by TNCs from developed countries, or through the transmission of technology by foreign affiliates of home-country TNCs. Another consideration is that the limited use of skilled, professional management may contribute to OFDI by emerging-market TNCs that is characterized by relatively modest economic benefits, both for the TNCs, as well as for the home countries.

Observers such as Wai-chung Yeung (2005) argued that globalization through OFDI and other channels will inevitably result in a greater use of professional managers in both domestic companies and TNCs headquartered in emerging markets, as well as in emerging-market TNCs adopting competitive strategies and practices that are similar to those of their developed country counterparts. The limited evidence suggests that this phenomenon has also been modest, as in the case of the convergence of governance practices.

To our knowledge, there has been little published research on the degree to which the use of professional managers in emerging markets has changed over time with increased globalization, or the extent to which corporate and competitive strategies in emerging-market TNCs have become more similar to those of their developed-country counterparts. The limited evidence does not unequivocally point to substantive convergence in corporate and competitive strategies on the part of TNCs from developed and emerging economies. For example, Duysters and Hagedoorn (2001) focused on global companies competing in the international computer industry. They used a number of variables related to the structures and strategies of the sample companies, including patent intensity, R&D intensity and relative share of sales outside the region of origin. Overall, they found little convergence over time across their sample of US, European and Asian companies.

As another example, Lee, Roehl and Choe (2000) assessed whether Korean management practices have changed over time with the increased international economic integration of the economy of the Republic of Korea. They concluded that there has been some convergence with Japanese management styles, although not in all relevant dimensions. There has been relatively little convergence with Western management practices. They argued that highly internationalized Korean firms were most active in learning from Japan because they have increasingly had to face severe competition with Japanese firms in many foreign markets.

12.4.3 Capital Formation and Exchange Rate Instability

As noted above, policy concerns about OFDI from emerging economies have focused not so much on limited efficiency benefits as on the potential short-run and long-run costs associated with capital outflows. In the short run, capital flight can potentially lead to serious foreign exchange crises. In the longer run, volatile capital flows can contribute to a permanent exchange rate risk premium being built into a country's international borrowing costs. Our interpretation of the evidence is that OFDI cannot be implicated as a significant contributor to either short-run currency crises or longer-run exchange rate volatility.[24] Most of the empirical evidence shows that FDI flows have much lower variance than flows of other forms of capital, and direct investment flows are also much less subject to sharp reversals in direction. Hence, we see no basis for condemning OFDI as a contributor to short-run or long-run macroeconomic instability in emerging markets.

Another broad concern is that OFDI results in less domestic capital investment in emerging markets with resulting adverse consequences for growth in per capita income and employment. However, we found no significant correlation between gross fixed capital formation intensity and OFDI intensity among our samples of developing countries. Moreover, available information clearly indicates that OFDI plays a very minor and indirect role in the overall savings and investment process in developing countries. Simply put, in the vast majority of developing countries, OFDI as a share of GDP is quite small compared to overall domestic savings as a share of GDP. This is particularly true for emerging Asian economies that account for a disproportionate share of emerging market OFDI. More generally, Edwards (2001) found evidence that countries with more open capital accounts outperform countries that have restricted capital mobility, although this may be truer for more developed countries.

Table 12.4 reports gross savings and gross capital formation as a share of regional gross national income for selected years. Several points are obvious from the table. First, gross savings rates in emerging Asia have been higher than gross capital formation rates over a 25-year period, reflecting in part the large trade surpluses of Asian countries. Even if one believes that emerging Asian economies should have invested more in domestic infrastructure, particularly in sectors such as transportation and environmental protection, a scarcity of domestic savings does not seem to be a direct constraint on such capital investments. Moreover, ratios of OFDI to GDP for emerging Asian markets are well below the reported ratio of gross savings as a share of gross national income, underlying the fact that OFDI is not a significant source of savings leakage in these countries.

A second point is that Latin America's experience is somewhat different from Asia's. Specifically, the gross capital formation ratio has generally exceeded the gross saving ratio, suggesting that increased domestic savings rates would have mitigated the need for as much external capital as was acquired by Latin American countries in the recent past; however, in the context of the major determinants of public and private sector savings, the relatively small flows of OFDI that have been undertaken to date by Latin American TNCs can hardly be considered an important factor. In particular, the political instability of the region is arguably far more important in depressing domestic savings rates than is the overseas investment of home-country TNCs. Indeed, the former may well be a strong encouragement to the latter.[25]

A third point is that recent increases in oil prices are contributing to a large savings surplus in Middle Eastern countries; a substantial share of these savings are presumably being recycled outside the region, given the disparity between the savings ratio and the gross capital formation ratio. In particular, the savings ratio is estimated to be 41 per cent in 2005, whereas the gross capital formation ratio is approximately 21 per cent. Against this

Table 12.4 *Gross savings and capital formation rates*

Region	Gross saving as share of Regional GNI (%)					Gross capital formation as share of Regional GNI (%)				
	1980–89	1990–94	1995–99	2000–04	2005p	1980–89	1990–94	1995–99	2000–04	2005p
United States	17.5	14.8	16.9	14.6	12.9	19.7	17.3	19.3	18.7	19.4
Japan	30.9	31.8	28.5	26.1	26.3	28.7	29.7	26.9	24.1	22.8
Europe[a]	21.5	20.8	21.1	20.5	20.3	21.7	21.2	20.2	19.9	19.8
Emerging Asia[b]	33.0	35.0	36.0	36.3	40.6	31.3	33.7	33.6	32.2	35.7
Emerging Latin America[c]	20.5	18.4	18.7	19.2	17.8	22.2	20.9	22.0	20.0	16.9
Middle East[d]	22.8	18.5	23.6	28.1	40.6	23.1	25.0	23.0	21.6	21.2

Notes:
[a] Austria, Belgium, Denmark, Finland, France, Germany, Greece, Ireland, Italy, Netherlands, Norway, Portugal, Spain, Sweden, Switzerland, United Kingdom.
[b] China, Hong Kong (China), India, Indonesia, Malaysia, Philippines, Republic of Korea, Singapore, Taiwan Province of China, Thailand. First column average for 1982–1989.
[c] Argentina, Brazil, Chile, Columbia, Ecuador, Mexico, Peru, Venezuela.
[d] Bahrain, Egypt, Iran, Jordan, Kuwait, Lebanon, Libya, Oman, Qatar, Saudi Arabia, Syria, UAR, Yemen. Data as share of regional GDP.
p preliminary

Source: Bosworth (2006).

background, it is obvious that even substantial increases in OFDI from the Middle East would have relatively little impact upon the availability of domestic savings to fund domestic capital investments.

Thus, although a major negative potential impact of OFDI for emerging economies is the effective reduction of domestic savings available to fund domestic capital investments, in fact this concern is unwarranted. As an empirical matter, many emerging markets enjoy large savings surpluses relative to domestic capital formation. Hence, even significant future increases in the relatively low current ratio of OFDI to GDP for these countries are unlikely to affect the ability of domestic investors to fund domestic capital expenditures from domestic savings. Furthermore, domestic savings rates in emerging markets are much more fundamentally affected by factors such as demographics, real economic growth, the efficiency of the financial sector and the security of property rights than by the saving and investment decisions of home-country TNCs.

As a theoretical matter, the overall impact of OFDI on domestic savings rates will reflect more than simply a direct deduction from domestic savings. For example, to the extent that OFDI contributes, directly or through augmenting other forces of globalization, to real income growth in emerging markets, it will probably contribute to higher savings rates in those markets. Furthermore, closer economic integration with developed countries, promoted in part by OFDI, will presumably better enable borrowers in emerging markets to raise capital in world markets at competitive rates. For example, as companies based in emerging markets become larger, partly as a consequence of OFDI, they can benefit from economies of scale in raising public capital. For another, the activities of foreign affiliates, particularly in developed countries, should raise awareness on the part of institutional and individual investors of the potential profitability of investing in emerging-market TNCs.

CONCLUSION

While it is not possible to quantify the impacts of OFDI on efficiency and capital formation in emerging economies, several prudent conclusions seem warranted. Perhaps the most unobjectionable conclusion is that there is no plausible basis for emerging-market governments to restrict or discourage OFDI by their TNCs. Specifically, there are no obvious negative externalities to the home country economy from OFDI. In particular, there is no basis for concluding that OFDI significantly restricts domestic capital formation rates in the home country. If anything, it seems more plausible that such capital formation is mildly encouraged by OFDI.

It is more difficult to conclude that emerging-market governments should actively encourage OFDI. The main point here is that external benefits to the home country economy from OFDI, while theoretically plausible, are difficult to identify empirically. It should be emphasized that higher profits realized by owners of home-country TNCs do not justify public policies that subsidize or otherwise lower the costs of undertaking OFDI for home-country TNCs. Such policies are potentially justified only if OFDI contributes to higher real income levels in the home country more generally. In other words, OFDI should also contribute to increased efficiency of the home economy that is manifested in higher real income levels of those who are not owners of TNCs.

Since OFDI is a component of globalization, one would expect it to contribute to improved efficiency of the home country. This is certainly the conclusion with respect to OFDI from developed countries; however, it can be argued that the linkages between OFDI, globalization and real income growth in developing countries are not as straightforward or as significant as in the case of developed countries. In particular, the efficiency benefits of technological and knowledge transfers are attenuated in the case of developing countries by limitations in their absorptive capacity.

Rather than suggesting the advisability of specific policies to promote the benefits of OFDI, the ostensibly weaker linkages between OFDI and the benefits of globalization point to the fundamental importance of policies focused on improving the capabilities of emerging economies and local companies to benefit from international economic integration more generally. Such policies have been extensively discussed and include obvious initiatives such as improving public sector governance, investing in education and physical infrastructure and so forth (Prasad *et al.* 2004). To the extent that changes in public sector governance play an important gatekeeper role to changes in corporate governance, the former might be a particularly important prerequisite to the growth of economically beneficial OFDI from emerging markets.

These conclusions are, of course, subject to several *caveats*. Our empirical analysis is based on a broad sample of countries and does not account for country-specific effects. This can be important since the BRICs are too small in number to be analyzed separately for statistical purposes, but they account for a substantial amount of OFDI. Similarly, the economy-specific factors associated with the success of Hong Kong (China), Israel, Singapore, the Republic of Korea and Taiwan Province of China are probably best observed 20 years ago, which is outside our sample period. Thus, a direct comparison of these economies 20 years ago with the BRICs today seems a fruitful direction for future research.

ACKNOWLEDGEMENTS

We acknowledge with gratitude the research assistance of Lisa Papania and the helpful comments of Karl P. Sauvant, Joseph Battat and two anonymous reviewers.

NOTES

1. Among the many studies, see Bergsten, Horst and Moran (1978), Globerman (1994), Horst (1976), Rugman (1987) and Reddaway, Potter and Taylor (1968). Kokko (2006) provides an extensive recent review of the literature.
2. Sauvant (2005) provides an overview of OFDI from the BRICs.
3. Kokko (2006) concludes that an important source of differing findings with respect to home country economic effects of OFDI is the nature of the assumed 'counter factual', that is, what assumption should one make regarding what would have transpired in the home country had the OFDI in question not taken place?
4. For summaries and analyses of OFDI patterns, see UNCTAD (2005b), Sauvant (2005) and World Bank (2006).
5. For purposes of convenience, we use the term 'globalization' as a synonym for international economic integration without regard to whether the integration is primarily intra-regional or extra-regional.
6. For a discussion of the conceptual linkages between OFDI, IFDI and intra-industry trade, see Graham (1994). Again, these relationships are difficult to identify in the statistical sense. Nevertheless, Lawrence and Weinstein (2001) suggest that imports lead to total factor productivity (TFP) growth because they promote innovation and learning by domestic firms. Urata (2001) found that trade enhances productivity for Asian countries and also links FDI and international trade.
7. The analog to this finding is that exporting countries may suffer adverse terms-of-trade effects to the extent that their direct and indirect exporting of technology enables other countries to build similar location advantages as the exporting country; however, to the extent that increased exports promote increased R&D and innovation activity in the exporting country, the location advantage of the exporting country might be maintained or even enhanced.
8. The main channels in this regard are imports of capital equipment, the operations of foreign-owned affiliates and transfers of foreign technology and practices to the home country through the activities of home-country TNCs.
9. In this regard, we note that several studies suggest that domestic firms are more productive when they engage in international activity, and part of the reason is their greater ability to absorb spillovers. Thus, foreign firms in the domestic market are more efficient than domestic firms only if the latter are confined to the domestic market (see, for example, Baldwin and Gu 2005).
10. Qian (2001) argued that the tight nexus between government and family-owned businesses can be a transitional institution during the process of economic development; however, as development proceeds, it is more and more of a liability to productivity and economic growth.
11. Hoskisson *et al.* (2005) provided a framework for evaluating the potential for refocusing among emerging economy business groups.
12. The majority of 'globalizing' Chinese companies are state-owned or state-controlled. See The Boston Consulting Group (2006).
13. In this regard, ownership of globalizing Indian companies is usually divided among private owners and the general public.

14. Oman and Blume (2005) identified a country's system of corporate governance as the formal and informal rules, accepted practices and enforcement mechanisms, private and public, which together govern the relationships between people who effectively control corporations, on the one hand, and all others who invest in the corporations, on the other hand.
15. For a contrary view, see Li (2005).
16. Morck, Wolfenzon and Yeung (2005) also suggested that 'openness' may create popular support for institutional reform in emerging economies. The World Bank (2006) focused on current impediments to OFDI such as bureaucratic constraints and the lack of business services.
17. Chen and Chen (1995), among others, discussed the possibility of the 'deindustrialization' of Taiwan Province of China as a consequence of resource-seeking OFDI.
18. Increased levels of domestic investment might be expected for the following reason: if TNCs increase their investing abroad, the expected rate of return to domestic capital formation should increase, all other things constant, since profitable domestic opportunities are presumably foregone by those TNCs in favor of more profitable opportunities abroad.
19. Although there is an increasing amount of South–North OFDI, particularly associated with several widely publicized acquisitions, it remains the case that the bulk of OFDI from emerging economies is South–South (Battat and Aykut 2005).
20. In order to avoid any confusion regarding classification, countries included in each sample are listed in Appendix A12.
21. It is not within the scope of this chapter to evaluate the reliability of OFDI data or to detail the potential problems associated with them. Suffice it to say that reliability problems exist.
22. There is evidence that corporate governance codes diffuse across countries, mainly developed ones, and that the impetus comes, in part, from the presence of foreign institutional investors (Aguilera and Cuervo-Cazurra 2004).
23. See, for example, Globerman and Shapiro (2002). An extensive review of the relevant literature is provided in Groslambert and Bouchet (2006).
24. For recent evidence on exchange rate instability that points to the importance of exogenous shocks in emerging markets, see Hausmann *et al.* (2004).
25. For some empirical evidence on the determinants of savings rates in emerging countries, see Edwards (1996).

REFERENCES

Aguilera, R.V. and A. Cuervo-Cazurra (2004). 'Codes of good governance worldwide: what is the trigger?' *Organization Studies*, 25(3), pp. 417–446.

Baldwin, J.R. and W. Gu (2005). *Global Links: Multinationals, Foreign Ownership and Productivity Growth in Canadian Manufacturing* (Ottawa: Statistics Canada, Cat. No. 11-622-MIE-no. 009).

Battat, Joseph and Dilek Aykut (2005). *Southern Multinationals: A Growing Phenomenon* (Washington, DC: FIAS), mimeo.

Bergsten, C. Fred, Thomas Horst and Theodore Moran (1978). *American Multinationals and American Interests* (Washington, DC: Brookings Institution).

Bernstein, Jeffrey and Pierre Mohnen (1998). 'International R&D spillovers between U.S. and Japanese R&D intensive sectors', *Journal of International Economics*, 44(2), pp. 315–338.

Blumenthal, Dan and Phillip Swagel (2006). 'Chinese oil drill', *The Wall Street Journal*, 8 June, A18.

Boston Consulting Group (2006). *The New Global Challengers* (Boston: BCG), mimeo.

Bosworth, Barry (2006). *United States Saving in a Global Context* (Washington: The Brookings Institute), mimeo.

Bris, Arturo and Christos Cabolis (2004). *Adopting Better Corporate Governance: Evidence from Cross-Border Mergers* (New Haven: Yale School of Management), mimeo.

Chen, T.Y. and Y.P. Chen (1995). 'Taiwanese foreign direct investment: the risks of de-industrialization', *Journal of Industry Studies*, 2(1), pp. 57–68.

Claessens, Stijn, Simeon Djankov and Larry Lang (2000). 'The separation of ownership and control in East Asian corporations', *Journal of Financial Economics*, 58(1–2), pp. 81–112.

Coe, D. and E. Helpman (1995). 'International R&D spillovers', *European Economic Review*, 39, pp. 859–887.

Doremus, P., W. Keller, L. Pauly and S. Reich (1997). *The Myth of the Global Corporation* (Princeton: Princeton University Press).

Dunning, J.H. (1973). 'The determinants of international production', *Oxford Economic Papers*, 25(3), pp. 289–336.

Dunning, J.H. (1981). 'Explaining the international direct investment position of countries: towards a dynamic or developmental approach', *Weltwirtschaftliches Archiv*, 119, pp. 30–64.

Dunning, J.H. (1988). *Explaining International Production* (London: Unwin Hyman).

Dunning, J.H., C. Kim and J. Lin (2001). 'Incorporating trade into the investment development path: a case study of Korea and Taiwan', *Oxford Development Studies*, 29(2), pp. 145–154.

Duran, Juan and Fernando Ubeda (2005). 'The investment development path of newly developed countries', *International Journal of the Economics of Business*, 12(1), pp. 123–137.

Duysters, Geert and John Hagedoorn (2001). 'Do company strategies and structures converge in global markets? Evidence from the computer industry', *Journal of International Business Studies*, 32(2), pp. 347–356.

Easterly, William (2001). *The Elusive Quest for Growth* (Cambridge, MA: MIT Press).

Edwards, Sebastian (1996). 'Why are Latin America's savings rates so low? An international comparative analysis', *Journal of Development Economics*, 51(1), pp. 5–44.

Edwards, Sebastian (2001). *Capital Mobility and Economic Performance: Are Emerging Economies Different?*, NBER Working Paper 8076 (January) (New York: National Bureau of Economic Research), mimeo.

Erdener, Carolyn and Daniel Shapiro (2005). 'The internationalization of Chinese family enterprises and Dunning's eclectic MNE paradigm', *Management and Organization Review*, 1(3), pp. 411–436.

Federal Reserve Bank of Dallas (2005). *Annual Report* (Dallas: Federal Reserve Bank).

Filatotchev, Igor, Mike Wright, Klaus Uhlenbruck, Laszlo Tihanyi and Robert Hoskisson (2003). 'Governance, organizational capabilities and restructuring in transition economies', *Journal of World Business*, 38, pp. 331–347.

Globerman, Steven (1994). 'The public and private interests in outward direct investment', in Steven Globerman, ed., *Canadian-Based Multinationals* (Calgary: University of Calgary Press), pp. 1–32.

Globerman, Steven and Daniel Shapiro (2002). 'Global foreign direct investment flows: the role of governance infrastructure', *World Development*, 30(11), pp. 1899–1919.

Globerman, Steven, Daniel Shapiro and Aidan Vining (2005). 'Location effects, locational spillovers and the performance of Canadian information technology firms', in Richard Lipsey and Alice Nakamura, eds, *Service Industries and the Knowledge-Based Economy* (Calgary: University of Calgary Press), pp. 167–204.

Graham, Edward M. (1994). 'Canadian direct investment abroad and the Canadian economy: some theoretical and empirical considerations', in Steven Globerman, ed., *Canadian-Based Multinationals* (Calgary: University of Calgary Press), pp. 127–150.

Groslambert, Bertrand and Michel-Henry Bouchet (2006). *Do Corrupt Countries Receive Less Foreign Capital After All?* (Paris: CERAM), mimeo.

Hausmann, Ricardo, Ugo Panizza and Roberto Rigobon (2004). *The Long-Run Volatility Puzzle of the Real Exchange Rate*, NBER Working Paper 10751 (September) (New York National Bureau of Economic Research), mimeo.

Horst, Thomas (1976). 'American multinationals and the U.S. economy', *The American Economic Review*, 66, pp. 149–154.

Hoskisson, Robert E., Richard A. Johnson, Laszlo Tihanyi and Robert E. White (2005). 'Diversified business groups and corporate refocusing in emerging markets', *Journal of Management*, 31(6), pp. 941–965.

Jaffe, Adam and Manuel Trajtenberg (1999). 'International knowledge flows: evidence from patent citations', *Economics of Innovation and New Technology*, 8, pp. 105–136.

Khanna, Tarun and Krishna Palepu (1997). 'Why focused strategies may be wrong for emerging markets', *Harvard Business Review*, 75, pp. 3–10.

Khanna, Tarun and Krishna Palepu (2004). 'Globalization and convergence in corporate governance: evidence from Infosys and the Indian software industry', *Journal of International Business Studies*, 35, pp. 484–507.

Khanna, Tarun and J.W. Rivkin (2001). 'Estimating the performance effects of business groups in emerging markets', *Strategic Management Journal*, 22, pp. 45–74.

Khanna, Tarun and Y. Yafeh (2005). 'Business groups and risk sharing around the world', *Journal of Business*, 78(1), pp. 301–340.

Khanna, Tarun and Y. Yafeh (2005a). *Business Groups in Emerging Markets: Paragons or Parasites?* ECGI Working Paper 92/2005 (Brussels: European Corporate Governance Institute), mimeo.

Kokko, Ari (1992). *Foreign Direct Investment, Host Country Characteristics and Spillovers* (Stockholm: Stockholm School of Economics).

Kokko, Ari (2006). *The Home Country Effects of FDI in Developed Economies* (Stockholm: The European Institute of Japanese Studies), mimeo.

Kumar, K. (1982). 'Third world multinationals: a growing force in international relations', *International Studies Quarterly*, 26(3), pp. 397–424.

Lawrence, Robert and David Weinstein (2001). 'Trade and growth: import led or export led? Evidence from Japan and Korea', in Joseph Stiglitz and Shahid Yusuf, eds, *Rethinking the East Asian Miracle* (New York: Oxford University Press), pp. 379–408.

Lee, Jangho, Thomas Roehl and Soonkyoo Choe (2000). 'What makes management style similar and distinct across borders? Growth, experience and culture in Korean and Japanese firms', *Journal of International Business Studies*, 31(4), pp. 631–652.

Li, Shaomin (2005). 'Why a poor governance environment does not deter foreign direct investment: the case of China and its implications for investment protection', *Business Horizons*, 48, pp. 297–302.

Li, Shaomin, Seung Ho Park and Shuhe Li (2004). 'The transition from relation-based governance to rule-based governance', *Organizational Dynamics*, 33 (1), pp. 63–78.

Lipsey, Robert E. (2000). *Interpreting Developed Countries' Foreign Direct Investment*, NBER Working Paper No. 7810 (New York: National Bureau of Economic Research), mimeo.

Lipsey, Robert E. (2002). *Home and Host Country Effects of FDI*, NBER Working Paper No. 9293 (New York: National Bureau of Economic Research), mimeo.

Liu, X., T. Buck and C. Shu (2005). 'Chinese economic development, the next stage: outward FDI?' *International Business Review*, 14, pp. 97–115.

Meyer, K.E. (2004). 'Global focusing: from domestic conglomerates to global specialists', *Journal of Management Studies*, 43(5), pp. 1110–1144.

Morck, Randal, Daniel Wolfenzon and Bernard Yeung (2005). 'Corporate governance, economic entrenchment and growth', *The Journal of Economic Literature*, XLIII, pp. 655–720.

Nachum, L. (2004). 'Geographic and industrial diversification of developing country firms', *Journal of Management Studies*, 41(2), pp. 273–294.

Oman, Charles and Daniel Blume (2005). 'Corporate governance: the development challenge', *Economic Perspectives*, 10, pp. 13–16.

Palepu, Krishna, Tarun Khanna and Joseph Kogan (2002). *Globalization and Similarities in Corporate Governance: A Cross-Country Analysis.* Working Paper No. 02–041 (Cambridge MA: Harvard University), mimeo.

Peng, Mike, Kevin Au and Denis Wang (2001). 'Interlocking directorates as corporate governance in third world multinationals: theory and evidence from Thailand', *Asia Pacific Journal of Management*, 18, pp. 161–181.

Peng, M., S.K. Lee and D. Wang (2005). 'What determines the scope of the firm over time? A focus on institutional relatedness', *Academy of Management Review*, 30(3), pp. 622–633.

Pitts, Gordon (2006). 'Temporary ties can stall Chinese buyers: report', *The Globe and Mail*, 24 May.

Prasad, Eswar, Kenneth Rogoff, Shang-Jin Wei and M. Ayhan Kose (2004). *Financial Globalizaton, Growth and Volatility in Developing Countries*, NBER Working Paper 10942 (December) (New York: National Bureau of Economic Research), mimeo.

Qian, Yingyi (2001). 'Government control in corporate governance as a transitional institution', in Joseph Stiglitz and Shahid Yusuf, eds, *Rethinking the East Asian Miracle* (New York: Oxford University Press), pp. 295–321.

Reddaway, N.B., S.T. Potter and C.T. Taylor (1968). *The Effects of UK Direct Investment Overseas* (Cambridge: Cambridge University Press).

Rugman, Alan (1987). *Outward Bound: Canadian Direct Investment in the United States* (Toronto: C.D. Howe Institute).

Sauvant, Karl P. (2005). 'New sources of FDI: the BRICs. Outward FDI from Brazil, Russia, India and China', *The Journal of World Investment and Trade*, 6(5), pp. 639–709.

Sula, Ozan (2006). *Surges and Sudden Stops of Capital Flows to Emerging Markets* (Bellingham: Western Washington University), mimeo.

Sula, Ozan and Thomas Willett (2005). *Reversibility of Different Types of Capital Flows to Emerging Markets* (Claremont: Claremont Graduate University), mimeo.

Tavares, Ana Teresa and Stephen Young (2005). 'FDI and multinationals: patterns, impacts and policies', *International Journal of the Economics of Business*, 12(1), pp. 3–16.

UNCTAD (2005). *World Investment Report 2005* (New York and Geneva: United Nations).

UNCTAD (2005a). *Linkages, Value Chains and Outward Investment: Internationalization Patterns of Developing Countries' SMEs*, TD/B/COM.3/69 (January)(New York and Geneva: United Nations), mimeo.

UNCTAD (2005b). *Internationalization of Developing-Country Enterprises through Outward Foreign Direct Investment*, TD/BCOM.3/EM.26/2 (November) (New York and Geneva: United Nations), mimeo.

Urata, Shujiro (2001). 'Emergence of an FDI-trade nexus and economic growth in East Asia,' in Joseph Stiglitz and Shahid Yusuf, eds, *Rethinking the East Asian Miracle* (New York: Oxford University Press), pp. 409–459.

Vahtra, Peeter and Kari Liuhto (2004). *Expansion or Exodus? Foreign Operations of Russia's Largest Corporations* (Turku: Turku School of Economics and Business Administration), available at www.tukkk.fi/pei/verkkojulkaisut/Vahtra_Liuhto_82004.pdf, (last visited 21 January 2007).

van Tulder, Rob and Ans Kolk (2001). 'Multinationality and corporate ethics: codes of conduct in the sporting goods industry', *Journal of International Business Studies*, 32(1), pp. 267–283.

Wai-chung Yeung, Henry (2005). *Globalizing Asian Business: Dynamics of Change and Adjustment* (Singapore: National University of Singapore), mimeo.

Woo-Cumings, Meredith (2001). 'Miracle as prologue: the state and the reform of the corporate sector in Korea', in Joseph Stiglitz and Shahid Yusuf, eds, *Rethinking the East Asian Miracle* (New York: Oxford University Press), pp. 295–321.

World Bank (2006). *Global Development Finance* (Washington: World Bank).

APPENDIX

Table A12.1   Country classifications for tables 12.1–12.3

Developed I	Developed II	Developing
Australia	Australia	Algeria
Austria	Austria	Antigua and Barbuda
Belgium	Belgium	Argentina
Canada	Canada	Bahamas
Denmark	China, Hong Kong SAR	Bahrain
Finland	China, Taiwan Province of	Barbados
France	Denmark	Belize
Germany	Finland	Bolivia
Greece	France	Bosnia and Herzegovina

Table A12.1 (continued)

Developed I	Developed II	Developing
Iceland	Germany	Botswana
Ireland	Greece	Brunei Darussalam
Italy	Iceland	Cameroon
Japan	Ireland	Chile
Netherlands	Israel	China, Macao SAR
New Zealand	Italy	Colombia
Norway	Japan	Congo
Portugal	Korea, Republic of	Cook Islands
Spain	Netherlands	Costa Rica
Sweden	New Zealand	Côte d'Ivoire
Switzerland	Norway	Cuba
United Kingdom	Portugal	Dominican Republic
United States	Singapore	Ecuador
	Spain	Egypt
	Sweden	El Salvador
	Switzerland	Fiji
	United Kingdom	Gabon
	United States	Ghana
		Guatemala
Transition economies	**BRIC**	Guyana
Albania	Brazil	Honduras
Armenia	China	Indonesia
Belarus	India	Iran, Islamic Republic of
Bulgaria	Russian Federation	Jamaica
Croatia		Jordan
Cyprus		Kenya
Czech Republic		Kuwait
Estonia		Lebanon
Georgia		Libyan Arab
Hungary		Jamahiriya
Kazakhstan		Malaysia
Kyrgyzstan		Mauritius
Latvia		Mexico
Lithuania		Morocco
Macedonia, TFYR		Namibia
Malta		Nicaragua
Moldova, Republic of		Nigeria
		Oman
Poland		Pakistan
Romania		Panama
Slovakia		Papua New Guinea
Slovenia		Paraguay

Table A12.1   (continued)

Transition economies	Developing
Tajikistan	Peru
Turkmenistan	Philippines
Ukraine	Qatar
	Saint Kitts and Nevis
	Saudi Arabia
	Serbia and Montenegro
	Seychelles
	South Africa
	Sri Lanka
	Swaziland
	Thailand
	Trinidad and Tobago
	Tunisia
	Turkey
	United Arab Emirates
	Uruguay
	Venezuela
	Zimbabwe

Sources: *OECD Member Countries*, available at www.oecd.org (select browse by country) (accessed 21 January 2007); *Handbook of Statistics*, UNCTAD Statistical Databases Online, www.unctad.org/Templates/Page.asp?intItemID=1890&lang=1 (accessed 3 August 2006); *Transition Economies: An IMF Perspective on Progress and Prospects*, available at www.imf.org/external/np/exr/1b/2000/110300.htm (last visited 21 January 2007).

13. What policies should developing country governments adopt toward outward FDI? Lessons from the experience of developed countries

Theodore H. Moran

INTRODUCTION

What policies should developing country governments adopt toward outward foreign direct investment (FDI)? Should developing countries actively promote outward FDI, adopting policies that explicitly favor home-country firms moving abroad? Or should developing countries restrain outward FDI, by discouraging home-country firms from moving abroad and/or granting preferences to firms that remain at home? Or, should developing countries design policies that are neutral to inward and outward investment – letting international market forces determine firm behavior – and intervene only to compensate for market failures or to generate externalities that can be captured at home?

Developing country strategists will choose among these three approaches on the basis of what impact they judge outward FDI to have on the economic and political objectives of their home countries. This will require empirical analysis of whether outward FDI strengthens or weakens the home country economy, and expands or diminishes the political capacities of the home country in the international arena.

To be sure, developing country policies toward outward FDI are related to much broader questions of enormous importance. For example, what are the pros and cons of overall capital account liberalization? How should developing country strategies for internal research and development (R&D), or external acquisition of knowledge (including brain-drain 'reversal') be designed? How do policies toward internal or external investment interact with national plans for education and training?

To keep the analysis manageable, this chapter deliberately narrows the focus to two extensive literatures examining outward investment from the developed world that developing country strategists can draw upon.

The first analyzes the implications of outward FDI flows on home-country firms, workers and communities; the second investigates the evolution of specific 'national champion' firms, initially launched by developed countries to further home country economic and political goals, as these 'national champions' move abroad.

These two literatures can help developing countries to address two questions that have preoccupied developed country policy makers:

- Does outward FDI hurt home country workers or help them, drain home country savings or enhance home country competitiveness (and ability to earn hard currency) in international markets?
- Does outward FDI augment national power or reduce national control over the pursuit of national economic and political objectives?

Examining developed country evidence may be useful to developing country strategists – by inference – in considering alternative policy approaches toward outward FDI. But ultimately these strategists should investigate whether the same results are observed when their own home-country firms engage in outward FDI.

The objective of this chapter is not simply to report findings from these two bodies of developed country literature, but to dissect the methodology of how to undertake rigorous investigation, so as to provide guidelines for developing country strategists to follow in appraising the effect of outward investment by their own firms.

Such an investigation is all the more important because developing country strategists cannot assume that they will discover similar results from outward investors as developed country investigators have observed. Elsewhere in this volume, Globerman and Shapiro (Chapter 12) point out that developing-country transnational corporations (TNCs) may exhibit very different corporate governance structures from developed-country TNCs. Developing country institutions may inhibit effects commonly recorded in developed economies. The indigenous absorptive capacity in developing countries may limit the transfer of technology or the creation of externalities that would be seen in developed home countries. On the other hand, as evidence uncovered by Cantwell and Barnard suggests (Chapter 5), South–South FDI may generate more spillovers than North–South FDI because external and internal firms operate within closer technological and managerial proximity. In any case, independent investigation of the impact of outward FDI on developing home countries is indispensable.

13.1 DOES OUTWARD INVESTMENT STRENGTHEN OR WEAKEN THE HOME COUNTRY ECONOMY?

What is the impact of outward FDI on the home country economy in the developed world?

Early analysts took an admirably expansive approach in raising issues related to outward FDI, asking, for example, whether home-country TNCs might be leaders in acquiring external inputs of R&D and act as catalysts in upgrading and restructuring the domestic industries in which they operated. As discussed below, the investigation of these broad possibilities has re-emerged in recent years.

But initial empirical analysis was almost entirely financial, focusing on whether outward FDI 'pays' in the sense of earning a higher return abroad than at home, whether outward investment (from Britain to the US 1860–1913) drained capital from the home country, and whether outward FDI affected the terms of trade or the balance of payments (Dunning 1970).[1]

Over the course of the past three decades, however, the bulk of developed country research on the impact of FDI on the home economy has taken a different bent, driven by a preoccupation with the fate of workers left behind as firms moved abroad. Is outward FDI from the United States to Mexico a win-win phenomenon for workers and communities on the home as well as the host side of the border, or does it constitute a 'great sucking sound' that destroys the dwindling supply of 'good jobs' at home? Does the movement of German, French and Italian companies to locales in Eastern Europe (and beyond) allow workers at home to be more productive, or does it merely undermine the social fabric and reduce the availability of high paying jobs in the domestic market? Should Japanese investment in China be seen as a benign 'flying geese' progression in which lower skilled jobs are moved to poorer neighbors while higher skilled activities are expanded at home, or a devastating process in which a 'hollowing out' of the domestic economy is the inevitable result?

While policy analysis of outward FDI from developed countries has occasionally been guided by active enthusiasm to help firms prosper abroad (see discussion of the doctrine of capital import neutrality and statements of TNC advocacy groups below), most analysis has started from a decidedly more skeptical stance than many developing country authorities currently exhibit (Sauvant 2005, pp. 639–709), that is, concern about 'runaway plants' within home country polities has generally dictated that the burden of proof is on the investigator to show that outward FDI does no harm and might do some good for the home economy.

13.1.1 The Impact of Outward FDI Flows on the Home Country Economy of Developed Countries

Developed country analysis of the impact of outward FDI on the home country economy begins with investigating whether production by home-country firms abroad complements exports from the home country, or simply substitutes would-be exports from the home country with offshore production.

Would export performance be stronger – and export-related jobs more abundant – if policies could be shaped to keep the firms at home, or might firms, workers and communities in the home economy actually suffer if obstacles were placed in the way of outward FDI?

To answer these questions requires comparing the export performance of home-country firms that do engage in outward FDI with the export performance of those that do not.

To undertake such a comparison, there is an analytical twist that has frequently ruined developed country analysis. In developed countries, TNCs and organizations representing them frequently point out that their participants export more, pay better wages, create more jobs and suffer fewer bankruptcies than average home-country firms (Emergency Committee for American Trade 1993). They cannot possibly be accused of undermining the home country economy, they argue, since their performance surpasses what can typically be achieved by other domestic companies. Quite to the contrary, they assert, their ability to invest at home or abroad as they wish is a prerequisite for maintaining their superior performance in the domestic economy.[2]

But firms that undertake outward FDI from developed countries are not average home-country firms. Just like Haier from China, Flextronics from Singapore, Ambev from Brazil or Infosys of India, IBM, Siemens, Ericsson and Mitsubishi tend to be larger, to do more R&D, to engage in more advertising and to have different labor relations from average home-country firms. To isolate the impact of outward FDI on the performance of those firms in the home country economy requires comparing apples with apples – that is, firms of similar size, R&D levels, advertising intensity and labor relations that undertake FDI with those that do not.

The need for structured comparisons of comparable firms that do and do not engage in FDI is important not merely for analytical integrity. It is also important because this procedure provides, for policy purposes, a clear look at the counterfactual – what would happen if home-country firms with a given set of characteristics were kept at home rather than allowed to engage in outward FDI?

A pioneer in this methodological approach was Horst, using US data. It is instructive to take a look at what would now be considered a rather primitive method to contrast the performance of firms that do undertake FDI with similar firms that do not before summarizing more sophisticated correlations, because of the perspective it gives to the stay-at-home option. Horst's early findings have been consistently replicated by researchers using more sophisticated methodologies ever since.

As illustrated in Table 13.1, Horst separated his sample of US firms according to company characteristics that might be expected to influence their capacity to export. He then compared the export levels of those that essentially stayed at home (column 1) with those that had begun to undertake outward FDI (column 2), those that had expanded their overseas operations (column 3), and those that had highest levels of outward FDI (column 4).

This progression of columns provides an easy visual presentation of what happens to the competitiveness of home-country firms (as represented by the level of exports as a percentage of domestic shipments) as they engage in outward FDI. As they establish distribution networks, transfer intermediate products for assembly and ship larger amounts of final products abroad, the percentage of domestic shipments that enter foreign markets rises. Outward FDI serves to pull exports out from the parent firms that expand abroad.

This positive relationship between outward investment and exports from developed countries holds for low-tech industries just as for high-tech industries, for low-advertising industries just as for advertising-intensive industries, and for heavily-unionized industries just as for non-unionized

Table 13.1   *Export performance of particular types of industries, by foreign investment level (exports as a percentage of domestic shipments) (%)*

Industry	1 Least amount or no foreign investment	2 Low middle range of foreign investment	3 High middle range of foreign investment	4 Most foreign investment
High tech	2.3	7.8	9.7	7.6
Low tech	1.3	3.0	2.5	3.5
High advertising	1.0	2.8	2.4	4.6
Low advertising	1.4	4.8	7.5	7.7
High unionization	1.9	5.5	4.4	3.8
Low unionization	1.3	3.2	7.0	7.8

Source: adapted from Bergsten, Horst and Moran (1978).

industries. Contrary to popular preconceptions, outward FDI is not somehow anti-labor – outward FDI creates more export-related jobs at home for low-tech workers and for unionized workers, just as for home-country workers in general.

This simple methodology also provides a clear picture of the counter-factual – what would happen in the home country economy if those firms that engaged in outward FDI had not done so. Their performance would resemble what appears in column 1 (stay-at-home firms with similar company characteristics). They export less, and thus show themselves to be less competitive, than firms that are expanding operations in external markets (columns 2–4).

A policy that prevents home-country firms from moving abroad, or that places obstacles in the way of outward FDI, would not lead to higher exports or larger numbers of export-related jobs. Just the reverse, such a policy would leave the home economy weaker, with fewer well-paying jobs available to domestic labor.

The structured comparisons in the early Horst analysis are only a prelude, of course, to sophisticated regression analysis subsequently done using data from the United States, Canada, Europe and Japan. Two-and-a-half decades of statistical investigations have consistently found comple-mentarity between outward investment and expanded levels of exports from the firms involved.[3]

It should be noted that these investigations do not claim to show that outward investment causes higher levels of exports in general. The empir-ical observation is limited to a comparison of the export performance of firms that do engage in outward FDI and that of similar firms that do not. This positive relationship between firms that undertake outward invest-ment and higher levels of exports from those firms holds for FDI that ends up at sites in both developing and developed countries. The complemen-tarity between outward investment and enhanced exports is more than large enough to offset exports from the investors' foreign affiliates to third countries that might replace shipments from the home country.

Since export-related jobs in developed countries pay wages 10 to 20 per cent higher than non-export related jobs, and offer 10 to 40 per cent higher benefits, outward FDI improves the proportion of good jobs (relatively high wages and benefits) to bad jobs (relatively lower wages and benefits) in home country labor markets (Richardson 2006).

Case studies of individual TNC behavior indicate that a large proportion of outward investment is 'defensive' in nature, and that the parent firm moves some operations offshore when headquarters expects those opera-tions to become non-viable at home over the next five-year period. It is pos-sible therefore, in some instances, that the home country workforce would benefit more over time with outward FDI taking place than not taking place, even if the immediate net job impact were to be negative, but not as negative as would be the case if the parent firm failed to build up distribution networks and assembly facilities abroad.

These findings have proven important to developed country policy makers because they show clearly that the preoccupation with 'runaway plants' and the loss of 'good jobs' in the home economy is unfounded empirically.

But even more weighty results are beginning to come into view. Developed country firms that are 'globally engaged' – that have higher levels of imports, exports and TNC operations – utilize cutting-edge processes in their home-country plants (at least in the US) more frequently, have higher levels of worker productivity and enjoy more rapid growth rates of overall productivity than home-country firms that do not (Bernard *et al.* 2005). This 'global engagement' generates a more competitive industrial base with a more stable job structure. Developed-country firms that invest abroad enjoy lower levels of bankruptcy, and are less likely to suffer job losses than counterpart firms that do not engage in outward investment.

Those communities in the home country that serve as a base for firms that invest abroad enjoy a higher level of economic well-being (even after controlling for size of city and geographical location) than communities that are less globally engaged. Some of this superior economic well-being can be traced directly to the higher paid workers and managers in TNCs. But the social value of the export-and-investment-related activities is larger than the benefits that can be captured by the international firms themselves and their workers. For the United States, there is evidence of spillovers and externalities to nearby firms and workers, and to the entire region clustered around the firms undertaking the outward investment (Richardson 2006).

It is a tricky question whether 'global engagement' – including outward FDI – causes this superior competitive performance of firms in the home economy, perhaps by acquiring technology and management techniques from a wider international font of knowledge, or merely accompanies superior competitive performance in a process of firm self-selection. But support for the idea of causation appears to be growing (Richardson 2006).

In any case, developing country strategists should set up their own structured comparisons to determine whether outward FDI is complementary to, or substitutes for exports from their home economies.

More broadly, they should investigate relative wages and benefits, productivity levels and bankruptcy frequencies among home-country firms that engage in outward FDI and similar firms that do not. They should search for externalities spilling over to the communities where developing country TNCs originate.

13.1.2   Policy Implications of the Overall Impact of Outward FDI on the Home Country Economy of Developed Countries

The decision of home-country firms to locate more operations at home or to deploy more operations to other countries depends upon many factors that home-country authorities can affect, such as support for indigenous R&D, expansion of local education and training efforts, and improvement in domestic infrastructure – a list that could be continued at some length.

Among these factors, tax treatment may not rank near the top. But at the margin, tax treatment of home-country firms is increasing in importance.[4] And in the debate about outward investment from developed countries, tax issues have occupied a prominent place. The alternatives for tax policy are 'National Neutrality', 'Capital Import Neutrality' and 'Capital Export Neutrality' (Hufbauer and Roou 1992). As discussed below, tax treatment can then be augmented by other official policies aimed at achieving the same objective as the tax policy.

The National Neutrality approach is the most restrictive toward outward FDI. While it does not prohibit the movement of indigenous firms abroad, National Neutrality aims at keeping the operations of domestic companies at home and maximizing the home country tax take from their activities. For example, National Neutrality tax policy does not allow a foreign tax credit for taxes paid by home-country firms abroad, but rather only allows the firms to deduct foreign taxes as a cost of doing business. Thus, if the tax rate abroad is equal to the tax rate at home, or higher, the home-country firm engaging in outward FDI would suffer a considerable amount of double taxation, paying the full tax burden twice and subtracting the foreign taxes only as a business expense. If the tax rate abroad is lower than the tax rate at home (or the foreign locale offers tax breaks or tax holidays), the home-country firm would nonetheless have to pay the full rate to home-country authorities, negating the impact of the tax break or tax holiday abroad.

If empirical investigation substantiated the hypothesis that production abroad substituted for exports, with home-country firms able to stay at home and replace overseas production with shipments from the domestic economy, the National Neutrality approach might have some justification. But the discovery that outward FDI from developed countries is complementary to exports, strengthens the competitiveness of home-country firms and bolsters home-country labor markets, undermines the rationale for the National Neutrality effort to discourage outward FDI. In practice, a National Neutrality policy would impose a huge burden on the ability of home-country firms to compete in international markets, with adverse consequences for associated indigenous workers and communities.

Moreover, the adoption of National Neutrality by some individual states, to try to keep their firms at home and/or pull them back from abroad, would have beggar-thy-neighbor consequences for their neighbors and trading partners. Other states might well be tempted to emulate the National Neutrality policy to try to shift production back to their own home economies. The spread of technology, management and capital that underpins the dynamic comparative advantage of the contemporary international economic system would be undercut via the multiplication of National Neutrality policies.

At the other end of the policy spectrum is 'Capital Import Neutrality'. This is named for the proposition that firms engaging in outward FDI should be taxed in overseas sites at the same rate as other firms located there. Capital Import Neutrality aims to ensure that outward investors do not suffer any competitive disadvantage to rivals wherever they are located.

In practical terms, Capital Import Neutrality effectively exempts the profits of home-country firms from any home-country tax whatsoever. Home-country firms would thereby reap all the benefits from tax breaks and tax holidays abroad, owing no home-country taxes on operations offshore under any conditions. This in effect provides home-country firms with an added incentive to move abroad.

The Capital Import Neutrality approach is consistent with the finding that outward investment benefits the competitive position of home-country firms, helping workers to gain export-related jobs with high wages and high benefits, and underwrites the stability of communities where those firms are located. But whether the movement of home-country firms should be 'promoted' through what is essentially a preference is debatable, unless there are clear externalities – positive benefits to the home country greater than what is collected by the firms, workers and communities themselves – associated with outward FDI. (The research summarized earlier provides indications of possible externalities, at least in the case of the United States.)

Capital Import Neutrality introduces tax considerations into the strategic decision making of TNCs about where to locate plants. But there is no reason to suspect that international comparative advantage will be served by having TNC activities concentrated artificially in low-tax locations. At the same time, unfortunately, Capital Import Neutrality promotes a race-to-the-bottom competition among nations seeking to attract FDI via tax breaks, giveaways and subsidies – a danger to developing as well as developed countries that will be highlighted below. Finally, the practice of awarding a tax preference to selected outward investors on the basis of possible spillovers opens the door to a long list of other home-country supplicants (telecom firms, biotech firms, venture capital firms, hospital builders, home builders, sports stadium builders) making the same argument.

In between these two approaches is the doctrine of Capital Export Neutrality. This takes its name from the proposition that home-country business operations should be taxed to the same extent whether those operations remain at home or make and deliver goods and services abroad. The goal is to prevent tax considerations from distorting the locational decisions of TNCs.

To implement Capital Export Neutrality, outward investors are taxed on their global operations, while receiving a foreign tax credit for taxes paid abroad. As a result, managers of TNCs can then ignore income tax considerations when they decide whether to locate a plant in the home country or abroad. Individual countries cannot try to shift FDI in their direction via tax breaks or tax holidays, since TNCs will still have to pay their home-country tax rate on operations undertaken in a low-tax jurisdiction.

The Capital Export Neutrality approach recognizes the benefits that empirically have been found to accrue to home-country firms, workers and communities from outward investment from developed countries, but does not 'push' companies abroad through tax preferences. The Capital Export Neutrality rationale is bolstered by the argument that business operations are allocated most efficiently on a worldwide basis without artificial distortion.

The empirical results derived from the investigation of the positive impact from outward FDI on the home-country economy has led developed-country authorities to adopt some version of Capital Import Neutrality or Capital Export Neutrality. Germany, France, the Netherlands and Canada, for example, take the Capital Import Neutrality approach, exempting the profits of their firms' foreign subsidiaries and branches from home-country tax altogether. The United States follows the Capital Export Neutrality approach, taxing the global operations of home-country firms, but allowing a foreign tax credit for external taxes up to the US rate. (In reality, the US provides a slight preference for outward investment through allowing 'deferral' of taxes owed to the Internal Revenue Service (IRS) from low-tax jurisdictions overseas until the profits are repatriated. This might be considered a tax-free loan of such obligations to the IRS as long as profits are kept abroad.)

In addition to crafting tax policy toward outward investors, developed-country governments engage in other official operations to help home-country firms evaluate offshore opportunities in the same way they do domestic investment prospects. Most developed countries assign to their foreign service or commercial service officers the task of helping domestic companies uncover promising FDI opportunities (as well as export opportunities) in the countries where those officers are stationed. Since there are large information asymmetries for firms trying to locate potential sites abroad, and appropriateness problems for successful first movers (first movers take large risks in 'trying out' any given new FDI site while rivals copy their successes too rapidly to compensate the first movers adequately for those risks), there may be a market-failure justification for the expenditure of public funds to help with FDI site identification.

At the same time developed countries have, with few exceptions, become members of multilateral investment guarantee programs (the Multilateral Investment Guarantee Agency of the World Bank group, and equivalents in the Asian Development Bank, InterAmerican Development Bank and the European Bank for Reconstruction and Development). These provide political risk insurance that corrects for market failure in contract markets for countries that have a weak record in making 'credible commitments' to foreign investors. Many developed countries also offer government-sponsored political risk insurance – like the Export Credit Guarantee department (ECGD) of the UK or the Overseas Private Investment Corporation (OPIC) of the US – that serves the same purpose.

The conclusion from this first body of literature is that the home economy is strengthened overall by a generally neutral policy, predisposed toward eliminating market failures that might impede home-country firms from engaging in FDI.

Does the same conclusion hold from examining not all home-country firms – anonymous, impersonal home-country firms across all sectors – but just 'national champion' firms that have been created to serve explicit home-country economic and political objectives?

13.2   THE EVOLUTION OF NATIONAL CHAMPIONS AS ECONOMIC AND POLITICAL TOOLS OF THE HOME GOVERNMENT WHEN THEY INTERNATIONALIZE THEIR OPERATIONS

The second body of literature that might be useful for developing countries as they watch their own firms move abroad shifts from examination of home-country firms in general, to investigation of the evolution of specific 'national champion' firms in particular targeted industries as they internationalize their operations.

Do individual national champion firms continue to serve the purposes for which they were created as they interact with international market forces? Can these companies be counted on to continue to fulfill the economic and political objectives of the home government, or do firms that have been born and bred as national champions become increasingly independent of national wishes or commands?

13.2.1 Developed Country Experience with National Champion Firms

To examine whether national champion firms can be relied on to pursue the political and economic goals for which they were created, it is first necessary to examine the three interlocking rationales for their creation.

The first rationale is to ensure that there are national firms participating in sectors of the home economy that are considered particularly valuable because they provide good jobs and/or high value-added business operations. This might be called the industrial policy justification for creating national champions.

The second rationale, more narrowly focused, is to ensure that the home country has a national champion presence in sectors in which economies of scale are especially large, barriers to entry especially high and rents and externalities especially abundant, in the face of possible preemption of such sectors by firms of rival states. This has acquired a rather arcane characterization as the strategic trade justification for creating national champions.

The third rationale, which overlaps with the second, is to create firms of home country nationality to avoid dependence on external suppliers who might delay, deny or place conditions on the provision of goods or services crucial for the functioning of the home economy (or its military forces). This is the national security justification for creating national champions.

What has been the experience of developed countries in using national champion firms to achieve the objectives for which they were created? What observations about the evolution of national champions from developed countries might be useful for developing countries as their own firms enter international markets?

Looking first at post-World War II Europe, there was considerable diversity in the degree to which individual governments designed an explicit 'industrial policy' to create or sustain national champions (Jacquermin 1984; Pearce and Sutton 1986; Vernon 1974). Some governments (for example, Italy) provided direct subsidies to designated national firms, and other governments provided more indirect and implicit support (such as, France's 'indicative planning'), while others (for example, West Germany, the UK) provided gentle manipulation to market forces via competition policy and government procurement. In Asia, Japan offered a combination of direct support and trade protection to allow the emergence (or re-emergence) of powerful *keiretsu* to preside over the growth of the domestic economy in the postwar period.

In all cases, however, the objective was the same: to ensure that there were national players in desirable industrial sectors to build plants and create jobs rather than leaving impersonal market forces to determine the composition of domestic economic activity or the nationality of market participants (Servan-Schreiber 1968). Fiat's duty was to foster development of the Mezzogiorno. Michelin's duty was to expand operations in vital French locales. Philips' duty was to reduce unemployment during the period of the 'Dutch disease'. Volkswagen and Siemens were to be the centerpiece of the German domestic 'economic miracle'. Tokyo's support for Mitsubishi, Mitsui, Hitachi, NEC and other great Japanese companies aimed to rebuild home country economic strength better than the impersonal workings of international markets would do alone.

Contemporary research on the results of post-World War II industrial policy – more detailed for Asia than for Europe – shows a mixed record of successes and failures (Dobson and Lipsey 1987; Jacquermin 1984; Noland and Pack 2003; Pearce and Sutton 1986). To conduct a successful industrial policy requires that public bureaucrats are able to select economic sectors and support specific companies better than the market does on its own, and avoid imposing burdens on or denying resources to other unfavored industries and companies. This rarely appears to have been accomplished on a sustained basis. It also requires keeping the award of special help free from contamination by parochial politics. Here the record is even more dismal. Political pressures regularly trumped careful economic analysis. In both Europe and Asia, 'sunset industries' and 'sunset firms' – from antiquated shipyards, to duplicative steel mills, to faltering petrochemical plants, to small farm agriculture – consistently received more support than 'sunrise industries' or 'sunrise firms'.

Whatever the costs and inefficiencies associated with industrial policy in Europe and Japan, more interesting – for the purposes of developing-country strategists wanting to forecast the evolution of their domestic companies – is to examine how the behavior of specific national champion firms changed as they were exposed to international competitive forces and began to move abroad.

The opening of borders to trade and investment exposed national champions to competitive pressures that posed a quandary for their role as servants of the home government. The national champion had either to look out for its own corporate interests ever more firmly, or else become increasingly uncompetitive and dependent upon the public dole.

However much allegiance a particular company might have owed to the home government that helped it launch, adherence to commands from that home government rendered the survival of the company increasingly precarious (Vernon 1974). Fiat could devote only limited attention to locating activity in the Mezzogiorno as its international rivals began moving operations abroad. Fiat's CEOs chose to locate operations in Argentina and Brazil even while laying off workers in Italy. Michelin began building three plants overseas for every one it constructed in France. Volkswagen's output in Brazil grew to more than a quarter of what remained in Germany; revenues from the VW Beetle assembled in Mexico became one of the parent's largest cash cows. The Parliament in The Hague complained when Philips increased electronics assembly in Asia as unemployment rose around Eindhoven. The Siemens workforce in the United States surpassed the number of employees in Germany even while German unemployment rates climbed to double digits.

In the Japanese case, the initial drive of Japanese auto companies to move car plants and parts manufacturers into the United States to jump over actual or threatened trade barriers, and of Japanese electronics firms to carry out increasing amounts of labor-intensive assembly in Southeast Asia, took place during a period of near-full employment and booming output in the home market. With the arrival of economic stagnation in the 1990s, however, the globalization of production on the part of Japanese TNCs led to charges that these erstwhile national champions were 'hollowing out' the industrial base at home.

What has been the record of developed countries with national champion firms created to serve 'strategic trade' purposes?

In contrast to the industrial policy objective of trying to improve the composition of activities in the domestic economy overall, 'strategic trade' considerations narrow the home country policy attention to sectors where economies of scale are so large – often larger than the ability of any single national market to accommodate output efficiently – that many individual countries may be left off the list of sites where high value operations (flush with spillovers, externalities, rents) take place. In such a setting, home government sponsorship of a national champion can ensure that the state providing support becomes one of the lucky few locations for production.

The striking insight of strategic trade theory, however, was its potentially aggressive nature – that public backing might be deployed in a predatory fashion to drive rivals out of business (Brander and Spencer 1985; Krugman 1986). Home country subsidies for the national champion might be calibrated to reduce market opportunity for competitors to the point where those competitors would operate at suboptimal scale, lose money and perhaps exit the industry.

Strategic trade research has focused on the competition between Boeing and Airbus in the aerospace industry, and between US and Japanese companies in the semiconductor industry.[5] In both of these high profile duels, home-country authorities tempered inclinations to destroy rivals of all other nationalities with joint action to control the escalation of official support.

In the case of Boeing versus Airbus, home governments on both sides of the Atlantic took deliberate steps via the Civil Air Agreement (1992

US–EU Agreement on Large Civil Aircraft) to limit – imperfectly – the support parent authorities might devote to strengthening the position of their strategic champion. While the actual course of negotiations under the Agreement have been (and remain) highly contentious, the policy thrust has been to replace the strategic trade drive toward home country supremacy with a system of mutual surveillance and mutual complaint about what kinds and levels of public assistance are illegitimate, while leaving it to the corporations to use their own skill and expertise to compete for market share.

What is surprising in observing the behavior of the strategic trade champions themselves is, once again, the evolution in their own perception of how to strengthen their position around the world in the face of international competition. Adapting a practice first used to sell military aircraft, both Boeing and Airbus have gone to great lengths to erase their exclusive home country identity.[6]

General Dynamics was the pioneer in the strategy of diluting the national origin of its product to persuade the NATO partners to choose the American F-16 over the French Mirage F-1. Dangling joint production agreements in front of European aerospace suppliers, General Dynamics allowed NATO members that purchased the F-16 to build locally 40 per cent of the European version of the fighter, 10 per cent of the planes bought by the US Air Force, and 15 per cent of the planes sold elsewhere. Learning from success in gaining acceptance for the F-16, Boeing used the same approach to market AWACS (Airborne Control and Warning System) in competition with the arguably superior (and cheaper) British Nimrod. The unwieldiness of a transnational production strategy was substituted for all-US production because, in the words of Boeing's president, 'if we were to bleed off all of the aerospace production, we'd get a backlash that would cause more trouble than sharing to a degree' (Kraar 1980, p. 79).

In civilian aircraft, Boeing regularly lined up Rolls Royce in the UK or SNECMA in France to supply aircraft engines (the largest single component of each plane), and European aerospace companies to supply other inputs for Boeing planes marketed in the EU (Moran and Mowery 1994). Airbus replied with contracts to Pratt and Whitney and to General Electric for engines in planes sold to US airlines. Airbus boasts that 46 per cent of its procurement comes from the United States, amounting to $8.5 billion in 2005, supporting 174 000 US jobs.[7]

The rivalry between US and Japanese semiconductor companies was much less tidy (Flamm 1996; Tyson 1992, pp. 108, 137). Whether encouraged by Japanese government authorities or not, evidence emerged that Japanese semiconductor firms were intent on predation, with Hitachi, for example, explicitly ordering its subsidiaries to price their output 10 per cent below American quotes without regard to marginal cost (Tyson 1992, pp. 108, 137). The international negotiations that resulted to block any prospect of strategic trade dominance – the US–Japanese Semiconductor Agreement of 1989 – made the Civil Air Agreement appear like a model of rationality. The Semiconductor Agreement in essence created a worldwide cartel of Japanese semiconductor firms, administered by the Japanese Ministry of International Trade and Industry (MITI), to keep prices high enough for US companies to stay in business. With the emergence of new players bolstered by the high price levels – especially from the Republic of Korea and Taiwan Province of China – as well as resurgence of the semiconductor industry in the US and Europe, the prospect of market dominance by any single country became mute.

National security considerations add a further dimension to the justi-fication for support for national champion companies. National champion firms provide a vehicle to avoid dependence upon outsiders for goods or services that are 'crucial' or 'critical' for the functioning of the home economy, in particular the home country military forces. The fear is that outsiders might cut off or place obstacles in the way of delivery. National champion firms, in contrast, can be depended upon to ensure access to crucial or critical goods and services in timely fashion.

To be rigorous, a national security strategy for creating national cham-pions might be considered a variation of strategic trade analysis, applying only to industries with high barriers to entry and large economies of scale. Helping to simplify the identification of the sectors or companies that might genuinely qualify for national security protection or subsidy is this analytic insight: the threat of denial is credible only if the external suppli-ers are relatively few and the switching costs are high (Moran 1980, pp. 57–99). If there are more than four countries or four foreign companies that control more than 50 per cent of the international market for a par-ticular good or service, the likelihood of a successful campaign to delay, deny or place conditions on the provision of that good or service is quite low. But where suppliers are few and alternatives are scarce, and the threat of cut-off or cut-back is genuine, the likelihood is greater.

In the Suez crisis of 1956, for example, the mere allusion on the part of Secretary of State John Foster Dulles that US oil companies could be asked to cut supplies to Europe was a decisive factor in the British and French decision to withdraw their forces from occupation of the Canal since sub-stitute sources of petroleum were insufficient to meet their needs. Similarly, the Johnson Administration's order to IBM and Control Data to withhold advanced computer technology from de Gaulle's *force de frappe* caused French work on the hydrogen bomb to 'come to a grinding halt', since these two companies had a virtual monopoly at the time on high speed computational capabilities (*The Economist* 1966, p. 1229). These instances of actual or threatened denial reinforced the conclusion in Europe that they needed 'their own' oil firms and computer firms to serve national needs rather than to find themselves dependent upon US TNCs.

Once again, however, the evidence shows that national champion firms suffer an attenuation in their ability – and willingness – to act as a conduit of home country policy directives as these firms internationalize their operations, especially if authorities elsewhere issue contrary instructions.

Perhaps the starkest evidence of this came during the US–European confrontation over the Soviet gas pipeline in 1982 (Hufbauer *et al.* 1990). After declaration of martial law in Poland, President Reagan unilaterally suspended export licenses to the Soviet Union for many high-tech products and prohibited US subsidiaries and non-US licensees of American technology from carrying out duly signed contracts for sales to the USSR. In response, British, German and Italian governments ordered firms of their own nationality that were operating under US licenses to proceed with shipments to the Soviet Union, and France ordered the French subsidiary of Dresser Industries (headquartered in Dallas) to proceed with the delivery of 21 pipeline booster compressors as required by a prior legal contract.

As operations increasingly globalized, firms of all nationalities found themselves caught in the middle, facing severe penalties no matter whose directive they obeyed. Creusot-Loire of France and John Brown Engineers of the UK, working on the pipeline with US-licensed technology, faced retaliation from the US government within US borders if they complied with their home government's mandate. Senior Dresser executives noted that their only real choice was whether to report to prison in the United States or in France. The result was a stalemate as negotiations about how to deal with the Soviet Union proceeded on the higher political plane among the sovereign governments involved. It is noteworthy that during this process, Dresser's senior management orchestrated an energetic private campaign in the US capital to get the sanctions lifted. Corporate interest trumped compliant obedience to home country political leadership.

A close look at the historical record shows that even national champion oil companies have not been immune to moving in a non-national direction as they spread abroad – all the more surprising yet when government ownership is present. During the 1973–4 oil embargo, when Prime Minister Ted Heath demanded that British Petroleum (with more than half a century of support from Her Majesty's government and still 48 per cent government-owned) give preference to the British market in delivering oil supplies, BP refused, noting that it would adhere to contractual obligations rather than to 'instructions from shareholders' (Stobaugh 1975, p. 189). Subsequent analysis revealed that all international oil companies, including Royal

Dutch Shell, ENI of Italy and Elf-ERAP and CFP of France, spread the pain of cutbacks evenly among their customer base rather than favoring their home countries (Stobaugh 1975).

What are the policy implications for developing countries from observing the experience of developed countries with national champion firms, as those national champions moved abroad?

13.2.2 Policy Implications from the Evolution of National Champions

For many developed countries, industrial policy was intended to be the vehicle to create and maintain national champion companies at the cutting edge in especially desirable sectors – high tech, rapid growth, 'sunrise' industries – so that their workers and the communities surrounding them could enjoy good jobs and high value-added economic activity.

The historical record in Europe and Asia shows developing countries how difficult this is likely to be in the contemporary period. Public sector authorities have to devise a means to pick winning and losing sectors better than the market, and then identify winners and losers among specific local companies to produce a roster of viable national champion companies. The most promising industrial policy interventions have taken place where there have been clear market failures that prevent the emergence of national firms and/or clear externalities that are derived from their operations. But market failures and externalities have proven notoriously hard to identify in any rigorous fashion, and the selection among potential claimants is highly prone to political pressure.

Japan, for example, was long heralded as a model for industrial policy and national champion prowess. But careful retrospective analysis fails to find any evidence that subsidies or preferential tax policies contributed in positive fashion to total factor productivity growth in targeted sectors (Beason and Weinstein 1996, pp. 286–295). As for trade protection, the evidence suggests that Japanese growth would have been even more rapid, with greater openness and expanded exposure to new, improved or highly specialized intermediate inputs (Lawrence and Weinstein 2001). Selective public sector interventions were so skewed toward noncompetitive 'backward' industries (agriculture, mining, coal, stone, glass, textiles, chemicals) – for political reasons – that the much-vaunted manufacturing sector in Japan actually suffered from negative net resource transfers (Noland and Pack 2003, p. 36). Public interventions to help individual national champion manufacturing firms might thus be seen as a compensatory policy for an overly burdened economic sector. But the record here again is far from consistent: MITI helped Isuzu and Mitsubishi Motors. Toyota, Honda, and Suzuki were ignored, but rose through the entrepreneurial energy of their founders, without public help. Canon and Nikon developed cutting-edge processes for photo-lithography etching on chips while remaining outside the official very-large scale integrated circuits (VLSI) initiative. The Japanese government focus on single vector computing rather than parallel processing held back Fujitsu and Toshiba.

The European experience shows considerable diversity in the willingness of different countries and governments to adopt an explicit industrial policy to promote specific sectors. France and Italy showed more comfort with dirigiste measures to target particular industries and companies, while Germany and the UK showed less. There has been, therefore, no overall assessment of the efficiency with which EU public resources have been deployed to enhance the performance of the home economies. As in Asia, however, it is nonetheless evident that political interests pulled more resources toward declining industries than pushed resources toward those where dynamic comparative advantage pointed toward the future (Dobson and Lipsey 1987).

Whatever the aggregate calculus of costs and benefits of industrial policy initiatives in general, however, all European governments and the UK showed a willingness to use the levers of public policy – competition policy, supervision of mergers and acquisitions, government procurement, as well as tax policy and subsidies – to create national champions that might respond to domestic needs more faithfully than firms of foreign ownership. But as shown above, once those champions became exposed to international competitive pressures, their behavior began to replicate the behavior of rivals of other nationalities.

The record of both Europe and Asia shows national champions losing their ability – and willingness – to response to home country economic and political needs if such actions run contrary to their own corporate self-interest. Competition does not make all firms behave in identical fashion, to be sure, and international companies may retain home-country management styles. But the tendency to match the behavior of rivals under international market pressure has led the analytical community in the developed countries to look critically at whether there are systematic differences in behavior among similar companies of different nationality. As any such differences decline, the significance of the nationality of firms correspondingly diminishes (Sapsford and Shirouzu 2006). The logical conclusion is that any company that improves productivity in the use of domestic resources, pays higher wages, conducts local R&D and generates spillovers and externalities that benefit the internal economy should be favored as much as any other such company, independent of who owns the equity shares (Reich 1990, pp. 53–64).[8]

Moving from national champions in general to strategic trade national champions in particular, in industries with especially high barriers to entry and large economies of scale, there are similar problems of having public bureaucrats target in a manner superior to the market while keeping the targeting process free of political contamination. Easiest might seem to be champion firms created for national security reasons, since the circumstances in which public sector intervention might be justified are reasonably objective – dependence upon suppliers whose numbers are so small (four firms or four countries controlling 50 per cent or more of the international market) that denial of some crucial good or service is plausible and would have devastating consequences.

In practice, however, the record in developed countries shows that it is difficult to limit candidates for national security support to situations that meet a rigorous justification – rather, 'national security' opens the door to a plethora of claimants, from steel (for guns), to footwear (boots), to textiles (uniforms), to trucks, autos and other transportation equipment, to ball bearings, to machine tools, to all manner of electronics, to energy, to food. Drawing the line around which sectors and companies deserve special support or protection on national security grounds because the goods and services they supply are 'critical' for the functioning of the home country has proven extremely difficult for developed country polities to accomplish in any rigorous fashion.

Moreover, the historical record suggests that, even here, national security/national trade champions – as their operations become more internationalized – may well become less amenable to responding to home government commands when such actions run counter to what best serves their own interests.

13.3 DEVELOPING COUNTRY POLICY OPTIONS TOWARD OUTWARD FDI

Developing-country strategists can survey the entire array of policy alternatives within developed countries about how to treat outward investment. At one end of the policy spectrum is the option to promote outward FDI actively, providing positive incentives to encourage home-country firms to move abroad. At the other end of the policy spectrum is the option to discourage firms from moving abroad, pressing them instead to keep their operations at home. In between is the option to maintain policy neutrality toward firm decisions about where to locate operations.

As in the developed countries, developing country strategists should choose among these policy approaches on the basis of how they evaluate the impact of outward FDI on the economic and political interests of the home country.[9]

To accomplish this, the first analytical task is to contrast the performance of home-country firms that undertake outward FDI with the performance of those of similar size, technology-intensity (and other characteristics) that do not undertake outward FDI. Do the former make themselves more competitive, export more and provide better high-wage high-benefit jobs than the latter, or not?

In the developed countries, the somewhat counterintuitive result has been that home-country firms that invest abroad show superior performance in the home market than those that do not. They export more, demonstrating that outward FDI and exports are complements, not substitutes. Their export-related jobs pay higher wages and have higher associated benefits. Keeping firms at home, in contrast, is not a viable option for strengthening the local job base, maintaining the stability of local communities or enhancing the competitiveness of home-country companies.

Developing-country strategists should set up their own structured comparisons to determine whether outward FDI is complementary to, or a substitute for exports from their home economies. They should investigate relative wages and benefits, productivity levels and frequency of bankruptcies among home-country firms that engage in outward FDI and similar firms that do not. They should search for externalities spilling over to the communities where developing-country TNCs originate. They should investigate whether developing-country TNCs act as channels for external acquisition and vehicles for increased competition and sectoral renovation at home.

As noted at the outset of this chapter, it cannot be assumed that outward investment from developing countries will produce the same results for the home economy as outward investment from developed countries. As argued earlier, there are good reasons to expect that the impact of outward FDI on developing home economies might be different.

Nonetheless, are there any indications that developing countries might in fact discover similar results as have been found for outward FDI from developed countries?

Here the Korean experience – using data from as early as 1980, well before the Republic of Korea became an OECD member (1996) – may be instructive. Hongshik Lee found that Korean firms that engaged in outward FDI were larger, paid higher wages and were more productive than counterpart Korean firms that did not (Lee 2003). Chang-Soo Lee showed that the relationship between outward FDI by Korean firms and exports from the Republic of Korea were positive and statistically significant in most years from 1991–1999 (Lee 2002).

Findings such as these suggest that developing countries may want to adopt policies toward outward FDI roughly along the lines of Capital

Export Neutrality, which tries to avoid biasing firm investment decisions on the basis of tax policy alone. Capital Export Neutrality offers home-country firms a foreign tax credit on profits earned abroad, allowing them to avoid double taxation.

Alternatively, if developing countries discover broader and more consistent externalities for their home economies from outward investment, they may want to adopt policies more along the lines of Capital Import Neutrality, exempting home-country firms from all home-country taxes on profits earned abroad.

The Capital Export Neutrality or Capital Import Neutrality approach might then be bolstered with light-handed public policies to overcome information asymmetries and other market failures that hinder outward FDI, such as instructing foreign service agencies to supply information on investment opportunities abroad (such as China, Malaysia, Singapore and Thailand already do) (Brooks 2005; Lim 2005; Mirza 2005; Yean 2005).[10] Developing countries will also want their home firms to become eligible for multilateral political risk insurance (from MIGA, the Asian Development Bank, the InterAmerican Development Bank, the ERBD) to compensate for contractual instability in FDI destinations. They will want to continue the process of signing bilateral investment treaties (BITs) and double taxation treaties (DTTs).

The analysis of policies toward outward FDI would not be complete without noting the need for multilateral initiatives to place a ceiling on, and reduce locational incentives. The past decade has seen a steep escalation in tax breaks, free factory space and other forms of subsidy on the part of both developed and developing countries (Thomas 2000). Conventional wisdom has held that tax advantages have a small impact on corporate strategy, and that – in any case – there is little competition between developed country and developing country sites over where plants are located. Contemporary econometric research shows both of these assumptions to be faulty. The evidence shows that TNCs are becoming more responsive to locational incentives, and that the competition between developed and developing country sites is in fact growing (Mutti 2003; Altshuler *et al.* 1998). There is a genuine race-to-the-bottom in giveaways to international investors.

At the same time, developing countries are attempting to design an optimal tax strategy to deal with outward FDI, and therefore their interests would be well served to join with developed countries in a common initiative to rein in subsidies designed to attract TNCs (Moran 2006).

Some developing countries – most notably Russia and China – have raised an issue that has not been prominent in developed country policy discussions on outward FDI, namely, whether FDI might be worrisome as a channel for capital flight or capital 'round-tripping' in order to secure special privileges associated with inward investment (Crane *et al.* 2005, pp. 405–444; Mirza 2005). With regard to the first, however, the preferred vehicles for capital flight are instruments whose value is easily identifiable and whose purchase or sale requires least specialized information.[11] By these criteria, cash and money market instruments are most preferred, followed by government bonds and widely traded equities. Much further down the list is commercial real estate. Buying industrial plants and other facilities abroad, or disposing of industrial plants and other facilities at home as a capital transfer mechanism – rather than as part of the parent firm's international corporate strategy – would appear to be particularly cumbersome. Appearing to validate this perception, FDI flows consistently show less fluctuation than other forms of capital transfers, even in the midst of currency crises and financial upheaval (Reisen and Soto 2001, pp. 1–14; World Bank 1999, p. 55).[12]

Turning from outward investors as a class of companies to specific 'national champion' firms created and nurtured to serve the economic and political interests of the home country, the evidence from developed countries shows surprising results as the national champions face the pressures of international competition and begin moving into international markets themselves. The national champions are forced to devise strategies to enhance their own competitive position that may or may not correspond to the objectives their home governments have in mind for them. This does not mean that they abandon their national origins completely, or become unresponsive to home country allegiances. But it does mean that the margin within which they are able – or willing – to alter their behavior to accommodate home country wishes or commands may narrow.

Developing-country strategists will want to monitor, therefore, the extent to which systematic differences between the behavior of home country national champions and firms of other nationalities persist, to judge whether 'their own' firms become more non-national as conditions change.

Here Brazil's experience with the country's two largest orange juice companies – Cutrale and Citrosuco – might be instructive (Hart 2004).[13] The Brazilian government fought hard to defend its national interest in maximizing domestic orange exports, with congressional deputies and indigenous companies organizing vigorous opposition to US import restrictions. Once Cutrale and Citrosuco hedged their own bets with sizable FDI in Florida in the 1990s, however, the Brazilian companies' stance shifted to acquiescence – or perhaps even quiet support – for the continuation of the US tariff on orange juice.

Similar dynamics can be observed with Mittal Steel of India (or London or Amsterdam). As an exporter to the United States, Mittal opposed US import duties and anti-dumping penalties against external steelmakers trying to penetrate the US market. But once Mittal acquired US steel plants, the corporation shifted to active support for US steel protection.

CONCLUSION

Might this be a small taste of larger things to come for developing countries?

It will be interesting to see whether developing countries will witness what developed countries have learned, that the responsiveness of home country national champions to what home countries consider the national interest – even high-tech strategic champions, even national oil companies, even champions created to supply goods and services vital to national defense – may become more problematic, as time goes on.

ACKNOWLEDGEMENTS

I am grateful to Gary Hufbauer, Ted Truman, John Williamson, Karl P. Sauvant and anonymous readers for valuable comments and suggestions.

NOTES

1. Safarian (1993) focuses on developed countries as recipients of FDI, not sources of FDI.
2. There is evidence to suggest that TNCs from developing countries are growing accustomed to making similar assertions.
3. For a summary of evidence, see Lipsey *et al.* (2000) and Markusen and Maskus (2003).
4. As discussed below; see Mutti (2003) and Altshuler *et al.*(1998).
5. High-definition TV, robotics and superconductors have also been subjected to scrutiny (Busch 1999).
6. Multiple 'home countries' in the case of Airbus, whose owners include France, Germany, Spain and the UK. Germany and the UK privatized their government ownership shares.
7. *See* www.airbus.com/en.worldwide/north_america/us_indus_partners/.
8. In the United States, this is referred to as the 'Who-Is-Us?' debate.
9. For path-breaking work on outward FDI from developing countries, see UNCTAD (1995).
10. Singapore has gone so far as to build industrial parks for Singapore investors in Vietnam.
11. I am indebted to Edwin M. Truman and John Williamson at the Institute for International Economics for help with this analysis (Reuter and Truman 2005).
12. This does not mean that TNCs necessarily refrain from measures to protect their interests in the midst of a currency crisis, such as accelerating income repatriation, leads and lags in payments, hedging and shifting the locus of short-term finance.
13. I am grateful to Sidney and Jerry Haar for this citation.

REFERENCES

Altshuler, R., H. Grubert and S. Newlong (1998). *Has US Investment Abroad Become More Sensitive to Tax Rates?* Working Paper No. 6383 (Cambridge, MA: National Bureau of Economic Research), mimeo.

Beason, Richard, and David E. Weinstein (1996). 'Growth, economies of scale, and targeting in Japan (1955–1990)', *Review of Economics and Statistics* 78(2), pp. 286–295.

Bergsten, C. Fred, Thomas Horst and Theodore H. Moran (1978). *American Multinationals and American Interests* (Washington: Brookings Institution Press).

Bernard, Andrew B., J. Bradford Jensen and Peter K. Schott (2005). *Importers, Exporters and Multinationals: A Portrait of Firms in the U.S. that Trade Goods*, Working Paper No. 11404 (Cambridge, MA: National Bureau of Economic Research), mimeo.

Brander, James A. and Barbara J. Spencer (1985). 'Export subsidies and international market share rivalry', *Journal of International Economics*, 18(1), pp. 83–100.

Brooks, Douglas H. (2005) 'Outward FDI from developing Asia', Paper presented at the Asian Development Bank conference *Outward Foreign Direct Investment from Developing Asia*, 28–29 November, Bangkok, mimeo.

Busch, Marc L. (1999). *Trade Warriors: States, Firms, and Strategic-Trade Policy in High-Technology Competition* (New York: Cambridge University Press).

Crane, Keith, D.J. Peterson, and Olga Oliker (2005). 'Russian investment in the Commonwealth of Independent States', *Eurasian Geography and Economics*, 46(6), pp. 405–444.

Dobson, Wendy and Robert Lipsey, eds (1987). *Shaping Comparative Advantage* (Toronto: C.D. Howe Institute).

Dunning, John H. (1970). *Studies in International Investment* (London: George Allen and Unwin).

The Economist (1966). 'America says no' *The Economist*, (16 June), p. 1229.

Emergency Committee for American Trade (1993). *Mainstay II: A New Account of the Critical Role of U.S. Multinational Companies in the U.S. Economy* (Washington: ECAT).

Flamm, Kenneth (1996). *Mismanaged Trade? Strategic Policy and the Semiconductor Industry* (Washington: Brookings Institution Press).

Hart, Ezequiel (2004). *The U.S. Orange Tariff and the 'Brazilian Invasion' of Florida: The Effect of Florida's Brazil-based Processors on the Political Debate over the U.S. Orange Juice Tariff*, Master of Arts in Law and Diplomacy Thesis (Waltham, MS: The Fletcher School, Tufts University).

Hufbauer, Clyde, Jeffrey J. Schott and Kimberly Ann Elliott (1990). *Economic Sanctions Reconsidered: History and Current Policy* (Washington: Institute for International Economics).

Hufbauer, Gary Clyde with Joanna M. Van Roou (1992). *U.S. Taxation of International Income: Blueprint for Reform* (Washington: Institute for International Economics).

Jacquemin, A., ed. (1984). *European Industry: Public Policy and Corporate Strategy* (Oxford: Oxford University Press).

Kraar, Luis (1980). 'Boeing takes a bold plunge to keep flying high', *Fortune*, 25 September, p. 79.

Krugman, Paul R. (1986). *Strategic Trade Policy and the New International Economics* (Cambridge, MA: MIT Press).

Lawrence, Robert Z. and David E. Weinstein (2001). 'Trade and growth: import led or export led? Evidence from Japan and Korea', in Joseph E. Stiglitz and Shahid Yusuf, eds, *Rethinking the East Asian Miracle* (Oxford: Oxford University Press).

Lee, Chang-Soo (2002). *Korea's FDI Outflows: Choice of Locations and Effect on Trade*, Working Paper 02-07 (Seoul: Korean Institute for International Economic Policy), mimeo.

Lee, Hongshik (2003). *The Decision to Invest Abroad: The Case of Korean Multinationals*, Working Paper 03-12 (Seoul: Korean Institute for International Economic Policy), mimeo.

Lim, Hank (2005). 'Outward foreign direct investment from developing Asia: Singapore'. Paper presented at the Asian Development Bank conference *Outward Foreign Direct Investment from Developing Asia*, 28–29 November, Bangkok, mimeo.

Lipsey, Robert E., Eric D. Ramsterrer and Magnus Blomstrom (2000). *Outward FDI and Parent Exports and Employment: Japan, the United States, and Sweden*, Working Paper 7623 (Cambridge, MA: National Bureau of Economic Research), mimeo.

Markusen, James R. and Keith E. Maskus (2003). 'General-equilibrium approaches to the multinational enterprise: a review of theory and evidence', in E. Kwan Choi and James Harrigan, eds, *Handbook of International Trade* (London: Blackwell).

Mirza, Hafiz (2005). 'Chinese outward foreign direct investment'. Paper presented at the Asian Development Bank conference *Outward Foreign Direct Investment from Developing Asia*, 28–29 November, Bangkok, mimeo.

Moran, Theodore H. (1980). 'The globalization of America's defense industries: managing the threat of foreign dependence', *International Security*, 15(1), pp. 57–99.

Moran, Theodore H. (2006). *Harnessing Foreign Direct Investment for Development* (Washington: Center for Global Development).

Moran, Theodore H. and David C. Mowery (1994). 'Aerospace and national security in an era of globalization', in David C. Mowery, ed., *Science and Technology Policy in Interdependent Economies* (Boston MA: Kluwer Academic Publishers).

Mutti, J. (2003). *Taxation and Foreign Direct Investment* (Washington: Institute for International Economics).

Noland, Marcus and Howard Pack (2003). *Industrial Policy in an Era of Globalization: Lessons from Asia* (Washington: The Institute for International Economics).

Pearce, J. and J. Sutton (1986). *Protection and Industrial Policy in Europe* (London: Routledge and Kegan Paul).

Reich, Robert B. (1990). 'Who is us?' *Harvard Business Review*, 90, pp. 53–64.

Reisen, Helmut and Marcelo Soto (2001). 'Which types of capital inflows foster developing-country growth?' *International Finance*, 4(1), pp. 1–14.

Reuter, Peter and Edwin M. Truman (2005). *Chasing Dirty Money: The Fight Against Money Laundering* (Washington, DC: The Institute for International Economics).

Richardson, J. David (2006). *Global Forces, American Faces: US Economic Globalization at the Grass Roots* (Washington: Institute for International Economics).

Safarian, A.E. (1993). *Multinational Enterprise and Public Policy: A Study of the Industrial Countries* (Cheltenham UK: Edward Elgar).

Sapsford, Jathon and Norihiko Shirouzu (2006). 'Mom, apple pie and . . . Toyota? Ford says it's patriotic to buy a Mustang, but Sienna is made in Indiana with more U.S. parts', *Wall Street Journal*, 11 May, p. B1.

Sauvant, Karl P. (2005). 'New sources of FDI: The BRICs: outward FDI from Brazil, Russia, India, and China', *The Journal of World Investment and Trade*, 6, pp. 639–709.

Servan-Schreiber, Jean-Jacques (1968). *The American Challenge* (New York: Avon).

Stobaugh, Robert (1975). 'The oil companies in crisis', *The Oil Crisis in Perspective* (special issue) *Daedalus*, 104(4), p. 189.

Thomas, Kenneth P. (2000). *Competing for Capital: Europe and North America in a Global Era* (Washington: Georgetown University Press).

Tyson, Laura D'Andrea (1992). *Who's Bashing Whom: Trade Conflict in High-Technology Industries* (Washington: Institute for International Economics).

UNCTAD (1995). *World Investment Report 1995: Transnational Corporations and Competitiveness* (New York: United Nations), pp. 344–393.

Vernon, Raymond, ed. (1974). *Big Business and the State* (Cambridge, MA: Harvard University Press).

Yean, Tham Siew (2005). 'Outward foreign direct investment from Malaysia: an exploratory study'. Paper presented at the Asian Development Bank conference *Outward Foreign Direct Investment from Developing Asia*, 28–29 November, Bangkok, mimeo.

World Bank (1999). *Global Development Finance* (Washington, DC: The World Bank), p. 55.

14. Will emerging markets change their attitude toward an international investment regime?

Edward M. Graham

INTRODUCTION

Will emerging markets change their attitude toward an international invest-ment regime? One can infer from this wording that emerging markets, meaning the big middle income countries such as Brazil, China, India and ten or so others, have been less than enthusiastic about implementing formal rules in the World Trade Organization (WTO) or elsewhere dealing with international investment.[1] Indeed, the lack of progress toward such a regime can be explained in some large measure by the lack of enthusiasm of these emerging markets; or, otherwise put, had a single one of these countries voiced enthusiasm for such a regime, the issue of 'trade and investment' would probably still be on the Doha agenda. However, at the Cancun meeting of the World Trade Organization in September 2003, one of a number of ministerial-level meetings of the WTO in recent years that have ended in discord, the issue of trade and investment was simply dropped from the agenda of the Doha Round of Multilateral Trade Negotiations. This happened essentially because none of the negotiating parties, including the emerging markets, showed any enthusiasm whatso-ever for continuing discussions on the issue. It was one of the so-called 'Singapore issues', added to the WTO agenda at the Singapore Ministerial meeting in 2000. Indeed, then and ever since, the issue has been addressed with what could only be termed a lack of enthusiasm by most emerging markets.

The issue thus becomes: will these countries ever become more enthusi-astic about an international investment regime?

The temptation is simply to say 'no' and to stop writing at this point. Indeed, nothing in recent months or years suggests any increase in the enthusiasm of these countries for international investment rules. The rele-vant question to ask is: why so?

To begin, it should be pointed out that a case could be constructed to indicate that an international investment regime might be in the interests of such countries. The case rests on two pillars. The first is that international investment and, in particular, foreign direct investment (FDI), conveys benefits to emerging markets, benefits that indeed might be hard to achieve in the absence of such investment. The second pillar is that an international regime of some sort could act to increase the rate at which these countries receive this investment. This case is explored in section 14.1 of this chapter.

But if such a case can be constructed, the question poses itself: why are these countries then not enthusiastic *demandeurs* for an international investment regime, rather than parties that are reluctant to support negotiations that could lead to such a regime? In section 14.2 of this chapter, several hypotheses are explored to explain this reluctance. These are: (1) international regimes have been 'oversold' to these countries such that the benefits of participating in them have often proved, in effect, disappointing. This hypothesis applies not specifically to an international investment regime, but rather to international trade and investment regimes writ larger than one to cover investment alone; (2) in particular, emerging markets were sold on the benefits of the Uruguay Round Agreement on Trade-Related Intellectual Property Protection (TRIPS). But leaders of most of these countries do not believe that benefits have come their way as the result of this Agreement; indeed, in some cases, such countries perceive net transfers from their economies to the coffers of transnational corporations (TNCs), and thus perceive that this Agreement has done them harm rather than conferred benefits upon them. In the light of this experience, leaders of these countries are reluctant to enter into an investment agreement that they feel has the potential to offer similar results: the promise of benefits will not be realized, but rather, their economies might be penalized were they to participate in an international investment agreement.

The concluding section then returns to the issue: will they change their minds? The answer is still: probably not.

14.1   WHAT IS THE CASE FOR AN INTERNATIONAL REGIME FOR INVESTMENT FROM THE POINT OF VIEW OF THE EMERGING MARKETS?

As outlined above, this case rests on two pillars: first, that international investment (and especially FDI, upon which this chapter will focus) will bring to an economy benefits that might be impossible or difficult to garner via other means; and second, that participation in an international regime will enable an economy to attract more direct investment than would probably flow in the absence of this participation.

14.1.1   Will FDI Bring Benefits that Cannot be Obtained via Other Means?

The first pillar is easier to establish than the second. The two benefits that FDI are most likely to achieve in an emerging market are enhanced rates of economic growth and positive externalities. These two benefits are not independent of one another (positive externalities are likely to boost economic growth) but they have been separately investigated empirically, and hence are separately discussed here. We need to be careful to define these two benefits.

By 'enhanced rates of economic growth', we mean that FDI must cause economic growth that would not be achieved by alternative means of financing capital formation. Thus, for example, let us posit that an economy's desired gross investment is x per cent of GDP, but that all forms of domestic savings are y per cent of GDP, where $y < x$. To finance investment, then, the country must import savings from the rest of the world. These imported savings can come in the form of FDI (which really is a misnomer, because FDI is a source of finance for investment and not the investment itself), or it can come in some other form. What we require is that, if the imported savings do come in the form of FDI, the result is a higher rate of economic growth of the economy than if the imported savings come in some other form. The higher rate of growth might be achieved, for example, because FDI, in addition to being a source of savings, also brings with it technology transfer, which enhances the rate of total factor productivity in the economy, whereas another form of imported savings might not bring with it any such technology transfer. By a 'positive externality', we mean that FDI enables the creation of economic gains that are captured neither by the operations funded by FDI, nor direct suppliers to these operations, nor to the consumers of products created by these operations. The usual example of such a positive externality is a 'spillover' of technology into the economy. If firms that compete with the FDI-funded operations, for example, are able to observe and imitate technologies used in these operations, and thus become more efficient than they otherwise would be, such an externality is generated. It is clear that these two examples are not independent events, because a technological spillover is likely to boost total factor productivity and thus to contribute to enhanced growth. On the other hand, the enhanced growth could come about even without the FDI generating positive externalities.

Does FDI enhance growth in the sense just discussed, or generate positive externalities? There is a growing empirical literature addressing both of these issues. Importantly, this empirical literature supports neither that FDI does enhance economic growth nor that FDI generates positive externalities unequivocally; however, the preponderance of the evidence in both cases does point in a positive direction. While what follows is not a comprehensive review of the relevant literature, let us look at some of the main findings.

First, let us examine the empirical findings regarding FDI and economic growth. Most studies that have been done used 'panel' data, that is, data to compare results in different countries over extended periods of time. Most of these studies found a positive and significant relationship between growth rates and FDI, although a number of the results must be qualified. One important study, however, concluded that there is no such relationship; but, again, this conclusion itself must be qualified. Until very recently, such studies were performed using ordinary least squares (OLS) estimators, a technical matter touched upon below. Among these are results reported by:

- Blomström, Lipsey and Zejan (1994), who found that FDI positively affects growth if and only if a national wealth threshold is reached. By their finding, FDI does not positively affect growth if a country is quite poor.
- Balasubramanyam, Salisu and Sapsford (1996), also found a positive relationship, but only if the country is open to international trade. This result is not inconsistent with Blomström *et al.* because, in recent history, poorer countries have tended to be less open to trade than richer countries.
- Borzenstein, de Gregorio and Lee (1998), who also found a positive relationship, but only if a country meets a threshold level of education. Again, this finding is generally consistent with the earlier results because poorer countries tend to have less well-educated populations than do richer ones. It should be noted, however, that Blomström *et al.* did consider education as a conditioning variable but found it not to be significant.
- Alfaro *et al.* (2004), who again found a positive relationship, but only in countries with well-developed financial markets; this is (roughly) consistent with earlier findings because richer countries have better developed financial markets than do poorer ones.
- Blonigen and Wang (2005), who found, using a later and larger data set than Blomström *et al.*, that FDI affects growth more strongly in developing (poorer) countries than in rich ones. This lattermost finding is of course not consistent with the other and earlier ones and

might be explained by a number of factors, including that the data are more recent and hence are strongly affected by growth in China. Moreover, it is possible that, because most FDI in rich countries in recent years has been created by cross-border merger and acquisition, as opposed to greenfield FDI, the former type of FDI simply generates less growth than the latter.[2] By contrast, the majority of FDI in certain developing countries, most especially China, has been of the greenfield variety.

Kumar and Pradhan (2005) used instead of an OLS estimator an Arellano-Bond (modified General Method of Moments) estimator to test whether FDI in South Asia has had a positive impact on growth. They concluded in the affirmative. This study is of note because an Arellano-Bond estimator is now accepted as a more appropriate tool with which to analyze panel data than the more commonly used OLS estimator.

In addition to studies based on panel data, there have been studies of individual countries based on time series. We note an unpublished study in particular (Dayal-Gulati and Husain 2001) focusing on China. Comparisons of regions within China reveal that, in the years subsequent to China becoming more open to FDI in 2001, there was an acceleration of economic growth in those regions that received significant amounts of FDI. By contrast, this acceleration in economic growth was not observed in those regions where such FDI did not flow. The findings thus are consistent with a claim that FDI does accelerate economic growth. The growth in China is also linked to exports, because foreign affiliates are the largest generators of export growth. Indeed, it is difficult to sort out whether increased exports or the underlying FDI is the main causal agent, a fact that bears on points made below.

One major study, however, concluded that FDI does not exert a robust and exogenous effect on economic growth (Carkovic and Levine 2005). They, like Kumar and Pradhan, applied an Arellano-Bond estimator to panel data, but the former used a longer and larger data set than the latter. Their finding is of particular importance because (1) their data are extensive and (2) as just noted, the Arellano-Bond estimator is more appropriately used to analyze panel data than an OLS estimator; an OLS estimator can, in particular, yield 'false positives' when applied to panel data. However, even Carkovic and Levine's results indicated a robust relationship between FDI and economic growth unless the conditioning variables include a variable for trade openness; when such a variable is included in the conditioning variables, Carkovic and Levine showed that the effect of FDI on growth remains positive but is no longer robust. Melitz (2005) questioned whether this should be interpreted as wholly contradictory to the hypothesis that FDI does positively affect economic growth robustly (the interpretation that Carkovic and Levine themselves favor); rather, Melitz argued that FDI and trade, which are as noted associated with each other, jointly and positively affect growth.

If Melitz is correct, the joint effect of FDI and trade on growth is almost surely brought about by the efficiencies that result from increased trade. These result from efficiencies at a micro, or firm, level. In addition to achieving economies of scale, TNCs can lower transaction costs by sourcing materials and knowledge through their own intra-firm trade rather than having to negotiate with third parties. Globally integrated procurement practices, deployment of research and development (R&D) and the ability to hire skilled workers from a multiplicity of nations and utilize existing skill sets by employees to maximum potential, enable firms to lower costs and compete better to the ultimate benefit of consumers and society. Thus, to the extent that FDI leads not only to increased trade in goods and services, but also to increased transfers of knowledge, it magnifies the benefit to the economies in which investment is directed and linked. This leads to the issue of whether FDI generates positive externalities.

As with the empirical evidence regarding FDI and growth, there is an empirical literature on FDI and externalities, and the reported results are mixed. A recent survey of the rather extensive literature (Lipsey and Sjöholm 2005), however, notes a curious fact: whereas older studies tended both to support and not support the hypothesis that FDI does create positive externalities, newer studies more consistently find in favor of this hypothesis than do the older ones. The authors concluded that one of two possibilities is correct: either, in recent times, the externalities themselves have been more prevalent and perhaps stronger than in earlier times, or methodologies have improved such that externalities that have long existed but once escaped detection are now more readily discerned than in the past. Either way, the recent evidence does seem to point toward the probable existence of positive, and mostly technology-based, externalities being generated by FDI.

The bottom line is that the literature generally supports that FDI brings economic benefits to economies that probably cannot be achieved via alternative means to finance the same amount of capital formation. This conclusion is not unequivocal; rather, it must be qualified. At minimum, to capture these benefits, certain conditions have to be met, for example, the country must have a reasonably well-educated workforce, and the economy must meet some threshold of openness to international trade.

Moreover, the literature certainly does not support a contention that FDI brings economic harm to an economy. Thus, for example, is the finding that FDI enhances economic growth a robust one? The discussion of the empirical findings above indicates that the answer is contentious (but, even so, likely to be yes). Importantly, however, there is no finding that FDI might retard economic growth. Likewise, the findings on whether FDI generates positive externalities are not unequivocal, but there are no findings that empirically demonstrate negative externalities being generated by FDI.[3]

Thus, we assume that FDI is generally desirable from the point of view of the economic interests of an emerging market. It is probably true that the leadership of some emerging markets remains unconvinced that FDI indeed is in their interest, and this lack of conviction might help explain why such countries are generally unenthusiastic about an international investment regime. But now the question is: if FDI is desirable, is there a case that an international regime will help emerging markets to attract more of it? On this question, the second pillar of a case for such a regime, the evidence is much more equivocal than for the first pillar.

14.1.2   Will an International Regime Attract More FDI?

Why is the evidence equivocal? Because, in fact, there really is not much evidence at all. And this is so for the simple reason that there is no international regime on FDI, and hence, no experience on which to judge whether such a regime would be effective as a means to enlarge the amount or share of FDI going to emerging markets. Some limited evidence can be gleaned from regional or bilateral investment regimes, such as exist in the North American Free Trade Area (NAFTA) or the US–Chile Free Trade Agreement.

In the former case, that of NAFTA, there is little doubt that FDI flows to Mexico, especially from the United States but also from the European Union, accelerated markedly after NAFTA came into effect (Hufbauer and Schott 2005, Table 1.5). That the FDI flows to Mexico from the European Union rose after NAFTA came into force might seem irrelevant to the issue of whether NAFTA had an effect on FDI flow, because the European Union is not a party to the NAFTA. However, Mexico has extended its obligations regarding investment as indicated in NAFTA Chapter 11, Part A, to investors from all countries on a most-favored-nation basis, even though its commitment to submit to investor-to-state dispute settlement procedures as according to NAFTA Chapter 11, Part B, apply only to investors from NAFTA parties (that is, the United States and Canada). Moreover, since NAFTA has come into effect, the share of US FDI going to Mexico as a percentage of all US FDI has increased.

In the case of the US–Chile Free Trade Agreement, which contains provisions for FDI somewhat along the lines of the NAFTA, there seems also to be an upturn in US FDI to Chile that has occurred since the agreement was signed. However, this happened only recently, and it is simply too early to claim that this upturn is significant in any statistical sense. With time, it might prove that this agreement was associated with a significant upturn but, unfortunately, confirmation of this, if any, must wait until enough data have accumulated to make an assessment meaningful.

Thus, the bottom line seems to be that there is not enough evidence to determine empirically whether an international investment regime would result in significantly greater FDI being placed in emerging markets or not. On this matter, it is important to note that this lack of evidence does not mean that such a regime would be against the interests of these countries. The reason why this assertion is of importance is that there are non-governmental organizations (NGOs) of an anti-globalist bent that have argued that such a regime would bring about negative results from the point of view of these countries; such views in fact figured in the failure of the OECD countries to conclude negotiations of a Multilateral Agreement on Investment (MAI) during the late 1990s.[4] However, just as the evidence is scant that an international regime on direct investment might bring benefit to emerging markets, the evidence is also scant that such a regime would bring harm or embody hidden dangers. In particular, anti-globalist activists have argued that the investor-to-state dispute resolution procedures created under Chapter 11, Part B of the NAFTA have created unprecedented rights for TNCs to sue governments and that these rights to sue will have a chilling effect on the ability of governments to pass or enforce needed regulations, for example, environmental or health regulations. However, review of experience with the NAFTA fails to reveal any marked tendency in the direction that the activists have feared. To date, one case has gone against the outcome that environmentalists sought, but several cases have actually gone in their direction. Moreover, there has been no marked trend or tendency for NAFTA Chapter 11 cases to compel weakened enforcement of environmental law.[5]

So, if there is at least some evidence that an international regime on direct investment might work to benefit emerging markets but little evidence that such a regime would do any harm to these nations, why are they against such a regime? A number of hypotheses are explored in the following section.

14.2 WHY ARE EMERGING MARKETS SO UNENTHUSIASTIC OVER AN INTERNATIONAL REGIME ON INVESTMENT?

Let us explore four hypotheses that might explain why emerging markets are unenthusiastic about an international regime on investment. These are:

- Hypothesis 1: Spooked by the MAI?
- Hypothesis 2: Tripped up by TRIPS?
- Hypothesis 3: Disillusioned with multilateral trade agreements?
- Hypothesis 4: We can do it by ourselves, if 'it' is what we really want to do.

14.2.1 Spooked by the MAI?

As noted in the previous section, the MAI was a failed effort to negotiate a comprehensive regime on investment that was undertaken in the Organisation for Economic Co-operation and Development (OECD). The negotiations were undertaken according to the Ministerial Declaration of the OECD in May 1995. Three and a half years later, in late 1998, the unfinished negotiations were suspended, and they have not since been revived; thus it is fair to say that they ended in failure, albeit that in a legal sense they simply remain suspended rather than terminated. The reasons for failure are several, and one of these reasons has been alluded to already: opposition by NGOs. Indeed, among certain NGOs, the cessation of the MAI negotiations is still seen as one of the greatest triumphs of the anti-globalist movement to date, perhaps even a greater triumph than the ability of some of the same NGOs to disrupt thoroughly the WTO Ministerial Meeting in Seattle a year later. But NGO opposition to the MAI was by no means the only reason for its failure: the negotiations were on a path to nowhere even before the NGOs injected themselves on to the scene. The reasons the negotiations were on such a path include: a major impasse between some of the negotiating parties on the issue of whether there would be an exception (as opposed to a national 'reservation') for so-called 'cultural' industries; inept political handling of the negotiations or, perhaps more to the point, lack of strong support for a positive outcome by the top political leadership in at least certain of the key negotiating parties; and, in the end, lack of strong support within the business communities of at least some of the negotiating parties.[6]

The MAI was envisaged as an agreement to which all nations on earth, rich or poor, could sign up. But the OECD itself is an international organization whose membership is restricted by and large to the world's high per capita income countries, and this membership in 1995 did not include any of the emerging markets.[7] Given that OECD members themselves would surely want these latter countries in particular to join the MAI, if and when it came into existence, the choice of the OECD as the negotiating venue seems a rather strange one because it could have readily been foreseen that emerging markets would be reluctant to join an international regime from which they had been excluded during the negotiation phase. Indeed, at a meeting organized by the OECD Secretariat held in 1996 in Hong Kong (China) to explain the MAI to the governments of the East Asian countries, representative after representative of these countries stood up to denounce their government's exclusion from the negotiating process. The logic among the OECD membership for this choice of venue was that it would be relatively easy for the negotiations to be concluded successfully among the OECD members because, with respect to investment, they were 'like-minded'. Moreover, or so went the logic, once the OECD members had created what was touted as a 'state-of-the-art' investment agreement embodying 'high standards', other countries would be readily persuaded of the benefits of joining the agreement. Of course, as matters happened, neither element of this dubious logic – putative ease of negotiating the MAI inside the OECD and ready acceptance by nations outside the OECD – proved to have any traction whatsoever.

Is the failure of the MAI a matter that still spooks emerging markets, causing them to be reluctant with respect to any future international regime on investment? It is, for two reasons: first, by placing the negotiations in the OECD itself, the OECD countries that initially sponsored the MAI played into the hands of the many opponents of an international regime on investment in emerging markets who would argue that such a regime serves only the interests of the richest countries and large TNCs based in these countries. If such an agreement were in the interests of developing countries, these opponents could argue, why should it not have been negotiated in a venue in which such countries were represented and party to the negotiations? Thus, the perception was built, and is still strong, that the MAI or any international regime on investment is likely to work against the interests of emerging markets. This perception might, in fact, be at least partially belied by the actual experience of Mexico in the NAFTA and certain other emerging markets in bilateral arrangements, where it has already been argued that this experience has been, by and large, positive; but it can take a long time for a perception, once it becomes widespread, to be dispelled by such contrary evidence. Second, the MAI did become the *bête noire* of NGOs, and some of these organizations do have major influence inside the governments of at least some emerging markets. They can be expected to oppose vigorously what they perceive as any effort to revive the MAI, and especially via what they term 'migration of the MAI to the WTO'.

14.2.2   Tripped up by TRIPS?

Suspicion of an international regime on investment on the part of at least some emerging market nations has doubtlessly been exacerbated by actual experience with the TRIPS Agreement that was concluded as part of the

Uruguay Round. From the time when it was included in the Uruguay Round, the TRIPS Agreement itself was treated with suspicion by the governments of emerging markets. This suspicion probably began with the fact that this Agreement was fervently sought by a number of large TNCs whose business activities could be protected or enhanced by stronger intellectual property protection worldwide. Urged on by these firms, US negotiators in particular, during the Uruguay Round, were especially keen to see the TRIPS Agreement concluded and implemented. Thus at least some countries were wary of TRIPS from the beginning on grounds that, if implementation of this Agreement were so fervently sought by the US, it simply could not wholly be in these countries' interests. However, this suspicion is not the end of the story. In fact, experience since the conclusion of the Uruguay Round more than ten years since has, if anything, bolstered suspicions.

The Agreement committed WTO member countries to minimum substantive and enforcement-related standards with respect to patents, copyrights, trademarks, industrial designs, trade secrets, and (for semiconductor products) layout designs.[8] Intellectual property protection is a second-best approach to solving a market failure: innovation of new products, processes or designs that lead to technological progress or creative output entails sunk costs that can be substantial to the innovator; but once demonstrated, these products, processes or designs can be imitated by competing firms without these firms having to incur sunk costs of comparable magnitude. The upshot is that competition can reduce returns to the innovator to the point at which incentives to innovation are destroyed. The (second-best) solution is to allow the innovator, via intellectual property rights, to hold some degree of market power over those commercial activities created or enabled by the innovation. Exercise of this market power causes prices of the relevant products or services to be higher than would be the case with unrestricted competition, and the elevated prices lead to social welfare losses. Moreover, the exercise of market power can lead to a reduced rate of diffusion of the innovation. However, these losses are meant to be more than offset by a greater rate of innovative activity than would occur in the absence of intellectual property rights.

It follows that a trade-off exists between the benefits of short-run competition and the benefits of long-run, dynamic competition in markets for products that are subject to the protection of intellectual property rights.[9] The exact level or type of intellectual property protection needed to optimize this trade-off is not easily determined, and indeed, might vary by specific activity. Given that there is no model to determine what protection is optimal, the propensity has been for intellectual property standards to be set via a bargaining process, where holders of intellectual property rights can be expected to argue that the more such protection, the better for society as a whole, but where buyers of the relevant products argue to the contrary.

In an international setting, countries that have strong capabilities to innovate commercially desired products would be expected to seek 'high' international standards for intellectual property protection. They do so not only because they are swayed by political constituencies created within their economies that stand to benefit from such standards, but also because, via international trade and investment, these countries can earn higher rents if other countries, those without strong innovative capacities, nonetheless enforce strong intellectual property rights.

Emerging markets are not, by and large, at the stage at which domestic innovative capacity is so high that they can capture rents from the international enforcement of strong intellectual property rights. They do stand to benefit from higher overall rates of innovation, so they face a trade-off between the benefits of lower prices occasioned by relatively weak intellectual property rights and enforcement and the benefits of higher rates of innovation occasioned by strong rights and enforcement.[10] However, this trade-off, in their case, is often such that their preference would be for weaker rights and enforcement than would be preferred by those countries that have stronger innovative capacities.

However, and in implicit recognition of this last point, the countries seeking a strong agreement on intellectual property rights held out in the Uruguay Round the following argument: those countries, and especially emerging markets, that enforced strong intellectual property rights would be ones to which TNCs would be willing to transfer technology. By contrast, if countries maintained weak intellectual property rights and enforcement, they created disincentives to such a transfer. Technology transfer is strongly associated with FDI, and thus countries with weak intellectual property protection would be at a major disadvantage in attracting FDI relative to countries with strong protection. This line of reasoning proved compelling and doubtlessly led to countries accepting the TRIPS Agreement that might not have done so but for fear of losing FDI to countries that did sign up to the Agreement. This line of reasoning is developed more fully in Maskus (2000), who noted a number of nuances not reflected above, for example, that FDI flows are most likely to be increased by high intellectual property protection for activities marked by new and complex technologies that are relatively easily imitated, but that high intellectual property protection is unlikely to stimulate FDI in activities marked by mature technologies that change slowly. Also, to the extent that strong intellectual property protection leads to innovating firms increasing their willingness to license technologies, it is possible that higher protection could in some instances lead to lower FDI. Whether or not this happens is a function of the extent to which the relevant commercial activities are subject to economies of internalization; the greater likelihood of increased intellectual property protection leads to greater FDI.[11]

There is both theoretical and empirical support for the proposition that stronger intellectual property rights can lead to higher rates of inward FDI and technology transfer or, perhaps more accurately stated, that weak intellectual property rights create significant disincentives to this investment and transfer. In addition to the sources cited in the previous paragraph, Ferrantino (1993), Hagedorn, Cloodt and van Kranenburg (2005), Lee and Mansfield (1996), Markusen (2000), Maskus (1998), Saggi (2000), Seyoum (1996), Smarzynska (2002), and Yang and Maskus (2003 and 2000) examine these issues. Unfortunately, of course, most of these studies appeared following completion of the Uruguay Round.

The problem, however, is that since then, little evidence has accumulated to suggest that the higher intellectual property standards created under the TRIPS Agreement have resulted in any significant acceleration in the rates of inward technology transfer or inward flow of FDI to emerging markets. Indeed, while most of the studies cited above indicate that a low degree of intellectual property protection could lead to reduced incentives to FDI and technology transfer, they provide scant evidence that standards achieved via TRIPS actually created additional incentives for technology transfer to emerging markets. But by contrast, there does seem to be widespread belief in these countries that TRIPS has enhanced the market power enjoyed by certain firms in certain sectors – pharmaceuticals is most often mentioned. The standard claim is that, as a result of TRIPS, firms that, prior to the implementation of the TRIPS Agreement, might have supplied 'generic' variations of patented pharmaceuticals to emerging markets have often been forced to cease doing so, with the result that prices of products have risen. With regard to this last matter, I say 'the standard claim' because I am unaware of empirical studies that conclude thusly; rather, I am merely citing anecdotal evidence which, if cited widely enough, can create a strong impression that might not prove true but nonetheless shapes public opinion and perhaps even public policy.

Thus, the story that one hears, over and over, from emerging markets is that implementation of TRIPS obligations has actually done harm to these countries. But the question remains open: on what evidence is it asserted that this harm actually has been done? Again, I am not sure that the evidence exists on which one might confidently give an answer.

Suppose, however, that there has been harm to emerging markets or, barring harm, that the promised benefits simply have not materialized in any clearly identifiable way. Does the lack of benefit from the TRIPS

Agreement (or even positive harm) support the argument that an international regime for investment would be bad for these countries? Of course, not necessarily: the TRIPS Agreement is simply not the same as an international regime for investment. Indeed, earlier in this chapter, it was argued that a case could be made in favor of such a regime. However, even if largely anecdotal, the evidence against TRIPS does give ammunition to those who, for whatever reason, oppose an international regime for investment. And while the argument made might be little more than 'beware of Greeks bearing gifts' (or, otherwise put, 'don't accept another "gift" from the same people who gave you TRIPS'), the argument resonates. As summarized below, this line of argumentation might go beyond the (thin) nexus between TRIPS and an international regime on investment.

14.2.3   Oversold on Multilateral Agreements More Generally?

An end result of the Uruguay Round, the advent of the World Trade Organization and the new agreements associated with the WTO was termination of a number of provisions of the predecessor GATT that granted what has been termed 'special and differential treatment' to developing countries, including certain of what are now termed the emerging markets. As with the implementation of TRIPS, the ending of special and differential treatment was meant to bring benefit to them. But, as with TRIPS, there is widespread belief within these countries that the promised benefits largely have not materialized and in the meantime, they have been stripped of policy options that they once could exercise without being in violation of international trade rules. Again, I am aware of no hard empirical evidence to indicate that the changes brought on by the implementation of the Uruguay Round agreements to end special and differential treatment have actually done harm to emerging markets. But, as with TRIPS, what might matter is not tangible evidence of harm, but rather, the perception of harm, even if this perception is not buttressed by strong empirical evidence. Moreover, as argued above, even if the changes in the trade rules brought on by the Uruguay Round have not done harm to developing countries, there is a dearth of evidence that these changes have resulted in tangible benefits.

Once again, the fact that there is a lack of hard evidence that changes in the trade rules as agreed under the Uruguay Round have created benefits to developing countries is not an argument that an international regime on investment will not bring benefit to them. Again, as stressed throughout this chapter, because no such regime exists, it is truly hard to assess whether benefits would follow from it. Nonetheless, disillusionment with the results of the Uruguay Round surely has dampened enthusiasm within the emerging markets for a new regime.

14.2.4 We Can Do it All by Ourselves

An alternative to an international regime for investment is unilateral liberalization of investment policy, and indeed, much liberalization has occurred over the past decade and a half.[12] Under unilateral liberalization, of course, a country can liberalize as much or as little as it wishes to, and on a schedule of its own choosing rather than one mandated by some international organization. The revealed preference of emerging markets has been for such an approach. Thus, while the governments of almost all of them have been quite unenthusiastic about an international regime for investment, most of them nonetheless have significantly liberalized investment policy on their own.

Is there anything wrong then with unilateral investment liberalization? There can be. If the liberalization undertaken is unaffected by special interest politicking, this is fine and good. However, international investment policy can, as can international trade policy, be captured by special interests whose agenda is inconsistent with maximizing the overall welfare of a country. An international regime offers some degree of protection against such capture; it is far harder, after all, for the government of a country to rescind a law or policy where to do so would bring the government out of compliance with an international obligation than to rescind a law or policy that is not affected by such an obligation. Alleged violations of international obligations by any country, if these violations cause some sort of harm to other countries, are subject to dispute settlement procedures; but measures taken by a government, if these measures do not violate international obligations, are generally not challengeable by other governments, even if the measures do create harm to other countries. To be sure, none of this works to protect a country that is determined (or misled by special interests) to 'shoot itself in the foot' by enacting measures that are not really in its interests, even if these measures are inconsistent with international obligations, if the measures cause no harm to other countries. Governments are sovereign and, with few constraints, they can do what they choose to do, even to do their citizens harm. The only real constraint these governments face is the wrath of other countries if harm is thereby done to these other countries.

Thus the ultimate problem with unilateral liberalization of law and policy relating to international investment is that the process within a country by which law and policy is set might not take the liberalization far enough (in the sense of maximizing welfare gains to the country) or, even if it does, the liberalization runs the risk of being rolled back at some point in the future. By contrast, an international regime provides some impetus for liberalization to go a few steps further than it might under a unilateral approach, and also, it offers some insurance against rollback. Even so, there is no guarantee of an ideal outcome.

CONCLUSION

So, will emerging markets change their attitude toward an international investment regime? This chapter has argued that there is a strong case to be made that these emerging markets should change their attitude. But, even so, there is scant evidence that such a change is imminent.

Could any set of events bring about a change in attitude? Yes, but the circumstances under which such a change might be achieved could themselves be highly undesirable. These circumstances would be a worldwide rollback of both liberal international trade and liberal international investment policies, followed by a major economic downturn, followed by a reinstatement of the liberal policies. This was the course of events observed during the 1930s and 1940s. The Smoot-Hawley tariffs imposed by the United States in 1930 and the retaliatory tariffs imposed by other countries in reaction to the US tariffs led to a worldwide economic downturn – indeed, the worst global depression in all of history. But eventually, the Great Depression convinced many world leaders that policies meant deliberately to suppress international commerce (both trade and investment) are not wise. Following the conclusion of World War II, therefore, a new and liberalizing international economic architecture was negotiated and put into place. If history were to repeat itself such that a new worldwide depression were to happen, the response might again be that governments not only restored the liberal order, but also advanced it, including the creation of new rules on FDI. But this scenario, even if it does lead to the right outcome, is a most unpleasant one, and we surely should wish to avoid it.

In the meantime, it has been argued that a number of developing nations are increasingly becoming not simply 'hosts' (recipients) to FDI, but also 'homes' to this investment (that is, they have become sources of FDI flowing to other countries, as the result of the international expansion of locally-based firms that grow to become TNCs in their own right). Accordingly, it is argued, governments of these countries should increasingly favor international policies that work in the interests of TNCs based inside their economies. These TNCs, in turn, would seek to be able to establish themselves in other markets on non-discriminatory terms, and hence would be inclined to favor international investment rules that are based on principles of non-discrimination. Thus, governments of these countries might be expected to lower their opposition to new international rules in the WTO (or elsewhere) to FDI and perhaps even over time reorient their position to favor such rules.

This last possibility is something of a 'reach'. While I do not rule out that at least certain emerging markets might soften their opposition to an international investment regime in response to the interests of 'their' TNCs, the rise of TNCs from emerging markets is not likely to lead to a wholesale shift of position of the governments of these nations. Why not? The main reason hails back to the MAI experience. As discussed in this chapter, the MAI represented an attempt at the OECD to negotiate such a regime, where virtually all of the governments party to the negotiations were home to TNCs. But also, all of these governments were hosts to FDI from other countries as well. And in the negotiations, the positions of most OECD governments seemed to reflect their status as host country more than as home country. Thus, even within the OECD, the demands for exceptions and reservations to the proposed new rules – demands more consistent with a country's role as host to FDI than as a home – were such that the negotiations ended in discord and without any new regime coming into effect.

Moreover, despite the fact that certain of the emerging markets have become significant homes to locally-based TNCs, the investment positions of such countries are likely in the foreseeable future to be that inward investment greatly exceeds outward investment. In other words, these countries are, and will probably remain, net hosts to FDI. And if, as with a number of OECD members, the overall positions of the governments of these emerging markets continue to reflect their status as host to FDI rather than home, it is unlikely that their opposition to an international regime on investment will be reversed. To be sure, opposition by these governments to some sort of international regime on investment might, with time, soften. But it seems far-fetched that any of these governments will advocate such a regime in the foreseeable future.

NOTES

1. Progress on addressing investment issues in the WTO is addressed in Bora and Graham (2005). This article is two years old, but no major developments have transpired to date since its publication. It should be noted that, following the establishment of the Working Group on Trade and Investment in the World Trade Organization following the WTO Singapore Ministerial meeting in 1996, the governments of some emerging markets (mostly in Latin America) did express some enthusiasm for moving toward some sort of WTO agreement on investment. However, as noted just below, this (rather muted) enthusiasm seems largely to have evaporated by the time of the WTO Cancun Ministerial meeting in 2003.
2. Greenfield FDI occurs when a foreign investor creates a new affiliate that then creates new plant and equipment, as opposed to a foreign investor acquiring an extant, ongoing operation from local investors.

3. This lack of evidence, alas, does not stop anti-globalists from arguing that TNCs do harm developing countries.
4. On these failed negotiations, see Graham (2001).
5. Graham (2005) contains a review and analysis of recent cases.
6. Further details are provided in Graham (2001).
7. Mexico and the Republic of Korea would, however, soon become members.
8. See Schott (1994) for a detailed description of the TRIPS Agreements.
9. This trade-off might not exist, however, if intellectual property rights are too strong. In this case, firms holding such rights to mature technologies might experience so low a rate of competition from imitators as to have no incentive to improve the technology. See, for example, Helpman (1993).
10. Some of the additional innovation might even take place within their own borders, given that a greater degree of intellectual property protection creates incentives for innovative activity. However, to the extent that this happens, it is likely to be a long-run benefit and not one that is quickly realized.
11. On these issues, see also Dunning (1993), Chapters 11 and 12.
12. See UNCTAD (2006).

REFERENCES

Alfaro, L., A. Chanda, S. Kalemli-Ozcan and S. Sayek (2004). 'FDI and economic growth: the role of local financial markets', *Journal of International Economics*, 64, pp. 89–112.

Balasubramanyam, V.N., M. Salisu and D. Sapsford (1996). 'Foreign direct investment and growth in EP and IS countries', *Economic Journal*, 106, pp. 92–105.

Blomström, Magnus, R.E. Lipsey and M. Zejan (1994). 'What explains developing country growth?' in William Baumol, R. Nelson and E. Wolff, eds, *Convergence and Productivity: Gross National Studies and Historical Evidence* (Oxford: Oxford University Press).

Blonigen, Bruce A. and Miao Grace Wang (2005). 'Inappropriate pooling of wealthy and poor countries in empirical FDI studies', in Theodore H. Moran, E.M. Graham and M. Blomström, eds, *Does Foreign Direct Investment Promote Development?* (Washington, DC: The Institute for International Economics), pp. 221–243.

Bora, Bijit and Edward M. Graham (2005). 'Investment and the Doha Development Agenda', in Ernst-Ullrich Petersmann, ed., *Reforming the World Trading System: Legitimacy, Efficiency, and Democratic Governance* (London: Oxford University Press), pp. 335–356.

Borzenstein, E.J. de Gregorio and J.W. Lee. (1998). 'How does foreign investment affect growth', *Journal of International Economics*, 45, pp. 115–72.

Carkovic, Maria and Ross Levine (2005). 'Does foreign direct investment accelerate economic growth', in Theodore Moran, E.M. Graham and M. Blomström, eds, *Does Foreign Direct Investment Promote Development?* (Washington, DC: The Institute for International Economics), pp. 195–220.

Dayal-Gulati, A. and A.M. Husain (2000). *Centripetal Forces in China's Economic Take-off*, International Monetary Fund Working Paper WP/00/86, available at www.imf.org/External/Pubs/FT/staffp/2002/03/pdf/gulati.pdf (last visited 16 February 2007).

Dunning, John (1993). *Multinational Enterprises and the Global Economy* (London: Addison Wesley).

Ferrantino, Michael J. (1993). 'The effect of intellectual property rights on international trade and investment', *Weltwirtschaftliches Archiv*, 129, pp. 300–331.

Graham, Edward M. (2001). *Fighting the Wrong Enemy: Antiglobal Activists and Multinational Enterprises* (Washington, DC: The Institute for International Economics).

Graham, Edward M. (2005). 'Economic issues raised by NAFTA Chapter 11 investor-to-state dispute settlement cases having environmental implications', in Lorraine Eden and Wendy Dobson, eds, *Governance, Multinationals, and Growth* (Cheltenham, UK: Edward Elgar), pp. 272–296.

Hagedoorn, John et al. (2005). 'Intellectual property rights and the governance of international R&D partnerships', *Journal of International Business Studies*, 36, pp. 175–186.

Helpman, Elhanan (1993). 'Innovation, imitation, and intellectual property rights', *Econometrica*, 61, pp. 1247–1280.

Hufbauer, Gary C. and Jeffrey J. Schott (2005). *NAFTA Revisited: Achievements and Challenges* (Washington, DC: The Institute for International Economics).

Kumar, Nagesh and Jaya Prakash Pradhan (2005). 'Foreign direct investment, externalities, and economic growth in developing countries: some empirical evidence', in Edward M. Graham, ed., *Multinationals and Foreign Investment in Economic Development* (London: Palgrave Macmillan), pp. 42–84.

Lee, J.-Y. and Edwin Mansfield (1996). 'Intellectual policy protection and U.S. foreign direct investment', *Review of Economics and Statistics*, 78, pp. 181–186.

Lipsey, Robert E. and Fredrik Sjöholm (2005). 'The impact of FDI on developing countries: why such different answers?' in Theodore Moran, E.M. Graham and M. Blomström, eds, *Does Foreign Direct Investment Promote Development?* (Washington, DC: The Institute for International Economics), pp. 23–43.

Markusen, James R. (2000). 'Contracts, intellectual property rights, and multinational investment in developing countries', *Journal of International Economics*, 53(1), pp. 189–204.

Maskus, Keith E. (1998). 'The international regulation of intellectual property', *Weltwirtschaftliches Archiv*, 134, pp. 186–208.

Maskus, Keith E. (2000). *Intellectual Property Rights in the Global Economy* (Washington, DC: The Institute for International Economics).

Melitz, Marc. J. (2005). 'Comment', in Theodore Moran, E.M. Graham and M. Blomström, eds., *Does Foreign Direct Investment Promote Development?* (Washington, DC: The Institute for International Economics), pp. 273–277.

Saggi, K. (2000). *Trade, Foreign Direct Investment, and International Technology Transfer*, Policy Research Working Paper 2349 (Washington, DC: The World Bank).

Schott, Jeffrey J. (1994). *The Uruguay Round: An Assessment* (Washington, DC: The Institute for International Economics).

Seyoum, B. (1996). 'The impact of intellectual property rights on foreign direct investment', *Columbia Journal of World Business*, 31, pp. 50–59.

Smarzynska, Beata K. (2002). *The Composition of Foreign Direct Investment and Intellectual Property Rights*, Policy Research Working Paper 2786 (Washington, DC: The World Bank), mimeo.

UNCTAD (2006). *World Investment Report 2006: FDI from Developing and Transition Economies: Implications for Development* (New York and Geneva: UNCTAD).

Yang, Guifang and Keith E. Maskus (2003). *Intellectual Property Rights, Licensing, and Innovation*, World Bank Policy Research Working Paper No. 2973 (Washington, DC: The World Bank).

Yang, Guifang and Keith E. Maskus (2000). *Intellectual Property Rights and Licensing: an Econometric Investigation*, (Colorado: University of Colorado, Economics Department), mimeo.

15. The need for an adequate international framework for FDI

Joseph E. Stiglitz

INTRODUCTION

The thesis of my book *Making Globalization Work* (Stiglitz 2006) is that, in many ways, globalization has not lived up to its potential. I explain, for instance, the ways in which globalization has not benefited everybody. It has not been the case that a rising tide lifts all boats: there are some people and countries who are actually worse off. But the problems are not inherent in globalization; it is the way in which globalization has been managed. In the book I try to describe a number of reforms that would help make globalization work, or at least work much better than it has so far for a lot of people.

15.1 A PERSPECTIVE ON TNCs

In one chapter of my book I talk about transnational corporations (TNCs). This is very natural, because TNCs are the principal mechanism through which many of the benefits of globalization are achieved, but also through which many of its problems are realized. This is why you hear different views about these corporations. They are the vehicle through which knowledge is transferred. A large part of the knowledge is produced in the advanced industrial countries, and then gets transferred through TNCs to emerging markets. Training that occurs in many developing countries by TNCs helps close the knowledge gap between the developed and developing countries, and increasingly development economists see this knowledge gap as the central problem facing developing countries.

To some extent, TNCs also play a role in shifting capital from developed to less developed countries, but that is a less important role in many of the countries in which there has been heavy investment, like China, which has a savings rate of 42 per cent and is not really in desperate need for outside capital. In fact, the liberalization of capital markets in the Republic of

Korea was really more a source of problems than benefits. Capital came in, contributed a bit to growth, but then as it rushed to leave in 1997, it brought on a crisis. In Latin America, capital inflows have mainly helped support consumption binges, and when financial market attitudes toward particular countries change (as they inevitably do), they were not able to sustain such binges. Volatility in these economies has been in part brought about by the volatility of investment, mostly short-term investment, but also long-term investment.

But the concerns about TNCs go beyond these macroeconomic concerns and extend to the role of TNCs in facilitating corruption and bribery, degrading the environment and getting special protection that distorts the economy. There are a whole host of complaints about work conditions, many of which have some validity to them. One of the questions that I try to address in my book is why there are so many of these problems and why they seem to be worse internationally than they are domestically.

15.2   ECONOMIC GLOBALIZATION NEEDS POLITICAL AND MINDSET GLOBALIZATION

Underlying my book is a general thesis that economic globalization has outpaced political globalization and the globalization of our mindsets. It may be a simplistic way of putting it, but I think it captures many of the problems posed by globalization. Economic globalization has meant that we have become more integrated, more interdependent, and that means that there is greater need for collective action. But we do not have the political institutions or the mindset with which to address problems in a democratic and effective way.

One way of seeing what is at issue is to think about the parallel between the problems that occurred some 150 years ago as the nation-state, like the United States, developed, and the problems today. Some 150 years ago, for instance, as the Civil War was ending in the US, there was a realization that a national economy was in the process of emerging. The US put banking regulations into place in 1863, and then, over time, the interstate commerce clause was repeatedly invoked to establish a basis for national commercial regulation in a whole host of areas. Today, bankruptcy is governed by national legislation. The US still has state anti-trust laws, but the national competition (anti-trust) laws clearly have a paramount role. We could go through each of the areas that affect commerce: it is clear that today, the United States has basically what you might call a national legal structure with varying degrees of federalism in various parts. One aspect of this, of course, is that you can enforce, although not perfectly, judgments that cross state borders. Unfortunately, this is not the case in the global economy today: more broadly, at the national level we can enforce (albeit imperfectly) a lot of contracts that extend beyond state borders, but internationally things are more difficult.

The thesis I develop in *Making Globalization Work* is that we have been working to create a global economy, but we do not have much of the global institutional infrastructure that really would make it work in an effective and fair way, and we do not have the political institutions to help bring about that infrastructure.

15.2.1 Assymetric Globalization

These problems are made worse in some ways by the fact that the way globalization has proceeded has been very asymmetric. We have liberalized capital far more rapidly than we have liberalized labor. Why is that important? Because firms can say, 'If you do not have what I want – weaker environmental regulations, weaker labor laws, lower wages, a whole host of things – we will move somewhere else'. This asymmetrical liberalization completely changes the bargaining power of the two sides. In terms of optimal tax theory, it means, of course, that you cannot impose a high tax on capital, because if you do, capital will leave. The one thing that cannot leave is land, but the next least mobile factor is unskilled labor. So both in terms of bargaining theory and in terms of tax policy, the burden of taxation is shifted to unskilled labor and away from capital. That asymmetry too often leads to a race to the bottom, so that in the competition to attract businesses and TNCs, there is an attempt to persuade firms to come by lowering social protection, lowering taxes or overlooking environmental regulations.

As an aside, I should mention that the liberalization of labor has a far greater effect in increasing global GDP than the liberalization of capital. Ironically, the argument that we often use for capital market liberalization is that it is good for the global economy; but in a contest between liberalization of labor and capital, in terms of what is more important for the global economy, there is no competition; the liberalization of labor markets would lead to an increase in global GDP an order of magnitude greater than that which results from the liberalization of capital. In other words, if increased global efficiency is the objective, then we need to focus on labor liberalization. But that is not what is being done, and everyone knows the politics behind that stance. It is obvious how the agenda has been set and why it has been set in the way that it has.

15.2.2   Enforcement of Regulations

Making matters worse is the problem I mentioned already, of enforcement of existing regulations across borders. For instance, consider the Bhopal incident, where hundreds of thousands of people were injured by the Dow Chemical–Union Carbide episode. The Government of India wanted to prosecute the CEO of the company which was responsible. It asked the US to extradite him, and without comment, the United States refused to allow him to be subjected to a trial in India, even though India is a country that has very sophisticated legal institutions.

There are, in addition, a number of instances in which corporations take advantage of limited liability. This was supposed to be something to encourage investment, not encourage bad behavior. What happens over and over again is that a limited liability company will be created to extract natural resources from a country. It will extract the resource and pay out dividends to shareholders, but when the time comes to clean up the environmental damage that may have been created, the company may claim that there are no funds to do so, that they have all been distributed. Unfortunately at that point there is very little that can be done.

One famous case occurred in Papua New Guinea, where, after a major mining company admitted that it had vastly underestimated the magnitude of the environmental damage, it recognized the mistake and offered to turn over all its shares to the Government. In other words, it offered to turn over a negative net worth enterprise to the Government of Papua New Guinea. In fact, the cost of cleaning up may have been greater than the total value of the royalties that the country had received, so the whole mine may have been a negative value-added gambit for the country as a whole. However, GDP rose. This is an example of a case in which GDP provides a very misleading measure of economic success, as it does not take into account the degradation of the environment or where funds are going, as royalties that leave the country are still part of GDP. In many of these countries, royalties are as low as one, two or three per cent, so the country receives little from the mine, except environmental degradation. But still the value of the extracted resource is part of GDP, even though the income generated by the resource is shifted outside. Outsiders may claim that such projects are good for the country because GDP increases and a few jobs are created, but in the long run, if royalties are low and the environment is degraded, the value added by such projects to the host country may well be negative.

If something like that happened inside the US, there would be a tort claim; but of course, if a limited liability company were involved, it might be hard to collect. These problems are even worse internationally. Domestically, quite often public pressure is brought to bear. No one likes to have the reputation at home of being a rogue investor. People do not like to feel as though they are poisoning their neighbors, but somehow they do not mind as much poisoning people who live several thousand miles away. Then they do not see the effects and so are more tolerant of adverse environmental and health effects; they assuage their conscience by thinking about the contribution they are making to the country by creating jobs and contributing to the government's revenues. Particularly troublesome is that, even as some of the better mining and oil companies have taken aboard these issues and do believe in a sense of corporate social responsibility, they confront other players for whom these issues are not important, such as privately held mining companies that do not have any public accountability, and increasingly companies from the Third World. These companies say that the TNCs who came into their countries did not pay attention to these issues, so why should they behave any differently? Increasingly, the companies that are creating environmental degradation in many countries, such as in the case of illegal logging in Papua New Guinea, will be from other developing countries. (The problems are even more serious in areas of human rights violations. Even as US companies and, to a lesser extent, European companies, are withdrawing from Sudan to put pressure on the Sudanese Government on the issue of genocide in Darfur, Chinese and Indian companies are willing to come in and extract oil.)

15.3   SOME STRATEGIES FOR IMPROVEMENT

15.3.1   Bribery

In some ways, though, things are better in some areas than they used to be. We have all heard much of the discussion in past years about corruption in developing countries. The point is that every bribe involves both a briber and a bribee; and too often, at least it used to be, the briber is somebody from a TNC. During the Carter Administration, the US passed an anti-bribery law. I was the US representative to the OECD ministerial in 1996, and US companies felt very strongly that they were unfairly constrained by not being allowed to bribe. To some of them it did not seem to matter very much; they found creative ways of evading the restrictions (although at least one major US company that may have thought that it had successfully done so is now being tried for violating the Foreign Corrupt Practices Act). But the Act did put US firms at a disadvantage, so they put a lot of pressure on the US Government to make this an OECD issue. At the time, several European countries gave tax deductions to bribes, as though it was a legitimate business expense necessary to get business. Maximizing profits means minimizing cost, and it is cheaper to pay a US$5 million bribe and get oil at a much lower price than to pay the full price of oil. In some interpretations of standard economic theory, Adam Smith had said that that was what firms were supposed to do – maximize profits by minimizing costs. The pursuit of self-interest and maximizing profits is supposed to lead to general well-being and, in this context, it means that you should bribe. Of course, this is a misinterpretation of economic theory: maximizing profits does not necessarily lead to societal well-being, and it certainly does not do so when that entails bribery. Fortunately, the OECD eventually adopted an anti-bribery instrument, as did the UN later. There have been very few enforcement cases, but at least the legal structure is there.

  More recently, firms in the extractive industries have recognized that, short of bribery, even just giving funds to corrupt dictators, like those in Angola or Chad, allows them to maintain their dictatorship and perpetuate themselves. A recent initiative called the Extractive Industries Transparency Initiative requires that firms should at least make sure that the citizens of the countries involved know how much money is being paid to the government. A few companies have taken the lead on this, such as BP and Hydro (a Norwegian oil company), for instance in Angola, and have done exactly as the Initiative asks. The Government of Angola was not pleased, and other companies, interested in keeping the Government on their side, said in effect, that they would not disclose their payments. However, there are a few governments, like that of Nigeria, that have indicated that they at least want to seem less corrupt or that they want to create an environment which is less corrupt, and they have actually adopted the Extractive Industries Transparency Initiative. Otherwise, relatively few countries have done so. It would be easy for the advanced industrial countries to promote this initiative: all they would need to do is extend the same principle that we discussed before. In the past, many governments had allowed firms to deduct bribes from their taxes, and then we prohibited this, because in effect the government is paying half the bribe. This in turn reduced the incentives to bribe. We could use tax policies to promote the Extractive Industries Transparency Initiative by stipulating that unless payments to these countries are transparent, they cannot be deducted. In other words, anything claimed as a tax deduction has to be disclosed. This would fundamentally change the relationship between some dictatorships and TNCs. At a minimum, it would reduce the scope for corruption in these countries.

15.3.2 Banking

The fact is that we have not created a legal environment that is as conducive as it could be to corporations helping countries develop. Perhaps the most important example is our continued toleration of secret bank accounts in places like the Cayman Islands. Some $500 billion are in banks there, and not because the Cayman Islands have a particular good climate for banking. Rather, there is a climate of tax avoidance and of avoidance of other regulations; but also, the corrupt dictators that get bribes from TNCs can hide their money there.

This, too, is a problem the industrial countries could address. In fact, the OECD took an important initiative to reduce bank secrecy, but in August 2001 the US, under the Bush administration, vetoed that effort. The Administration said, in effect, it likes to have competition in this area. In September of 2001 we discovered, of course, that not only do drug dealers and corrupt dictators use secret bank accounts, terrorists do as well. Since then we have shown that we can stop bank secrecy when we want to, but we have only wanted to do so in connection with terrorism. Bank secrecy continues in all other areas.

This is an example of the way in which legal structures and political globalization have not kept pace with economic globalization. We would not tolerate this if it were all inside our country, but globally we do, because it is outside our borders, it is somebody else's problem, it is tax evasion or corruption in some other country, although, unfortunately, it is often also happening in our own country.

15.3.3 Balanced Investment Agreements

The asymmetry that I described before is manifested in several other ways as well, and it exacerbates the problems that I have just described. For the most part, international investment agreements focus on protecting investors, not protecting the country being invested in. For example, while such agreements are concerned with expropriation, about nationalistic or populist governments seizing assets, they are not concerned about TNCs despoiling the environment, leaving behind all kinds of problems of environmental damage without any remediation. A balanced investment agreement would address the issues that are important to both sides, but the focus of most of the negotiations in multilateral investment agreements has been to protect the investors and not the countries or communities where the investment occurs. That is a reflection of the same kinds of asymmetries that we see in other aspects of globalization, so we should not be surprised.

In fact, bilateral investment treaties have exacerbated the imbalances that I have described. For example, Chapter 11 of the NAFTA Agreement was described as an investor protection agreement. I was in the White House when NAFTA was being discussed and advocated, and no one ever said that Chapter 11 was anything other than investment protection against the threat of a populist Mexican Government nationalizing investor assets. But, of course, Chapter 11 has a provision protecting investors from measures that are 'tantamount' to an expropriation. An example of that is a Mexican village that decided it did not want to have toxic waste dumps in the middle of the village, which one would think is a perfectly reasonable regulation. But a US firm had a piece of property that it had intended to use to construct a toxic waste dump, so it claimed that the value of its property had been diminished by this regulation and was thus a regulatory taking for which it should be compensated. In the end, the Government of Mexico had to pay the US firm for not polluting, for engaging in what many would argue are sound environmental practices. (As is so often the case, there are disagreements about the interpretation of the decision: for instance, was compensation demanded because the environmental regulations were imposed in a discriminatory manner? Would Mexico have had to pay compensation if it had acted to protect the environment in another way?) There are currently many lawsuits of this kind, potentially worth hundreds of millions, even billions, of dollars, and there remains uncertainty about their full consequences.

The real irony is that at the very time that the Clinton administration was pushing this provision of NAFTA, it was also resisting the anti-environmentalists in Congress who were trying to pass a domestic regulatory taking provision. The anti-environmentalists like regulatory takings provisions because they make environmental regulation virtually impossible. I, and the other members of the Council of Economic Advisers, believe these regulatory takings laws are bad public policy. They will lead to inefficiencies, and US courts have sustained the view that they are undesirable. The Clinton Administration was successful in resisting this initiative in Congress; but while the Administration was opposing this in Congress, it was negotiating a regulatory takings provision in NAFTA. As far as I know, this provision was never mentioned in the White House during the many discussions of NAFTA.

Perhaps inspired by this kind of questionable environmental legislation embedded in a treaty, Europe and the United States have been steadily working to extend these bilateral investment treaties and to include these and other provisions that are equally or more adverse to the interests of developing countries. The full impact of these treaties remains uncertain. In my recent visits to developing countries, I have sensed their anxiety. We will not know for years what these agreements really will mean, and the US government often does not fully disclose the agreements while they are under negotiation (except perhaps to the business interests that they are advancing).

For instance, one set of clauses that is giving rise to heightened anxiety involves pre-investment (pre-establishment) protection. Under earlier regulatory taking provisions, if a firm made an investment and a change in a regulation or law decreased the value of the investment, the firm would be compensated. Now, apparently, an effort is being made to provide for pre-investment protection. For example, if an investor from the United States went to Bolivia or Ecuador and undertook a feasibility study, and then the regulations changed to make that investment impossible or less profitable, the country might have to compensate the investor as if he had already made the investment; and the compensation is not limited to offsetting what he actually spent but is based on the potential future profit that might have been realized if the investment had gone forward. One can imagine that developing countries do not have much enthusiasm for this kind of provision.

In *Making Globalization Work* I provide several ways in which we should begin to redress these problems, what we might do to help create the necessary legal infrastructure as we create a global economy. We cannot continue to operate in the way that we have so far. For instance, in the area of competition law, we know there is an uneven battle. If Microsoft goes to battle with a smaller developing country, Microsoft's annual income may well be higher than the GDP of that country, and the size of its legal staff may well be bigger than that of the developing country. It is not a fair battle. In a sense, Microsoft admitted that it had monopoly power when the Government of the Republic of Korea attempted to stop what it considered to be anti-competitive practice. Microsoft indicated that it would leave the country if the Government pursued its course of action. The response to such a threat in a competitive sector should be indifference: it makes no difference if one competitive firm leaves the country. But if a firm is a monopolist, or has significant market power, leaving the country has an effect. Microsoft admitted indirectly its market power and that it was willing to use that power to shut down a valid prosecution of anti-competitive behavior of the kind that had been sustained in the United States and Europe.

There is a growing recognition that countervailing global monopolies requires global action. Proceeding piecemeal, one country after another, does not achieve this; fragmenting the legal process is costly and undermines its effectiveness. Of course, monopolies like fragmentation: in a battle against each of the separate enforcement agencies they are more likely to prevail. There should be either a global competition court or the ability to consolidate the cases into a single case.

For example, I filed an *amicus curiae* petition in the *Epigram* case a year ago. The issue was an interesting one: it was a class action suit of a large number of plaintiffs against the vitamin cartel that had raised prices. The defendant settled with all the Americans, and then claimed that they could no longer be sued in the American courts. Then the question was: could that case still go on? The US Supreme Court ruled that it could not; but at least one of the Supreme Court Justices seemed to recognize that there is now a real problem in enforcing global competition effectively in a world with fragmented jurisdictions.

There are also issues of extradition, to which I referred earlier. If there is to be accountability, we have not only to be able to extradite those individuals who may be culpable, but also be able to pierce the corporate veil. The corporate veil, the corporation, is a social construction that has an enormous set of benefits; but when that social construction is being used (or abused) in the way that it has been in many countries, we need to pierce the corporate veil.

Let me end by raising a fundamental question: why is there a need for investment treaties in the first place? The argument for these agreements is that you have to swallow this bitter medicine of various demanding provisions because it is good for you – because if you swallow this medicine, you will attract more investment. But if these provisions are as good for the developing countries as the US claims, why do developing countries not implement them on their own, without investment treaties?

This question has never really been adequately answered, and the obvious implication is that maybe these agreements – or at least the most noxious provisions within them – are not as good for developing countries as the US and the EU claim. Maybe these agreements are being forced on them: the developed countries are trying to persuade the developing countries to do things that are not in their best interest. Maybe the developing countries know better what is in their own best interest than the advanced industrial countries, or at least their trade negotiators, who are often closely aligned with commercial interest. (There is an obvious analogy: the IMF tried to get countries around the world to liberalize their capital markets for short-term speculative capital flows, and then it discovered several years later, after a lot of damage had been done all over the world, that it was not the best policy, that it led to more instability and not to more growth).

There is one final problem with the bilateral investment agreements that many people are increasingly disturbed about: the processes by which disputes are adjudicated. Do the courts (arbitration panels) where these agreements are enforced provide the judicial safeguards that we have come to expect and demand? The procedures are often not as transparent and do not satisfy the kind of judicial standards that we have domestically (in the US, many jurisdictions allow either party to demand a jury). These standards have evolved for good reason: we cannot have confidence in the justice in the outcomes if we do not have confidence in the procedures through which justice is administered and disputes adjudicated. We have yet to develop international commercial courts in which there is widespread confidence. It seems to me that, if we were to establish international courts, or even ad hoc panels to adjudicate the disputes which inevitably arise out of investment treaties, we ought to make sure that we incorporate all that we have learned about fair and transparent procedures within each of our jurisdictions, and not look for frameworks that are potentially biased toward one side or the other, particularly toward corporations in the industrial countries.

CONCLUSION

In conclusion, I really do think that TNCs can have enormous benefits for developing countries, and in many cases they have lived up to this potential. However, in some countries they have had quite negative effects. The question is: how can we restructure incentives in such a way as to make positive effects more likely and negative effects less likely? We learned domestically that we must have legal structures which will provide the correct incentives that lead corporations to socially desirable behavior in relation to the environment, competition, labor and a whole host of other standards to which corporations are held domestically. The challenge before us is finding ways of extending those standards to the global arena.

REFERENCES

Stiglitz, Joseph E. (2006). *Making Globalization Work* (New York: W.W. Norton).

PART V

Conclusion

Conclusion

16. The rise of TNCs from emerging markets: threat or opportunity?
Lorraine Eden

INTRODUCTION

This edited book is based on a conference held at Columbia University in October 2006. The theme of the conference was the rise of transnational corporations (TNCs) from emerging markets, and the impact of this rise on home and host countries and the international community. The purpose of my chapter is to sum up – or to distill – a few observations based on looking across the conference (and the book chapters) as a whole. My comments focus on broad themes and do not cover all of the points or even cover all of the chapters. Rather, I focus on selections which illustrate what I saw as some of the key themes emerging from the conference.

16.1 WHICH ARE THE EMERGING MARKETS?

The first issue is definitional: which countries are included in the term 'emerging markets'? Which firms are considered to be 'emerging market firms'? How broad or narrow are the terms that scholars and policy makers should be using?

The most commonly used definition of emerging markets in the management literature is: 'Emerging economies are low-income, rapid-growth countries using economic liberalization as their primary engine of growth' (Hoskisson *et al.* 2000, p. 249). Their definition included 51 rapid-growth developing countries in Asia, Latin America and the Middle East identified by the International Finance Corporation, and 13 transition economies in the former Soviet Union and China identified by the European Bank for Reconstruction and Development, making a total of 64 countries.

The core characteristics that identify this group of emerging markets are that (1) they are dynamic economies; (2) their institutional environments were buffeted in the 1990s by a contagious tidal wave of policy shocks (liberalization, privatization, deregulation); and (3) they suffer from missing or weak market-based institutions, particularly in terms of property rights and legal infrastructure.

These country characteristics have been important for the way firms from emerging market countries have internationalized. Chapter 8, by Dunning, Kim and Park, for example, shows that emerging-market firms have gone international much earlier than their developed-country predecessors. The authors argue that liberalization and deregulation at home lowered the costs of investing abroad while raising competitive pressures at home. Thus, emerging-market firms may have been both pushed and pulled 'out of the nest' well before their own firm-specific advantages might have propelled them into becoming TNCs.

As a result, Dunning *et al.* argue that emerging-market TNCs are more likely to engage in strategic asset-seeking FDI, designed to supplement their weaker firm-specific advantages. In addition, these firms are more likely to engage in FDI that internalizes their home country advantages, and more likely to stay close to home in terms of their locational choices. Rugman's chapter (Chapter 6) makes somewhat similar points for TNCs from the People's Republic of China. He argues that Chinese TNCs' firm-specific advantages draw from China's country-specific advantages in low-cost, low-skilled labor. Moreover, he argues that China's TNCs are home-country (or at best regional) corporations, with the bulk of their sales and activities located either in or close by the home market. He does not foresee that situation changing over the next ten years.

The Dunning *et al.* and Rugman chapters raise the question: are Chinese TNCs representative of all emerging-market TNCs? Can or should we use a broad brush that paints all TNCs from emerging economies the same?

16.2   EMERGING MARKETS ARE NOT ALL THE SAME: DIFFERENCES DO MATTER

While Hoskisson *et al.* (2000, p. 259) cautioned researchers that 'emerging market economies are not homogeneous, even within the same region', researchers have focused on their similarities more than their differences. At least two chapters in this volume, however, do focus on the differences among emerging markets and their implications for emerging-market firms.

In fact, Chapter 5, by Cantwell and Barnard analyzes developing countries not emerging markets, but their analysis is pertinent for both the broad group of developing countries and the narrower group of emerging markets. The authors make the sensible argument that: 'In determining whether developing country firms benefit from investing abroad, a first point is that firms need some initial ownership advantages to enable them to invest abroad'.

Following Dunning's eclectic paradigm, the authors argue that the ownership advantages of firms from developing countries depend partly on the strengths of their home country's locational advantages. Two country-level factors are examined: resource abundance and market size. The authors argue that large, resource-rich emerging markets are a home-country advantage that encourages outward foreign direct investment (OFDI) by emerging-market firms in resource-based industries and low research-intensive manufacturing. As examples, they give Petrobras (Brazil), BT Bumi (Indonesia) and Cemex (Mexico). Small emerging markets that are poor in natural resources tend to be heavily engaged in OFDI in services; for example, Asia Netcom (Hong Kong (China)) and Neptune Orient Lines (Singapore). Using *World Investment Report* data on all cross-border mergers and acquisitions (M&As) between 1995 and 2004, they categorize the M&As by type of home and host country and find that large, resource-rich and small, resource-poor emerging markets do have differing patterns of OFDI, as they predicted. TNCs from larger, richer emerging markets do come disproportionately from the natural resource and manufacturing sectors, whereas TNCs from small, resource-poor emerging markets are more typically in services.

Chapter 12, by Globerman and Shapiro, focuses on differences between developed and emerging markets in terms of their trade, inward FDI and OFDI patterns. Two subgroups within emerging markets are examined: transition economies and the BRICs (Brazil, Russia, India, China). The authors find that emerging markets, not surprisingly, are much less internationalized in terms of trade and FDI patterns than their developed market counterparts.

However, there are interesting differences among the emerging markets over the 1995 to 2004 period. Transition economies have higher rates, and BRIC countries lower rates, of inward FDI flows as a percentage of GDP than do other emerging markets (4.5 per cent and 2.4 per cent versus 3.4 per cent, respectively; see Table 12.1 in their chapter). Similarly, transition economies are more trade intensive, and BRIC countries less trade intensive, than other emerging markets (103.1 per cent and 36.0 per cent versus 82.2 per cent, respectively), measured by exports plus imports as a share of GDP. In terms of the topic of interest at this conference – emerging-market TNCs – it is the OFDI statistics that are most relevant. Here, the difference exists but is less pronounced: OFDI as a share of GDP for transition economies and BRIC countries are both lower than other emerging-markets, suggesting that their emerging-market firms have been less engaged in outward internationalization strategies (0.3 per cent and 0.4 per cent versus 0.5 per cent, respectively).

Moreover, Globerman and Shapiro review the literature linking trade and FDI, which gives strong evidence that the two are 'relatively strong complements', not substitutes, for developed-market economies. In this situation, the potential for a virtuous circle emerges whereby trade, OFDI and inward FDI all increase in tandem over time. However, this is not the case for emerging markets, where the authors find much weaker complementarities as a whole, and significantly weaker and possibly declining complementaries between trade and FDI for the non-transition, non-BRIC transition economies. Globerman and Shapiro also find no evidence that an exogenous shock or disturbance to emerging markets (for example, liberalization of capital controls) generates permanent effects. Coupling the weak complementarities with the lack of permanent effects from shocks suggests that exogenously determined increases in OFDI might not generate the same virtuous cycle of OFDI–trade–inward FDI in emerging markets that one sees in developed economies.

A clear contribution of the Cantwell and Bernard and the Globerman and Shapiro chapters is therefore to point out that emerging markets, while usefully analyzed as a group, in fact have quite different trade and FDI patterns. These differences are important for understanding the likely impacts of emerging-market TNCs on both their own home countries and the host countries where they locate.

16.3   PUBLIC POLICIES SHOULD BE TAILORED: ONE SIZE DOES NOT FIT ALL

Emerging markets in the pre-1990s were typically characterized by high degrees of protection, monopoly and limited industry competition that negatively affected the international competitiveness of their domestic firms. Political instability, inefficient and underdeveloped capital markets and inadequate legal protections generated high uncertainty, raised transaction costs and crippled investment. The 1990s radically changed the environment for domestic firms in most emerging markets. However, institutional infrastructure in emerging markets is still not robust, particularly in the transition economies.

Globerman and Shapiro (Chapter 12) question whether weak and missing institutions might be the underlying reason why exogenous shocks do not appear to have permanent FDI impacts on these economies, arguing that deep integration requires strong infrastructure. The policy implication of their work is that public policies aimed at encouraging OFDI from emerging markets might not have large-scale, synergistic effects on economic growth at home. The key appears to be reforming governance practices and developing better institutions in emerging markets.

Moran (Chapter 13) reaches a similar policy conclusion through analyzing the effects of OFDI from emerging markets on home-country firms, workers and communities. He reviews the literature on the economic effects of OFDI on home developed-market economies, where typically TNCs show superior performance at home than non-TNCs. Moran notes that similar studies done on emerging-market home countries are few and far between. While weak evidence suggests the same positive performance difference, Moran recommends fairly neutral policies toward OFDI. In terms of tax policy, this means giving home country firms a foreign tax credit on profits earned abroad (preserving capital export neutrality). He also recommends that emerging market governments should strengthen their multilateral policy ties through signing more bilateral investment treaties and double tax treaties, encouraging their firms to buy political risk insurance (for example from the Multilateral Investment Guarantee Agency, MIGA), and setting up national agencies to provide information to emerging-market firms about OFDI opportunities.

Graham (Chapter 14) like Globerman and Shapiro, reviews the literature on home country impacts from OFDI. He concurs that the literature to date is very thin, but concludes, on a more positive note than Globerman and Shapiro, that OFDI should bring enhanced economic growth and spillovers to emerging markets. As a result, Graham agrees with Moran's public policy prescription: emerging-market governments should strengthen their multilateral FDI policies. However, Graham does not believe that emerging-market governments are willing to support a multilateral investment regime. While many emerging markets have become homes to TNCs, the bulk of FDI flows are still inward and most emerging-market governments are suspicious of the foreign firms in their midst. As long as emerging markets are 'net hosts' to FDI, Graham believes they will prefer a piecemeal approach to regulating FDI, one that he worries is open to capture by vested interest groups. Moreover, he worries that emerging-market governments see multilateral agreements such as TRIPS and TRIM as primarily benefiting developed-market TNCs, and view new multilateral proposals with a skeptical eye.

Looking at the public policy debate from the reverse lens, or from the perspective of host countries toward emerging-market TNCs, Goldstein (Chapter 9) argues that the rise of TNCs from emerging markets has generated new issues for OECD public policy debates, many of these reminiscent of the 1980s debates about Japanese FDI in the United States. First among these is the investor's nationality. Goldstein argues that, when the general public has a negative appreciation of a country, TNCs from that country face much higher liability of foreignness problems arising from the country of origin effect. Moreover, since many emerging-market TNCs do not have strong firm-specific advantages, they are doubly hampered. The absence of strong firm-specific advantages makes it difficult for emerging-market firms to compete with local firms in developed markets; it also means that these firms have smaller firm-specific advantages to 'bring to the table' when they enter developed markets. From a political perspective, emerging-market firms may also face additional liabilities in terms of national security, particularly those with some degree of home-country state ownership. Goldstein reviews two recent cases (CNOOC and Dubai Ports World) in the United States and concludes that assuming that emerging-market TNCs are acting as instruments of their home country governments is 'somewhat naive'. For all these reasons, Goldstein concludes that an active dialogue between developed- and emerging-market policy makers is much needed.

16.4   WHERE DO WE GO FROM HERE?

Sachs's keynote address at the conference (Chapter 2) made the clear point that the world is facing a 'major rebalancing of global power' as the processes of convergence bring the economic power and size of emerging markets to a position where they parallel, and possibly surpass, western economies. Sachs argues that the geopolitical impacts will be comparable to those from the Industrial Revolution. Transnational corporations are agents of change, and in this transition (as in previous ones), TNCs will be both the bellwether and the lightning rod.

The purpose of this conference – and of this volume – was to encourage a debate about emerging-market TNCs and their impact on home and host countries. There is a rich menu of materials in here to stimulate both scholarly and public policy discussions. I have touched on a few of the broad themes that emerge from the book; I hope my comments whet your appetite.

REFERENCES

Hoskisson, R.E., L. Eden, C.M. Lau and M. Wright (2000). 'Strategy in emerging economies', *Academy of Management Journal*, 43, pp. 249–267.

17. Outward foreign direct investment from emerging markets: annotated bibliography

Zenaida Hernández[1]

Although overseas investment by emerging-market transnational corporations (TNCs) has received a significant amount of attention recently, relatively little is known about this phenomenon. This bibliography contains a few key resources to help those who want to learn more about recent trends and drivers in foreign direct investment (FDI) from these countries. The first set of resources is global in scope, while the rest is organized by region to reflect the patterns of actual investment flows.

GLOBAL

Aykut, Dilek and Dilep Ratha (2003). 'South-South FDI flows: how big are they?' *Transnational Corporations*, 13(1), pp. 149–176.

This note calculates the volume of South–South FDI flows in the 1990s. Indirect estimates suggest that more than one-third of such inflows into developing economies originate in other developing economies. South–South FDI is driven by 'push' and 'pull' factors similar to those that drive North–South flows. A non-negligible part of South–South investment may reflect round-tripping of capital motivated by policies that favor foreign investors over domestic ones.

Aykut, Dilek and Andrea Goldstein (2006). *Developing Country Multinationals: South-South Investment Comes of Age*, Working Paper No. 257 (Paris: OECD Development Centre), mimeo.

Large Western corporations have long invested overseas to penetrate markets, seek resources and increase efficiency. After the explosion of inward FDI to the South in the 1990s, it is now the turn of the largest companies from emerging and transition economies, including the BRICs, to intensify their outward FDI through mergers and acquisitions as well as greenfield investments. The contours of this emerging phenomenon are described in this paper, with a focus on the quantification of the weight of South–South FDI flows and their developmental consequences.

Bartlett, Christopher and Sumantra Goshal (2000). 'Going global: lessons from late movers', *Harvard Business Review*, 78, pp. 132–142.

Conventional wisdom says that companies from the periphery of the global market cannot compete against established global giants from Europe, Japan and the United States. Companies from developing countries have entered the game too late; they do not have the resources. But the authors of this paper disagree. The problem for most aspiring TNCs from peripheral countries is that they enter the global marketplace in low-margin businesses at the bottom of the value curve, and they stay there. But it does not have to be that way: each company in the study overcame the same core challenges. They broke out of the mindset that they were unable to compete successfully on the global stage. They adopted strategies that made being a late mover a source of competitive advantage. They developed a culture of continual cross-border learning. And they all had leaders who drove them relentlessly up the value curve.

Beausang, Francesca (2003). *Third World Multinationals: Engine of Competitiveness or New Form of Dependency?* (London: Palgrave Macmillan).

This book uses case studies from Brazilian and Chilean firms to compare TNCs from the developed world to those from the Third World. In the end, the characteristics of Brazilian and Chilean TNCs did not provide consistent evidence of a Third-World TNC category. The conclusions drawn from this study were that Brazilian and Chilean TNCs are not fundamentally different from developed-country TNCs.

Bray, John (2005). *International Companies and Post-Conflict Reconstruction*, World Bank Social Development Paper, No. 22 (Washington, DC: World Bank), mimeo.

This paper studies the role of TNCs in post-conflict reconstruction as an essential complement to the work of international aid agencies. The most active foreign investors in the smaller post-conflict states are niche players with a higher tolerance of risk or regional companies with regional development strategies. This is evident in the oil sector. State-owned companies from developing countries – such as Malaysia's Petronas, India's ONGC-Videsh or China's CNPC – face the challenge of establishing a niche against competition from the established western TNCs and believe that their greater willingness to take political and security risks may be an advantage.

Casanova, Lourdes (2004). 'East Asian, European, and North American multinational firm strategies in Latin America', *Business and Politics*, 6(1), p. 1074.

Over the past decade, TNCs have entered Latin America with three main objectives: efficiency seeking, growth seeking and resource seeking. Natural markets – those sharing a common history or language or having a high level of physical proximity with the MNC country of origin – can explain the relative successes of TNCs from regions such as Europe (mainly Iberia), the United States and Asia. By looking at the successes of Latin American TNCs, East Asian TNCs may infer some lessons on how to best leverage their competitive advantage.

Citigroup (2005). *Emerging Market Acquirers in Developed Markets: A Growing Force* (New York: Citigroup).

Leading emerging-market companies have recently focused their sights on developed markets. This report reviews all cross-border acquisitions by emerging-market companies since 1981. Fourteen economies have displayed the greatest cross-border acquisition activity. These economies have collectively grown at a faster pace than developed countries and other developing markets, despite the fact that several individual economies experienced sustained periods of decline during this period.

Dunning, John H., Roger van Hoesel and Rajneesh Narula (1997). 'Third World multinationals revisited: new developments and theoretical implications', in John H. Dunning, ed., *Globalization, Trade, and Foreign Direct Investment* (New York: Elsevier), pp. 255–286.

Distinguishes between 'first wave' and 'second wave' developing country MNCs, as explained by Lall (technology accumulation) and the investment development path (later stage). The second wave is also the result of increased globalization and regionalization due to dramatic technological advances and the opening of markets.

Ettinger, Stephen, Shelly Hahn and Georgina Dellacha (2005). *Developing-Country Investors and Operators in Infrastructure, Phase 1 Report* (Washington, DC: Public-Private Infrastructure Advisory Facility).

Based on a database of 1100 projects of PPI in developing countries between the years 1998 and 2003, the authors found that investors from developing countries (mostly nearby) supplied approximately 11 per cent of the value of investments. 'Developing foreign investors' (South–South) in infrastructure are a growing trend as a share of the number of sponsors: 13 per cent in 2003, compared to 7 per cent in 1998–2000. They are very important in Africa (from South Africa), significant and growing in the Middle East and South Africa, small but growing in the Eastern Caribbean, significant and stable in Latin America, but barely extant in East Asia and the Pacific. Of the 25 largest investors, 7 are from developing countries. Within the period studied, the authors found a modest shift from developed countries to developing countries.

Goldstein, Andrea (2007). *Multinational Companies from Emerging Economies: Composition, Conceptualization and Direction in the Global Economy* (Hampshire, UK and New York: Palgrave Macmillan).

This is a comprehensive study of Southern TNCs. It describes recent trends, theories and case studies and poses questions for future study. Emerging-market firms are heterogeneous in their transnationalization patterns and begin to expand their businesses at an earlier development stage than their industrialized nation counterparts. Asian investors play an important role in Southern outward FDI. Public policies and migration are inherent in the overseas investment decisions of TNCs from emerging markets. Southern TNCs tend to have closer ties with their governments than their OECD peers.

Goldstein, Andrea, Federico Bonaglia and John Mathews (2006). 'Accelerated internationalization by emerging multinationals: the case of white goods', submitted for 'International Expansion of Emerging

Market Businesses', in a focused issue of the *Journal of International Business Studies*.

The emergence of a 'second wave' of developing-country TNCs in a variety of industries is one of the characterizing features of recent globalization. These new TNCs did not delay their transnationalization until they were large, as did most of their predecessors, and often become global as a result of direct firm-to-firm contracting. It is a further interesting hypothesis to investigate the extent to which such firms, born as suppliers of established incumbents, have leveraged on their 'latecomer' status to accelerate their transnationalization. This paper investigates how three latecomer TNCs pursued global growth through accelerated transnationalization combined with strategic and organizational innovation. Haier (China), Mabe (Mexico) and Arçelik (Turkey) emerged as dragon TNCs in the large home appliances (so-called 'white goods') industry.

Goldstein, Andrea, Nicolas Pinaud, Helmut Reisen and Xiaobao Chen (2006). *The Rise of China and India: What's in it for Africa?* (Paris: OECD Development Centre).

African economies are affected differentially by Asian economic growth. Complementary effects are possible in certain cases, as producers benefit from increased Asian demand. Further, China and other countries may want to secure more raw materials and may want to improve export infrastructure in selected African countries, while offering project finance, FDI and other forms of trade-linked capital flows. In other cases where Asian economies indirectly divert investment resources away from African economies, interests may be competitive rather than complementary. Although on balance the short-term opportunities of Asia's ascendancy and the concomitant effects on South–South trade may outweigh the economic costs for Africa, serious long-term risks may be involved. These risks are related to inadequate institutions and governance systems, which may lead to the misallocation of revenues from higher raw material prices and from disincentives for investment in tradable activities in the non-traditional sector that are required in order to distribute the benefits of global trade more equitably among sectors.

Hoskisson, R.E., L. Eden, C.M. Lau and M. Wright (2000). 'Strategy in emerging economies', *Academy of Management Journal*, 43(3), pp. 249–267.

This paper considers the nature of theoretical contributions on the strategy of TNCs in emerging economies. The research is classified in this article into four categories of TNCs: (1) firms from developed economies entering emerging economies, (2) domestic firms competing with emerging economies, (3) firms from emerging economies entering other emerging economies, and (4) firms from emerging economies entering developed economies. Among the four perspectives examined (transaction cost theory, agency theory, resource-based theory, institutional theory), the most dominant seems to be institutional theory. Much more research needs to be done to answer questions regarding the third and fourth categories.

Khanna, Tarun and Krishna G. Palepu (2006). 'Emerging giants: building world-class companies in emerging markets', *Harvard Business Review*, 84(10), pp. 60–69.

In this article, the authors, citing the results of their six-year study of 'emerging giants', describe the three strategies these businesses used to become effective global competitors despite facing financial and bureaucratic disadvantages in their home markets. Some have capitalized on their knowledge of local product markets: some have exploited their knowledge of local talent and capital markets, thereby serving customers both at home and abroad in a cost-effective manner; and some emerging giants have exploited institutional voids to create profitable businesses.

Sauvant, Karl P. (2005). 'New Sources of FDI: the BRICs. Outward FDI from Brazil, Russia, India and China', *The Journal of World Investment and Trade*, 6, pp. 640–709.

FDI integrates production activities internationally through the corporate production systems established by TNCs. All countries are involved in this 'deep integration' process. Brazil, the Russian Federation, India and China (the BRICs) have participated in it primarily through inward investment. But firms from these four countries are becoming sources of outward FDI (as part of the growth of such investment from emerging markets in general), to establish portfolios of locational assets as increasingly important sources of their international competitiveness. Although these countries are on the verge of becoming important outward investors, many of their firms still need to acquire the necessary know-how, and their governments need to put in place an appropriate enabling framework.

UNCTAD (2004). 'South-South investment agreements proliferating'. *Press release* UNCTAD/PRESS/PR/2004/036, 23 November.

Agreements on investments between developing countries have increased substantially in both number and geographical coverage over the past decade. Agreements represent one aspect of cooperation within the developing world aimed at achieving development goals and covering a wide range of activities and areas, such as trade and labor. This wave of South–South international investment agreements includes 653 bilateral investment agreements, 312 double taxation treaties and 49 preferential trade and investment agreements among developing countries. This note describes the nature of these agreements.

UNCTAD (2005). *Linkages, Value Chains and Outward Investment: Internationalization Patterns of Developing Countries' SMEs*, Note by the UNCTAD secretariat TD/B/COM.3/69, 5 January, mimeo.

This note examines key developments in the area of enterprise transnationalization to identify major factors that could enhance the international competitiveness of developing-country firms, given the changing environment and rapid globalization. It discusses opportunities and threats created by globalization for developing-country SMEs and how the latter can better use these opportunities and become global players themselves. In particular, it discusses recent trends in outward investment from developing-country firms as a means of accessing strategic assets, technology, skills, natural resources and markets, and improving efficiency. It also examines possible forms of integrated production networks, with specific reference to TNC–SME linkages and global value chains.

UNCTAD (2006). *World Investment Report 2006: FDI from Developing and Transition Economies: Implications for Development* (Geneva: United Nations).

This report states that the rise of TNCs from developing and transition economies is part of a profound shift in the world economy. The unprecedented rate of transnationalization by TNCs based in emerging markets has been encouraged by many factors, including soaring export revenues and rapid economic growth in a number of these economies, as well as the burgeoning industrial and business prowess of their firms. Perhaps most significantly, emerging-market firms have come to realize the necessity of accessing international markets and connecting to global production systems and knowledge networks. This change, from a domestic vision to an international one, underscores the nature of the structural shift taking place in the global economy. The report goes on to explore, in detail, the implications for development, both at the home country and host country level. South–South FDI is a significant facet, especially because developing-country TNCs invest proportionally more in developing countries than do their developed-country counterparts. Partly based on a series of surveys, the report establishes a model to research further and understand better this dynamic phenomenon, especially recognizing the diverse nature and unique characteristics of emerging-market TNCs – stemming, as these do, from a multiplicity of origins and sources of competitive advantage.

World Bank (2006). *Global Development Finance 2006: The Development Potential of Surging Capital Flows* (Washington, DC: World Bank).

Chapter 4 of this annual World Bank publication focuses on financial flows among developing countries. Capital flows among developing countries (South–South flows) are now growing more rapidly than North–South flows, particularly FDI. South–South trade rose to $562 billion in 2004, up from $222 billion in 1995, and in 2004 accounted for 26 per cent of developing countries' total trade. South–South FDI also rose, reaching $47 billion in 2003, up from $14 billion in 1995, and in 2003, accounted for 37 per cent of developing countries' total FDI. Much South–South FDI originates in middle-income country firms, and is invested in the same region, for example, Russian and Hungarian firms investing in Eastern Europe and Central Asia, and South African companies investing elsewhere in southern Africa. About half of China's FDI, however, went to natural resources projects in Latin America.

Yeung, Henry Wai-chung (1999). 'Competing in the global economy: the globalization of business firms from emerging economies', in Henry Wai-chung Yeung, ed., *The Globalization of Business Firms from Emerging Economies* (Cheltenham, UK: Edward Elgar), pp. xiii–xlvi.

This chapter reviews material published between 1973 and 1998 on the globalization of business firms from emerging economies. There have been more than100 articles published on this topic. The early phase of transnationalization in Asia and Latin America was largely confined to intra-regional operations. Transnationalization has been an incremental process, less driven by competitive pressures than by the search for alternative markets in the home regions in order to become greater global players. TNCs started in the nineteenth century and were primarily organized through social and family networks. Today political institutions play a vital role in creating and sustaining the competitiveness of emerging economies. They can play the role of both a constraint and an enabling mechanism. This paper also analyzes Dunning's investment development cycle model, the location-specific advantage theory and the extended product life cycle hypothesis.

EAST ASIA

Asia-Pacific Foundation of Canada and China Council for the Promotion of International Trade (2005). *China Goes Global: A Survey of Chinese Companies' Outward Direct Investment Intentions* (Vancouver and Beijing: Asia-Pacific Foundation of Canada and China Council for the Promotion of International Trade).

This report presents the results of a survey of approximately 300 Chinese companies conducted in May–June 2005. The objective of this survey was to gain a better understanding of outward FDI by Chinese companies under the government's 'going global' strategy. More specifically, it aimed to understand who intends to invest, where and why.

Bain and Company (2005). *China Goes West: An Opportunity for the German Economy* (Munich: Bain and Company).

This study includes two surveys of 50 Chinese companies conducted between November 2003 and January 2004, that were used to investigate the motivations and needs underlying their investment decisions. All the companies surveyed were either present in Europe or were planning to enter the market. The study answers the following questions: What is the foreign investment strategy being followed by Chinese companies? What are the location requirements of the Chinese, and what is currently in need of improvement in Germany? Which sectors are favored by Chinese making foreign investment, and how can German companies use this knowledge in strategic partnerships?

Frost, Stephen (2004). *Chinese Outward Direct Investment in Southeast Asia: How Much and What are the Regional Implications?* South-South

East Asia Research Center Working Paper Series, no. 67 (Hong Kong: City University of Hong Kong), mimeo.

China is becoming an important source, not just a recipient, of outward FDI. This paper adds to the literature on mainland investment in ASEAN and is a preliminary attempt at presenting some ideas about the ramifications for the region of what is a rapidly growing and under-reported investment phenomenon. There are different theories on the motives for Chinese OFDI among economists and social scientists. Frost also notes that it is difficult to measure OFDI because figures are not reported. Thailand hosts the largest number of companies, but Singapore is the recipient of most investment capital. Indonesia receives the largest average investment. There is also South Asian interest in attracting Chinese money.

Gao, Ting (2005). 'Foreign direct investment from developing Asia: some distinctive features', *Economics Letters*, 86(1), pp. 29–35.

This paper finds that, compared to FDI from developed countries, FDI from East and South East Asian developing economies exhibits several distinctive features: it is less sensitive to host-country income and attenuates more rapidly with distance. Asian direct investors tend to invest in low-income countries and in countries nearby. This paper presents evidence of these empirical regularities and provides some possible explanations. Ethnic Chinese networks play a significant role in international trade, especially in differentiated goods. The rise of the newly industrialized economies and other countries in Asia as FDI sources turns out to be a blessing for developing Asia. A prime example is China, which received large FDI inflows that fueled its rapid economic growth in recent decades. From where has China drawn its inward FDI? Nearly 70 per cent of China's inward FDI has come from developing Asia.

Gutierrez, Hernan (2004). *Oportunidades y Desafíos de los Vínculos Económicos de China y América Latina y el Caribe*, ECLAC Serie Comercio Internacional, no. 42 (Santiago de Chile: ECLAC Serie Comercio Internacional).

The paper describes the economic relationships between China and Latin America and discusses the future challenges and opportunities for trans-Pacific investment. The author mentions that Chinese investment in Latin

America has been relatively small but has grown in recent years. According to Chinese statistics, China's investment stock in Latin America was \$1.2 billion in 2002. Chinese FDI projects in Latin America are usually of small size, on average \$3–5 million, and it is estimated that 80 per cent of Chinese FDI is in the natural resources sector. The author also describes the growing ties between the Chinese government and those of Latin America, translated into bilateral investment agreements and economic and technical cooperation agreements. However, Chinese investment in Latin America lags behind that of other Asian countries. And in Latin America, especially in Mexico and Central America, China is perceived as a competitor in attracting FDI flows from the United States.

Jomo, K.S. (2002). *Ugly Malaysians? South-South Investments Abused* (Durban, South Africa: Institute for Black Research).

This book examines recent Malaysian investment overseas, in particular in other Third World countries, and questions the cronyism involved in some of the controversial investments. Among the topics covered is Malaysian investment in Cambodia, South Africa and Tanzania.

Khanna, Tarun, Felix Oberholzer-Gee and David Lane (2005). *TCL Multimedia*. Harvard Business School Case 705–502 (Boston, MA: Harvard Business School).

A rewritten version of an earlier case, this abstract considers the underlying logic behind the globalization of TCL, one of China's most prominent companies. TCL and similarly prominent companies in China are in the forefront of China's emergence as one of the world's preeminent economic powers. The abstract discusses how TCL's approach to globalization compares with that of other Chinese companies and that of companies from other developing countries.

Matsuno, Hiroshi and Elly Lin (2003). *The Globalization of Chinese Companies and Advances into Japan*. Nomura Research Institute Papers, no. 68 (Tokyo: Nomura Research Institute).

This paper touches on China's need to continue to grow by looking to reinvest the inflow of FDI outward. The article goes through the history of overseas investment in China. Currently China continues to increase its amount of outward FDI, the major recipients of which include Hong Kong and South East Asia. The country is strongly pursuing investment in Japan to increase market size, but the cost of human resources is high. The paper goes on to describe what China needs to do to become a thriving force in the Japanese market.

Sim, Ah Ba and J. Rajendren Pandian (2003). 'Emerging Asian MNEs and their internationalization strategies: case-study evidence on Taiwanese and Singaporean firms', *Asia Pacific Journal of Management*, 20(1), pp. 27–50.

There is limited empirical research on the transnationalization process, strategies and operations of Asian TNCs. Drawing on primary data from 12 case studies of emerging Taiwanese and Singaporean TNCs in the textile and electronics industries, this paper analyzes their transnationalization and strategies, including motivations, patterns and sources of competitive advantage. The findings indicate that the emerging Taiwanese and Singaporean TNCs, although exhibiting characteristics such as that described in extant theories, also show some differences. The empirical findings, limitations and areas for further research are discussed.

Sung, Yun-Wing (1996). *Chinese Outward Investment in Hong Kong: Trends, Prospects, and Policy Implications*, OECD Development Centre Technical Papers, no. 113 (Paris: OECD Development Centre), mimeo.

Over the previous decade, China had been an important outward investor among developing countries, and Hong Kong was the foremost destination of Chinese investment. However, China's outward investment has been grossly understated in official statistics due to avoidance of China's foreign exchange controls. This paper tries to appraise those investment flows both quantitatively and qualitatively. It examines the many estimates of Chinese investment in Hong Kong, tracing their sources and bases of estimation. Most of these estimates are found to be crude guesses with very little empirical support. However, from the data on asset value and market capitalization of listed Chinese companies in Hong Kong, and also from interviews with knowledgeable sources, it is possible to gauge the rough size of Chinese investment in Hong Kong.

UNCTAD (2003). 'China: an emerging FDI outward investor', *E-brief Note* UNCTAD/PRESS/EB/2003/08, 4 December.

The Chinese government has encouraged Chinese firms to invest abroad, in particular to secure the supply of resources to meet the growing demand at home and to transfer matured technologies in which Chinese firms have a comparative advantage (for example, electronics, textiles, garment processing industries). Increased FDI flows to various countries underline China's role as an emerging home country of TNCs.

UN Department for International Development (2005). *The Effect of China and India's Growth and Trade Liberalization on Poverty in Africa* (London: UN Department for International Development).

This paper focuses on both trade and FDI in and out of China and India to sub-Saharan Africa. Trade and FDI can have an impact on poverty through their effects on production and factor markets, through changes in the prices of consumer goods, or via effects on government revenues and expenditure. The effect of OFDI from China and India on developing countries in Africa has so far been slight, even relative to the effects of trade and in comparison to their investment in other regions. Given the lack of Africa's success in attracting FDI in general, the inflow from Asian countries may actually make a significant contribution. The sector in which Chinese and Indian investment has been concentrated is in oil and mining, and given this, the investment will have little positive effect in terms of directly benefiting the poor.

Von Keller, Eugen and Wei Zhou (2003). *From Middle Kingdom to Global Market: Expansion Strategies and Success Factors for China's Emerging Multinationals* (Shanghai: Roland Berger Strategy Consultants).

Fifty leading firms in China were surveyed to identify and analyze the motivations, target markets and business structures involved in their international projects. The greatest impetus came from internal corporate dynamics (such as excess production capacity) and the least amount from the competitive environment. Sixty per cent of China's top 50 firms sought new markets, 20 per cent went for natural resources, and 16 per cent of the firms responded that obtaining advanced technology and related brand equity was the strongest motivation. Developed economies were the preferred destination for investment, with growing interest in South East Asia, Latin America, South Asia, Eastern Europe and the Commonwealth of Independent States.

Wong, John and Susan Chan (2003). 'China's outward direct investment: expanding worldwide', *China: An International Journal* 4(2) (September), pp. 273–301.

China has become a capital-surplus economy, and its overseas investment has grown apace. Although its outward investment is still small in absolute terms, especially compared to the huge inward flows, China's TNCs have been quietly gaining importance as new sources of international capital. These enterprises are now globally diversified and involved in a wide variety of sectors, including banking, manufacturing and natural resource exploitation. In the coming years, Chinese outward investment is expected to accelerate.

World Bank (2004). 'Patterns of Africa-Asia trade and investment: potential for ownership and partnership'. Paper prepared for *TICAD Asia-Africa Trade and Investment Conference*, Tokyo, Japan, 1–2 November, mimeo.

This paper discusses mainly trade relations between Asia and Africa. It addresses Asian investment in home-country markets, African markets and global markets.

Yang, Dexin (2005). *China's Offshore Investments* (Cheltenham, UK: Edward Elgar).

Presenting a thorough analysis of China's outward FDI in the past quarter of a century – something little explored in the literature – this book explores the rationale behind its emergence and development. China's outward FDI exhibits unique features in respect of timing, pace and geographical distribution that defy the existing mainstream theories of FDI. China's outward FDI fits into the framework of a network model of FDI, which is developed by applying economic norms to ideas of networks in business analysis. This network model has been designed specifically for the purpose of theorizing the changing pattern of FDI in the era of globalization in general and interpreting China's FDI in particular.

Zeng, Ming and Peter J. Williamson (2003). 'The hidden dragons', *Harvard Business Review* 81(10), pp. 92–103.

Chinese brands are starting to push into world markets. This article discusses four types of Chinese companies that are becoming increasingly powerful global competitors: national champions, dedicated exporters, competitive networks, and high-tech start-ups. The strengths and weakness of each of these groups of emerging global competitors are assessed along with their likely impact on global competition.

Zhang, Yongjin (2003). *China's Emerging Global Businesses* (Basingstoke: Palgrave Macmillan).

China is well-known as the largest FDI recipient among developing countries. Little is known so far about the fact that China has become one of the most significant Third World investors in the global economy. This book traces the evolutionary path of China's outward investment activities and examines the political economy of the rapid rise of China's global businesses in the context of the economic reforms since 1978. The analysis of changing policy regimes for China's outward investment is complemented by detailed investigations of the rise and operation of three pioneering Chinese TNCs to illustrate this new thrust of China's engagement with the global economy.

SOUTH ASIA

Khanna, Tarun, Rajiv Lal and Merlina Manocaran (2005). *Mahindra and Mahindra: Creating Scorpio*, Harvard Business School Case 705-478 (Boston, MA: Harvard Business School).

This case details the emergence of a private-sector automobile manufacturer in India that has created globally competitive and cheap versions of an SUV commonly available worldwide. The authors ask us to think about the parent corporation's next steps in leveraging this success. In particular, to what extent does it make sense to expand overseas versus entrenching the company within the home market, India?

Pradhan, Jaya Prakash (2005). *Outward Foreign Direct Investment from India: Recent Trends and Patterns*, Gujarat Institute of Development Research Working Paper No. 153 (Ahmedabad: GIDR), mimeo.

This paper provides an overview of the changing patterns of outward FDI from India from 1975 to 2001. It shows that the increasing number of

Indian TNCs during the 1990s has been accompanied by a number of changes in the character of such investments, which notably include the overwhelming tendency of Indian outward investors to have full or majority ownership, expansion into new industries and service sectors, and the emergence of developed countries as the most important host countries for trans-border activity.

Sen, Rahul, Makul Asher and Ramkishen Rajan (2004). 'ASEAN-India economic relations: current status and future prospects', *Economic and Political Weekly* (17 July), pp. 3296–3307.

This paper analyzes recent trends in merchandise trade, services, investment and manpower flows between India and ASEAN and assesses future prospects for economic cooperation. Since India's 'Look-East' policy was initiated in the early 1990s, there has been steady progress in economic cooperation and supporting institutional structures between India and ASEAN. There has also been a welcome diversification of India's trade with ASEAN both in terms of the share of individual members in total trade and of goods and services being traded. The analysis in the paper is consistent with the view that India's economic structure is largely complementary to ASEAN economies, and therefore there are significant opportunities for mutual gain.

UNCTAD (2004). *India's Outward FDI: A Giant Awakening?* Note UNCTAD/DITE/IIAB/2004/1, 20 October.

Indian firms began investing abroad in the late 1990s, but investment flows have increased since 2000 due to recent policy changes. Now, two-thirds of outward FDI from India goes to developing countries. Motivations and drivers for OFDI have been the desire for access to markets, natural resources, distribution networks, foreign technologies, strategic assets like brand names, and improvement of owner-specific advantages, including financial capability. Tax haven countries are specifically targeted, and in some cases this leads to 'round-tripping'. India's membership in regional trade agreements such as BIMSTEC and SAFTA will also provide a favorable platform to strengthen the presence of Indian firms in partner countries. Most outward FDI goes to the manufacturing sector, with an emphasis on pharmaceuticals. OFDI in the services sector is increasingly moving toward developed countries and away from the developing world.

CENTRAL AND EASTERN EUROPE

Andreff, Wladimir (2003). 'The newly emerging TNCs from economies in transition: a comparison with third world outward FDI', *Transnational Corporations*, 12(2), pp. 73–118.

This article describes the emergence of outward FDI from post-communist economies in transition during the 1990s. The Russian Federation has been by far the most significant home country with respect to the absolute volume of outward FDI. Its share in the overall outward FDI stock from economies in transition rose from 46 per cent in 1995 to 57 per cent in 2000. Two economies in transition remain as hubs for western FDI: Hungary toward Central and Eastern Europe and Estonia toward the Baltic States. Outward FDI from these two countries certainly contains a non-negligible share of indirect investment. The author argues that TNCs from transition economies share a number of common features with Third World TNCs in their first stage of development in the late 1970s. The future of the newly emerging transnational corporations is expected to follow a trend similar to that of outward FDI from newly industrializing countries.

Erdilek, Asim (2003). 'A comparative analysis of inward and outward FDI in Turkey', *Transnational Corporations*, 12(3), pp. 79–105.

This article presents a comparative analysis of inward and outward FDI in Turkey. It hypothesizes that the country's negative business climate is caused by both economic and political factors and is a major determinant of both. This article investigates why, compared to many developing countries that have attracted and benefited from significant FDI inflows, Turkey is conspicuous as a country that has not done so, despite its increasing openness to international trade. After showing that Turkey's outward investment has surged recently, the author relates the causes of such a surge, especially compared to the meager inward investment flows. It concludes that recent institutional reforms and increasing economic and political stability can make Turkey an important host country for FDI in the future.

Heinrich, Andreas (2004). 'EU enlargement and the challenges for the internationalization of companies from Central and Eastern Europe: insiders and outsiders in the energy sector'. Paper presented at the *Elites and EU Enlargement Second International Conference*, University of Bremen, 1 May, mimeo.

This paper analyzes the internationalization strategies of firms from new EU member states in the energy sector. Competitive pressure from established western companies as well as Russian energy firms trying to gain access to the EU markets is driving energy firms in Central and Eastern Europe to expand internationally. This paper presents case studies of MOL from Hungary and PKN Orlen from Poland. It also analyzes the strategy of Russia's Gazprom, which has entered the downstream markets of most new EU member countries.

ICEG EC and Corvinus (2005). 'Hungarian foreign direct investment outflow to Southeast European Countries', *SEE Monitor*, 2005/1, pp. 3–5.

Hungary became a significant foreign investor in the South East European region. Some large Hungarian enterprises gained a foothold in mainly Bulgaria, Croatia, Macedonia and Romania. This process is unique among the Central and Eastern European (CEE) countries, and it only began in this decade or a few years ago. In the future, the increase of this foreign activity is expected to continue due to the progressing privatization process, high economic growth and the improving business climate.

Jaklič, Andreja and Marjan Svetličič (2001). 'Slovenia's outward direct investment in the states of former Yugoslavia: a strategic or a defensive response?' *Economic and Business Review*, 3(3/4), pp. 299–321.

Slovenian outward FDI experienced an increase and diversification in the 1990s, yet it remained strongly concentrated in the region of the former Yugoslavia. The article analyses the characteristics of Slovenian OFDI through a comparison of investment locations. Contrary to a defensive state's response to OFDI, surveys among outward investors have demonstrated more of a strategic response to globalization and regionalization. Companies investing in the states of the former Yugoslavia do not differ significantly from companies investing elsewhere. OFDI in the region of the former Yugoslavia often reflects the strategy of becoming a regional leader or the first step toward wider internationalization.

Jaklič, Andreja and Marjan Svetličič (2001). 'Does transition matter? FDI from the Czech Republic, Hungary and Slovenia', *Transnational Corporations*, 10(2), pp. 67–105.

The authors studied outward FDI from the Czech Republic, Hungary and Slovenia after the change in their systems and explained their growth primarily as a response to globalization pressures, EU accession and certain country-specific factors like keeping economic ties developed within the previous regime. The internationalization of firms has proven to be more a spontaneous bottom-up firm activity than any planned macro-economic strategy of the countries concerned. It is undertaken predominantly as a way to keep market shares abroad (export facilitation) and the manifestation of firm-specific advantages mostly realized as 'knowing how to do business' in a specific market rather than innovative technological capabilities.

Jaklič, Andreja and Marjan Svetličič (2003). 'The outward direct investment from CEECs: can their firms compete in the global market?' *Journal of Eastern European Management Studies*, 8(1), pp. 67–83.

The authors analyze firm-specific advantages of CEEC investing firms in relation to their geographical presence and location-specific advantages. Investing firms ranked marketing knowledge as their most important advantage, followed by technological and organizational skills, though their applicability was most efficient in markets that are less developed. Only firms with advantages in all three areas realized international growth without strong geographical concentration.

Jaklič, Andreja and Marjan Svetličič (2003). *Enhanced Transition Through Outward Internationalization: Outward FDI by Slovenian Firms* (Aldershot, UK: Ashgate).

The authors present a comprehensive study of Slovenian outward investment to understand the role of outward FDI in Slovenia's economic development and transition process. The importance of outward FDI as an entry mode into the global economy is discussed from various angles, beginning with the context of the development strategy and the transition process, geographical distribution, trends and sectoral allocation of such outward FDI, as well as the major motives, barriers and problems. The study is based on extensive empirical research and focused case studies of seven investing firms. The analysis offers learning opportunities for other transition economies, and may be used as a starting point for similar studies in the region.

Jaklič, Andreja and Marjan Svetličič (2005). *Izhodna Internacionalizacija in Slovenske Multinacionalke* (Ljubljana: Fakulteta za družbene vede).

The monograph (in Slovenian) provides an extensive overview of the outward internationalization process of Slovenian firms. It presents the major characteristics of outward direct investment (motivation, geographical spreading, competitive advantages, effects, development implications) and suggestions for further internationalization on the micro- and macro-economic level.

Kalotay, Kálmán (2003). 'Outward FDI from Central and Eastern European Europe', *Economics of Planning*, 37(2), pp. 141–172.

This article looks at the reasons why outward FDI in Central and Eastern Europe has not yet become as prominent a factor in the region's reintegration into the world economy as trade liberalization used to be in the early 1990s or inward FDI is currently. To put the question into an analytical context, it refers to the investment development path paradigm as originally suggested by Dunning. According to significantly improved statistics, in 2002 the region's outward stock reached $59 billion, of which Russia represented the lion's share with $40 billion. Nevertheless, the author warns about data limitations. The article argues that a combination of the latecomer status of the region's TNCs and the transition shock can explain most of that laggard situation. The paper also discusses government policies toward outward FDI and their variations from country to country.

Kalotay, Kalman (2005). 'The late riser TNC: outward FDI from Central and Eastern Europe', in Kari Liuhto and Zsuzsanna Vincze, eds, *Wider Europe* (Lahti and Tampere, Finland: Esa Print Oy), pp. 199–223.

In Central and Eastern Europe, outward FDI was not until recently a prominent factor in the region's reintegration into the world economy, especially when compared to trade liberalization in the early 1990s or inward FDI in the late 1990s. In the terminology of the investment development path, with the notable exception of the Russian Federation, the region is in stage 2, whereby inward flows are still growing faster than outward flows. This article argues that a combination of the latecomer status of the region's TNCs and the transition shock can explain most of that laggard situation.

Lisitsyn, Nikita, Sergi F. Sutyrin, Olga Y. Trofimenko and Irina V. Vorobieva (2005). *Outward Internationalisation of Russian Leading Telecom Companies*. Electronic Publications of Pan-European Institute, vol. 1 (Turku, Finland: Turku School of Economics and Business Administration).

The internationalization of Russian telecommunication firms (MTS, VimpelCom, MegaFon) started in 2001–2002 when the Russian telecom market was near saturation. Russian mobile operators have contributed to the development of the telecom sector in Belarus, Ukraine, Kazakhstan, Uzbekistan, Turkmenistan and Tajikistan and have shown interest in other countries in the region. The authors conclude that the next step for Russian telecom operators may extend beyond former Soviet countries.

Pelto, Elina, Peeter Vahtra and Kari Liuhto (2004). 'Cyprus investment flows to Central and Eastern Europe: Russia's direct and indirect investments via Cyprus to CEE', *Journal of Business Economics and Management*, V(1), pp. 3–13.

This paper studies Russian investments in ten Eastern European countries (new EU members). Eastern Europe has been an important destination of Russian FDI, mostly in the energy sector. The authors give special attention to the changing role of Cyprus as a transit point for Russian capital and to the effects that Cyprus's accession to the EU will have on the investment behavior of Russian companies. The study is not able to quantify the amount of Russian transit capital, but it notes that Cyprus ranks among the ten largest investors in some Central and Eastern European countries. The paper shows some evidence that Russian capital started to move away from Cyprus even before Cyprus's accession to the EU in 2004 as the legislation became more transparent along with EU integration.

Svetličič, Marjan (2003). *Transition Economies' Multinationals: Are they Different from Third World Multinationals?* (Ljubljana, Slovenia: Centre of International Relations, Faculty of Social Sciences, University of Ljubljana) mimeo.

The article first evaluates the recent expansion of selected Central European firms' outward FDI and compares this expansion with that of Third World TNCs. Differences and similarities are identified. In both cases the most advanced countries prove to be the biggest investors abroad. The motives are similar, although there are some differences, particularly those that are specific to the system/transition[2] and starting base. Similarities are stronger if we compare the starting phases of both groups of firms. Both groups of investors followed certain stages in which the macroeconomic strategy of the home countries proved to be important. There are also many differences between groups and within them. One is the more important role of pull factors (globalization) in the case of latecoming investors abroad stemming from transition economies.

Svetličič, Marjan (2005). *Slovenian Outward FDI* (Ljubljana, Slovenia: Centre of International Relations, Faculty of Social Sciences, University of Ljubljana) Slovenia, August, mimeo.

The paper studies the evolution of outward FDI by Slovenian firms. Outward investment dates back to the late 1950s when Slovenia was still part of Yugoslavia. The systemic factors explaining the early internationalization also explain the reverse sequence of Slovenian internationalization (outward FDI started before inward FDI). Slovenian firms are investing abroad through greenfield as well as through acquisitions and privatization overseas.

Svetličič, Marjan and Matija Rojec, eds (2003). *Facilitating Transition by Internationalization: Outward Direct Investment from Central European Economies in Transition* (Aldershot, UK: Ashgate).

This book presents a collection of papers exploring outward FDI from transition economies. The authors present empirical evidence on outward FDI and internationalization of firms from the Czech Republic, Estonia, Hungary, Poland and Slovenia. These are the most advanced transition economies. The articles study whether the internationalization of firms from transition economies follows similar patterns to that of firms from developed or developing countries, whether it is sustainable or a temporary phenomenon, and how strongly it is embedded in the transition process. One of the main conclusions of the study is that investing abroad has been strongly influenced by managers who are courageous enough to undertake such a risky operation at the early stage of development of firms in very risky markets. One of the implications of this is that firms coming from more advanced transition countries have developed transition management-specific advantages that they can 'cash in' in other less-developed transition countries.

Svetličič, Marjan, Andreja Jaklič and Anže Burger (2007). Internationalization of Small and Medium-sized Enterprises from Selected Central European Economies. Eastern European Economics, 45(4), pp. 36–65.

The authors examine the differences in the outward FDI activity between small and medium-sized enterprises (SMEs) and large enterprises in five Central European Economies (CEEs). The impact of firm size on motives, barriers and competitive advantages in outward investment is examined on the basis of a survey of 180 firms. The results indicate more similarities than differences in the internationalization pattern, and show that SMEs are capable in their internationalization strategies. The results also show that differences found in theoretical propositions and previous empirical studies apply to a large degree to companies from CEEs although the specific characteristics of both types of firms and the intensity of differences are not yet as pronounced as in other developed countries, which is to some extent a transition-specific phenomenon. The differences identified suggest possible modifications in policy support programs for the internationalization of SMEs.

Svetličič, Marjan, Matija Rojec and Andreja Jaklič (2000). 'Strategija pospeševanja slovenskih neposrednih investicij v tujino', *Teorija in Praksa*, 37(4), pp. 623–645.

The article (in Slovenian) elaborates on the need for an outward investment promotion strategy at the national level. The authors propose a promotion policy and a set of instruments, ranked as the most effective based on a survey among Slovenian firms that directly invest abroad.

Vahtra, Peeter (2006). *Expansion or Exodus? Trends and Developments in Foreign Investments of Russia's Largest Industrial Enterprises.* Electronic Publications of Pan-European Institute, vol. 1 (Turku, Finland: Turku School of Economics and Business Administration).

The report is a follow-up to the earlier publication *Expansion or exodus? Foreign operations of Russia's largest corporations,* by Peeter Vahtra and Kari Liuhto. The report also initiates a series of publications concerning foreign investment and the activities of Russian companies. The report provides an update on overall developments in the foreign operations of

Russian largest enterprises, along with recent data on Russia's international investment position, as well as the implications of Russian investments in target countries.

Vahtra, Peeter and Kari Liuhto (2004). *Expansion or Exodus? Foreign Operations of Russia's Largest Corporations*, Electronic Publications of the Pan-European Institute, vol. 8 (Turku, Finland: Turku School of Economics and Business Administration).

The study is a comprehensive description of Russian corporations' activities abroad by sector. The authors map their recent activities, motivations and target markets. The most active outward investors are in the oil and gas sector. Few companies outside resource-based sectors rank among the top global corporations in Russia, with some exceptions such as heavy machinery manufacturer OMZ. However, there are signs of growing internationalization in manufacturing.

Varblane, Urmas, Priit Vahter and Jaan Masso (2006). 'The impact of outward FDI on the home country employment in the low cost transition economy'. Paper presented at the *European Association for Comparative Economics Studies (EACES) 9th Bi-annual EACES Conference: Development Strategies – A Comparative View*. Brighton, UK, September, pp. 7–9, mimeo.

The home-country employment effect has been the subject of a large number of empirical studies, but almost exclusively in the case of investment from high-income and high-cost home countries. The paper analyzes the home-country employment effect of the outward FDI from Estonia as a low-cost medium-income transition economy. It uses regression analysis and propensity score matching on the firm-level panel data about the whole population of Estonian firms between 1995 and 2002. The results indicate that outward FDI was positively related to home-country employment growth and suggest differences between home-country employment effects for direct and indirect outward FDI.

Weiner, Csaba (2006). *Russian FDI in Central and Eastern Europe Countries: Opportunities and Threats*. Working Paper Series, no. 168 (Budapest, Hungary: Institute for World Economics, Hungarian Academy of Sciences), mimeo.

Russian outward FDI has been showing a very promising performance in recent years. The Central and Eastern European (CEE) countries have become a key destination, but this is often viewed with suspicion by host countries. The paper begins with the quantity and geographical distribution of Russian capital investment, pointing to differences between estimates and official outward FDI data reported on a balance-of-payments basis by the Central Bank of Russia. The paper investigates the companies behind the transactions and their various motives for expanding abroad. The bulk of the outward FDI has been coming from natural resource-based companies, Russia's largest exporters, earning well from high world market prices for energy sources and raw materials.

SUB-SAHARAN AFRICA

Games, Diana (2003). *The Experience of South African Firms Doing Business in Africa: A Preliminary Survey and Analysis* (Braamfontein, South Africa: South African Institute of International Affairs).

The study is part of a three-year research project undertaken by the South African Institute of International Affairs to complement its Nepad Good Governance project, with the goal of developing policy recommendations to develop a sustainable business environment in Africa. This study looks at four sectors (banking, telecommunications, retail and food, mining) and four destination countries (Morocco, Ghana, Mozambique, Uganda) and is based on a diverse range of sources such as interviews, questionnaires, reports and press articles. The paper provides a description of South African firms' international operations in these sectors and countries. It then shifts to list investment climate issues in other African countries and describes the role that South African businesses can play as an engine of growth in Africa.

Games, Diana (2004). *An Oil Giant Reforms: The Experience of South African Firms Doing Business in Nigeria* (Braamfontein, South Africa: South African Institute of International Affairs).

This report is based on a series of interviews conducted both in Nigeria and South Africa in 2004. Twenty-two companies were interviewed in both countries. The study identifies some of the pitfalls associated with doing business in Nigeria, as well as the advantages of entering sub-Saharan Africa's most populous state and second largest economy. Two important points are raised: the first is the difficulty in business relationships. South

Africans have been accused of being patronizing, bringing in local partners and then ignoring their advice, and undermining local goods and services. The Nigerians, on the other hand, have been described by some South Africans as being corrupt, exploitative and inclined to think only of short-term gain rather than long-term partnerships. The second point raised is that the large investment by MTN has persuaded a number of South African businesses that Nigeria is a market worth exploring, whereas the debacle by Vodacom has raised concerns about corporate governance in Nigeria and respect for contractual obligations.

Gelb, Stephen (2005). 'South-South investment: the case of Africa', in Jan Joost Teunissen and Age Akkerman, eds, *Africa in the World Economy: The National, Regional and International Challenges* (The Hague: Fondad), pp. 200–206.

This chapter focuses on South–South FDI, particularly as it relates to Africa, on which there has been very little analysis to date. The chapter reflects initial thinking and background work done for a research project which is still underway, rather than the results of detailed research.

Goldstein, Andrea (2004). *Regional Integration, FDI, and Competitiveness in Southern Africa* (Paris: OECD Development Center).

An in-depth analysis of the structure of FDI flows in the 14 countries that make up the Southern Africa Development Community (SADC), including trends, sectors and development impact and frameworks for FDI in these countries. South African investors have been very enthusiastic about investment in SADC countries, much more than OECD members. Several factors explain the internationalization of South African firms: competition in the home country; the fact that most South African large firms operate in capital-intensive sectors where global consolidation is a reality; and the country's strategic interest in improving economic conditions in the continent. Two features distinguish South Africa from other emerging economies: the relatively high levels of internationalization of its corporations and the 'financial hollowing out' due to transfer of primary listing abroad.

Goldstein, Andrea, Neo Chabane and Simon Roberts (2006). 'The changing face of big business in South Africa: ten years of political democracy', *Industrial and Corporate Change*, 15(3), pp. 540–577.

Under the apartheid regime, South African business was marked by a high degree of concentration, both in terms of ownership and activities; indeed, it could be argued that this concentration was both created by and reinforced the exclusions linked to apartheid. This paper identifies the main changes that have characterized South Africa's big business since democracy in 1994 – the unbundling of traditional conglomerates, the transfer of primary listing to overseas stock exchanges, and the slow emergence of black-owned economic groups. These changes are related to key policy actions taken by government, including liberalization, black economic empowerment policies and competition policies.

Grobbelaar, Neuma (2004). *Every Continent Needs an America: The Experience of SA Firms Doing Business in Mozambique* (Braamfontein, South Africa: South African Institute of International Affairs).

Based on a survey conducted in November 2003 of 20 South African companies doing business in Mozambique, this publication tracks the experience of South African firms in that country, including difficulties with the business environment. South Africa has become the main investor in Mozambique, accounting for 49 per cent of total FDI to Mozambique between 1997 and 2002. The success of large projects such as Mozal or Sasol has played a critical role in improving business confidence in Mozambique. Smaller investors are more exposed to the difficulties of doing business there. Overall, linkages to the local economy are limited, but the goods sold by South African firms have improved available supply to consumers, contributed to price stability and increased consumer awareness.

Kabelwa, George (2004). *Technology Transfer and South African Investment in Tanzania*, Globalization and East Africa Working Paper Series, no. 10 (Dar es Salaam, Tanzania: Economic and Social Research Foundation).

The paper measures the impact of 29 South African companies investing in Tanzania between 1996 and 2000, compared with 97 companies from the OECD and developing countries. An econometric model is developed to estimate technology spillovers from foreign investment. The paper concludes that South African companies have a significant potential to improve the country's low technological base and complement modern technology brought by companies from western countries through technology transfer and spillovers.

Page, Sheila and Dirk Willem Te Velde (2004). *Foreign Investment by African Countries* (London, UK: Overseas Development Institute), mimeo.

A comprehensive write-up on African firms investing in Africa and beyond, the report is based on available statistics, academic papers, information on mergers and acquisitions, and case studies. In the case of South Africa, the report uses the outward FDI stock from the Reserve Bank, due to the volatility of FDI flows. South Africa is an important source of FDI in other African countries, yet its FDI stock in Europe commands the highest share. Only $1.4 billion of South African outward stock was in other African countries. Mauritius, Nigeria, Libya, Liberia, Botswana, Ghana and Ethiopia are also providers of FDI but at a smaller share than South Africa. Ninety per cent of South African FDI within Africa goes to southern African countries. Mozambique alone accounts for half of South African FDI outward stock in Africa, followed by Mauritius, Namibia, Zimbabwe, Botswana, Swaziland, Lesotho and Zambia. Just $129 million, or 9 per cent of total stock of South African FDI in Africa, goes to other African countries, mainly to Tanzania and Uganda.

South Africa Foundation (2004). *South Africa in Africa: Development Partner or Investment Predator?* Occasional Paper No. 3/2004 (Johannesburg, South Africa: South Africa Foundation), mimeo.

This paper studies the role of South African companies in Africa. Two opinions dominate this debate: (1) South African companies are not doing enough to revitalize the continent; (2) South African firms are the new 'colonizers' in Africa. The paper examines the growing activity of South African firms in the continent in the past ten years. It describes the expansion of destination countries for South African FDI from the Southern Africa Customs Union (SACU) countries to other Southern and East African countries and more recently to the West African coast. South African firms have invested in most sectors, from mining and energy to financial services, telecom and so forth. The analysis focuses on cross-border activity, including trade, projects and investment. Project (investment and service exports) data are based on a database from the consulting firm Africa Project Access. The paper mentions a 2003 study of companies listed on the Johannesburg Stock Exchange that put South African investment in Africa during the 1990–2000 period at $12.5 billion.

Southern African Regional Poverty Network (2004). *Stability, Poverty Reduction and South African Trade and Investment in Southern Africa. Papers presented at the Southern African Regional Poverty Network and the EU's CWCI Fund Conference*, Pretoria, South Africa, 29–30 March, available at www.sarpn.org.za/documents/d00004755/papers.php, last visited 25 October 2007.

This collection of short papers highlights different aspects of South African economic involvement in southern Africa, including trends of South African FDI to the region, main sectors and firms, country-specific studies of the presence and impact of South African FDI (Mozambique and Zambia), and an overview of Vodacom's strategy and lessons learned from investment in African countries.

MIDDLE EAST AND NORTH AFRICA

Goldstein, Andrea and Federico Bonaglia (2006). 'Outward foreign investment from Egypt', *International Journal of Emerging Markets*, 1(2), pp. 107–127.

This article analyzes the process of internationalization of TNCs from emerging economies and, more broadly, tests the investment development path (IDP) hypothesis for Egypt. It uses a combination of data analysis and company case studies to assess the extent to which and the way Egyptian companies are internationalizing. The theoretical background is the IDP hypothesis, according to which the net outward investment position of a country depends on its level of development. The article highlights how countries with a poor investment climate and a difficult, broader geopolitical situation receive limited FDI inflows, while outward FDI is limited in size and scope. Despite this climate, two TNCs have successfully expanded abroad, following different strategies.

LATIN AMERICA AND THE CARIBBEAN

Barragán, Juan Ignacio and Mario Cerutti (2003). 'CEMEX: del mercado interno a la empresa global'. Paper presented at the *V Congresso Brasileiro de História Econômica e 6a Conferência Internacional de História de Empresas*, Caxambu, Brazil, 7–10 September, mimeo.

This case study traces the story of CEMEX, arguably the first Mexican global firm. CEMEX's experience in Mexico allowed it to recognize opportunities in other emerging markets and confront the risks inherent to them, anticipating changes in consumption and growth caused by the higher instability in these markets.

Chudnovsky, Daniel and Andrés Lopez (2000). 'A third wave of FDI from developing countries: Latin American TNCs in the 1990s', *Transnational Corporations*, 9(2), pp. 31–73.

The paper studies the wave of outward FDI from Latin American countries during the 1990s. Despite data limitations, evidence shows growing FDI outflows from Mexico, Argentina, Chile and Brazil. The authors describe the different patterns of this wave of FDI from developing countries. First, internationalization is associated with the process of liberalization and structural reforms. Although most domestic firms were not able to compete in the new environment, a few firms were capable of upgrading their managerial, technological and productive capacities to meet the challenge of globalization. There are some weaknesses in the internationalization process of Latin American firms related to their smaller size compared to traditional MNCs and their difficulties in accessing finance, human resources and technology.

Cyrino, Alvaro Bruno and Moacir Miranda de Oliveira Júnior (2003). *Emerging Global Players: Evidence from the Internationalization Processes of Brazilian Firms*. (Nova Lima, MG: Fundação Dom Cabral-CI 0311).

This paper summarizes the results of a study carried out on a sample of 109 of the 1000 largest Brazilian companies. Most large Brazilian companies operate only in the internal market (27 per cent) or are still in the simple exporting phase (51 per cent). The main barriers to internationalization come from the Brazilian competitive environment (high tax load for 77 per cent of respondents and lack of financing lines for 75 per cent), followed by internal or organizational barriers and barriers imposed by foreign countries. Aspects associated with technological, market and managerial knowledge do not constitute major barriers to internationalization. (Thirty per cent of respondents consider them important barriers now.)

Del Sol, Patricio (2005). *Why Join a Chilean Firm to Invest Elsewhere in Latin America?* Documento de Trabajo no. 182 (Santiago de Chile:

Pontificia Universidad Católica de Chile, Departamento de Ingeniería Industrial y de Sistemas), mimeo.

One of the most surprising responses of Chilean firms to the economic liberalization trend that began in Chile in 1975 and spread through Latin America from 1985 onward was the outbound FDI undertaken by these companies throughout the region during the 1990s. Their pursuit of this regional strategy was very often supported by Chilean and foreign strategic alliances. This paper shows that being part of a Chilean group and having a partner from a developed country boosted the effectiveness of outbound Chilean FDI. More surprisingly, it demonstrates that firms from developed countries benefited from having a Chilean partner even if the investment was not located in Chile. Chilean firms added value by offering distinctive capabilities acquired through Chile's experience as the first Latin America country to liberalize its economy.

Del Sol, Patricio and Pablo Duran (2002). 'Responses to globalization in Asia and Latin America: Chilean investment alliances across Latin America', Latin America/Caribbean and Asia/Pacific Economics and Business Association (LAEBA) Working Papers, no. 5. Paper presented at the *Strategic Management Society Annual Conference*, Paris, France, 22 September, mimeo.

This paper describes Chilean firms' responses to the economic liberalization in the region, focusing on their investment throughout Latin America. The paper analyzes empirically whether Chilean and foreign alliances add value to these investments. The authors found that foreign investments made by firms affiliated with business groups are more profitable than those made by unaffiliated firms and that foreign investments made with partners from developed countries are more profitable than those made without them. In contrast, the authors did not find evidence that foreign investments made with local partners are more profitable.

Del Sol, Patricio and Joe Kogan (2004). *Regional Competitive Advantage Based on Pioneering Economic Reforms: The Case of Chilean FDI* (Santiago de Chile: Pontificia Universidad Católica de Chile), 4 June, mimeo.

This paper compares the profitability of foreign affiliates of Chilean companies operating in Latin America between 1994 and 2002 with that of local firms. Chilean affiliates are more profitable, but this difference decreases over time. The authors argue that the result can be explained by the competitive advantage that Chilean firms developed by learning to adapt to economic reforms, which started ten years earlier in Chile, and then applying this knowledge in other markets. This hypothesis is supported by two case studies of Chilean firms successfully investing abroad: Endesa, an electricity generator, and Provida, a pension fund. These are not isolated cases, and the authors observe that the link between the two industries is that both were affected by reforms.

Dom Cabral Foundation (2005). 'Brazilian foreign direct investment'. Paper presented at the seminar *Global Players from Emerging Markets: Brazil*, organized by the Ministry for Development, Industry and Foreign Trade, UNCTAD and Fundação Dom Cabral, São Paulo, Brazil, 30 May.

This paper describes recent developments in Brazilian outward FDI. It also describes the fiscal and regulatory framework for Brazilian firms with investments abroad. According to the Brazilian Central Bank, net capital exit through Brazilian direct investment abroad in 2004 amounted to $9.47 billion. Out of the 2004 total amount, $6.6 billion was due to the increase in participation, out of which almost $5 billion resulted from the exchange of assets between Ambev and Interbrew. Service-sector activities accounted for almost 97 per cent of Brazilian direct investment in 2003. The United States, Uruguay and the 'fiscal havens' were the main destinations for Brazilian capital in 2003. The Cayman Islands, the Bahamas and the British Virgin Islands together account for 62 per cent of Brazilian FDI, which supports the hypothesis that capital leaves the country mainly for financial reasons, including tax evasion and speculation.

Goldstein, Andrea (2005). 'Un jugador global Latinoamericano se dirige a Asia: Embraer en China', *Boletín Informativo Techint*, No. 316.

This paper analyzes the development of the Brazilian aircraft company Embraer since its creation and especially focuses on the Embraer strategy to establish itself in the Chinese market. The author mentions that it is too early to evaluate its complex investment in China; but like other investors, the experience in China is unlikely to be easy for Embraer.

Iglesias, Roberto M. and Pedro Motta Veiga (2002). 'Promoção de exportações via internacionalização das firmas de capital Brasileiro', in A.C. Pinheiro, R. Markwald and LV. Pereira, eds, *O Desafio das Exportações* (Rio de Janeiro: Brazilian National Economic and Social Development Bank), pp. 367–446.

This paper studies the reasons behind the low levels of FDI among Brazilian firms, with a special focus on investments to support exports. The authors suggest three hypotheses to explain it: a macroeconomic framework not favorable to investment in general, an export structure too concentrated on commodities and the low coefficients of exports and sales for most Brazilian exporters. The paper also analyzes the demand for FDI to support exports and identifies the types of restrictions (financial and institutional) preventing Brazilian firms from investing abroad. It also describes some examples in international experience in public support for outward FDI, including the European Union, Turkey and the Republic of Korea.

Martínez, Jon I., José Paulo Esperança and José de la Torre (2003). *The Evolving Multinational: Management Processes in Latin American Operations* (Santiago de Chile: ESE – Escuela de Negocioes, Universidad de Los Andes), mimeo.

This paper, based on a firm-level survey, compares the management processes of 58 foreign MNCs competing in Latin America with those of 40 local companies that have gone abroad and expanded operations within the region. These new or 'emerging' TNCs from the region are named *multilatinas*. These present special characteristics when compared to TNCs. They are at an earlier stage of development, smaller in size and less geographically diversified in sales, and have lower levels of R&D investment and rate of introduction of new products. MNCs make more use of processes – such as formalization of corporate relationships, strategic planning and budgeting, and corporate control and reporting – as vehicles to integrate, coordinate and control operations of subsidiaries located in different Latin American countries, as compared to *multilatinas*.

Mendes de Paula, G. (2003). *Estratégias Corporativas e de Internacionalização de Grandes Empresas en América Latina*, ECLAC Serie Desarrollo Productivo, No. 137 (Santiago: Economic Commission for Latin America).

This paper is a literature survey of recent studies about the strategies of large Latin American firms. The article focuses on three areas: corporate strategies, especially the special characteristics of diversified business groups; internationalization strategies; and cooperation strategies, such as joint ventures. In each of these areas, the article summarizes recent academic literature, including theory and case studies of firms based in Brazil, Argentina, Chile and Mexico. The author concludes from the case studies that outward investment by Latin American firms is concentrated in the natural resource sector. The most studied examples (Gerdau, CEMEX, PDVSA) belong to this sector. Other characteristics from those firms with higher degrees of internationalization are that (1) they operate in markets with oligopoly structure, (2) their competitive advantage is their capacity to adapt available technologies and (3) they operate in mature markets.

Ramírez R., Carlos Enrique and Johann Rodríguez-Bravo (2004). *Inversión Extranjera Directa entre Países en Desarrollo y una Aproximación al Caso de la Comunidad Andina de Naciones* (Cali, Colombia: Universidad ICESI), mimeo.

This paper offers an overview of the theories behind the motivation of firms from developing countries to invest abroad. It then looks at FDI flows among the members of the Andean Community of Nations. Intra-regional FDI has been small, representing only 1.2 per cent of total FDI to the region between 1992 and 2002. Colombia has been the main investor, with important investments in Venezuela and Ecuador. Colombia and Bolivia have been the main recipients of FDI originating in other Andean countries.

Salas-Porras, Alejandra (1998). 'The strategies pursued by Mexican firms in their efforts to become global players', *CEPAL Review*, 65, pp. 133–153.

This article describes and analyzes the various internationalization paths and strategies of Mexican firms. The drive for internationalization took place against the background of an open export-oriented economy and growing integration with the United States and Canada. The article examines in depth the internationalization experiences of three firms: Vitro, CEMEX and Televisa. The three companies had some similarities in their strategy, such as an explicit foreign investment strategy, an aggressive approach to expanding their international presence, and taking advantage of synergies. The article examines the paths and preferences of Mexican firms seeking to become TNCs, the obstacles they have had to overcome and the consequences of their international activities.

UNCTAD (2004). 'Outward FDI from Brazil: poised to take off.' *Occasional Note* UNCTAD/WEB/ITE/IIA/2004/16, 7 December.

This note describes recent trends in FDI outflows from Brazil and lists the main Brazilian MNCs. Brazil's outward FDI stock was likely to reach $66 billion in 2004. In 2003 it was the largest outward stock held by any country in the region, and the largest in the developing world (excluding Hong Kong, Singapore and Taiwan Province of China). There were altogether more than 1000 Brazilian firms that had invested abroad (TNCs) in the late 1990s (a number of them foreign affiliates). Among them, Petrobrás, CVRD and Gerdau figured on the list of the top 50 non-financial TNCs from developing countries compiled by UNCTAD. A good part of outward FDI from Brazil appears to involve capital flows seeking shelter from taxation or undertaking currency transactions, rather than establishing production affiliates in manufacturing or services, which is corroborated by the fact that, in 2003, the Cayman Islands headed the list of host countries for Brazil's outward FDI stock.

NOTES

1. This bibliography was originally prepared by Zenaida Hernández and Saira Haider, Foreign Investment Advisory Service, for the International Conference *Southern Multinationals: A Rising Force in the World Economy*, organized by the International Finance Corporation and *Financial Times*, Mumbai, 9–10 November, 2005. It was revised and updated by Zenaida Hernández for the international conference *The Rise of TNCs from Emerging Markets: Threat or Opportunity?* Columbia University, New York, 24–25 October 2006.
2. The author used this expression in the abstract. It means the economic/political system and the process of transition (from communism).

Index

Note: The following abbreviations have been used throughout the index: FDI for foreign direct investment; TNCs for transnational corporations.